Seventh Edition

PRINCIPLES OF CLASSROOM MANAGEMENT

A PROFESSIONAL DECISION-MAKING MODEL

James Levin
Pennsylvania State University

James F. Nolan
Pennsylvania State University

Boston   Columbus   Indianapolis   New York   San Francisco   Upper Saddle River
Amsterdam   Cape Town   Dubai   London   Madrid   Milan   Munich   Paris   Montréal   Toronto
Delhi   Mexico City   São Paulo   Sydney   Hong Kong   Seoul   Singapore   Taipei   Tokyo

Vice President and Editorial Director:
    Jeffery W. Johnston
Vice President and Publisher: Kevin M. Davis
Vice President, Director of Marketing: Margaret
    Waples
Editorial Assistant: Lauren Carlson
Marketing Manager: Joanna Sabella
Senior Managing Editor: Pamela D. Bennett
Production Project Manager: Liz Napolitano

Manager, Central Design: Jayne Conte
Cover Designer: Suzanne Behnke
Cover Image: ©Krivosheev Vitaly/Shutterstock
Full-Service Project Management: George Jacob/
    Integra Software Services Pvt. Ltd.
Composition: Integra Software Services Pvt. Ltd.
Printer/Binder/Cover Printer: Courier/
    Westford
Text Font: 10/12 ITC Garamond Std.

Credits and acknowledgments for material borrowed from other sources and reproduced, with permission, in this textbook appear on the appropriate page within the text.

Every effort has been made to provide accurate and current Internet information in this book. However, the Internet and information posted on it are constantly changing, so it is inevitable that some of the Internet addresses listed in this textbook will change.

Photo Credits: Valerie Schultz/Merrill, **p. 7**; © Chmura Frank/Prisma Bildagentur AG/Alamy, **p. 14**; Katelyn Metzger/Merrill, **pp. 27, 99, 101, 156**; Stockbyte/Getty Images, **p. 31**; Triangle Images/Getty Images, **p. 38**; Anthony Magnacca/Merrill, **p. 39**; Radosław Brzozo/Fotolia, **p. 76**; Michael Weber/ imagebroker/Alamy, **p. 78**; GeoStock/Getty Images, **p. 82**; Laura Bolesta/Merrill, **p. 132**; © Richard G. Bingham II/Alamy, **p. 177**; Monkey Business/Fotolia, **p. 186**; Image Source/Fotolia, **p. 188**; © Corbis, **p. 212**; Monkey Business Images/Getty Images, **p. 228**; Monkey Business Images/Shutterstock, **p. 231**; Maria B. Vonada/Merrill, **p. 268**.

Library of Congress Cataloging-in-Publication Data
Levin, James
    Principles of classroom management : a professional decision-making model/James Levin,
    Pennsylvania State University, James F. Nolan, Pennsylvania State University.—Seventh edition.
       p. cm.
    ISBN-13: 978-0-13-286862-4
    ISBN-10: 0-13-286862-8
    1. Classroom management—United States—Problems, exercises, etc.   2. Teaching—
    United States—Problems, exercises, etc.   I. Title.
    LB3013.L475 2014
    371.102'40973—dc23
                                                                        2012036986

10 9 8 7 6 5 4 3 2 1

ISBN-10:   0-13-286862-8
ISBN-13: 978-0-13-286862-4

To Sylvia and Herman Levin, Jim and Mary Nolan, Rocky and Andy, Heidi, Sarah, Geoff and Dan for their support, encouragement, and understanding.

PREFACE

Principles of Classroom Management: A Professional Decision-Making Model offers teachers an alternative to the coercive cookbook approach that is common in many popular classroom management texts. Rather than assuming that children need to be controlled through the teacher's use of rewards and punishments, this text asserts that children are better influenced to behave appropriately through the use of competent instruction, positive student-teacher-family relationships, intrinsic motivation, pro-social self-esteem, encouragements and natural/logical consequences. Similarly, rather than treating teachers like technicians by providing them with a cookbook of steps or strategies to follow, this text asserts that teachers are professionals. Therefore, the text expands on a variety of principles, theoretical perspectives, and empirical findings so that teachers have a depth and breadth of knowledge from which they are able to make professional decisions with respect to classroom behavior issues.

As in the previous editions, in this seventh edition, we identify and expand on two foundational beliefs that guide teachers' behavior. First and foremost, we believe that teachers cannot control student behavior. Thus, teachers influence student behavioral change by controlling or managing their own behavior, that is, by making professional decisions. Throughout the entire text, the reader will encounter language that consistently emphasizes the teacher's responsibility to make decisions and act in ways that will influence students to behave appropriately and be successful academically. Second, students who enjoy positive relationships with teachers are more likely to be successful academically and engage in pro-social behavior. Such positive relationships are potentially jeopardized by rewards and punishments and are likely enhanced by encouragements and natural/logical consequences.

WHAT'S NEW IN THIS EDITION

Although the basic approach of the text and the underlying principles remain consistent, we have made several changes, which were sparked by contemporary educational issues, comments from educators who have used the text, and detailed reviews of the sixth edition.

Based on feedback from the users and reviewers of the text, and the authors' own experiences, we made the following changes:

- Although the authors have always believed that students choose how to behave and that the teacher's role is to influence student behavior, we noted in previous editions of the text that the language did not always match those beliefs. In previous editions of the text, we sometimes talked about managing behavior or coping with behavior. In this edition, we have worked diligently to ensure that the language throughout the text conveys the message that the teacher's role is to use professional knowledge to decide how to act in order to influence students to choose to behave appropriately. This change in language is exemplified in the new titles for Chapters 8, 9, and 10.

- The power of building positive relationships with students and their families has taken a much more prominent role in the earlier chapters of this edition of the text. This edition also devotes an entire chapter, Chapter 7, to relationship building as well as devoting considerable attention to various dimensions of proactively building positive relationships in Chapters 3, 4, 5, and in working with students who display unremitting disruptive behavior in Chapters 10 and 11.

- In contrast to many texts that provide a list of do's and don'ts for building relationships, Chapter 7 in this text is intended to enable the teacher to generate strategies for relationship building by using professional knowledge about authority bases, self-esteem, and motivation. By employing professional knowledge, the teacher can create respectful and caring relationships, enhance student success expectations through the development of an internal locus of control, and influence the development of an internal value structure that enhances the value of desired student outcomes.

- The role of culture and cultural differences has been taken up more prominently in this edition. As the teaching force in the United States has become increasingly more white and middle class, the students in our nation's classrooms have become more culturally diverse and poorer. Thus, it is critically important that teachers understand the role that culture can and should play in thinking about how they should behave in order to influence students to choose to behave appropriately and to expend effort to be successful academically. In this seventh edition, the role of culture and cultural differences is discussed in reference to many topics, including understanding student behavior, appropriate use of teacher authority bases, teacher expectations, building relationships, breaking the cycle of discouragement, and in working positively with families.

- In the sixth edition of the text, we provided three cases, one elementary, one middle, and one high school, that could be used for iterative analysis on the part of the reader as a way of assessing how the text was influencing the reader's understanding of and response to the cases. In this edition, we have included six cases for iterative analysis, two at each level.

- In each chapter of this edition, we have also provided pre- and postreading activities focused on the "Principles of Teacher Behavior That Influence Appropriate Student Behavior" as an opportunity for the reader to reflect on how his or her understanding of the principles grows over time.

- In Chapter 2, we have included an expanded section on new uses of technologies including cyberbullying, cybercheating, and sexting that alerts teachers to some of the problems that can be created through student access to these technologies. Obviously technology can bring powerful benefits to the instructional process, but it can also create new sorts of problems.

- In Chapter 3, the concepts of motivation and self-esteem are defined and then used to analyze students' disruptive behavior. The understanding gained from the analyses enables the professional teacher to target specific components of motivation and self-esteem for intervention to influence students to behave appropriately.

- In Chapter 4, we have changed our terminology from "teacher power bases" to "teacher authority bases." This change in terminology reminds us that teachers derive their authority and the ability to influence students by using professional knowledge to determine their classroom behavior. The notion of relationship building also plays a more prominent role in the discussion on referent authority.

- In Chapter 5, we have included a new section on student-teacher relationships and effective teaching and updated the research on effective teaching using concepts from current research on instruction.
- We have reworked Chapter 6 so that it focuses on designing the physical environment and effectively establishing and teaching classroom guidelines. We have expanded our discussions on effectively teaching both procedures and rules to ensure that students have a clear understanding of what appropriate behavior looks like and also that they are capable of behaving in the expected way.
- In Chapter 9, we have added a discussion that relates the concept of cultural stereotyping to the cycle of discouragement for students who exhibit chronic behavior problems or who underachieve.
- In Chapter 11, we have expanded our discussion of working collaboratively with families when outside assistance is needed to work effectively in resolving problems and have added a new section on alternatives to suspensions that reports some of the empirical findings concerning the negative outcomes associated with out-of-school suspensions.
- In addition to adding the three new cases to the iterative case analysis sections, we have updated the references (which are now all located after Appendix C), added new case studies within chapters, and updated/revised/added exercises included throughout the text.

HOW TO USE THIS TEXT: A FOCUS ON PEDAGOGY

This text presents in detail a professional decision-making model. The model requires teachers to use their professional knowledge base to change their behavior (teaching practices) in order to influence students to choose to behave appropriately.

Conceptualizing and implementing teaching as a way of influencing students is an inherently challenging endeavor requiring a high level of expertise. Additionally, it is an approach that is contrary to the unexamined beliefs, past experiences, and current practices of many educators. Therefore, it is incumbent upon educators who wish to practice this approach to develop a deep understanding of the content of this text so that they can employ the approach in classrooms with confidence and, when called upon, can explain the approach to administrators, professional peers, families, and students.

To fully understand this model, it is necessary to have a thorough grasp of the model's foundational concepts, principles, and classroom applications. The principles, found at the beginning of each chapter, are statements that relate two or more concepts. Without these integrative statements the concepts would stand alone, and their connection to teaching practices would be relatively meaningless. The interpretation of the principles into classroom practices and the decision-making hierarchies are applications of the model.

The first four chapters of the text focus on foundational concepts that the wise teacher must consider in building a set of operational beliefs about influencing student behavior and its connection to teaching. These concepts include teaching, learning, discipline problems, motivation, self-esteem, rewards, punishments, authority bases, and theories of teacher influence. Chapters 5 through 7 focus on concepts and principles that teachers can employ to create a learning and instructional environment that will influence students to behave appropriately and strive for academic success. These concepts include effective teaching, teacher expectations, classroom design, guidelines for behavior, and encouragement. Chapters 8 through 11 focus on concepts and principles that teachers can employ using a hierarchical approach to influence and redirect student behavior from inappropriate to appropriate behavior.

To aid readers in learning the professional decision-making model, the authors deliberately designed the text with pedagogy in mind. The many pedagogical features to aid the learner include the following:

Iterative Case Studies   Six iterative case studies are provided at the beginning of the text and repeated at three points later in the text. The case studies enable readers to continually revise their analyses of real classroom events as they proceed through the text, applying their new understandings of how to influence students to behave appropriately. Comparisons of earlier with later analyses should clearly show readers their growth in understanding and applying the concepts and principles. Instructors and students are also encouraged to use additional cases studies of their own that they have experienced or observed.

Pre- and Postreading Activity of Explaining Principles   In each chapter, "Principles of Teacher Behavior That Influence Appropriate Student Behavior" are presented at the beginning and end of each chapter. Readers are asked to explain the principles before they read the chapter and then again after reading the chapter. It is a readiness and closure activity that focuses the reader's attention on how the principles integrate the various concepts and how the principles are applied to the classroom.

Prereading Questions   This readiness activity is intended to enable readers to uncover and examine their initial thinking about some of the major concepts that will be covered in each chapter.

Flow Charts   Flow charts are presented at the beginning of each chapter. These flow charts illustrate the hierarchy of teacher knowledge and how the present content relates to what was previously learned.

Exercises   Exercises are found at the end of each chapter and provide readers with the opportunity to analyze and apply the chapter's concepts and principles.

Embedded Cases   Each chapter presents multiple cases that illustrate the concepts and principles in practice. The cases are drawn from real classroom, school, and community events that the authors have experienced, witnessed, or been told about.

Tables and Figures   Throughout the book, tables and figures are used to illustrate the content being read.

Appendices   At the end of the book there are three appendices. Appendix A Analysis Inventory of Teacher Behavior that Influences Appropriate Student Behavior is a tool that the classroom teacher can use to reflect upon her behavior used to influence appropriate student behavior. Appendix B summarizes teacher behavior that is congruent with the text for Working with Students With Special Needs. Appendix C Decisions and Tasks for Beginning the School Year lists important tasks and decisions that teachers should consider that will get the school year off to a good start.

SUPPLEMENTS

A **Test Bank** that includes multiple choice, true/false, and discussion questions and a **PowerPoint**® **Presentation** for each chapter are available online. Instructors can access these supplements by contacting their local representative for a password.

ACKNOWLEDGMENTS

We are especially grateful to the following reviewers who completed very helpful reviews of our work on this edition: Kelechi Ajunwa, Delaware County Community College; Beverly Doyle, Creighton University; Mary Estes, University of North Texas; Marilyn Howe, Clarion University of Pennsylvania; Anita Welch, North Dakota State University; and Eleanor Wilson, University of Virginia. A special thanks goes to Andrew Thompson, during his senior year did an extensive literature search regarding influences on students' behavior and alternatives to suspension which are used in the text.

Ultimately, the authors' goal is to present a contemporary approach to classroom management that will improve teaching and learning for today's teachers and students. Please feel free to let us know if we have been successful.

BRIEF CONTENTS

CONTENTS

Iterative Case Study Analyses

Six case studies of discipline problems at different grade levels are described. One or more of the case studies can be analyzed four times.

The first analysis should be completed before you begin to read and study the text. This analysis will serve as a baseline from which you can reflect on your growth of understanding and ability to analyze complex student behaviors as you study the text and reanalyze the cases.

The second analysis occurs after you have read and studied Section 1, Foundations, which includes Chapters 1 through 4. The third analysis should incorporate the concepts discussed in Section 2, Prevention, which includes Chapters 5, 6 and 7. The fourth and final analysis should use the concepts found in Section 3, Interventions for Common Behavior Problems, and Section 4, Interventions for Chronic Behavior Problems, which include Chapters 8 through 11.

For each reanalysis, consider what has changed and what has stayed the same from the previous analysis/analyses. As you read each chapter and gain additional understandings and skills, you are encouraged to reconsider everything you have written in earlier analyses. For example, even though the definition of teaching is first introduced in Chapter 1, if what you read in later chapters causes you to reexamine the definition, do so and discuss the change in your analyses.

Iterative Case Study Analyses

First Analysis

Select one or more of the case studies. Before studying the text, how would you analyze the case study? In your analysis, consider why the students may be choosing to behave inappropriately and how you might intervene to influence them to stop the disruptive behavior and resume appropriate on-task behavior.

Elementary School Case Studies

"I don't remember"   During silent reading time in my fourth-grade class, I have built in opportunities to work individually with students. During this time, the students read to me and practice word work with flash cards. One student has refused to read to me but instead only wants to work with the flash cards. After a few times, I suggested we work with flash cards this time and begin reading next time. He agreed. The next time we met, I reminded him of our plan, and he screamed, "I don't remember. I want to do word cards." At this point, I tried to find out why he didn't like reading and he said, "There's a reason, I just can't tell you," and he threw the word cards across the room, some of them hitting other students. What should I do?

"Let's do it again"   Cathy is in my third-grade class. Whenever I ask the class to line up for recess, lunch, or to change classes, Cathy is always the last to get in line. When she does, she pushes, shoves, and touches the other students. When this happens, I usually demand that all the children return to their seats, and we repeatedly line up again and again until Cathy lines up properly. I thought that peer pressure would cause Cathy to change her behavior, but, instead, it has resulted in my students being late to "specials" and having less time for recess and lunch.

Middle School Case Studies

"It makes me look cool"   I can't stop thinking about a problem I'm having in class with a group of 12-year-old boys. They consistently use vulgar language to one another and to some of the shy kids in the class, especially the girls. In addition, they are always pushing and shoving one another. I've tried talking to them about why they keep using bad language when they know it's inappropriate.

The response I get is that "it makes me look cool and funny in front of my friends." I have asked them to please use more appropriate language in the classroom, but that has not worked. I haven't even started to deal with the pushing and shoving. What should I do?

"My parents will be gone all weekend"   One of my seventh-grade girls was passing notes to a boy two rows over. After the second note, I made eye contact with her and it stopped for about half an hour. When I saw her getting ready to pass another note, I went over to her desk and asked her to give me the note and told her that that the note passing had to stop. She looked very upset, but she did give me the note. I folded it and put it in my desk drawer. When class ended, she ran out of the room crying. My personal policy is not to read students' notes but, instead, give it back to the student at the end of class or throw it away. However, this time, maybe because of her reaction, something told me to read the note. It said, "Mike, my parents will be away Saturday don't you and John sleep will be fun. I promise I'll do whatever you want me to do and that you and John can do anything you want to me." What should I as the teacher do?

High School Case Studies

"Homo"   This past week I had a student approach me about a problem he was experiencing in our class. This eleventh-grade student had recently "come out" as a homosexual. He said he was tired and upset with the three boys who sit near him. These boys frequently call him a "homo" and a "fag" every time they see him, both in and out of class.

"Why don't you get out of my face?"   A twelfth-grade student came up to me the first day of class and said, "My name is Ted. I don't want to be here, so just leave me alone and we'll get along just fine." I did not react to his comment but, instead, said, "After you see what we will be learning, I think you will find the class interesting." Ted walked away and took a seat in the back of the room. Later that week, I noticed Ted was reading a magazine while everyone else was working on an in-class assignment. Without making it obvious, I walked by Ted's desk and quietly asked him to put away the magazine and begin working on the assignment. Ted turned to me and said, "Maybe you don't understand; I asked you not to bother me. I'm not bothering you so why don't you get out of my face"

3

1

The Basics

The Basics

Conceptualizing the Process of Teaching • Understanding Principles of Teacher Behavior That Influence Appropriate Student Behavior • Understanding the Professional Decision-Making Hierarchical Approach

PRINCIPLES OF TEACHER BEHAVIOR THAT INFLUENCE APPROPRIATE STUDENT BEHAVIOR

1. The single most important factor in determining the learning environment is teacher behavior. Intentionally or unintentionally, teachers' verbal and nonverbal behaviors influence student behaviors.

2. Teachers have the professional responsibility for assuming the role of instructional leader, which involves employing techniques that maximize student on-task behavior.

3. Teachers who have clearly developed ideas of (a) the relationship between teaching and discipline, (b) the factors influencing student behavior, (c) their own personal expectations for student behavior, and (d) a systematic plan to influence appropriate student behavior have classrooms characterized by a high percentage of on-task student behavior.

4. A preplanned decision-making hierarchy of intervention strategies increases the likelihood of influencing appropriate student behavior.

PREREADING ACTIVITY: UNDERSTANDING THE PRINCIPLES OF TEACHER BEHAVIOR

Before reading Chapter 1, briefly describe your understanding of the implications of the principles for a classroom teacher.

Principle 1:

Principle 2:

Principle 3:

Principle 4:

PREREADING QUESTIONS FOR REFLECTION AND JOURNALING

1. Educators generally believe that teaching is a profession. What does it mean for a teacher to be a professional?

2. Influencing appropriate student behavior is a challenging process. As you think about your experiences as student and teacher, are there any guidelines that you could suggest to teachers to make this process more effective?

INTRODUCTION

Many years ago both authors had the opportunity to take a graduate class entitled "Classroom Management." It was our first formalized instruction in this area. A significant change in the appropriate way to conceptualize "classroom management" has occurred in the 30 years since the authors were graduate students. Then, the goal was "coping" with disruptive behavior and/or managing student behavior. Now, the goal is "influencing" appropriate behavior. This change is not trivial or just semantic; it represents a major change in how teachers view discipline problems and how teachers interact with students who exhibit disruptive behaviors.

A catalyst for this change is a basic understanding that the only person a teacher can control is herself,[1] or, in other words, the only behavior a teacher can control is her own. Therefore, a teacher does not control students but rather influences them by changes in her own behavior she can control. Additionally, the dictionary.com definition of *coping* is "to handle something successfully" with synonyms including *manage, handle, deal with*. The dictionary.com definition of *influence* is "to have an effect on the outcome of something or the behaviors of others" with synonyms including *guide, impact, transform* (thesaurs.com). Furthermore, coping with discipline problems infers an inevitability that there will be discipline problems that the teacher must endure. It is reactive and pessimistic in that it implies the teacher can do little about future student behavior other than cope with it when it occurs.

In contrast, influencing infers discipline problems need not be inevitable but may actually be preventable. Influencing is proactive, taking place before any

---

[1]To foster equality without being cumbersome, gender pronouns will be alternated by chapter. Chapter 1 will have female pronouns; Chapter 2, male; Chapter 3, female; and so forth. The new Chapter 7 will have both gender pronouns.

discipline problems even exist, and optimistic in that the teacher can impact students to behave appropriately, greatly reducing the frequency of discipline problems. The authors have chosen this orientation because it offers an optimistic approach to teaching based on a clear understanding of what teachers can control and whom they can influence. The result is increased teacher empowerment and efficacy that comes from thinking about the possibility of influencing students to choose appropriate behavior and to strive for academic success. A conscious effort has been made to orient the content of the text toward influencing positive behavior rather than coping with misbehavior. This becomes very evident in the next section in which teaching is defined.

At that time when we were enrolled in the graduate course, little research had been conducted on the subject of how teachers influence students to behave appropriately. Even with this limitation, the instructor did an excellent job of organizing what was available into a systematic approach for influencing students who display disruptive behavior to behave appropriately. Throughout the course, however, students continually asked the instructor to define teaching and explain how teaching and influencing students were related.

Unfortunately, the instructor was never able to give a satisfactory answer. Questions about the relationship between teaching and influence continually arose: Should a teacher plan objectives for appropriate behavior in her lesson plan? How do various teaching strategies increase or reduce the likelihood of students behaving appropriately? Should a student's grades be affected by misbehavior?

The lack of a definition of teaching not only plagued this class but also several other education courses. Even today, many texts still use the term *classroom management*, and many teachers who use various "management techniques" still lack a clear definition of teaching and an understanding of how teachers influence students. This is most unfortunate because teaching and influencing students cannot exist independently of each other.

Therefore, we begin by setting forth a definition of teaching and explaining how influencing behavior is part of the teaching process. The rest of this chapter presents a structural overview of the text. First, we present the principles of teacher behavior that influence students to behave appropriately. These principles form the text's foundation. Second, we provide an explanation of the decision-making hierarchical approach to intervention. Last, we offer a flowchart of the knowledge, skills, and techniques that make up a hierarchy of teacher behaviors that result in successful classrooms in which teachers are free to teach and students are free to learn.

DEFINING THE PROCESS OF TEACHING

Each year, colleges and universities educate and graduate thousands of students who then enter the teaching profession. All of these new teachers have accumulated many credit hours of coursework in their chosen area of specialization, in professional knowledge, in methodology, and in practical experiences. Armed with this background, they enter classrooms and teach for an average of approximately 20 years or more. The average number of years of teaching experience of in-service teachers is 16.1 years with close to 40 percent of teachers having more than 20 years experience (National Education Association, 2010). Even with this background, however, many teachers, seasoned professionals as well as recent graduates, are unable to provide an adequate operational definition of teaching. Some argue that a formal definition is not necessary because they have been teaching for years and whatever they do seems to work. For those of us who consider teaching a professionally sophisticated endeavor, however, experience, although invaluable in many teaching situations, is not the only factor that should be used to develop and plan instruction. Furthermore, this "gut-reaction" approach is sorely limited when the old "proven methods" seem not to work, and there is a need for modifying or developing new instructional or management strategies. This is conspicuously evident in today's technology-enhanced classrooms, which are characterized by increases in student diversity and students with special needs. Others, when asked, define teaching as the delivery, transference, or giving of knowledge or information. Definitions such as these give no clue to how knowledge is transferred and the strategies that are used to deliver it. They limit teaching to only the cognitive domain, thus failing to recognize the extraordinary level of competence needed for making hundreds of daily content and pedagogical knowledge-based decisions in complex and dynamic classroom environments.

Teaching always has emphasized the cognitive domain. However, when teaching is viewed as concerned solely with cognitive development, teachers limit their effectiveness when working with students who exhibit disruptive behavior. These students often need growth and development in the affective domain, such as cooperating with others, valuing others' viewpoints, volunteering, and developing motivation and interest, as well as in cognitive areas. Teachers who understand the critical nature of the affective domain are in a much better position to work with students who exhibit disruptive behavior. Indeed, many exceptional teachers actually approach their work with the attitude that the students need teachers because there are behaviors that seriously interfere with teaching and learning (Haberman, 1995). Teachers with this attitude are better prepared to work effectively with all students. They do not get as frustrated or feel as if they are wasting their time because they understand that teaching is helping students mature not only cognitively but also affectively.

When teaching is defined, teachers have a clearer perception of what behaviors

Through careful lesson planning, teachers can design strategies that have an increased probability of gaining students' interests and preventing discipline problems.

constitute the practice of their profession. Before we present our formal definition, however, we must consider an important assumption that underlies it. One of the major tenets of the theory of psychology developed by Alfred Adler is that each individual makes a conscious choice to behave in certain ways, either desirable or undesirable (Sweeney, 1981). Building on this tenet, we believe that individuals cannot be forced to change their behavior they must choose to do so. Therefore, individuals cannot be forced to learn or to exhibit appropriate behavior. In other words, teachers do not control student behavior. Students control their own behaviors. If this idea is accepted, it follows that a teacher changes student behavior only by *influencing* the change through changes in her own behavior, which is the only behavior over which she has total control. In the classroom, then, a teacher is continually involved in a process in which student behavior is monitored and compared with the teacher's idea of appropriate behavior for any given instructional activity. When actual student behavior differs from appropriate student behavior, the teacher attempts to influence a change in student behavior by changing her own behavior. For the skilled veteran teacher, the monitoring of student behavior and the appropriate adjustment of teacher behavior are automatic, transparent, and seamless to the outside observer. The behavior the teacher decides to employ should be one that maximizes the likelihood that student behavior will change in the appropriate way. The probability of choosing the most effective behavior increases when teachers have a professional knowledge of instructional techniques, cognitive psychology, and child development and use it to guide the modification of their own behavior (Brophy, 1988).

With this background, we can define teaching as *the use of preplanned teacher behaviors, founded in learning principles and child development theory and directed toward both instructional delivery and classroom behavior that increase the probability of effecting a positive change in student behavior.* The significance of this definition in trying to change any student's behavior is threefold. First, teaching is concerned with what the teacher controls, her own behavior, and this behavior is preplanned. Teaching is not a capricious activity. Second, the preplanned behaviors are determined by the teacher's professional knowledge. This knowledge guides the teacher in selecting appropriate behaviors. It is the application of this specialized body of professional knowledge and knowing why it works that makes teaching a profession (Tauber and Mester, 1994). Third, many teaching behaviors are well founded in professional knowledge. The teacher's challenge is to select those behaviors that increase the probability that a corresponding behavioral change will take place in the student. For this to occur, the teacher not only must know the students' initial behaviors but also have a clear picture of desired student behaviors for any given instructional activity.

The emphasis on the use of professional knowledge to inform teacher behavior is critical. The public should expect no less from teachers than it does from physicians, engineers, or other professionals. When a physician is asked why she performed a certain procedure, we expect her answer to be more scientifically based than "It seemed like a good thing to do at the time" or "It worked before." If teaching is a profession, teachers must understand and be able to explain the knowledge and beliefs that lie behind their teaching decisions. If a teacher is asked why she interacted with a student in a particular manner or why she used a particular instructional strategy, her response should be based on pedagogical or psychological research, theory, or methodology.

Case 1.1 illustrates the application of the definition of teaching to instructional delivery. Ms. Kelly was aware of the present student behavior and had a clear picture of what she wanted the behavior to become during questioning. To effect this change, she analyzed her behaviors and how they affected her students. Because changes in teacher behavior influence changes in student behavior, the former is often termed "affecting behavior" and the sought-after student behavior is termed "target behavior" (Boyan and Copeland, 1978). Using her professional knowledge, Ms. Kelly modified her behavior to improve her practice of teaching and bring about the target behavior. The behaviors she chose to employ were well founded in the educational literature on questioning methodology (see Chapter 5). Ms. Kelly performed as a professional.

CASE 1.1

Getting Students to Respond

Ms. Kelly believes that students must actively participate in class activities for learning to take place. She prides herself on her ability to design questions from all levels of the cognitive domain; she believes that students benefit and enjoy working with questions that require analysis, synthesis, and evaluation. However, she is sorely disappointed because very few students have been volunteering to answer questions and those who do volunteer usually give very brief answers.

Observation of Ms. Kelly's class indicates a fairly regular pattern of behaviors during questioning. Standing in front of the class, she asks the first question: "Students, we have been studying the westward movement of pioneers during the 1800s. Why do you think so many thousands of people picked up and moved thousands of miles to a strange land knowing that they would face incredible hardship and suffering during the long trip?" Two hands shoot up. Ms. Kelly immediately calls on Judy. "Judy, why do you think they went?" "They wanted new opportunities," she answers. Ms. Kelly immediately replies, "Great answer. Things where they lived must have been so bad that they decided that it was worth the hardships that they would face. In a new land, they would have a new beginning, a chance to start over. Another thing might be that some of the pioneers might not have realized how difficult the trip would be. Do you think that the hardships continued even after the pioneers arrived in Oregon and California?"

After discussion, Ms. Kelly realizes how her behaviors are affecting student behavior. Instead of increasing participation, they actually hinder participation. After further discussions and reading about questioning strategies, Ms. Kelly decides to change her questioning behavior. She begins to ask questions from different locations throughout the room. She also waits three to five seconds before calling on any student. After a student answers, she again waits at least three seconds and then points out the salient parts of the response, rephrases another question using the student's response, and directs this question to the class.

As before, her behaviors affect student behavior. However, this time more students volunteer initially, responses are longer, and additional students are willing to expand on initial answers.

Case 1.2 illustrates the relationship between teacher behavior and targeted student behavior in classroom management. Like Ms. Kelly, Mr. Fox changed his behavior to one that reflected a well-accepted educational practice. With this change came corresponding changes in student behavior.

How do teachers become aware of the methodology and theory to support their behaviors and from where do the methodology and theory come? The methodology and theory are generated by research, often conducted by educational psychologists in controlled laboratory settings. Their findings are then applied to classroom situations, where they may or may not be applied properly and may or may not result in expected outcomes. Research about teaching moved into the modern era only within the past 35 years. When reliable, replicable studies began to be conducted in actual classrooms with real teachers (Berliner, 1984), research developed rapidly. Indeed, research now shows that a set of teacher behaviors, referred to as *effective teaching* or *effective instruction*, is present in many classrooms in which students make noteworthy gains in learning. Teachers need to incorporate these behaviors into their daily instruction. They may do so by becoming thoroughly familiar with the professional literature that synthesizes and summarizes the research (see also Chapter 5). Some teachers may prefer a more experiential approach. These individuals may wish to participate in many of the formalized workshops that use the research to develop effective teaching practices, such as Marzano, Frontier, and Livingston's "Effective Supervision" (2011), Charlotte Danielson's "Framework for Effective Teaching" (2007), and Dean et al.'s "Classroom Instruction That Works" (2012).

Although not as plentiful, there now is a body of knowledge concerning effective classroom management (Charles and Senter, 2010; Curwin, Mendler, and Mendler 2008; Emmer and Evertson, 2008; Evertson and Emmer 2009; Kounin, 1970; Redl and Wineman, 1952).

CASE 1.2

"Why Study? We Don't Get Enough Time for the Test Anyway!"

Mr. Fox has a rule that test papers will not be passed out until all students are quiet and in their seats with all materials, except a pencil, under the desk. He explains this to the class before every test. Without fail, he has to wait five to ten minutes before everyone in the class is ready. Typically, some students complain: "Why do we have less time just because a few other kids take their good old time?" Sometimes students will get visibly angry, saying, "This isn't fair," "This is stupid," or "Why study? We don't get enough time for the test anyway!" Mr. Fox dreads test days.

During a discussion of this situation with another teacher, Mr. Fox is introduced to the concept of logical consequences; in other words, allowing students to experience a logically related consequence of their behavior. Employing this concept, Mr. Fox announces to the class that he will pass out tests on an individual basis. "Once you are ready, you receive a test." He walks down the aisles giving students who are ready a test paper and passing by without comment those who are not. As a result of his changed behavior, student behavior changes. Complaining stops, and in a few minutes, more students are ready to take the test.

As stressed throughout this text, positive student behavior is closely connected to effective instruction. Effective instruction prevents many discipline problems by increasing on-task behavior. Without effective instructional practices, teachers are unlikely to be able to successfully maintain appropriate student behavior. However, although effective instruction is absolutely necessary, it is not in itself sufficient to guarantee that classrooms are free from disruptive behavior. Even the best teachers experience some disruptive behavior.

PRINCIPLES OF TEACHER BEHAVIOR THAT INFLUENCE APPROPRIATE STUDENT BEHAVIOR

As a result of the research on effective instruction, student behavior, and positive classroom learning environments, a number of well-accepted principles governing teacher behavior to prevent and successfully intervene with disruptive behavior have emerged. Some of these principles are quite specific to a particular philosophical underpinning (see Chapter 4), whereas others are philosophically generic. This text presents 38 generic principles of teacher behavior that influence appropriate student behavior developed through years of experience, research, and study. Each of the remaining 10 chapters emphasizes some of these principles and discusses in detail how they may be incorporated by the teacher into effectively influencing students to behave appropriately.

The following paragraphs summarize the contents of each chapter and its relevant principles. These paragraphs are followed by an explanation of the decision-making hierarchical approach to influence appropriate classroom behavior. Just as it is good classroom practice to provide the learner with an anticipatory set before in-depth instruction, these sections provide the reader with the scope, sequence, and structure of this text.

Chapter 2 discusses the nature of the discipline problem. First, there is a review of the limitations of current definitions of what behaviors constitute a discipline problem. Offering a new operational definition of the term *discipline problem* rectifies these limitations. This definition is then used to classify common classroom behaviors. Second, misbehavior is analyzed historically by frequency and type to determine what schools are like today. Research concerning the effect of disruptive behavior on both teachers and students is presented. Finally, the use of technology is examined. As beneficial as technology can be for teaching and learning, it is also being used by students to bully others 24/7 and by some students to cheat on tests and assignments.

The related principles of teacher behavior that influence appropriate student behavior are the following:

A discipline problem exists whenever a behavior interferes with the teaching act, interferes with the rights of others to learn, is psychologically or physically unsafe, or destroys property.

   For effective teaching to take place, teachers must be competent in influencing appropriate student behavior so as to maximize the time spent on learning. Such teachers enjoy teaching more and have greater confidence in their ability to affect student achievement.

Chapter 3 explores the underlying complex influences on student behavior and provides multiple reasons why children misbehave. Societal changes have created an environment vastly different from that in which children of previous generations grew up. How these out-of-school changes have influenced children's attitudes and behaviors is examined first.

Like adults, children have strong personal, social, and academic needs. At the same time, they undergo rapid cognitive and moral development. Also, schools are more culturally diverse than in any previous time. The chapter goes on to describe typical behaviors associated with children's attempts to meet their needs as well as normal developmental behaviors. Behaviors that may appear when the home or school fails to recognize and respond to these needs and developmental changes are detailed. The analysis of motivation and self-esteem coupled with a concept called a *parallel process* is presented as a means to understand disruptive behavior. A particularly negative way to meet one's needs is through the use of bullying behavior. In-person bullying and cyberbullying are examined from both the bully and the bullied perspectives. Bullying is a widespread and serious problem with particularly long-term negative effects. The concepts of *resiliency* and *protective factors* are discussed and used to explain how many students overcome negative experiences to become competent adults.

Student mobility is increasing mostly as a result of economic pressure. When these students attend their new schools, their academic performance often decreases and disruptive behavior increases. Finally, new neuroscience findings are starting to explain that adolescent behavior that was once considered problematic is most likely normal and is a result of brain maturation.

We emphasize that the teacher has little control over many of the changes that occur in society and in children. However, she does have total control over her instructional competence. Excellent instruction is a significant way to lessen the effects of uncontrollable factors and to prevent misbehavior.

The following principles of teacher behavior that influence appropriate student behavior are found in Chapter 3:

An awareness of the influences of misbehavior, which are often beyond the schools' control, enables teachers to use positive intervention techniques rather than negative techniques, which stem from erroneously viewing misbehavior as a personal affront.

Satisfaction of basic human needs such as food, safety, belonging, and security is a prerequisite for appropriate classroom behavior.

The need for a sense of significance, competence, virtue, and power influences student behavior.

Cognitive and moral developmental changes result in normal student behavior that often is disruptive in learning environments.

Instructional competence can lessen the effects of negative outside influences as well as prevent the misbehavior that occurs as a result of poor instruction.

Chapter 4 invites the reader to explore the connection between teacher behavior and teacher beliefs as related to influencing student behavior. Different strategies for influencing students are presented as either compatible or incompatible with certain schools of thought. When teachers employ behaviors that are inconsistent with their beliefs about children, they feel emotionally uncomfortable and usually do not see the desired change in student behavior.

Teachers exert influence through the use of four authority bases. In this chapter, each authority base is placed along a continuum, which begins with those most likely to engender students' control over their own behavior and proceeds to those bases that foster increasing teacher direction of student behavior.

The second section of the chapter describes three theoretical models of classroom management. A series of nine questions helps the teacher define her beliefs about classroom management. These questions are then used to analyze, compare, and contrast the three models. It is the teacher's underlying beliefs concerning how children learn and develop and who has the primary responsibility for controlling a child's behavior that determine which model provides the best fit.

The principles of behavior that influence appropriate student behavior that are found in Chapter 4 are the following:

Theoretical approaches to classroom management are useful to teachers because they offer a basis for analyzing, understanding, and influencing student and teacher behavior.

As social agents, teachers have access to a variety of authority bases that can be used to influence student behavior.

The techniques a teacher employs to influence student behavior should be consistent with the teacher's beliefs about how students learn and develop.

Chapter 5 explores the effective instructional techniques used by the professional teacher. Effective teaching prevents most discipline problems. The discussion of effective teaching is divided into three parts. The first part, Positive Student-Teacher Relationships and Effective Teaching, explores the relationship between the teacher's instructional effectiveness and the types of relationships that the teacher develops with students. The second section, Basics of Effective Teaching, describes the knowledge gained from research on teacher effects. This research focuses on teacher behaviors that facilitate student achievement on lower-level cognitive tasks as measured by paper-and-pencil tests. The third section of the chapter, Beyond the Basics, describes more recent conceptualizations of teaching and learning, which focus on student cognition and higher-order cognitive learning tasks.

Chapter 5 emphasizes the following principles:

Developing positive relationships with students will enhance the teacher's instructional effectiveness and exert a greater influence on student learning.

Student learning and on-task behavior are maximized when teaching strategies are based on what educators know about student development, how people learn, and what constitutes effective teaching.

Chapter 6 details how to structure the learning environment to minimize disruptive behavior. Many classroom behavior problems arise because students are either unaware of or unclear about what types of behaviors are expected of them

Many teachers need to keep up to date on the latest techniques by attending professional development workshops.

or why certain procedures must be followed in the classroom. This lack of awareness usually occurs when the teacher herself is unclear about how and why she wants her students to behave. Thus, developing meaningful classroom guidelines is extremely necessary.

The processes for designing classroom guidelines, i.e., procedures and rules, are presented with emphasis on the importance of having both a rationale and stated consequences for each rule. Techniques to communicate guidelines to students in a way that maximizes understanding and acceptance are offered. Ways to plan for teaching procedures, rules and appropriate behavior are discussed.

The principles of Chapter 6 include the following:

When environmental conditions are appropriate for learning, the likelihood of disruptive behavior is minimized.

Students are more likely to follow classroom guidelines if the teacher models appropriate behavior; explains the relationship of the guidelines to learning, mutual student-teacher respect, and protection and safety of property and individuals; and obtains student commitment to follow them.

Teaching students appropriate behavior increases the likelihood that disruptive behavior will be prevented.

Enforcing teacher expectations by using natural and logical consequences helps students learn that they are responsible for the consequences of their behavior and thus are responsible for controlling their own behavior.

Chapter 7 highlights the importance of developing proactive, positive relationships with all students and their families. The initial section of the chapter discusses the influence of cultural background on teacher and student values, norms, and expectations for appropriate behavior. In addition, the chapter advocates the use of cooperative learning activities and the teaching of social skills as techniques for creating classroom group norms that are supportive of pro-social behavior and student engagement in learning activities.

The benefits to students and teachers of positive student, teacher, and family relationships are outlined in the later sections of the chapter. Building positive student-teacher relationships using teacher authority bases, student motivation based on values and expectations for success, and student self-esteem are examined. Building proactive family-teacher relationships using three criteria that reinforce the value of parental support is detailed in the final section of the chapter.

The principles described in Chapter 7 include the following:

When classroom guidelines and rules match the culture of the students' home community, the likelihood that students will behave appropriately is increased.

When the teacher creates group norms that are supportive of engagement in learning activities, the likelihood that students will behave appropriately is increased.

When teachers use their professional knowledge base to build positive student-teacher relationships, the likelihood that students will behave appropriately and demonstrate higher academic achievement is increased.

When teachers proactively build relationships with families that communicate that home support for school endeavors is important, that families have the ability to help, and that the school welcomes and encourages their involvement, the likelihood that students will behave appropriately and demonstrate higher academic achievement is increased.

Chapters 8 and 9 explore how teachers can effectively influence students to behave appropriately through the use of a three-tiered hierarchical decision-making model of nonverbal and verbal behaviors called *intervention skills.*

Research reviewed in Chapter 8 reveals that the majority of misbehaviors are verbal interruptions, off-task behavior, and disruptive physical movements. The frequency of these surface disruptions can be greatly reduced with proper planning, instructional strategies, environmental structure, and verbal and nonverbal teacher behaviors.

Chapter 8 covers the first tier of the decision-making hierarchy. It discusses the appropriate use and limitations of four nonverbal intervention skills: planned ignoring, signal interference, proximity interference, and touch interference. The chapter includes an intervention decision-making model that hierarchically orders nonverbal behaviors teachers can use to influence student behavior. The hierarchy begins with those nonintrusive techniques that give students the greatest opportunity to control their own behaviors and proceeds to intrusive strategies in which the teacher assumes more responsibility for managing student behavior. Five implementation guidelines are also presented.

Chapter 8 covers the following principles:

Teacher intervention techniques need to be consistent with the goal of helping students become self-directing individuals.

Use of a preplanned hierarchy of remedial interventions improves the teacher's ability to influence appropriate behavior.

The use of a hierarchy that starts with nonintrusive, nonverbal teacher behaviors gives students the opportunity to exercise self-control, minimizes disruption to the teaching/learning process, reduces the likelihood of student confrontation, protects students' safety, and maximizes the teacher's alternative interventions.

Chapter 9 discusses in detail the second and third tiers of the decision-making hierarchy: verbal intervention, and the application of logical consequences. Twelve verbal intervention techniques are presented along with nine guidelines for their appropriate use as well as their limitations. Once again, these techniques are ordered along a continuum that ranges from nonintrusive student control to intrusive teacher management of behavior. The use of verbal intervention is founded on the assumption that teachers do have effective alternatives to angry, personal, sarcastic confrontations with students. Such alternatives typically defuse rather than escalate misbehavior.

The third tier of the decision-making hierarchy, the use of logical consequences, is a powerful technique in influencing student behavior. The concept of logical consequences is explained in detail along with the guidelines teachers use to develop effective logical consequences for a wide range of misbehavior. The assertive delivery of logical consequences is also discussed.

The following principles are dealt within Chapter 9:

An intervention hierarchy that consists of nonverbal intervention, followed by verbal intervention, and application of logical consequences, when necessary, seems most effective in coping with common behavior problems.

Some forms of verbal intervention defuse confrontation and reduce misbehavior; other forms of verbal intervention escalate misbehavior and confrontation.

Chapter 10 looks at long-term and short-term classroom interventions for students who exhibit chronic behavior problems. Two long-term problem-solving strategies—relationship building and disrupting the cycle of discouragement—are presented. In addition, the use of conversation and conferencing to solve problems is discussed. Most strategies used with chronic behavior problems involve referral outside the classroom. However, there are four effective field-tested, in-classroom techniques: self-monitoring, anecdotal record keeping, functional behavior assessment, and behavior contracts. The effective use of these techniques assumes that the teacher's classroom behaviors have met the prerequisites discussed in previous chapters and reviewed here. The step-by-step implementation of these strategies is described, and a detailed discussion of the critical communication skills that can make the difference in successfully resolving chronic misbehavior is presented. Last, teacher-controlled exclusion from the classroom, an interim step between in-classroom interventions and outside referral, is explained.

The following principles are part of Chapter 10:

When dealing with students who pose chronic behavior problems, teachers should employ strategies to resolve the problems within the classroom before seeking outside assistance.

Breaking the cycle of discouragement in which most students with chronic behavior problems are trapped increases the likelihood that the problems can be resolved within the classroom.

When teachers talk with students privately and use effective communication skills with students who have chronic behavior problems, the likelihood that the problems can be resolved within the classroom increases.

Interventions that require students to recognize their inappropriate behavior and its impact on others increase the likelihood that the problems can be resolved within the classroom.

Interventions that require students who exhibit chronic behavior problems to be accountable for trying to control their behavior on a daily basis increase the likelihood that the problems can be resolved within the classroom.

The final chapter, Chapter 11, offers advice on seeking assistance. When in-classroom techniques have been exhausted and have not resulted in appropriate student behavior, it is necessary to seek outside assistance. Teachers are offered guidelines to follow when deciding whether or not outside consultation is warranted. The concept of a *success/failure ratio* is explained along with a discussion of how this ratio contributes to persisting misbehavior.

Other students may need outside referral even though they do not display any forms of chronic misbehavior. These students may exhibit signs of emotional stress or family dysfunction. The chapter discusses six warning signs of these problems. A referral process that stresses multidisciplinary team consultation is offered as an effective means of working with these students. The roles of the counselor, families, administrator, and school psychologist are presented along with the legal issues that must be considered when making outside referrals.

Family support and cooperation with the school is critical when working with students who misbehave chronically. The chapter outlines specific guidelines that teachers can use to decide when families need to be contacted. Techniques on how to conduct family conferences to facilitate and enhance parental support and cooperation are discussed.

The principles of teacher behavior that influence appropriate student behavior in Chapter 11 are these:

Professional teachers recognize that some chronic misbehavior problems are not responsive to treatment within the classroom or are beyond their expertise and necessitate specialized outside assistance.

When outside assistance must be sought to manage a chronic misbehavior problem adequately and appropriately, the use of a multidisciplinary team is the most effective approach.

Family support and cooperation with the school are critical when attempting to influence a student who exhibits chronic behavior problems. Careful planning and skilled conferencing techniques are essential in developing a positive homeschool working relationship.

PROFESSIONAL DECISION-MAKING HIERARCHY

Professionals, regardless of their fields, use the specialized body of knowledge they possess to make decisions in their area of expertise. For example, engineers rely on their knowledge of science and mathematics to make engineering decisions, and physicians rely on their knowledge of biology and medical science to arrive at medical decisions. Educators who make hundreds of instructional decisions on a daily basis do so after considering their specialized knowledge in pedagogy, cognitive psychology, and child development.

In these professions and in others, hierarchies, taxonomies, and classification systems are used to organize vast amounts of isolated bits of data into manageable, comprehensible bodies of knowledge. Some common examples of classification systems to organize scientific information are the periodic table of elements in chemistry, the taxonomy of the plant and animal kingdoms in biology, and the electromagnetic spectrum in physics. In the social sciences, there are the taxonomies of cognitive, affective, and psychomotor abilities in education and stages of cognitive and moral development in psychology, as well as many more.

Hierarchies may be used for more than just organizing information may also be used to guide professional decisions. Scientists, who use the scientific method to guide their inquiries, and doctors, who diagnose and treat patients by using a step-by-step approach, are using hierarchical approaches. The advantages of using a hierarchical approach are twofold: (1) it allows for the systematic implementation of the knowledge that informs the practice of a given profession, and (2) it provides the practitioner with a variety of approaches rather than a limited few. Thus, the hierarchical approach increases the likelihood that successful outcomes will result. The hierarchical strategies are based on professional knowledge, and if early strategies are ineffective, numerous other strategies may produce positive results.

Applying a hierarchical approach to classroom decisions allows teachers to employ knowledge effectively in order to understand and influence student behavior. When such an approach is not used, a teacher may find herself with few alternatives for influencing student behavior. Consider, for example, Case 1.3.

Needless to say, Ms. King's approach to handling a common student behavior was a gross overreaction. It not only led to an administrator-initiated meeting but also probably to an increase in student misbehavior because students recognize the discrepancy between the minimal student behavior and maximum teacher response. Furthermore, Ms. King's approach left her with few if any alternatives in influencing other students who called out answers in the future. It is highly unlikely that parents, students, administrators, or other teachers would support this approach. The technique of exclusion from class is usually reserved for use after many less intrusive strategies have been attempted. In other words, changes in student behavior are best accomplished when the teacher employs intervention strategies in a hierarchical order.

When teachers use a professional body of knowledge to make decisions, the decisions made are usually professionally acceptable and defendable, and they result in desired changes in students' behaviors. When teachers make "gut" or emotional decisions, sometimes called *reactions,* the decisions more often than not result in unexpected and undesirable student behaviors. Additionally, they may not be professionally acceptable and defendable. The principles of teacher behavior and the hierarchy of intervention skills presented in this text have served many educators well in making effective decisions concerning how to influence student behavior.

Two hierarchies are presented in this text. The first is a summary of how the concepts and principles that underlie effective teacher behavior can be organized, presented, studied, and used. The four sections into which the chapters are grouped represent this hierarchy. The first section, Chapters 1 through 4, presents the foundational knowledge base. The second section, Chapters 5, 6, and 7, addresses prevention strategies or teacher behaviors that influence students to behave appropriately The third section, Chapters 8 and 9, deals with teacher behaviors that influence students to stop common discipline problems and return to acceptable behavior. The fourth and final section, Chapters 10 and 11, addresses teacher behaviors that are used for working with students who exhibit chronic misbehavior problems.

The second hierarchy concerns the implementation of intervention strategies initiated by the teacher when discipline problems become evident. This hierarchy is a decision-making model that uses specific techniques that have been shown to influence students to stop the inappropriate behavior and increase the likelihood

CASE 1.3
The Vice-Principal Wants to See Whom?

Ms. King decides one way to maintain discipline in her eighth-grade class is to be firm and consistent with the enforcement of classroom rules and procedures from the beginning of the school year. One of her rules is that students must raise their hands to be called on before answering questions. She explains this rule to the class: "By eighth grade, I'm sure you all understand that everyone has an equal chance to participate. For this to happen, everyone must raise his or her hand to be called on. I hope I will have to tell you this only once."

During the year's first question-and-answer session, Jill calls out the answer.

Ms. King reminds her, "Jill, you must raise your hand if you want to answer. I do not expect this to happen again." However, it isn't much longer until Jill calls out again. This time, Ms. King says, "Jill, please leave the room and stand in the hallway. When you feel that you can raise your hand, come back and join us."

In a few minutes, Jill returns to class and as before calls out an answer. This time, Ms. King says, "Go to the office and speak with the vice-principal." Within minutes, Jill is sent back to class. Later that day, Ms. King receives a message in her mailbox requesting her to set up a meeting with the vice-principal to discuss the matter.

of students exhibiting continuous appropriate behavior. Using the decision-making model, the teacher finds a variety of nonintrusive strategies that provide the student with the opportunity to manage her own behavior while curbing the common forms of classroom misbehavior efficiently and effectively (Shrigley, 1985). As the teacher moves down through the intervention hierarchy, the techniques become more and more intrusive, with the teacher playing an increasingly larger role in influencing student behavior. The overall hierarchy of the text is shown in Figure 1.1. In addition, each chapter begins with a flowchart depicting those parts of the hierarchy that have been covered in previous chapters and the specific parts of the hierarchy that are now to be discussed. We hope this arrangement provides a systematic, step-by-step approach to building a comprehensive system that teachers can use to influence students to choose appropriate behavior with the ultimate goal of having students become self-regulating.

Section 1   Foundations (Chapters 1–4)

Conceptualizing the process of teaching
Understanding principles of teacher behavior
   that influence appropriate student behavior
Understanding the decision-making hierarchical
   approach
Defining a discipline problem
Understanding the extent of discipline problems
   in today's schools
Understanding how discipline problems affect
   teaching and learning
Understanding the impact of cybercheating and
   cyberbullying on students
Understanding societal change and its influence
   on children's behaviors
Recognizing student needs
Recognizing bullying
Understanding developmental changes and
   accompanying behaviors
Recognizing the importance of instructional
   competence
Understanding resiliency
Understanding the impact of mobility on
   students' behavior
Understanding and employing different
   teacher authority bases
   Referent
   Expert
   Legitimate
   Reward/Coercive

Understanding theories of classroom management
   Student directed
   Collaborative
   Teacher directed

Section 2   Prevention (Chapters 5–7)

Developing effective teaching strategies
   Building positive student-teacher relationships
   Designing effective lessons
   Enhancing student motivation using
     teacher variables
   Communicating high teacher expectations
     to all students
   Employing classroom questioning effectively
   Maximizing time-on-task
   Teaching for understanding
   Creating learning communities
   Teaching for multiple intelligences
   Differentiating instruction
   Enhancing student motivation using
     student variables
Designing the physical environment
Establishing classroom guidelines
   Determining procedures
   Determining rules
   Determining consequences
     Natural • Logical • Contrived
   Communicating rules
   Obtaining commitments
   Teaching rules and appropriate behavior

FIGURE 1.1   A Hierarchical Approach to Successful Classroom Management.

Building Relationships
Understanding cultural embeddedness of behavior
Creating positive group norms
Building student-teacher relationships
Building family-teacher relationships

Section 3   Interventions for Common Behavior Problems (Chapters 8–9)

Using proactive intervention skills
Using preplanned remedial nonverbal interventions
Planned ignoring
Signal interference
Proximity interference
Touch interference
Using preplanned verbal interventions
Adjacent reinforcement
Calling on the student
Humor
"I message"
Direct appeal
Positive phrasing
"Are not for's"

Reminder of rules
Glasser's triplets
Explicit redirection
Canter's "broken record"
Applying logical consequences

Section 4   Interventions for Chronic Behavior Problems (Chapters 10–11)

Relationship building
Disrupting the cycle of discouragement
Talking to solve problems
Using self-monitoring
Using anecdotal record procedure
Using behavioral contracts
Understanding the nature of persisting misbehavior
Recognizing when outside assistance is needed
Making referrals
Counselors
Administrators
School psychologists
Working with families
Considering alternatives to suspension
Protecting student rights

FIGURE 1.1   continued

Summary

This chapter first discussed a critical premise concerning teachers influencing students to behave appropriately that the reader should clearly understand before continuing. Teaching is defined as *the use of preplanned behaviors, founded in learning principles and child development theory and directed toward both instructional delivery and classroom behavior that increase the probability of effecting a positive change in student behavior.*

Therefore, by deliberately changing her behavior, the teacher can influence positive changes in students' academics as well as classroom behaviors.

Second, the principles and the hierarchical approach to teacher decision making, on which the entire text is based, were explained. These serve as the foundation on which specific strategies to influence student behavior are developed throughout the rest of the text.

Exercises

1. Many teachers define teaching as the delivery of knowledge or the giving of information. In your opinion, are these definitions adequate? If so, explain why. If not, what are the limitations?

2. What problems may arise when teachers base most of their decisions on "gut reactions"? Give specific examples.

3. In recent years, there has been much discussion over whether or not teaching is a profession. In your opinion, is teaching a profession? If yes, explain why. If no, why not and what must occur to make it a profession?

4. Review the definition of teaching presented in this chapter. Do you agree with it or should it be modified? If you agree, explain why. If not, what should be changed?

5. The definition of teaching in this chapter focuses on the teacher changing her behavior to influence students because that is the only behavior over which she has control. Given this, how might you reply to a principal who believes that teachers should be able to control their students' behavior?

6. This chapter discusses how teacher behaviors (affecting) influence changes in student behavior (targeted). For each targeted behavior that follows, suggest an appropriate affecting behavior and explain why such a teacher behavior would increase the likelihood of a positive change in the student's behavior.

Situation	Targeted Behavior	Affecting Behavior
calling out answers	raising hand	
not volunteering	volunteering	
daydreaming	on-task	
forgetting text	prepared for class	
short answers to questions	expanded answers	
few students answer questions	more participation	
passing notes	on-task	
walking around room	in seat	
noisy during first five minutes of class	ontask from start of class	

7. Suggest some ways that a busy teacher can keep up with the latest research on effective teaching.

8. This text offers 38 principles of teacher behavior. Principles are usually quite broad statements. How can a teacher use these principles to guide her teaching practice and specific management techniques?

9. This text chapter supports the use of a decision-making hierarchical approach to teacher influence. Discuss the advantages as well as the disadvantages to such an approach.

10. **Principles of Teacher Behavior** After reading Chapter 1 and doing the exercises, use what you have learned to briefly describe your understanding of the implications of the principles listed at the beginning of the chapter for a classroom teacher.

Principle 1:

Principle 2:

Principle 3:

Nature of the Discipline Problem

Nature of the Discipline Problem
Defining a Discipline Problem • Understanding the Extent of Discipline Problems • Recognizing the Problems in Today's Schools • Understanding How Discipline Problems Affect Learning • Addressing a New Concern: Technology

---

PRINCIPLES OF TEACHER BEHAVIOR THAT INFLUENCE APPROPRIATE STUDENT BEHAVIOR

1. A discipline problem exists whenever a behavior interferes with the teaching act, interferes with the rights of others to learn, is psychologically or physically unsafe, or destroys property.

2. For effective teaching to take place, teachers must be competent in influencing appropriate student behavior so as to maximize the time spent on learning. Such teachers enjoy teaching more and have greater confidence in their ability to affect student achievement.

PREREADING ACTIVITY: UNDERSTANDING THE PRINCIPLES OF TEACHER BEHAVIOR

Before reading Chapter 2, briefly describe your understanding of the implications of the principles for a classroom teacher.

Principle 1:

Principle 2:

PREREADING QUESTIONS FOR REFLECTION AND JOURNALING

1. What makes a problem a discipline problem? How do discipline problems differ from other problems that teachers must address?

2. Why is it important that teachers differentiate discipline problems from non-discipline problems?

3. What effect do you think discipline problems have on teachers, students, and schools in general?

4. How has technology, particularly the Internet and cell phones, been used by students to negatively impact teaching and learning?

INTRODUCTION

When educators, public officials, or parents with school-age children discuss schooling, the topic of classroom discipline inevitably arises. Discipline and classroom management are topics that have been widely discussed by both professionals and the public for a considerable period of time.

In these discussions, it is generally assumed that everyone knows what is meant by a discipline problem and understands the major problems that discipline poses for educators. However, when we have asked pre- or in-service teachers at workshops, "What is a discipline problem?" there has been no consensus whatsoever in their responses. Thus, contrary to popular belief, there does not seem to be a professional operational definition of what behaviors constitute a discipline problem. So what would seem to be the obvious starting point for effective classroom management, that is, the definition of a discipline problem, has yet to be adequately formulated.

A second common topic among educators, public officials, and parents is the magnitude of discipline problems in today's schools. Many think that our schools are plagued by crime, violence, and frequent disruptive classroom behavior, but is this true? Do today's schools differ greatly from those of 10 or 20 years ago? How does the lack of an agreed-upon definition of a discipline problem affect the gathering of statistics to assess the extent of disruptive behavior?

Although almost everyone agrees that it is important for students to behave properly in a classroom, a survey of pre- and in-service teachers shows no agreement on why it is important. What are the actual effects of misbehavior on students and their learning and on teachers and their teaching?

Finally, technology has had many positive impacts on teaching and learning. In some disciplines, technology has fundamentally changed the way teachers teach and students learn. However, technology has also been used by students in ways that have very negative impacts on academic integrity (cybercheating) and on the well-being of students (cyberbullying). What are these impacts and how extensive are their influences?

In this chapter, we (1) develop a working definition of what is a discipline problem in a classroom, (2) assess the magnitude of the discipline problem in today's schools, (3) determine the effect of misbehavior on both students and teachers, and (4) describe how technology is used by students to cheat and bully other students.

DEFINING A DISCIPLINE PROBLEM

Teachers often describe students who exhibit discipline problems as lazy, unmotivated, belligerent, aggressive, angry, or argumentative. These words at best are imprecise, judgmental, and descriptive of a wide range of behaviors. After all, a student can be lazy or angry and yet not be a disruptive factor in the classroom. Furthermore, attribution theory (Weiner, 1980) tells us that our thoughts guide our feelings, which in turn guide our behavior. Therefore, when they describe children using negative labels, teachers are much more likely to feel and behave negatively toward those children (Brendtro, Brokenleg, and Van Bockern, 1990). Negative teacher behavior is ineffective in helping children learn appropriate behavior and actually influences students to continue to display inappropriate behavior (Levin and Shanken-Kaye, 2002). Thus, for a definition of a discipline problem to be useful to a teacher, it must clearly enable a teacher to differentiate student behavior that requires immediate corrective action from behavior that does not.

The amount of material that has been written on discipline and classroom management is staggering. Hundreds of books and articles on this subject have been produced for both the professional and the general public, the great majority of them appearing since the mid-1970s. They typically cover such areas as the types and frequency of behavior problems, the causes of student misbehavior, and the strategies that teachers can employ to improve classroom management. However, surprisingly, the most basic question, "What types of student behaviors are discipline problems?" has rarely been considered.

A teacher's ability to differentiate from a myriad of student behavior that which is a discipline problem needing immediate teacher attention is a prerequisite of effective classroom management. Without this ability, it is impossible for teachers to design and communicate to students rational and meaningful classroom guidelines, to recognize misbehavior when it occurs, or to employ intervention strategies effectively and consistently.

In developing an operational definition, it is helpful to examine some inadequate definitions found in the literature. Kindsvatter (1978) defined discipline in terms of student behavior in the classroom, or "classroom decorum." He uses terms such as *behavior problems* and *misbehavior* but never gives meanings or examples for them. However, he does associate discipline with student behavior (which we will see does not always have to be the case).

Feldhusen (1978) used the term *disruptive behavior*, which he defines as a violation of school expectations interfering with the orderly conduct of teaching. This definition is significant because it states that misbehavior is any student behavior that interferes with teaching. In defining disruptive behavior in this manner, Feldhusen attempts to provide teachers with a guideline for monitoring student behavior: any behavior that keeps the teacher from teaching is a disciplinary problem; any behavior that does not interrupt the teaching process is not a discipline problem.

Using this guideline, it seems relatively easy to identify discipline problems. Or is it? Let's test it by applying it to a number of common classroom behaviors: (1) a student continually calls out while the teacher is explaining material, (2) a student quietly scratches his name into his desk with a pencil, and (3) a student quietly passes notes to his neighbor. According to Feldhusen's definition, only the first student is exhibiting a discipline problem because his calling out interferes with the teacher's ability to teach. Unless a teacher were quite observant, the second and third behaviors could go unnoticed. Even if the teacher were aware of these behaviors, he could easily continue to teach. However, how many teachers would agree that scratching one's name on a desk and passing notes are not discipline problems? Teachers realize inherently that such behaviors are discipline problems and must be dealt with. Therefore, Feldhusen's definition is inadequate.

Emmer and colleagues (1989) offer a more comprehensive definition: "Student behavior is disruptive when it seriously interferes with the activities of the teacher or of several students for more than a brief time" (p. 187). Under this definition, disruptive behavior interferes not only with the teacher or teaching act but also with students or the learning act. This is an important enhancement because it recognizes the right of every student to learn (Bauer, 1985), and most of the time in a classroom, the need of the group must override the need of an individual student (Curwin and Mendler, 1980).

Unfortunately the definition includes the terms *seriously, several,* and *brief time.* Although these terms are used to generalize to a wider range of situations, they allow room for disagreement and misinterpretation. First, a brief time or a serious interference for one teacher may not be a brief time or serious interruption for another. Second, is it only when several students are disrupted that a discipline problem exists? If we apply this definition to the three types of behaviors listed previously, the student who calls out and possibly the note passer would be identified. The student who is defacing the desk would not be covered.

By far one of the most comprehensive definitions come from Shrigley (1979), who states that any behavior that disrupts the teaching act or is psychologically or physically unsafe constitutes a disruptive behavior. This definition includes behaviors that do not necessarily interfere with the teaching act but are definitely psychologically or physically unsafe, such as running in a science lab; unsafe use of tools or laboratory equipment; threats to other students; and bullying, teasing, and harassing of classmates. However, the same problem is evident in this definition as in Feldhusen's: name scratching and note passing would not be considered discipline problems because they do not interfere with teaching and are not unsafe.

In examining contemporary texts, identifying or defining discipline problems is addressed in three ways. The first approach suggests that misbehavior or a discipline problem exists if the behavior is inappropriate for the particular setting and the behavior is done willfully (Charles, 2002). This definition is very subjective because inappropriateness is open to as many interpretations as there are teachers and willfulness requires the teacher to be an interrogator or mind reader. Thus, agreement among teachers as to whether or not a given behavior is a discipline problem would be difficult.

The second approach is not to provide any criteria to judge whether a discipline problem exists but instead to place student behavior into categories of magnitude ranging from non-problematic to serious issues that may spread to other students (Evertson et al., 1994). There are many issues regarding this approach, for example, what is considered a non-problem—talking among students and inattentiveness may require more immediate attention from the teacher than a behavior listed as a major problem, such as not doing assignments. Additionally, there are no guidelines as to how the teacher should address the behaviors in each category.

The third approach is to define discipline as *what teachers do to teach students how to behave appropriately* (Charles, 2002; Iverson, 2003; Maag, 2004). This definition focuses on teacher behavior and is not useful for identifying students' behavior that are inappropriate or, in other words, students' behaviors that are discipline problems.

When teachers are not prepared to start classes on time, discipline problems can result.

It should be clear from this discussion that any definition of the term *discipline problem* must provide teachers with the means to determine instantly whether or not any given behavior is a discipline problem. Once this identification has been made, the teacher can then decide what specific teacher intervention should be employed to influence students to act appropriately.

Consider the following six scenarios. For each, ask yourself the following questions:

1. Is there a discipline problem?
2. If there is a discipline problem, who is exhibiting it?
3. Why is or isn't the behavior a discipline problem?

Scenario 1:   Marisa quietly enters the room and takes her seat. The teacher requests that students take out their homework. Marisa does not take out her homework but instead takes out a magazine and begins to flip quietly through the pages. The teacher ignores Marisa and involves the class in reviewing the homework.

Scenario 2:   Marisa quietly enters the room and takes her seat. The teacher requests that students take out their homework. Marisa does not take out her homework but instead takes out a magazine and begins to flip quietly through the pages. The teacher publicly announces that there will be no review of the homework until Marisa puts away the magazine and takes out her homework.

Scenario 3:   Marisa quietly enters the room and takes her seat. The teacher requests that students take out their homework. Marisa does not take out her homework but instead takes out a magazine and begins to flip quietly through the pages. The teacher begins to involve the class in reviewing the homework and at the same time moves closer to Marisa. The review continues with the teacher standing in close proximity to Marisa.

Scenario 4:   Marisa quietly enters the room and takes her seat. The teacher requests that students take out their homework. Marisa does not take out her homework but instead takes out a magazine and begins to show the magazine to the students who sit next to her. The teacher ignores Marisa and begins to involve the class in the review of the homework. Marisa continues to show the magazine to her neighbors.

Scenario 5:   Marisa quietly enters the room and takes her seat. The teacher requests that students take out their homework. Marisa does not take out her homework but instead takes out a magazine and begins to show the magazine to the students who sit next to her. The teacher does not begin the review and, in front of the class, loudly demands that Marisa put the magazine away and get out her homework. The teacher stares at Marisa for the two minutes that it takes her to put the magazine away and find her homework. Once Marisa finds her homework, the teacher begins the review.

Scenario 6:   Marisa quietly enters the room and takes her seat. The teacher requests that students take out their homework. Marisa does not take out her homework but instead takes out a magazine and begins to show the magazine to the students who sit next to her. The teacher begins the homework review and, at the same time, walks toward Marisa. While a student is answering a question, the teacher, as privately as possible, assertively asks Marisa to take out her homework and put the magazine away.

If you are like many of the teachers to whom we have given these same six scenarios, you probably have found answering the questions that preceded them somewhat difficult. Furthermore, if you have taken time to discuss your answers with others, you undoubtedly have discovered your answers differ from theirs.

Much of the difficulty in determining what is a discipline problem can be avoided using the following definition, which recognizes that discipline problems are multifaceted: *a discipline problem is behavior that (1) interferes with the teaching act, (2) interferes with the rights of others to learn, (3) is psychologically or physically unsafe, or (4) destroys property.* This definition not only covers calling out, defacing property, or disturbing other students but also other common behaviors that teachers confront every day. Note, however, that the definition does not limit behavior to student behavior. This is very important, for it means the teacher must consider his own behavior as well as his students' behavior.

Using our new definition, review the six scenarios again and compare your analysis with ours. In Scenario 1, there are no discipline problems because neither Marisa's nor the teacher's behavior is interfering with the rights of others to learn. The teacher has decided to ignore Marisa for the time being and focus on involving the class with the homework review.

In Scenario 2, the teacher is a discipline problem because the teacher has interrupted the homework review to intervene with Marisa, who isn't interfering with any other students' learning. In this situation, it is the teacher who is interfering with the rights of the students to learn.

In Scenario 3, there is no evident discipline problem. Neither Marisa's nor the teacher's behavior is interfering with the other students' right to learn. The teacher has not decided to ignore Marisa but has wisely chosen an intervention strategy that allows the homework review to continue.

In Scenario 4, both Marisa and the teacher are discipline problems. Marisa is interfering with the other students' right to learn. Because Marisa is a discipline problem, by ignoring her, the teacher also interferes with the other students' right to learn.

In Scenario 5, Marisa and the teacher are again discipline problems. Marisa's sharing of the magazine is disruptive, but the teacher's choice of intervention is also a problem. In fact, the teacher is interfering with the learning of more students than Marisa.

In Scenario 6, Marisa is still a discipline problem. However, the teacher is not because the intervention strategy allows him to work with the class and, at the same time, attempt to influence Marisa to behave appropriately.

The guidelines provided by the definition make it far easier to determine whether or not a discipline problem exists, and if it does, who has the problem. Most non-discipline problems can be dealt with at some later time, after the other students have begun their work, during a break, or before or after class. When a discipline problem is evident, however, the teacher must intervene immediately because, by definition, an existing behavior is interfering with other students' rights or safety. When a teacher inappropriately or ineffectively employs management strategies that result in interference with the learning of others, he, in fact, becomes the discipline problem.

Let's examine Case 2.1. Did Tom's late opening of his book interfere with teaching or his classmates' learning? Was it unsafe or did it destroy property? Wasn't it Mr. Karis's behavior that caused escalation of a minor problem that would have corrected itself? Using our definition, Mr. Karis was the discipline problem. It is doubtful that any teacher intervention was necessary at all. See Chapter 7 for a full discussion of when teacher intervention is appropriate. Note that under the terms of the definition, inappropriate or ill-timed classroom procedures, public address announcements, and school policies that tend to disrupt the teaching and/or learning process are discipline problems.

PROBLEM STUDENT BEHAVIOR OUTSIDE THE DEFINITION

By now, some readers have probably thought of many student behaviors that are not covered by our definition, for example, students who refuse to turn in homework, who are not prepared for class, or who are daydreaming, as well as the occasional student who gives the teacher "the look" that says "I dare you to try to teach me." A careful analysis of these behaviors will reveal that under the terms of the definition, they are not discipline problems. They may be motivational problems because the student does not expect to be successful in the classroom or the student sees no value in what is being taught in the classroom, or possibly symptoms of problems that exist in a student's personal life outside school.

Motivational problems can occur because of low levels of self-confidence, low expectations for success, lack of interest in academics, feelings of lost autonomy, feelings of not being accepted by peers, achievement anxieties, or fears of success or failure (Levin and Shanken-Kaye, 2002; Stipek, 2001). Thus, working with students

CASE 2.1

Can a Teacher Be a Discipline Problem?

Usually when the bell rings, the students in Mr. Karis's ninth-grade social studies class have their books out and are quietly waiting to begin work. Today, when Mr. Karis is finishing taking roll and asking a few questions to review the previous day's work, he notices that Tom is just starting to get his book out. Mr. Karis asks Tom why he isn't ready. Tom replies that he has a lot on his mind. Mr. Karis then reminds Tom in a strong tone that when the bell rings, he is to be ready to start. Tom replies in a tone that makes it very clear that he is annoyed, "Look, you don't know what my morning's been like!" Mr. Karis tells Tom that he "is not to be spoken to in that tone of voice." Tom quietly mumbles to himself in a voice too low for anyone to really hear "Why the #### not?" Mr. Karis says, "Did you say something?" The rest of the class members are now either talking among themselves or deeply involved in the outcome of the confrontation rather than in social studies. By the time Tom decides it probably is not in his best interest to continue the escalating conflict, at least five minutes of class time have elapsed and no teaching or learning has taken place.

who have motivational or other problems often involves long-term individualized interventions and/or referrals to professionals outside the classroom.

A theoretical in-depth coverage of motivation is beyond the scope of this book; however, Chapter 5 presents an introductory coverage of motivation from both teachers' and students' perspectives, along with practical strategies to address motivational problems. Students with low motivation typically exhibit behavior (daydreaming, lack of participation, unfinished assignments) that is not disruptive to other students' learning. However, some of the suggested strategies used to address motivation problems disturb the learning of others or reduce the time spent on learning. Therefore, it is best to work with these students individually *after* involving the rest of the class in the day's learning activities. Doing so allows the teacher to protect the other students' rights to learn and to maximize the time allocated for learning. Chapters 8–11 detail intervention strategies used to address discipline problems.

Some of these strategies, particularly anecdotal record keeping, can be used quite successfully for motivational problems. It cannot be stressed enough that motivational problems must be properly addressed, usually by focusing on the student's expectation of success and the value the student places on the learning activity, so that they do not develop into discipline problems (see Chapter 5). Case 2.2 illustrates how one teacher ensures that this does not occur.

Mr. Hill recognized that Bill's behavior did not interfere with the teaching and learning act and so did not need immediate action. He employed effective strategies that protected the other students' rights to learn. The strategies were the beginning of a long-term effort to build up Bill's interest (value) and confidence (expectation of success) in mathematics and to have him become an active, participating member of the class. Many readers have probably witnessed similar situations in which the teacher unfortunately chose to deal with the student's behavior in ways that were disruptive to the entire class.

CASE 2.2

Solving a Motivational Problem

Mr. Hill teaches fourth grade. One of his students, Bill, rarely participates in class and often is the last one to begin classwork. One day, the class is assigned math problems for seatwork. After a few minutes, Mr. Hill notices that Bill has not started. He calmly walks over to Bill, kneels down beside his desk, and asks Bill if he needs any help. This is enough to get Bill to begin his math problems. Mr. Hill waits until three problems are completed; he then tells Bill that because Bill understood them so well, he should put them on the board. After the class has finished the assignment, Mr. Hill begins to review the answers, stressing the correct procedures Bill used to solve the problems and thanking Bill for his board work.

Daydreaming students are not interfering with teaching or the rights of others to learn. Therefore, the teacher should first involve the rest of the class in the learning activity before individually influencing the daydreamer.

EXTENT OF THE PROBLEM

Public's Perceptions

According to all 43 Gallup polls of the "Public's Attitudes Toward the Public Schools," discipline is one of the most serious problems facing public schools. From the poll's inception in 1969 until 2000, the issue of discipline was the major concern on 16 occasions. For the next decade, the issues of financial support and overcrowded schools were the public's top concerns followed by discipline. In 2001, 15 percent of respondents reported discipline as a major problem; this fell to11 percent in 2006, and to 6 percent in 2011 (Bushaw and Lopez, 2011). In 2003, 35 percent of surveyed parents in a national sample identified discipline as an important aspect of schooling (Markow and Scheer, 2003).

Teachers' Perceptions

In a nationwide sampling of teachers in 1984, 95 percent believed that efforts to improve school discipline should have a higher priority than they then had (Harris, 1984). In a 1999 national survey, 65 percent of teachers said that discipline problems in their schools were very serious or fairly serious problems (Langdon, 1999). Additional studies all point to the importance teachers place on discipline. In 2003, 45 percent of a national sample of teachers stated that discipline was their first priority (Markow and Scheer, 2003); in 2004, 20 percent of new teachers identified classroom discipline as their greatest challenge (Markow and Scheer, 2004).

Students' Perceptions

Students are aware of the frequency of disruptive behavior. Nationwide in 1993, the majority of students in grades 8, 10, and 12 reported that student disruptions were fairly common occurrences in their classes. Sixteen percent of the eighth graders and 11 percent of the tenth graders surveyed reported that their teachers often interrupted instruction to manage disruptive student behavior (National Education Goals Panel, 1994). In 2000, 16 percent of the tenth graders surveyed reported frequently interrupted instruction (National Education Goals Panel, 2000).

Magnitude

In attempting to assess the magnitude of the discipline problem in the past, Doyle (1978) pointed out that serious historical investigation of student behavior was lacking and that the studies that were available at that time used data that were typically incomplete and in some cases unreliable. Doyle reviewed evidence from the few available sources and found that crime (violence and vandalism) was not a serious concern among school officials during the late 1800s to the early 1900s. However evidence exists that juvenile crime outside school was a problem during this period. In the early 1900s, less than 50 percent of the school-age population was enrolled in school. Of this, only 40 percent finished eighth grade, and only approximately 10 percent graduated. Thus, the children most likely to commit crimes were not in school (Hawes, 1971; Mennell, 1973; Schlossman, 1977). It was the growing concern over juvenile street crime that initiated a movement for public education. Authorities argued that street crime could be lessened if those youths responsible for it were brought under the influence of the school (Doyle, 1978). Doyle therefore concluded that youth behavior in the 1970s was no worse than it was in the past, but what was once a street problem was now a school problem, the result of more students attending school for longer periods of time.

Since the early 1980s, researchers have made a concerted effort to distinguish between crime (violence and vandalism) and common misbehavior (bothering other students, talking passing notes, etc.). Such a distinction is essential because crime and routine classroom misbehavior are inherently different problems that require different solutions, administered by different professionals both in and outside the school. Whereas teachers are responsible for handling routine classroom misbehavior, crime often must come under the control of the school administration and outside law-enforcement agencies.

Once crime is separated from common misbehavior, what do the schools of the 1980s to the early 2000s look like? In the later part of the twentieth century, Wayson (1985) stated that "most schools never experience incidents of crime and those that do, seldom experience them frequently or regularly" (p. 129), but disruptive behavior of "the kinds that have characterized school children for generations…continue to pose frequent and perplexing problems for teachers" (p. 127). After a thorough examination of studies, Baker (1985) concluded that there had been improvement, but "the level of disruptive behavior in the classroom is a major problem for public education" (p. 486).

These conclusions were supported by numerous studies reporting that teachers and administrators consistently ranked common classroom misbehaviors (excessive talking, failure to do assignments, disrespect, lateness) as the most serious and frequent disturbances, whereas they ranked crime (vandalism, theft, assault) as the least serious disturbance to their teaching or the least frequently occurring (Elam, 1989; Huber, 1984; Langdon, 1997; Levin, 1980; Thomas, Goodall, and Brown, 1983; Weber and Sloan, 1986).

Thus, the schools of the late 1980s and early 1990s were perceived as experiencing less crime than the schools of the 1970s; even though classroom misbehavior continued to be a major problem, it too was perceived as lessening. As we moved through the late 1990s and into the new millennium, there were indications that these trends were continuing. As discussed earlier in this chapter, although discipline problems remain a major concern, in 2007, the public ranked discipline problems as the second—after financial support—most serious problem facing public schools (Rose and Gallup, 2007). In 1999, only 7 percent of teachers ranked discipline as the most serious problem facing their schools (Langdon and Vesper, 2000).

Although it is difficult to believe if you watch the evening news, which disproportionally reports isolated incidents of extreme school violence, contrary to popular belief, crime and violent behavior in schools seem also to be trending downward. The latest data from the National Center for Education Statistics indicate that the total theft and violent and serious violent crime rates for students ages 12 to 18 all declined from 1992 to 2002 to 2008. The total student victimization rate fell from 10 percent to 5 percent to 4.7 percent, and the violent crime victimization rate declined from 4.8 percent to 2.4 percent to less than 1 percent (DeVoe et al., 2004; Robers,

Zhang, and Truman, 2010). Nationally, 2007–2009 aggregate data for rural, suburban, and urban schools indicate that serious crime and violence such as theft (3%), students' possession of weapons (6%), students being threatened or injured with a weapon (8%), and physical attacks on teachers (4%) are relatively infrequent occurrences (Robers et al., 2010). Irwin Hyman, a noted researcher on school violence, tracked violent behavior for more than 20 years and concluded as the millennium was ending that there were no indications that there had been an increase in school-based violence (Hyman and Perone, 1998). In fact, the data indicate a decrease in school-based violence.

Students are much more likely to be victims of serious crime away from school than when in school. For the 2008–2009 academic year, 15 student ages 5–18 were killed in school; for the same time period and age group, approximately 1700 student homicides occurred away from school. In 2008, the rate of nonfatal violent in-school crimes for students ages 12–18 was 4 per 1000 students, and the rate for the same crimes away from school was 8 per 1000 (Robers et al., 2010)

Schools continue to remain one of the safest places for children. Thus, as we continue in the new millennium, both discipline problems and serious crime and violence seem to be decreasing from the early 1990s, but they still remain a major concern of educators and the public. Successful teachers are those who continue to be effective in influencing students toward appropriate behavior and the use of nonviolent means to solve their conflicts.

THE EFFECT OF CLASSROOM DISCIPLINE PROBLEMS ON TEACHING AND LEARNING

Impact on Students

When classrooms are characterized by disruptive behavior, the teaching and learning environment is adversely affected. The amount of interference in the teaching and learning environment is related to the type, frequency, and duration of the disruptive behavior. Disruptive behavior also affects students' psychological safety, readiness to learn, and future behaviors.

For many years, we have had the opportunity to interact with thousands of college students preparing to become teachers as well as thousands of in-service teachers and school administrators who want to improve their own classroom management skills or those of the teachers they supervise. One of the first questions we always ask is, "Why do students have to behave in a classroom?" At first, we were somewhat embarrassed to ask such a basic question because we believed there was a universally obvious answer. However, to our surprise, the answer was not obvious to others. The answer, of course, involves the widely accepted learning principle that the more time spent on learning (time-on-task or engaged time), the more learning will take place (Brophy, 1988). In other words, disruptive, off-task behavior takes time away from learning, not only for the individual student but given our definition of a discipline problem developed earlier in this chapter, potentially many other students as well.

Case 2.3 illustrates the tremendous amount of time that can be consumed over a school year by some very minor off-task behaviors. Over a period of a week,

CASE 2.3

Discipline: A Costly Waste of Time

Mr. Kay is a seventh-grade social studies teacher who teaches five classes a day. He is content to allow his students, on entering the room, to stand around and talk rather than prepare their materials for class. As a result, class usually does not begin until five minutes after the bell has rung.

25 minutes that could have been directed toward learning are not. Over the 40-week school year, 1000 minutes are consumed by off-task behavior. This amounts to more than 22 class periods, or approximately one-ninth of the school year, that could have been directed toward learning goals. If the calculations also consider the 120 students Mr. Kay teaches per day, 2640 "student class periods" were not spent on learning social studies.

Some teachers are reported to spend as much as 25 percent (Lippman, Burns, and McArthur 2004) to 80 percent (Walsh, 1983) of their time addressing discipline problems. This figure simply highlights a previously mentioned basic fact of teaching: to be a successful teacher, one must be competent in influencing appropriate student behavior to maximize the time spent on learning.

Case 2.4 illustrates the fact that disruptive behavior can result in a "ripple effect." In other words, students learn misbehavior from observing it in other children (Baker, 1985). The off-task behaviors of Rebecca's friends draw her off task. This type of observational learning is often accelerated when the onlooking student notices the attention the disruptive student gains from both the teacher and his classmates.

Ripple effects are not limited to the initial misbehavior. The methods the teacher uses to curb the misbehavior and the targeted student's resultant behavior can cause

CASE 2.4

The Ripple Effect

Rebecca is a well-mannered, attentive fifth-grade student. For the first time since starting school, she and her two best friends are in the same class. Unlike Rebecca, her friends are not attentive and are interested more in each other than in class activities. The teacher often has to reprimand them for passing notes, talking to each other, and giggling excessively during class.

One day, Rebecca is tapped on the shoulder and is handed a note from her friend across the room. She accepts the note and sends one back. With this, her friends quickly include her in their antics. It takes the teacher a number of weeks to remove Rebecca from her friends' influence and reduce the off-task behaviors of the other two girls.

a second ripple effect (Kounin, 1970). Studies have shown that rough and threatening teacher behavior causes student anxieties, which lead to additional disruptive behaviors from onlooking students. Students who see disruptive students comply with the teacher's management technique and tend to rate their teacher as fair are themselves less distracted from their classwork than when they observe unruly students defying the teacher (Smith, 1969). Clearly, the dynamics that come into play with even minor classroom disruptions are quite complex. Aggressive teacher behavior toward students has also been related to students' poor emotional health and future disruptive behavior (Hyman and Snook, 1999).

Common day-to-day off-task student behaviors such as talking and walking around exist in all classrooms to some degree. Although less common, some classrooms, indeed some entire schools, are plagued by threats, violence, and vandalism. The most recent data, for 2007–2009, indicate that 32 percent of students ages 12–18 were bullied, 11 percent had been in a physical fight on school property, 6 percent carried a gun onto school property, and 4 percent had drunk alcohol and 5 percent had smoked marijuana at school. Additionally, 5 percent of students reported being victimized, including 3 percent reporting theft and 2 percent violent victimization (Robers et al., 2010).

Students use a variety of strategies to avoid being victimized, including avoiding certain locations in the school building, staying away from school-sponsored events, staying in groups while at school, and staying at home rather than attending school out of fear that someone might hurt or bother them. One study estimates that 1.1 million students fear for their safety while at school (Children's Defense Fund, 2002). Obviously, when students are fearful for their own safety or the safety of their property, their ability to concentrate on their schoolwork is diverted. Fear creates a hostile learning environment, increases a feeling of mistrust in the school, and reduces students' confidence in their teachers' ability to effectively work with students (Wayne and Rubel, 1982). Some studies indicate that a student's ability to learn in the classroom is reduced by at least 25 percent because of fear of other students (Dade County Public Schools, 1976; Lalli and Savitz, 1976).

In conclusion, minor and major misbehavior reduces learning time for both disruptive students and onlooking students. Less learning time equates to less learning. Although a clear cause-and-effect relationship has not been shown, there is a positive correlation between poor grades and all types of misbehavior (DiPrete, Muller, and Shaeffer, 1981).

Impact on Teachers

Classroom discipline problems also have a negative impact on teacher effectiveness and career longevity. We believe that the overwhelming majority of teachers choose to enter the profession because they enjoy working with children and are intrinsically motivated when they know that their efforts have contributed to the children's academic growth (Zabel and Zabel, 1996). Their motivation is high because they see their efforts such as lesson planning, classroom management, and building relationships with students as being successful by influencing what teachers value, that is, students' measurable academic growth and the display of appropriate behavior. High intrinsic motivation leads to a teacher's high self-esteem.

Coopersmith (1967) conceptualized self-esteem as the sum of significance (feeling good about yourself because people who are important to you like and respect you), competence (a sense of mastery of a discipline or a skill set), virtue (the ability and desire to help others), and power (the ability to control and change aspects of your environment). When a teacher has an appropriately behaving, academically achieving class, the teacher feels he is liked and respected, confident in his teaching abilities, and willing and able to help students and that his efforts are making a difference. In other words, he has high significance, competence, virtue, and power. The teacher has high self-esteem.

When a teacher's efforts are met with chronic disinterest and disruptive behavior, his motivation is most likely low because he sees his efforts as being unsuccessful in influencing what teachers value. Low motivation leads to low self-esteem. Teachers feel insignificant, incompetent, virtueless, and powerless.

Therefore, a teacher's motivation and self-esteem are quite vulnerable to students' academic growth and their classroom behaviors. No matter how careful teachers are not to allow their personal feelings to play a role in their interactions with students, it is inevitable that some will and when this occurs, their feelings will influence their behavior. Indeed, studies have shown that teachers interact differently with disruptive students than they do with nondisruptive ones (e.g., Walker, 1979). Such differential treatment is fueled by the negative beliefs and feelings many teachers have toward disruptive students and the disparaging labels they assign to these students (Brendtro et al., 1990). Unfortunately, differential treatment serves only to escalate inappropriate student behavior. Even the student who exhibits the most chronic disruptive behavior spends some time engaged in appropriate behavior. However, occasionally a teacher may become so angry with certain students that he tends to overlook the appropriate behavior and focuses only on the disruptive behavior. When this occurs, the teacher misses the few opportunities he has to begin to change disruptive behaviors to acceptable ones. At least two studies have concluded that teachers are much more likely to reprimand inappropriate behavior than to approve of appropriate behavior when interacting with disruptive students (Walker and Buckley, 1973, 1974). As a result, the student soon learns that when he behaves appropriately nothing happens, but when he misbehaves, he is the center of both the teacher's and other students' attention.

Any teacher can attest to the fact that students easily realize when rules and expectations are not consistently enforced or obeyed by either the teacher or the students. Even so, because teachers are so emotionally tied to the disruptive students, they often set and enforce standards for these students that are different from those for the rest of the class. These standards are often so inflexible and unrealistic that they actually reduce the chance that the disruptive student will behave appropriately.

Because students who exhibit disruptive behavior often have a history of inappropriate behaviors, they must be given the opportunity to learn new behaviors. The learning process is usually best accomplished in small, manageable steps that enable the student to have a high probability of success. This process requires behavioral standards to be realistic and the same as those for the rest of the class. The teacher must recognize and encourage what at first may be infrequent and short-lived appropriate behaviors. When behavioral standards are stricter for some students than for others, the teacher risks losing the confidence and support of even the nondisruptive students, whereas the student exhibiting disruptive behavior gains peer support.

As teachers begin to experience more discipline problems, their motivation to teach is often replaced by, at best, a "who cares?" attitude, which is actually a means to protect the teacher's self-esteem. If conditions do not improve, this attitude may develop into a "get even" one, which eventually overrides a teacher's motivation to assist students in learning, and the once supportive and effective teacher behaviors are replaced by revenge. Once a teacher operates from a basis of revenge, teaching effectiveness ceases and a teacher-student parallel process of shared negative affective experiences begins (Levin and Shanken-Kaye, 2002), with teacher-student power struggles becoming commonplace. Such power struggles often further fuel and escalate disruptive behavior and place the teacher in a no-win situation (Dreikurs, 1964).

Children who display disruptive behaviors are constant reminders to teachers that the classroom environment is not what they would like it to be. The time and energy needed to cope with some disruptive behaviors can be both physically draining and emotionally exhausting, negatively impacting a teacher's motivation to teach and feelings of self-esteem. New teachers identify classroom discipline to be their greatest challenge (APA, 2006; Zabel and Zabel, 1996). Stress related to classroom management is one of the most influential factors in failure among novice teachers (Levin, 1980; Vittetoe, 1977) and a major reason why they leave the profession (APA, 2006; Canter, 1989; Langdon, 1999).

Classroom management problems are a major cause of job-related stress for teachers.

Those teachers who do weather their first few years of teaching report that students who continually misbehave are the primary cause of job-related stress (Feitler and Tokar, 1992). According to the National Institute of Education (1980), teachers who report that they would not choose the teaching profession if they had to choose a profession again were much more likely to have experienced discipline problems than teachers who would choose teaching again (Curwin and Mendler, 1999; Haberman, 2004).

Discipline problems are also hypothesized as the catalyst for teacher burnout (Curwin and Mendler, 1999). Teachers who manage their classrooms effectively report that they enjoy teaching and feel a certain confidence in their ability to affect student achievement (Levin et al., 1985). Such feelings of efficacy lead to improvements in the teaching-learning process and job satisfaction, which ultimately result in gains in student achievement (Black, 2001).

NEW CONCERNS: TECHNOLOGY

Cybercheating

The Internet and new technologies including laptop computers, iPads, and smart mobile phones have significantly changed teaching and learning. As positive as these

Teachers who are effective managers have greater job satisfaction.

changes have been, the same technologies have been used by students in negative ways. Cheating on tests and assignments is as old as schooling, but the ways students cheat have drastically changed, often with serious unforeseen consequences. Writing a spelling list on the palms of hands has evolved into storing the list on his cell phone. Asking to be excused during a test to use the rest room where the students previously wrote notes on the wall has been replaced with texting a friend to look up answers to specific questions.

Cybercheating is the use of technology tools in inappropriate ways for academic work (Conradson and Hernandez-Ramos 2004). Many educators believe that cybercheating has reached epidemic proportions, and students continue to find innovative ways to use technology for the purpose of cheating. What was once considered mainly a college plagiarism problem is now soundly entrenched in secondary and even middle school and goes beyond plagiarism. In a 2002 Rutgers University study, 72 percent of the 4500 high school students surveyed admitted to seriously cheating (Schulte, 2002). In a 1998 survey of 21,000 middle and high school students, 70 percent reported cheating in school; by 2002, the percentage increased to 74 percent and by 2010, 59 percent of a sample of 40,000 students admitted to cheating in school (Josephson, 1998, 2002, 2010).

The technology most frequently used to cheat is the cell phone. Students store information on their cell phones and look at it during the exam. They text questions to friends who then text them back with answers. Some students take pictures of test questions and send them to friends, and others use the phone to search the web for answers. There are even websites that tutor students on how to cheat using technology, sell class notes and term papers, and edit papers with deliberately inserted misspellings and grammatical errors to avoid the suspicion of plagiarism (Conradson and Hernandez-Ramos, 2004).

Studies indicate that many students do not consider cybercheating to be a serious cheating offense, and some do not consider it to be cheating at all. A recent survey indicated that a fairly high percentage of students did not consider the following to be cheating: sending pictures of exams (23%), web surfing during an exam (19%), texting a friend for answers (20%), and storing notes on cell phones (22%; Commonsense Media, 2012). The reason given for cheating is to get better grades.

How should teachers address cybercheating in the classroom? In deciding what to do, the definition of a discipline problem needs be considered as well as the motivation that drives cybercheating. Earlier in this chapter, the definition of a discipline problem was stated as any behavior that (1) interferes with the teaching act, (2) interferes with the rights of others to learn, (3) is psychologically or physically unsafe, or (4) destroys property. Thus, unless the student is blatantly displaying his cheating, which is very unlikely, cybercheating is not considered a discipline problem, although it is a very serious problem. This means that the teacher does not have to intervene immediately but instead individually and as privately as possible while the other students are working on the assignment or exam. Next, the teacher needs to analyze the motivation that drives students to cheat. As was stated earlier, a detailed discussion of motivational theory is beyond the scope of this text, but such in-depth knowledge is not needed to obtain a basic understanding of the student's motivation to cheat. If motivation is a product of one's expectation of success and value (see Chapter 5), then the student expects to be successful in using cheating to obtain a good grade, which the student values. Punishing a student other than lowering grades or other academic actions, which are logical natural consequences will not work for long-term change (see Chapter 6). What is needed is changing a student's expectation of success, from one of cheating to learning and using more appropriate ways of being successful such as study skills and test-taking skills. Valuing good grades is perfectly acceptable, but helping students to value mastery and competence, which actually result in good grades, is a much longer-term, more widely applicable value.

Cyberbullying

Making fun of another student by calling him a nerd when passing in a hallway has become insignificant when compared to the magnitude of potential harm a student suffers when he is targeted as the subject of cyberbullying. Cyberbullying is a relatively new and particularly virulent form of online bullying. *Cyberbullying* is the willful and repeated harm to a person inflicted through electronic media. It enables bullies to post put-downs, nasty rumors, and humiliating pictures on e-mail, blogs, chat rooms, websites, instant messages, and cell phones. The latest statistics report that during the 2008–2009 school year, 28 percent of students ages 12–18 years were bullied at school and 6 percent reported they were victims of cyberbullying. The impact on the victims of cyberbullying ranges from embarrassment to in rare cases suicide. Chapter 3 presents in more detail the statistics and impact of bullying; cyberbullying; and a subset of cyberbullying, sexting.

Summary

This chapter has answered three questions that are critical for an understanding of discipline and classroom management: What is a discipline problem? What is the extent of the problem in today's schools? What is the effect of discipline problems on teaching and learning?

After a discussion of past definitions of discipline and their shortcomings, an operational definition was provided: a discipline problem is any behavior that (1) interferes with the teaching act, (2) interferes with the rights of others to learn, (3) is psychologically or physically unsafe, or (4) destroys property. According to this definition, teachers as well as students are responsible for appropriate behavior.

In response to the second question, we explored the belief that today's schools are plagued by violence, crime, and disruptive classroom behavior. Early studies were characterized by incomplete and in some cases unreliable data. Studies in the 1980s, which differentiated between crime and classroom misbehavior, characterized schools as having less crime than in the 1970s. This downward trend has continued into the present. Common classroom misbehavior also seemed to have lessened during this period, even though such behaviors still pose serious and perplexing problems for teachers. Recent studies indicate that the schools of the early 2000s are experiencing less disruptive classroom behavior, student crime, and violence.

Next, it was shown that disruptive behavior reduces the time spent on learning, encourages misbehavior by onlooking students because of a ripple effect, and may cause fear in other students, with a resultant decrease in school attendance and academic achievement. Teachers are also adversely affected by disruptive behavior, suffering decreased effectiveness, increased job-related stress, burnout, and decreased career longevity.

Finally, the practices of cybercheating and cyberbullying were introduced as new challenges that educators face. Both are increasing in frequency, and both can have significant present and future negative impacts on students.

Exercises

1. Is it important that all teachers have a consistent definition of the types of student behaviors that constitute discipline problems? Why or why not?
2. Do you agree with the definition of a discipline problem stated in this chapter? If so, why? If not, how would you modify it?
3. Give several examples of teacher behavior that would constitute a discipline problem.
4. Using the definition of a discipline problem stated in this chapter, categorize each of the following behaviors as a discipline problem or a non-discipline problem and explain your reasoning.

Behavior	Non-Discipline Problem	Discipline Problem	Rationale
a. A student consistently tries to engage the teacher in conversation just as class is about to begin.			
b. A student continually comes to class one minute late.			
c. A teacher stands in the hallway talking to fellow teachers during the first three minutes of class.			
d. A student does math homework during social studies class.			
e. A student interrupts a lecture to ask permission to go to the bathroom.			
f. A student often laughs at answers given by other students.			
g. A student doesn't wear safety goggles while welding in industrial arts class.			
h. A first grader continually volunteers to answer questions but never has an answer when he is called on.			
i. A fourth grader refuses to wear a jacket during recess.			
j. A seventh grader constantly pulls the hair of the girl who sits in front of him.			
k. An eighth-grade boy spends half of the time allotted for group work encouraging a girl to go out with his friend.			
l. A ninth-grade student consistently uses the last two minutes of class for hair combing.			
m. unkempt student can't get involved in group work because all students refuse to sit near him.			
n. A student continually asks good questions, diverting the teacher from the planned lesson.			
o. A student eats a candy bar during class.			
p. A student flirts with the teacher by asking questions about her clothes and personal life during class.			
q. A student consistently makes wisecracks that entertain the rest of the class.			

5. At this point in your reading, how would you handle each of the 17 behaviors listed? Why?

6. For each of the 17 behaviors, give at least one type of teacher behavior that might escalate the inappropriate student behavior.

7. According to the definition of a discipline problem, a student who refuses to do classwork is not a discipline problem. However, suppose other students start to say, "He is not working. Why do I have to work?" Does the student's refusal to work thus become a discipline problem?

8. Think back to your days as a student what extent would you say that discipline was a problem in your school? What types of discipline problems were most common?

9. Do you think that the discipline problem in schools has increased or decreased since you attended high school? On what evidence or information do you base your opinion?

10. Considering what a teacher's job entails and his relationship with students, why would he be prone to take discipline problems personally?

11. What are the dangers of personalizing student behavior? How might doing so affect the instructional effectiveness of a teacher?

12. How can teachers protect themselves from personalizing misbehavior?

13. Think back on your days as a student. Can you recall instances in which classroom discipline problems prevented you and others in the class from learning? How did you feel about the situation at the time?

14. When a student disrupts class and takes away the right of others to learn, does that student forfeit his right to learn? If you believe he does, what implication(s) does that have for teacher behavior? If you believe he doesn't, what implication(s) does that have for teacher behavior?

15. If youth violence seems to be on the decrease, why does the public perceive it as increasing?

16. What would you do as the teacher if a student told you that another student in your class had brought a gun to school?

17. Do you think that the national media overemphasize the actual amount of in-school violence? What is the effect of the media's portrayal of school violence?

18. Cybercheating was described as not being a discipline problem but instead a motivation problem. Motivation was defined as a product of a student's expectation of success and the student's values. If students involved in cybercheating expect to be successful because of their competence in using technologies and they value good grades, how might a teacher change the student's expectation of success and value so that the student would not be motivated to cheat?

19. **Principles of Teacher Behavior** After reading Chapter 2 and doing the exercises, use what you have learned to briefly describe your understanding of the implications of the principles listed at the beginning of the chapter for a classroom teacher.

Principle 1:

Principle 2:

3

Understanding Why Children Misbehave

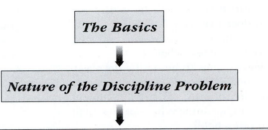

PRINCIPLES OF TEACHER BEHAVIOR THAT INFLUENCE APPROPRIATE STUDENT BEHAVIOR

1. An awareness of the influences of misbehavior, which are often beyond the schools' control, enables teachers to use positive intervention techniques rather than negative techniques, which stem from erroneously viewing misbehavior as a personal affront.

2. Satisfaction of basic human needs such as food, safety, belonging, and security is a prerequisite for appropriate classroom behavior.

3. The need for a sense of significance, competence, virtue, and power influences student behavior.

4. Cognitive and moral developmental changes result in normal student behavior that is often disruptive in learning environments.

5. Instructional competence can lessen the effects of negative outside influences as well as prevent the misbehavior that occurs as a result of poor instruction.

PREREADING ACTIVITY: UNDERSTANDING THE PRINCIPLES OF TEACHER BEHAVIOR

Before reading Chapter 3, briefly describe your understanding of the implications of the principles for a classroom teacher.

Principle 1:

Principle 2:

Principle 3:

Principle 4:

Principle 5:

PREREADING QUESTIONS FOR REFLECTION AND JOURNALING

1. As you think about changes in society that you have seen in your life, how have societal views of appropriate and inappropriate behavior changed? Are these changes positive or negative? Why?

2. Many students exhibit disruptive behaviors in school at one time or another. What are some factors that influence students to choose to behave in inappropriate ways?

3. How might changes in students' cognitive and moral development be a contributing factor in influencing students' behavior?

4. Why do many teachers and administrators ignore bullying in the schools?

5. Why does cyberbullying have such a negative impact on those being bullied?

6. What teaching strategies facilitate resilient student behavior?

INTRODUCTION

"Kids aren't the way they used to be. When I went to school, kids knew their place. Teachers wanted to teach and students wanted to learn. The students respected their teachers, and believe me, they sure didn't fool around in school like they do today." Adults frequently make these statements as they remember the "way it used to be," but are they true? Not entirely!

There have always been some behavior problems in our schools if only because of students' normal developmental changes. There also have always been some schools and homes that have been unable to provide adequately for children's needs. Even so, recent rapid societal changes—including the significant changes in society's beliefs about "the place" of all people in society, especially children—have been the catalyst for new behavior problems and have compounded existing ones (Levin and Shanken-Kaye, 2002). There have been significant shifts in the family structure, the distribution of wealth and knowledge in the United States, the cultural and racial makeup of the population, and world economies, as well as advances in technology that were only fantasized about a few decades ago. In addition, media reports of violence have increased disproportionately to actual violence in society. These changes have resulted in many students at risk for future problems. These changes are evident in students' thoughts, attitudes, and behavior. Nonetheless, students are still intrinsically motivated toward skill acquisition and competency (Stipek, 2001), and teachers still want to teach.

If, however, teachers want to maximize their teaching time, they must minimize the effect of societal changes on student behavior. Teachers must (1) not expect students to think and act the way they did years ago, (2) not demand respect from students solely on the basis of a title or position, (3) understand the methods and behaviors young people employ to find their place in today's society, (4) understand the ongoing societal changes and the influence these changes have on students' lives, and (5) be a catalyst for encouraging resiliency for at-risk students. To assist teachers in reaching these goals, this chapter describes some of the main factors that have influenced students to change and provides an explanation of why today's students behave as they do.

SOCIETAL CHANGES

For more than 100 years, it has been recognized that schools are microcosms of the larger society (Dewey, 1916; Kindsvatter, 1978). Therefore, discipline problems in the schools reflect the problems that face society. The social climate of the nation, city, or town and the community that surrounds each school has profound effects on students' perceptions of the value of education and their behavior in school (Menacker, Weldon, and Hurwitz, 1989).

It is widely recognized that our society is plagued by the ills of drug and alcohol use, crime and violence, unemployment, child abuse, adolescent suicide, and teenage pregnancy. It is no coincidence that if these problems exist, particularly in close proximity to the school, so do school discipline problems. This clear relationship between social problems and school discipline problems simply highlights the fact that many factors that contribute to discipline problems are beyond the schools' control (Barton and Coley, 2007; Bayh, 1978).

Even if there were no societal problems, disruptive behavior could still be expected in a school because it is an institution that brings together many of the conditions that facilitate misbehavior. Large numbers of young people, many of whom are still learning socially acceptable behaviors and would rather be elsewhere, are concentrated in one place for long periods of time. These young people come from a wide range of backgrounds, with different ethnic, racial, and parental attitudes and expectations concerning education. A school exposes all students to norm-violating behaviors and makes failure visible (Elliott and Voss, 1974; Feldhusen, 1978).

Children no longer grow up in a society that provides them with constant, consistent sets of guidelines and expectations. The intense, rapid technological advancements in mass communication of the past two decades have exposed young people to violence and a multitude of varying viewpoints, ideas, and philosophies. With this exposure, the direct influence of parents, community, and school has begun to wane. Role models have changed. Schools are now faced with children who are exposed to more varied types of information than ever before. As a result, these children think and act differently.

The Knowledge Explosion and the Erosion of Respect for Authority

Since the 1950s, when the Soviet Union launched *Sputnik*, the first satellite, there has been an unabated explosion in scientific knowledge and technological advancements. This explosion has resulted in products only dreamed of previously. Digital and satellite phones, DVDs, satellite dishes, CD-ROMs, powerful personal computers, personal digital assistants (PDAs), iPads, FAX machines, the Internet, e-mail, and other telecommunication devices that are used for instantaneous worldwide personal communications and access to an ever-expanding array of databases are common today.

To understand how great the explosion of knowledge has been, consider this. In the early 1970s, less than 20 years after *Sputnik*'s launch, it was estimated that by the time children born in 1980 reached the age of 50, the world's knowledge would have increased 32 times, and 97 percent of all knowledge would have been learned since they were born (Toffler, 1970). With the advances that have been made in the past 35 years, these estimates are probably much too low. Nothing illustrates this better than the emergence of the Internet.

Such a rapid expansion of knowledge has caused generation gaps characterized by discontinuities rather than mere differences. By the end of elementary school, many children possess knowledge that their parents only vaguely comprehend. This is poignantly clear in areas such as personal computing, information retrieval, ecology, biotechnology, and astronomy. In addition, because of the almost instantaneous telecommunication of national and world events, children are keenly aware of the state of the present world. They see famine; terrorist attacks; war; political corruption; drug busts; street violence; chemical spills; riots; accusations of sexual abuse against religious, education and political leaders; and reports of infidelity on a daily basis.

Such knowledge has caused many young people to view adults as ineffective in managing their own world. These young people perceive past solutions to life's problems as irrelevant to the world in which they live. Therefore, respect, which was once given to adults because of their worldliness and expertise, has eroded, and adults exercise less influence on the young than they once did. When talking to adolescents, it is common to hear such statements as, "My parents don't understand," "Why do we have to do it by hand when there are calculators that can do it for you?" "Why do I have to be honest when government officials are always lying and cheating?" and "Didn't you ever hear of spell check?"

As the world becomes a more complex and frightening place and as young people perceive their parents and teachers to be less relevant sources for solutions, the future for these young people becomes more remote, uncertain, and unpredictable, producing such feelings as "live for today." As far back as 1964, Stinchcombe demonstrated a direct relationship between adolescents' images of the future and their attitudes and behaviors. Those adolescents who saw little or nothing to be gained in the future from school attendance were likely to exhibit rebellious, alienated behavior. Unfortunately, even more young people today have this image of the future than there were in 1964. Clearly, then, a teacher's ability to maximize student success and demonstrate the present and future usefulness of the material to be learned plays an important role in students' perceived value of education.

The Knowledge Explosion, Teacher and Student Feelings of Frustration, and the Relevancy of Schooling

Students are not alone in their feelings of frustration. Teachers too perceive many school curricula to be irrelevant to today's world. They are frustrated because of the almost impossible task of keeping up with the expansion of knowledge and the new technologies. Changes in school curricula occur at a snail's pace when compared to the daily expansion of information and technological advances.

Many teachers have said that they find it impossible to keep abreast of developments in their content areas and the rapidly expanding array of new pedagogical models, many of which support the use of new technologies. In addition, many have found it difficult to integrate the new material into an already overloaded curriculum. They truly desire to restructure their curricula in meaningful ways and to integrate technologies into their instructional practices, but they often find that their schools lack the necessary resources or commitment to invest in the latest technologies, training, or teacher release time for curriculum development. Their feelings of frustration lead to job dissatisfaction and poor morale, which can spill into the classroom disguised as less-than-ideal teacher-student interactions. However, when schools are able to invest in the new technologies and teachers are properly trained in their use, powerful changes can occur for both teachers and students, as illustrated in Case 3.1.

CASE 3.1

"This Is the Greatest Thing That Has Happened to Me in 20 Years of Teaching"

At a national education conference, one of the authors met Mr. Lee, a 20-year veteran high school earth science teacher. Mr. Lee said that he felt he was no longer reaching his students who were disinterested and turned off. In his opinion, every day was an endless hassle. He was not sure he wanted to return to the classroom the next year.

A few years later, surprisingly, Mr. Lee was seen again at another national education conference. He said that not only had he remained in the classroom but that his enthusiasm for teaching was as high as it had ever been. Mr. Lee went on to say that shortly after meeting us, he had challenged himself to restructure his course to reflect contemporary earth science.

He had requested from his principal a small allotment of money for summer curriculum work to research the real-time meteorology and oceanographic databases accessible from the web. These databases were the same as those used by professional scientists. He said the integration of real-time data accessible by students was the best strategy he had ever used. For the first time in many years, visitation night was crowded with parents who had come to see what was going on in their sons' and daughters' science class. Many of the parents commented that their children were coming home talking about the neat things they were doing in science for the first time ever.

Just as students are positively affected by contemporary and innovative educational programs that meet their needs, they are negatively affected by those that do not. Frustration is a natural outcome when instructional methodology does not change, and students are expected to learn more in shorter periods of time. Traditional instructional practices used to deliver outdated content become meaningless and boring to youth who are growing up in a world significantly different from that of their parents. What teachers often label as only a lack of motivation (which is defined as the product of expectation of success and the value of what is being learned) may actually involve the students' inability to find any value or feel any affiliation with what is going on in the classroom (Gabay, 1991). Lack of affiliation leads to boredom and off-task, disruptive classroom behaviors.

Teaching only facts is not sufficient. To prepare students for their future rather than our past, they must be instructed in ways that facilitate their "learning how to learn" (see Chapter 5). However, such pedagogical outcomes are being significantly hampered by an educational climate that emphasizes accountability measured by high-stakes assessments. Thus, many teachers find themselves "teaching toward the test." Case 3.2 illustrates how students respond to different types of educational experiences, depending on their perceived relevancy. Obviously, Mary has a much better attitude about capitals than her sister. Although neither sister knew the requested capital, Mary knew one way to find it and was willing to follow through. Could it be that the different attitudes are related to the different instructional strategies that had been used in the girls' classrooms? Unlike Amy, Mary had an opportunity to use appropriate instructional technology and was taught a skill that facilitates her ability to be a self-learner. In other words, Mary was "learning how to learn."

Television and Violence

Unlike any stimulus available earlier in human history, including radio, television transmits incredible amounts of information and gives the viewer a "window on the world." Ninety-nine percent of 8- to 18-year-olds live in homes that have at least one television set (Rideout, Roberts, and Foehr, 2005). The average American child spends as much or more time watching television and using other media—approximately 28 to 40 hours per week (American Academy of Child & Adolescent Psychiatry et al., 2000; Rideout et al., 2005)—than she does in a classroom. Clearly, then, television has become a major source of information for and major influence on children. The inhabitants of the TV world, however, often act and think in ways that contrast sharply with the attitudes and behaviors of parents and teachers.

Most studies on the impact of television on children have concentrated on the amount of violence portrayed and its effects. In 1993, the American Psychological Association stated, "Nearly four decades of research on television viewing and other media have documented the almost universal exposure of American children to high levels of media violence" (p. 33).

Content analysis of television shows in the early 1950s indicated that, on average, there were 11 threats or acts of violence per hour (*Congressional Quarterly,* 1993). However, TV programs for children in the early 2000s were 50 to 60 times more violent than prime-time TV for adults. On average, there are 26 acts of violence per hour on weekend children's programming, with some cartoons having more than 80 acts

CASE 3.2

Who Really Cares?

The question that would win the game seemed simple: What is the capital of Kansas? Even so, none of the adults who were playing could remember. Don said, "How do they expect you to remember such ridiculous facts? This is exactly what bothers me about these games." He then called his two daughters over and said, "Hey, you learned the state capitals in fifth grade, didn't you? So what's the capital of Kansas?" Amy, who was in seventh grade, replied, "I hated that stuff. We had to memorize all 50 state capitals, take a stupid test, and we never used it again. Who really cares what the capital is!" Mary, who was finishing fifth grade, replied, "I don't remember, but it's not hard to find out. I can look it up right now on the web. I can 'Google' it. It's incredible. I don't know how it works but we also have a CD that has everything about geography on it. If you want, I can even view a map of the capital on 'Google Earth.'"

of violence per hour (American Psychiatric Association, 2002). Given the format for most TV programs in the United States—brief sequences of fast-paced action with frequent interruptions for unrelated commercial messages—the American Psychiatric Association (2002) predicted that the average child would witness 16,000 televised murders and 200,000 acts of violence by the age of 18.

Violence is not solely a characteristic of fictional TV programming. The "eyewitness" local news format frequently features violent stories. Content analysis in the 1980s indicated that stories about murder, rape, and assault are disproportionately covered by local news, whereas stories of international violence and crime predominate in national newscasts (Atkin, 1983). Television news collects and concentrates violence by practicing "bodycount journalism" (Simmons, 1994), which follows the axiom "if it bleeds it leads" (Kerbel, 2000). Although actual homicides have steadily declined over the past two decades, there has been an inversely proportional increase of 450 percent more homicide stories on the major networks (Grand Rapids Institute for Information Democracy, 2000), which accounts for 40 percent to 50 percent of all the airtime devoted to news (Klite, 1999).

The immediate emotional reaction that children have after watching a violent news story is the fear that what they just watched will happen to them. (Cantor, 1999; Rees, 2003). Children are particularly susceptible to this fear when the violence is real as on TV news. Longer-term effects include emotional, physical, and behavioral problems (Cantor, 2002; Kaiser Family Foundation, 2003a).

Although some psychologists in the 1950s suggested that TV violence had a cathartic effect and reduced a child's aggressive behaviors, by the 1980s, laboratory and field studies had cast serious doubt on the cathartic hypothesis (Pearl, Bouthilet, and Lazar, 1982). By 1993, the American Psychological Association stated, "There is absolutely no doubt that higher levels of viewing violence on television are correlated with increased acceptance of aggressive attitudes and increased aggressive behavior" (p. 33). Psychologists also suggest that the effects of TV violence may extend beyond viewers' increased aggressive behaviors to the "bystander effect," or the increased desensitization or callousness toward violence directed at others (*Congressional Quarterly,* 1993). In addition, the American Psychiatric Association stated, "The debate is over. Over the last three decades, the one overriding finding in research on the mass media is that exposure to media portrayals of violence increases aggressive behavior in children (2002, p. 1). The National Institute of Mental Health reported, "In magnitude, exposure to television violence is as strongly correlated with aggressive behavior as any other behavioral variable that has been measured" (cited in American Psychiatric Association, 2002, p. 1).

Some researchers have proposed that violence on TV produces stress in children. Too much exposure to too much violence over too long a time, they say, creates emotional upset and insecurity, leading to resultant disturbed behavior (Rice, 1981). A 1984 study has indicated that heavy TV viewing is associated with elementary school children's belief in a "mean and scary world" and that poor school behavior (restlessness, disruptiveness, inattentiveness, aggressiveness) is significantly correlated with the home TV environment (number of sets, hours of viewing, and type of programs; Murray, 1995; Singer, Singer, and Rapaczynski, 1984).

Of course, there have been many theories about the relationship between TV viewing and children's behavior (Pearl, 1984). The observational modeling theory, which is now more than 40 years old, is the most widely accepted. This theory proposes that aggression is learned from the models and real-life simulations portrayed on TV and is practiced through imitation (Bandura, 1973; Cantor, 2002). In trying to explain the effects of TV on school behavior, Rice, Huston, and Wright (1982) hypothesized that the stimuli of sound effects, exciting music, and fast-action images generate an arousal reaction, with an accompanying inability to tolerate the sometimes long conversations, explanations, and delays characteristic of the real world of school.

Eight- to 18-years-olds spend an average of 7 hours and 38 minutes per day or more than 53 hours per week using all types of media. This is an increase of 1 hour and 17 minutes per day over a period of five years (2004–2009). Although direct TV viewing has decreased by 25 minutes per day, total TV consumption has increased by 38 minutes when considering TV viewing on laptops, smart phones, iPods, and other MP3 players. When considering multitasking or the use of different media at the same time, a total of 10 hours 45 minutes of media content is consumed. This includes (with hours in parentheses) direct TV viewing (4:29), music (2:31), computers (1:29), video games (1:13), and print and movies (1:03; Kaiser Family Foundation, 2010).

In addition to viewing violence on TV shows, teenagers also spend considerable time day listening to music and watching music videos. (Children's Defense Fund, 2010). Music videos average more than one violent scene per minute, which is more than twice the rate on TV (Center for Media and Public Affairs, 1999).

Of more recent concern is that children can participate vicariously in violence by playing today's video games. Eighty-three percent of homes have video-game-capable technologies (Rideout et al., 2005), and 50 percent of young people report having a gaming console in their bedrooms (Kaiser Family Foundation, 2010). Content analyses of video games show that as many as 89 percent of games contain some violent content, and about 50 percent of the games include serious violent actions (Carnagey and Anderson, 2004).

Twenty years have passed since the American Psychological Association issued its statement on the definitive relationship between watching TV violence and aggressive behavior. Thus, it would be expected that the debate over the impact of TV violence on children would be over. Such is not the case; instead, the debate has been reinvigorated with the introduction of violent video games in the early 1990s. The level of violence in these games significantly surpasses that shown on TV. One of the most popular games rewards players for killing police, innocent bystanders and prostitutes.

Recent meta-analysis research indicates that exposure to violent video games is associated with increases in aggressive behavior, thoughts, and affect and antisocial behavior (Anderson, 2004a, 2004b). It has been hypothesized that this increase in aggressive behavior may be more than that associated with other violent media that are more passive than the hands-on active engagement necessary when playing violent video games.

Researchers in the 1980s and 1990s began to discover that in addition to short-term effects on children's behavior, media violence has long-term negative effects. One of the earliest longitudinal studies found a relationship between early TV viewing at age 8 and aggressive behavior at age 18. These same individuals were followed up at age 30 and again there was a relationship between TV viewing as a child and arrests and convictions for violent crime (Eron, 1982; Eron and Slaby, 1994). A more recent study found that even when the variables of prior aggressive behavior, family background, community environment, and psychiatric diagnosis were controlled for, there was a relationship between the number of hours of TV watched as a child and aggressive behavior at age 22 (Johnson et al., 2002). There is also empirical evidence that repeated exposure to violent media has a cumulative effect and is predictive of a person becoming habitually aggressive and occasionally a violent offender (Huesmann et al., 2003).

Repeated exposure to media violence increases aggressive behavior across the life span because it influences more positive attitudes toward aggressive solutions to conflict while decreasing negative emotional responses to violence; it makes violent behavioral scripts more cognitively available while decreasing the availability of non-violent scripts (Anderson, 2003).

Television and Alternative Role Models

Television also influences children's behaviors by presenting a wide range of alternative models and lifestyles. For instance, Music Television (MTV) broadcasts 24 hours a day the audio and video imagery of the latest rock music. What once were mostly inaudible lyrics are now visual depictions of songs, many of which concern drug and alcohol use, sexual promiscuity, hopelessness, and distrust of school and teachers.

Young people often look to professional athletes as role models. Yet in an alarming number of incidents, professional athletes model violence that goes beyond what is acceptable on the playing field and occurs both on and off the field. The violence is not only between players but also sometimes spills into the stands. Some recent noteworthy examples are the NBA Indiana Pacers' Ron Artest, who was previously suspended for throwing punches as he charged into the stands, celebrating a dunk with an elbow to the head of an opponent; the penalties imposed on the players, coaches, and management of the New Orleans Saints for placing bounties on opposing players; Texas Rangers' pitcher Frank Francisco throwing a chair into the stands; Todd Bertuzzi of the NHL's Vancouver Canucks assaulting from behind a player from the Colorado Avalanche; Raffi Torres of the Phoenix Coyotes, who launched himself to deliver a late, direct hit to the head of Chicago's Marian Hossa during the Stanley Cup Playoffs in April 2012; and heavyweight boxer Mike Tyson biting off the ear of Evander Holyfield. Each year, many professional athletes face charges of domestic violence and felonies, as well as allegations related to the use of steroids and other drugs. All of these acts of violence are highly publicized and replayed on national media outlets.

The recent proliferation of talk shows, especially during late afternoon hours, presents children with a glamorized view of oftentimes dysfunctional family life at a time when they are attempting to determine who they are, what they can do, and how far they can go in testing the limits of their parents' and teachers' authority. Television communicates to children pluralistic standards, changing customs, and shifting beliefs and values.

Although behavioral experimentation is both a prerequisite and a necessary component of the cognitive and moral developmental growth of young people, today's world is not as simple as it once was, and parents and teachers need to be aware of alternative models with which they compete.

Television's messages possibly have the most detrimental effects on children who live in poverty. These children usually are aware that they do not possess the things most other Americans have. They also know they lack the opportunities to obtain them in the near future. Thus, television's depiction of the "good life" may compound their feelings of hopelessness, discontent, and anger. Such feelings, coupled with the fact that many of these children believe they hold no stake in the values and norms of the more affluent society, lay the foundation for rage, which is often released in violent or aggressive behaviors directed at others (American Psychological Association, 1993). It is imperative for teachers to be aware of these outside influences on student behaviors in order to work constructively with and be supportive of today's youth. Teachers are in an ideal position to help youth understand how popular media attempt to manipulate feelings and behavior.

Changes in Ethnicity

Public schools today are being asked to educate students who are more racially and ethnically diverse than at any other time in our history. Approximately 49.4 million students attended school during the 2009–2010 school year (National Center for Education Statistics, 2011). In 2008, 44 percent of school-age students were from minority ethnic groups (Aud, Fox, and KewalRamani, 2010). This percentage is predicted to increase to more than 50 percent by 2040 when the majority of school-age students will be members of minority groups (Olson, 2000a). Minority students were in the majority in seven states (National Center for Education Statistics, 2003a). Demographers predict that there will be an increase in minority students in all but two states by 2015 (Olson, 2000a).

Whereas these significant changes in the population of students can offer unparalleled opportunities to enhance the learning environment and opportunities of all students, they can also raise major challenges for schools and teachers.

For example, in the nation's fifth largest school district, Broward County, Florida, students come from at least 52 countries and speak 52 languages (Olson, 2000b). Even more astonishing are the 80 languages spoken by students in the Houston school district, the nation's seventh largest public school system (Weaver, 2006).

While the percentage of students from minority groups increases, the percentage of teachers from minority groups remains at an all-time low of 17 percent (Strizek et al., 2006). Nearly half of all schools had no minority teachers (U.S. Department of Education, 1996; Weaver, 2005). In fact, Lisa Delpit (2012) argues that one of the most negative unintended consequences of the famous 1954 Brown vs. Board of Education the U.S. Supreme Court case that mandated school desegregation is a very significant decrease in the number of African American teachers. More than 38,000 African American teachers lost their jobs in southern and border states in the first decade following mandated desegregation.

Communication theory discusses the concept of *homophily*—the more two people are alike in background, attitudes, perceptions, and values, the more effectively they will communicate with each other (Abi-Nader, 1993). It is theorized that the disproportionate number of minority teachers leads to a lack of homophily or, in other words, a lack of cultural synchronization between minority students and their teachers. This can lead to misunderstandings, conflict, distrust, and hostility between students and the teacher as well as negative teacher expectations. This is especially problematic when a school's or classroom's philosophies and practices are characterized by a lack of understanding of minority students' cultural values, norms, styles, and language (Irvine, 1990). Typically, schools that are based on a white middle-class culture often deliver a curriculum that characterizes minority language as a corruption of English, minority familial structures as pathological, and historical contributions from minorities as absent or minimal (Ladson-Billings, 1994). Such learning environments create a negative learning climate in which the productive engagement of minority students in learning is greatly reduced, with a concomitant increase in disruptive behavior.

Understanding Behavior by Analyzing Motivation and Self-Esteem

Case 3.3 illustrates a lack of cultural synchronization and what commonly occurs when minority children are placed into learning environments for which they are psychologically and cognitively unprepared.

Marcus's behavior is very similar to that of other minority students in predominately white schools and can be understood if we consider Marcus's motivation and self-esteem. The construct of motivation was looked at earlier and will be covered again in more detail in Chapter 5. According to the social cognitive theory of motivation, motivation is the product of one's expectation of success multiplied by one's value of the outcome that success will bring. Using the equation $M = E \times V$, let's analyze Marcus's motivation. Does Marcus think that he will be successful in his new school? Probably not. So Marcus's expectation of success is low. Does Marcus perceive any value to what he is being taught? Probably not. So Marcus's value is also low. Using the equation for Marcus, $M = \text{low } E \times \text{low } V$. Therefore, Marcus's motivation is low; instead of doing class work, he sits by himself, does no work, and doesn't interact with others in the class.

CASE 3.3

Being Unprepared

Marcus, a tenth-grade boy from a poor black family, coming from an intercity school is bussed to a predominately white middle-class school with white middle-class teachers. Not only does he look different, he talks differently and dresses differently than his white classmates. Furthermore, he is in a highly competitive academic learning situation in which he has not yet developed the skills and knowledge that are rewarded. In other words, he is in an environment for which he is neither psychologically nor cognitively prepared. He sits by himself, doesn't participate, and when the opportunity arises, he rejects his white teachers and classmates by being disrespectful and aloof.

Self-esteem will be covered in more depth later in this chapter and in Chapter 10, but for now, let's consider Marcus's self-esteem. Self-esteem, or feeling good about yourself, is made up of four components:

Significance: a learner's belief that she is liked, accepted, and important to others who are important to her.

Competence: a learner's sense of mastery of age-appropriate tasks that have value to her.

Power: a learner's ability to control important parts of her environment.

Virtue: closely akin to significance, a learner's sense of importance to another person's well-being because of the care and help she provides to the other person.

Considering Marcus's situation, what are his feelings of significance, competence, virtue, and power? Probably all four are low. So Marcus is not feeling very good about himself. How might he improve his self-esteem and begin to feel better about himself? There is an old saying "If I can't be your best student, I can be your worst nightmare." In other words, if families, teachers, or communities fail to provide pro-social opportunities that allow students to experience a sense of significance, competence, power, and virtue, students are likely to express their significance, competence, power, and virtue in negative, distorted ways (Levin and Shanken-Kaye, 2002). Marcus does this by rejecting and being disrespectful to his teachers and classmates, and by behaving in a manner that communicates, "I'm not interested in what you have to teach me; it doesn't relate to my life."

When students exhibit signs of a lack of motivation, the teacher needs to look at students' expectations of success, and the value to the students of what is being taught, both of which the teacher influences. If a student begins to exhibit disruptive behavior, the teacher should consider how she could influence the student's significance, competence, virtue, and power. Chapter 5 explains the components of motivation and how the teacher can influence motivation.

Student Mobility

Student mobility refers to students changing schools for reasons other than grade progression (Hartman, 2002). The United States has high rates of student mobility. The 2004 census found that 15 percent to 20 percent of school-age students moved in the previous year (U.S. Census Bureau, 2004). The U.S. General Accounting Office found that one out of six children attended three or more schools by the end of third grade (U.S. General Accounting Office, 1994).

Students move when their families move. Families move for a variety of reasons, including military obligations of parents, job relocation of parents, separation and divorce, foreclosures, and poverty. Not all moves are for negative reasons. Positive moves include those for parents' job promotions or better paying jobs or moving to another neighborhood for better schooling choices. The reasons for the moves relate to student outcomes in their new schools. When the reasons for the move are positive, students seem not to experience any negative school consequences (Boon, 2010).

However, when the moves are for negative reasons, students are at risk of experiencing a number of serious consequences. School mobility has been linked to poor academics, behavior problems, difficulty with peer relationships, and an increased probability of dropping out of the new school (Hartman, 2002). Mobile students are more likely to come from disadvantaged backgrounds, single-parent homes, and homes with less educated parents. Therefore, it is uncertain if the outcomes are a result of the academic and social stresses of a new school environment or the preexisting risk factors (Rumberger, 2002).

Some school districts have adapted targeted strategies to increase the likelihood of a smoother transition from school to school. These include providing outreach programs for families, creating a buddy system by pairing new students with current students, sending a welcoming note and an invitation to chat with the guidance or counseling staff, and each teacher being friendly and offering to help the student acclimate to her new school.

FAILURE TO MEET CHILDREN'S BASIC NEEDS

The Home Environment

Educators have long recognized the significant influence of home life on a child's behavior and on academic progress. As case 3.4 illustrates it is crucial that the basic needs of the student be met by the home environment.

When considering Teresa's home environment, is it surprising that she has academic and behavior problems in school? Abraham Maslow's theory of basic human needs predicts Teresa's behavior. According to Maslow (1968), basic human needs align themselves into the following hierarchy:

1. Physiological needs: hunger, thirst, breathing
2. Safety and security needs: protection from injury, pain, extremes of heat and cold
3. Belonging and affection needs: giving and receiving love, warmth, and affection
4. Esteem and self-respect needs: feeling adequate, competent, worthy; being appreciated and respected by others
5. Self-actualization needs: self-fulfillment by using one's talents and potential

CASE 3.4

Hanging on the Corner

Teresa, a fifth-grade student, is on the school playground at 7:45 every morning, even though school doesn't start until 9:00. Often she is eating a bag of potato chips and drinking a can of soda. On cold, snowy mornings, she huddles in the doorway wearing a spring jacket and sneakers, waiting for the door to be unlocked. She brags to the other students that she hangs out on the corner with the teenagers in her neighborhood until 12:00 or 1:00 A.M. The home and school coordinator who has investigated her home environment has confirmed this.

Teresa is the youngest of four children. Her father left the family before she started school. Her mother works for a janitorial service and leaves for work by 7:00 A.M. When she returns home in the evening, she either goes out with her boyfriend or goes to sleep early, entrusting Teresa's care to her 16-year-old brother, who has recently quit school.

Teresa is two years below grade in both reading and mathematics. She is never prepared for class with the necessary books and materials, never completes homework assignments, and usually chooses not to participate in learning activities. Her classroom behavior is excessively off-task, characterized by noisy movements both in and out of her seat, calling out, and disruption of other students by talking to them or physically touching them. She occasionally becomes abusive to her fellow students and her teacher, using a loud, challenging voice and vulgarities.

If lower-level needs are not met, an individual may experience difficulty, frustration, and a lack of motivation in attempting to meet the higher-order needs.

Maslow's hierarchy also represents a series of developmental levels. Although the meeting of these needs is important throughout an individual's life, a young child spends considerably more time and effort meeting the lower-level needs than does an older child. From preadolescence on, assuming the lower-level needs are met, emphasis shifts to the higher-order needs of esteem and self-actualization. (Further discussion of self-esteem is found in a later section of this chapter and in Chapter 10.)

Academic achievement and appropriate behavior are most likely to occur when a student's home environment has met her physiological, safety, and belonging needs. This enables her to begin to work on meeting the needs of esteem and self-actualization both at home and at school.

Let's now examine Teresa's home environment in light of Maslow's hierarchy of basic needs. Her breakfast of potato chips and soda, her clothing (a light jacket and sneakers) on cold days, the lack of a father at home, and a mother who is rarely present are indications that her physiological, safety, and belonging needs are not being met. Because of her inadequate home environment, she has attempted to meet her need for belonging and esteem by bragging about hanging out with teenagers and by using loud, vulgar statements in class and disturbing other students. Given her situation, it is surprising that Teresa still attends school on a regular basis. If her home environment remains the same, if she continues to achieve below grade academically, and if she continues to exhibit behavior problems, she probably will quit school at an early age, still unable to control her own actions.

The results of a longitudinal study of third-, sixth-, and ninth-grade students (Feldhusen, Thurston, and Benning, 1973) provided clear evidence of the impact of the home environment on school behavior. Persistently disruptive students differed substantially from persistently pro-social students in a number of home and family variables:

1. Parental supervision and discipline were inadequate—too lax, too strict, or erratic.
2. The parents were indifferent or hostile to the child. They disapproved of many things about the child and handed out angry, physical punishment.
3. The family operated only partially if at all, as a unit, and the marital relationship lacked closeness and equality of partnership.
4. The parents found it difficult to discuss concerns regarding the child and believed that they had little influence on the child. They believed that other children exerted bad influences on their child.

In its 1993 publication, *Violence and Youth,* the American Psychological Association offered examples of the family characteristics of children with antisocial behaviors that were quite similar to the Feldhusen et al. findings. The examples included parental rejection, inconsistent and physically abusive discipline, and parental support of their children's use of aversive and aggressive problem-solving approaches. The study found lack of parental supervision was one of the strongest predictors of children's later conduct disorders.

Case 3.4, Feldhusen's longitudinal study, and the American Psychological Association summary describe homes that could be considered abusive or at least neglectful. Statistics from 2010 indicate that more than 3.3 million referrals were made to authorities regarding possible child abuse or neglect. Approximately 460,000 children were found to be victims of abuse or neglect (U.S. Department of Health and Human Services, 2011). Abuse and neglect have a negative impact on children's ability to learn and increase the vulnerability of children to future violent behavior and substance abuse (Children's Defense Fund, 2002d). Additionally, domestic violence poses a serious risk factor for child abuse (National Center for Injury Prevention and Control, 1999). Estimates indicate that from 1 million to 4 million women experience domestic violence each year (American Psychological Association, 1996; Bureau of Justice Statistics, 1995). Children who come from homes in which domestic violence occurs are 1500 times more likely to be victims of abuse than children who do not come from such homes (Department of Justice, 1993). The Children's Defense Fund (2002e) estimates that between 3.3 million and 10 million children witness domestic violence each year. These children are at risk for future behavioral, emotional, and academic difficulties and are much more likely to display violent and other delinquent behavior (Peled, Jaffe, and Edleson, 1995). However, many non-abusive or non-neglectful home environments also create situations that are quite stressful to children. This stress may be symptomatically displayed as behavior problems. Consider, for example, Case 3.5. Whereas Seth's home environment is significantly different from Teresa's, it too has a detrimental effect on behavior in school. Seth's situation is one that an increasing number of children face. As former U.S. Secretary of Education Terrel H. Bell said in an address given in 1984 to educational leaders, "The problems of American education today are at least partly attributed to changes that have taken place over the past decade in the lifestyle, stability, and commitment of parents." Bell's assertion that students' education can be negatively affected by home factors has been empirically demonstrated. Much of the failure that students experience in school can be predicted and explained by home factors, poverty, and the government's inadequate support of education. Specifically, four variables, all beyond the schools' control, were analyzed: being raised by a single parent, absentee rate, being read to by a parent, and the amount of time spent watching television. Regardless of what was going on in the school, using these four variables, researchers were able to account for two-thirds of the variance found in standardized academic tests (Barton and Coley, 2007).

What changes have occurred in the home environment of American children? During the past half century, the divorce rate increased more than 100 percent. In 1996, the divorce rate was approximately 50 percent of new marriages (Kreider and Fields, 2001). The total number of divorces in 2000 was approximately 1.1 million, up from approximately 950,000 in 1998 (National Center for Health Statistics, 2006). Although most divorced people eventually remarry (Kreider and Fields, 2001), remarriage often creates additional problems for children (Visher and Visher, 1978). Any form of marital conflict increases the likelihood that children will develop some type of behavioral problem (Rutter, 1978), but children of divorced or never-married parents are 2 times as likely to drop out of school, 3 times as likely to get pregnant as teenagers, 12 times as likely to be incarcerated if they are children of divorce, and 22 times as likely to be incarcerated if they are children of never-married parents (Public Broadcasting System, 2002).

Single-parent households are also increasing. The number of single mothers increased from 3 million in 1970 to 10 million in 2000, and the number of single fathers increased from approximately 400,000 to 2 million over the same time period (U.S. Bureau of the Census, 2001). The percentage of children younger than age 18 living with one parent has increased from 12 percent in 1970 to 32 percent in 2007 (Barton and Coley, 2007). Divorce not only changes the family structure but also

CASE 3.5
Marital Conflict

Seth was a typical eleventh-grade student from a middle-class home who attended a suburban high school. For the most part, he was motivated and attentive. He had to be reminded occasionally to stop talking or to take his seat when class started. His grades were Bs with a few Cs. He planned to attend a state college and major in liberal arts. Teachers enjoyed having Seth in their classes.

Now, at the end of eleventh grade, Seth has changed. He doesn't turn in homework and is often off-task, and his motivation is reduced. His future plans are to get a job after high school rather than attend college.

Conferences with his teachers and counselors reveal that Seth's parents have begun to discuss divorce. Because Seth is the oldest of three children, he often is involved in discussions with his parents concerning how the family will manage in the future. Both his mother and father now ask him for assistance in meeting family responsibilities rather than asking each other.

frequently results in a decrease in the family's standard of living, with an increasing number of children and their single mothers moving into poverty status (Kreider and Fields, 2001; Levine, 1984). In 2000, approximately 15.3 million children lived in female-headed households, 40 percent of which were at or below the poverty level (Children's Defense Fund, 2002b). In 2010, 22 percent (16.4 million) of all children younger than age 18 lived below the poverty level (Children's Defense Fund, 2010). These children are at a greater risk than others of developing academic and/or behavioral problems (American Psychological Association, 1993; Children's Defense Fund, 1997; Gelfand, Jenson, and Drew, 1982; Parke, 1978).

If, as Levine (1984) suggested, out-of-school experiences are stronger predictors of school behavior than in-school experiences, today's children need competent teachers more than ever before. Still, as the president of the Elementary School Principals Association noted, there never will be any lasting educational reform until there is parental reform (Whitmire, 1991).

The School Environment

PHYSIOLOGICAL NEEDS   Students are in school to learn. They are continually asked to demonstrate their new understanding and skills. In asking them to do so, schools are attempting to aid students in a process that Maslow calls self-actualization. When students successfully demonstrate new learning, they usually are intrinsically and extrinsically positively reinforced, which leads to the development of self-esteem and self-respect. Positive self-esteem further motivates students to learn, which results in the further development of self-actualization. The self-esteem, learning, self-actualization cycle can be maximized only if the home and school create environments in which the lower-level needs—physiological, safety and security, belonging and affection—are met.

Case 3.6 illustrates how a young child attempts to meet the physiological need of movement and activity. For some young children, no school activity takes more energy than sitting still. When the teacher demanded that Sarah sit and eventually removed her from recess, Sarah's physiological need was no longer being met. This resulted in Sarah's excessive movement around the room. When Sarah's needs were met, the disruptive behaviors stopped.

The importance of meeting students' physiological needs as a prerequisite to learning should be evident to everyone. Ask any teacher how much learning occurs on the first cold day of fall before the heating system is functional or on the first hot day of early spring before the heating system has been turned off. Unfortunately, many of our nation's schools are not new, and it is only recently that public attention has turned to correcting the dilapidated conditions that exist in many of the nation's schools. In 1995, it was estimated that 14 million children attended the 25,000 public schools in the most serious disrepair and that 22 percent of public schools—approximately 17,000 facilities—were overcrowded (National Center for Education Statistics, 2000). At a minimum, every classroom in every school should have adequate space and proper lighting and ventilation.

Somewhat less evident, but no less important than a school's environmental conditions, are concerns about hunger, overcrowding, noise, and frequent interruptions. Teachers have long known that students are less attentive in classes held just

CASE 3.6

Forgetting to Sit Down

Sarah, a second-grade student, is a bright, happy, active child. She is always the first one ready for recess and the last one to stop playing. When going to or from school, she is often seen skipping, jumping, or doing cartwheels.

Sarah's desk is second from the front. When given seatwork, she either stands at her desk or half stands with one knee on the chair. Her teacher always reminds her to sit, but no sooner has she sat down, then she is back up on her feet.

After a good number of reminders, Sarah is kept in from recess. When this occurs, she begins to walk around the room when class is

in progress. This leads to further reprimands by her teacher. Finally her parents are notified.

Sarah's parents inform her teacher that at home, Sarah is always jumping rope, playing catch, dancing, and even standing rather than sitting for piano lessons and practice. She even stands at the table at mealtimes. It is decided that Sarah's seat will be moved to the back of the room so that her standing doesn't interfere with the other students. After this is explained to Sarah, she agrees to the move. The reprimands stop. Sarah continues to do excellent work, and by the end of second grade, she is able to sit in her seat while working.

before lunch. When schools are overcrowded and/or lunch facilities are inadequate, lunch can span a three-hour period. Some students may eat lunch before 11:00 A.M., whereas others may not eat until after 1:00 P.M. This can produce a group of students whose long wait for lunch leaves them inattentive to learning tasks. In addition, some studies suggest that the typical school day, particularly when school begins early, does not match the circadian rhythms of students' "peak hours." This may negatively affect students' attentiveness and academic performance (Callan, 1998; Dahl, 1999).

Interruptions, noise, overcrowding, and fatigue produce in students, regardless of age, emotional uneasiness that may result in nervousness, anxiety, a need to withdraw, or overactivity. Emotional uneasiness interferes with on-task behavior and reduces the effectiveness of the teaching/learning environment. Schools must pay particular attention to minimizing distractions if they want to reduce student off-task behavior.

SAFETY AND SECURITY NEEDS   For the most part, schools create environments in which students feel safe from physical harm. Despite increased media coverage, incidents of school violence have decreased by half between 1992 and 2002. In 1992, there were 48 acts of violence per 1000 students; in 2002, this rate decreased to 24 acts of violence per 1000 students, and the latest figure is less than 1 violent act per 1000 students (DeVoe et al., 2004; Robers et al., 2010). In 2000, students were more than twice as likely to be a victim of violent crime and 70 times more likely to be a victim of homicide away from school than at school. Thus, schools continue to be one of the safest places for children (National Center for Education Statistics, 2003b). There are, however, occasions when students, such as Keith in Case 3.9, fear for their physical safety. Any incident of crime, violence, bullying, or coercion that is the catalyst for

CASE 3.7

There Must Be a Better Way

One university requires its secondary student teachers to follow a student's schedule of classes for an entire day. Student teachers are required to record their reactions to this experience. What follows are some common reactions:

No sooner were we in our seats in the first-period class than the V.P. was on the intercom system. She spent at least five minutes with announcements, mostly directed for the teachers' attention. The speaker was loud and very annoying. After the announcements, most of the students were talking among themselves. By the time we got down to work, 15 minutes had passed. Halfway through the period, a student messenger interrupted the class when he brought the morning office notices to the teacher. And believe it or not, five minutes before the end of class, the V.P. was back on the intercom with additional announcements. It was quite evident to me that these interruptions were a direct cause of inattentiveness and reduction in effective instruction.

Much time was wasted during the announcements and in obtaining student on-task behavior after the interruptions. There must be a better way.

Probably the most eye-opening experience I had was remembering how crowded and noisy schools can be. This was most evident to me when we changed classes. We had three minutes between classes. The halls were very crowded, with frequent pushing, shoving, and just bumping into one another. The noise level was so loud that it really bothered me. On arriving at the next class, all I really wanted to do was to sit quietly for a few minutes before starting to work. The changes from hallways to classrooms are dramatic. I can see why it is difficult for some students to settle down and get on task at the beginning of class. As bad as the hallways were, it didn't prepare me for lunch. The lunchroom was even noisier. By the time I waited in line, I had only 15 minutes to eat and then back to the hallways to class. By the end of the day, I was drained.

fear of one's safety compromises the learning environment. In 2008, approximately 629,900 violent crimes and 619,900 thefts occurred in our nation's schools (Robers et al., 2010).

Between 1995 and 2007, the percentage of students ages 12–18 who reported being victims of crime at school decreased from 10 percent to 4 percent. In 2009, the percentage of students in grades 9–12 who reported being threatened or injured with a weapon on school property was 8 percent. In 2007, 10 percent of students ages 12–18 reported that hate-related words were directed at them at school. Between 1993 and 2007, there was an increase from 5 percent to 32 percent of students who reported being bullied at school (National Center for Education Statistics, 2005; Robers et al., 2010).

Between 1993 and 2009, there was a decrease from 12 percent to 6 percent of students in grades 9–12 who reported carrying a weapon to school. In 2003,

CASE 3.8
Too Much Noise

Karen is a third-grade student who is well behaved and does well academically. One day, all of the third-grade classes are taken to the all-purpose room to observe a film. The classes are dismissed simultaneously, and the children in the hallway are excited and very noisy as a result. Karen is seen walking in the hallway with her hands over her ears. When she enters the room, she goes directly to the back corner and sits against the wall. The teacher asks her what is the matter. She says the noise hurts her ears; she feels like crying and she doesn't want to be there if it is going to be so noisy.

After the teachers quiet the students, Karen rejoins her class. Referral to an ear specialist discloses that Karen has no problems with her hearing that would have caused such a reaction.

21 percent of students reported that street gangs were present in their school. This was a decline from 29 percent in 1995 (National Center for Education Statistics, 2005; Robers et al., 2010).

Students in all schools experience anxiety and sometimes fear about walking to and from school, going to the restroom, dressing in locker rooms, or changing classes. However, this fear and anxiety among students has also decreased. In 1995, 12 percent of students ages 12–18 reported that sometimes or most of the time they were fearful at school, compared to 6 percent of students in 2003, and 5 percent in 2007. Similarly, there was a decrease in students who reported avoiding certain places in school for safety concerns from 9 percent in 1995 to 4 percent in 2003, but the percentage increased to 7 percent in 2007 (National Center for Education Statistics, 2005; Robers et al., 2010). The more students feel insecure about their physical safety, the less likely they will exhibit the on-task behaviors necessary for learning.

CASE 3.9
Afraid of Going to School

Keith, an eighth-grade student, achieves at an average level in his social studies class, which meets during the last period of the day. Approximately midway through the year, Keith's behavior in this class begins to change. He goes from a student who is attentive and participates freely to one who rarely participates and has to be called back to attention by the teacher. He is often seen nervously looking out the window and is the first out of his seat and room at the end of class.

After a few days of such behavior, the teacher asks Keith to stay for a few minutes after class to discuss his behavior. At this point, Keith tells his teacher that he has to be the first to leave school because Greg will beat him up if he sees him. Keith is fearful of Greg because Greg has threatened him for telling the gym teacher that he was throwing Keith's clothing around the locker room after gym class.

BELONGING AND AFFECTION NEEDS   Although belonging and affection needs are most often met by family at home or by the students' peers in and out of school, elements of caring, trust, and respect are necessary in the interpersonal relationships between teachers and students. In other words, the classroom climate should be caring and supportive. Such a climate is more likely to be created by teachers who subscribe to a referent power base in the classroom. The development of various teacher power bases will be studied in Chapter 4.

Withall (1969) stressed that the most important variable in determining the climate of a classroom is the teacher's verbal and nonverbal behaviors. Appropriate student behavior can be enhanced when teachers communicate the following to the learners:

Trust: "I believe you are able to learn and want to learn."

Respect: "Insofar as I try to help you learn, you are, by the same token, helping me to learn."

Caring: "I perceive you as a unique and worthwhile person whom I want to help to learn and grow" (Withall, 1979)

For students to learn effectively, they must participate fully in the learning process. This means they must be encouraged to ask and answer questions, attempt new approaches, make mistakes, and ask for assistance. However, learners engage in these behaviors only in settings in which they feel safe from being ridiculed or made to feel inadequate.

Case 3.10 illustrates what occurs in a class if the teacher is unable to establish a learning environment characterized by trust, respect, and care. As the year

CASE 3.10
Turning Off Students

Ms. Washington, a high school science teacher, is quite concerned over what she perceives to be a significant decrease in student participation throughout the year. She views the problem as follows: "I ask a lot of questions. Early in the year, many students volunteer but within a few weeks, I find that volunteering has almost ceased and the only way I can get students to participate is to call on them."

Arrangements are made to observe the class to determine the causes of the problem. Teacher questions, student responses, and teacher feedback are recorded. An example of one such interaction follows:

TEACHER QUESTION: "We know that man is in the family of Hominidae. What is man's taxonomic order?"

STUDENT RESPONSE: "Mammals."

TEACHER FEEDBACK: "No, it's not mammals. We had this material last week; you should know it. The answer is primates."

Further observation reveals that about 70 percent of Ms. Washington's feedback is totally or partially negative. Students note that they don't feel like being put down because their answer isn't exactly what Ms. Washington wants. One student states, "I only answer when I know I'm correct. If I don't understand something I often just let it go rather than be drilled."

CASE 3.11

"I'm Going to Be Sorry When Fifth Grade Is Over"

One afternoon last May, I overheard a group of fifth-grade students say, "I'm going to be sorry when fifth grade is over." I stopped and asked them if they would be willing to tell me why they felt this way. The following were their comments:

"She lets us give our opinions."

"If we say something stupid, she doesn't say anything."

"She lets us decide how we are going to do things."

"She gives us suggestions and helps us when we get stuck."

"You can say how you feel."

"She gives us choices."

"She tells us what she thinks but doesn't want us to think like her. Some teachers tell us their opinions, but you know that they really want you to think the same way."

"We learn a lot."

---

progressed, Ms. Washington failed to demonstrate her trust, respect, and caring for her students. Thus, her students were discouraged from fully participating in the learning process.

Comments such as, "Why do you ask so many questions?" "You should know this; we studied it last week," or "Everyone should understand this; there should be no questions" serve no useful purpose. Indeed, they hinder learner participation, confidence, and motivation and lead to off-task behavior. Glasser (1978) saw failure as the root of misbehavior, noting that when students don't learn at the expected rate, they get less "care" and recognition from the teacher. As the situation continues, students see themselves as trapped. Acceptance and recognition, it seems to them, can be gained only through misbehavior. In sharp contrast to the feelings of Ms. Washington's students are the feelings of the fifth-grade students in Case 3.11.

CHILDREN'S PURSUIT OF SOCIAL RECOGNITION AND SELF-ESTEEM

Social Recognition

Alfred Adler, the renowned psychiatrist, and Rudolph Dreikurs, Adler's student and colleague, believed that behavior can be best understood using three key premises:

1. People are social beings who have a need to belong, to be recognized, and to be accepted.
2. Behavior is goal directed and has the purpose of gaining the recognition and acceptance that people want.
3. People can choose how they behave; they can behave or misbehave. Their behavior is not outside their control.

Putting these key ideas together, Adler and Dreikurs theorized that people choose to try a wide variety of behaviors to see which behaviors gain them the recognition and acceptance they want. When socially accepted behaviors do not produce the needed recognition and acceptance, people choose to misbehave in the mistaken belief that socially unacceptable behaviors will produce the recognition they seek.

Applying these premises to children's conduct, Dreikurs, Grunwald, and Pepper (1982) identified four goals of disruptive behaviors: attention getting, power seeking, revenge seeking, and the display of inadequacy. According to this theory, these goals, which are usually sequential, are strongest in elementary-age children but are also present in adolescents.

Attention-seeking students make up a large part of the misbehaving population in the schools. These students may ask question after question, use excessive charm, continually need help or assistance, continually ask for the teacher's approval, call out, or show off. In time, the teacher usually becomes annoyed. When the teacher reprimands or gives these children attention, they temporarily stop their attention-seeking behavior. In Case 3.12, Bob was a child who felt that he was not getting the recognition he desired. He saw no chance of gaining this recognition through socially accepted or constructive contributions. He first channeled his energies into gaining attention. Like all attention-seeking students, he had the notion that he was important only when others took notice of him and acknowledged his presence. When attention-getting behavior no longer gives the students the recognition they want, many of them seek recognition through the next goal, power, which is exactly what Bob did when he began to confront the teacher openly.

Students who seek power through misbehavior believe that they can do what they want and that nobody can make them do anything they don't want to do. By challenging teachers, they often gain social acceptance from their peers. Power-seeking students argue, lie, ignore, become stubborn, have temper tantrums, and become disobedient in general to show that they are in command of the situation. Teachers feel threatened or challenged by these children and often feel compelled to force them into compliance. Once teachers enter into power struggles with power-seeking students, the students usually "win." Even if they do not succeed in getting what they want, they succeed in getting the teacher to fight, thereby giving them undue attention and time as well as control of the situation. If the teacher "wins" the power struggle, the winning reinforces the students' idea that power is what really counts.

With a power-seeking student, reprimands from the teacher result in intensified challenges or temporary withdrawal before new power-seeking behaviors reappear. As power struggles develop between a teacher and a student, both teacher controlling and student power-seeking behaviors usually become more severe and the student-teacher relationship deteriorates further (Levin and Shanken-Kaye, 2002). If the student sees herself as losing the power struggle, she often moves to the next goal—seeking revenge.

When students perceive that they have no control over their environment, they experience an increased sense of inferiority and futility. They feel that they have been treated unfairly and are deeply hurt by what they consider to be others' disregard for their feelings. They seek revenge by hurting others, often not just those that they think have hurt them. For instance, Bob sought his revenge on random individuals who

CASE 3.12

Seeking Faulty Goals

Bob is a sixth-grade student of average academic ability. On the first day of class, when students are asked to choose seats, Bob chooses the one next to the window in the back of the room. Between classes, he rarely interacts with classmates. Instead, he either bolts out of the class first or slowly swaggers out last.

During instructional times, he either nonchalantly leans back in his seat or jumps up and calls out answers. During seatwork, he often has to be reminded to begin, and once finished, he taps his pencil, wanders around the back of the room, or noisily moves his chair and desk.

Bob's behavior often improves for short periods of time after excessive teacher attention, ranging from positive reinforcement to reprimands. These periods of improvement are followed by a return to disruptive behaviors. Bob's attention-seeking behavior continues throughout the first half of the school year.

As time goes on, the teacher usually yells at Bob, sends him to the principal, or makes comments in front of the class that reflect her extreme frustration.

Eventually, the teacher's behavior is characterized by threats, such as, "You will stay after school longer every day until you begin to behave," or "Every day that you don't turn in your homework, you will have 20 more problems to do." Bob sees immediately the impossibility of some of the threats and boldly says, "If I have to stay after school longer each day, in two weeks I'll have to sleep here." Tremendous amounts of laughter come from his classmates at such comments. However, after a week or two, Bob says, "I'm not coming for your detention," and "You can't make me do homework if I don't want to." The teacher no longer feels annoyed but now feels threatened and challenged.

Whenever problems arise in the classroom, the teacher and students are quick to blame Bob. He is occasionally accused of things that he has not done, and he is quick to shout, "I didn't do it I'm always the one who gets blamed for everything around here." His classmates now show extreme annoyance with his behaviors, and Bob resorts to acts directed against individuals. He kicks students' chairs and intentionally knocks over others' books as he walks down the aisles.

One day one of the boys in the class accuses Bob of taking his book. Without warning, Bob flips the student's desk. The student falls backward, lands on his arm, and breaks it. As a result, Bob is suspended.

When Bob returns from his suspension, he is told that he will be sent to the office for any violation of a classroom rule. He is completely ignored by his classmates.

For the rest of the year, Bob comes in, goes to the back of the room, does no work, and bothers no one. At first, the teacher tries to get Bob involved, but all efforts are refused. The teacher thinks to herself that she has tried everything that she knows. "If he wants to just sit there, let him. At least he isn't bothering anyone anymore," she says.

happened to be sitting along his aisle. Revenge-seeking children destroy property, threaten other students and sometimes the teacher, engage in extremely rough play, and use obscenities.

When working with these students, teachers feel defeated and hurt and have a difficult time being concerned with what is best for the student. Teacher reprimands usually result in an explosive display of anger and abusiveness from the student. Over time, the teacher feels a strong desire to get even.

Unfortunately, revenge-seeking behaviors elicit dislike and more hurt from others. Revenge-seeking students continually feel a deep sense of despair and worthlessness. Their interactions with other people often result in negative feelings about themselves, which eventually move them to the last goal—the display of inadequacy. They cannot be motivated and refuse to participate in class activities. Their message is clear: "Don't expect anything from me because I have nothing worthwhile to give." They are often heard saying, "Why don't you just leave me alone I'm not bothering anyone"; "Mind your own business"; "Why try, I'll just get it wrong"; or "I can't do it."

Teachers often believe that they have tried everything with these students. Further attempts usually result in very little, if any, change in the students' refusal to show interest, to participate, or to interact with others. Bob's teacher actually felt somewhat relieved that he no longer was a disturbing influence in class. However, if the teacher had been able to stop his progression toward the display of inadequacy, Bob would have had a much more meaningful and valuable sixth-grade learning experience, and the teacher would have felt much more professionally competent.

Most of the goals of misbehavior are pursued one at a time, but some students switch back and forth between them. Goal-seeking misbehaviors can also be situational. The decision-making hierarchical approach to classroom management presented in this book offers many strategies for working with children seeking these four mistaken goals. In addition, specific intervention techniques for each goal are discussed in detail in Charles and Senter (2004), Dreikurs et al. (1982), Dubelle and Hoffman (1984), and Sweeney (1981).

Self-Esteem

Self-esteem, or a feeling of self-worth, is a basic need that individuals continually strive to meet. Without a positive sense of self-esteem, a child is vulnerable to a variety of social, psychological, and learning problems (Gilliland, 1986).

Introduced earlier in this chapter, Stanley Coopersmith (1967) wrote that self-esteem is made up of four components:

Significance: a learner's belief that she is liked, accepted, and important to others who are important to her.

Competence: a learner's sense of mastery of age-appropriate tasks that have value to her.

Power: a learner's ability to control important parts of her environment.

Virtue: closely akin to significance, a learner's sense of importance to another person's well-being because of the care and help she provides to the other person.

The feeling of self-worth or self-esteem is such a strong human drive that if families, teachers, or communities fail to provide pro-social (socially acceptable) opportunities that allow students to experience a sense of significance, competence, power, and virtue, students are likely to express their significance, competence, power, and virtue in negative, distorted (socially unacceptable) ways (Levin and Shanken-Kaye, 2002).

It is possible to express the concept of self-esteem mathematically. Notice that it is a summation of the four components. Being a sum, any decrease in one or more components can be compensated for by a corresponding increase in one or more of the remaining components.

$$\text{Self-Esteem} = \text{Significance} + \text{Competence} + \text{Power} + \text{Virtue}$$

Students who exhibit chronically disruptive behavior have low levels of pro-social significance because typically they are not liked or accepted by their teachers, peers, and sometimes even their parents. Their levels of pro-social competence are depressed because they rarely achieve academically or are socially competent or involved in extracurricular activities. In addition, because these students rarely choose or are rarely selected by the teacher to interact responsibly with others, their sense of pro-social virtue is low. Therefore, as the self-esteem equation indicates, the only component left to build the self-esteem of a student who exhibits chronic misbehavior is power. This is illustrated by noting which components of self-esteem are lowered and which are increased:

$$\text{Self-Esteem} = \text{Significance (down)} + \text{Competence (down)}$$
$$+ \text{ Power (up)} + \text{Virtue (down)}$$

It is exactly this striving for power, or control of the environment, that is operating when students choose to behave disruptively. In fact, such a student can be viewed as the most powerful individual in the classroom. How she behaves often determines the amount of time spent on learning in the classroom and whether the teacher leaves the classroom with a headache or, in some cases, leaves the profession. It is, however, important to note that this is not pro-social power but distorted power. The display of distorted power (socially unacceptable) provides the student with a distorted sense of significance and competence that is evident in a comment such as, "The other kids know that they can count on me to get Mr. Beal to go ballistic and liven this class up a bit."

A PARALLEL PROCESS   Students are not the only ones to use distorted power, so do teachers. Unless a teacher is very careful, she can become significantly influenced by a student's self-esteem and vice versa. Two people sharing the same affective experiences engage in a parallel process. With regard to self-esteem, the process begins when the teacher in this case treats a student harshly and disrespectfully. "Tara let me see you pass a note again and I'll see that your butt gets passed down to the principal's office. This isn't junior high." Tara replies, "No kidding when my butt is in the principal's office, I'll be sure to tell her what a good teacher you are, ha!" The students began to laugh and the teacher says, "You're out of here." The teacher's public humiliation of the student may have been because of the teacher's frustration brought on by the student's continuing inappropriate behavior or a myriad of other reasons. The important point is not why the teacher acted that way, but how her comments influenced the student. Naturally, the student is upset with the teacher and the teacher is upset with the student.

Using the equation for self-esteem, it becomes clear what is happening:

$$\text{Self-Esteem (T)} = \text{Significance (down)} + \text{Competence (down)}$$
$$+ \text{ Power (up)} + \text{Virtue (down)}$$

The teacher's self-esteem is characterized by a lowered significance (teacher probably does not feel trusted or respected by the student), a lowered competence (teacher probably does not feel she has the skills it takes to deal with the student), and a lowered sense of virtue (teacher probably does not feel she has helped the student). The only path the teacher has left to raise her self-esteem is power, and she displays her power in a distorted manner, by her public scolding of the student.

Now let's look at the student's self-esteem:

$$\text{Self-Esteem (S)} = \text{Significance (down)} + \text{Competence (down)}$$
$$+ \text{Power (up)} + \text{Virtue (down)}$$

The student's self-esteem looks the same as the teacher's self-esteem. The student has a lowered significance (student probably does not feel trusted or respected by the teacher), a lowered competence (student probably does not feel successful in this teacher's class), and a lowered sense of virtue (student probably does not feel she is a valued member of this teacher's class). The only path left for the student to raise her self-esteem is power, which she displays in a distorted manner by her public disrespect of the teacher.

The understanding of self-esteem and the parallel process has important implications. These include the misconception that students who exhibit chronic discipline problems have low self-esteem. In fact, they have high self-esteem, at least in some dimensions, but it is distorted and not pro-social. In other words, they feel good about being bad. Also, the parallel process indicates that quite often teachers and students feel the same way about each other; it is not a one-way street. Finally, if the teacher wants to decrease the likelihood of disruptive behavior, which is distorted power, she needs to find ways to influence the student to obtain a sense of pro-social significance, competence, and virtue.

Some readers might be wondering how a teacher ends this negative cycle. The answer is that the teacher needs to end the cycle because the teacher is the professional, understands what is occurring, and has a higher level of cognitive and moral development than most of her students. Being at a formal stage of cognitive processing, the teacher can think abstractly and plan for the future by asking the question, "How can I teach this student to be respectful?" Using the definition of teaching developed in Chapter 1, the answer is changing your behavior to influence a change in the student's behavior. Throwing the student out of the class and public humiliation are not congruent with our definition. Because the student is likely in the concrete stage of cognitive processing, what is real now, is what is real; she cannot necessarily grasp what may happen in the future.

Needless to say, a parallel process involving self-esteem can operate in a positive manner whereby both the teacher and students have pro-social components of self-esteem. Chapter 10 provides more information on breaking this cycle of mutual negative influence.

Bullying

Bullying in the school environment is a widespread serious problem that has a long-term negative impact on the victims and bullies. As a result of the fear of bullying,

CASE 3.13

"Get Out of My Face"

Rob, Tom, Jason, Tanya, Margo, and Beth are talking in the hallway outside their seventh-period classroom door. Ms. Wertz comes out of her room and screams across the hall, "Jason, get to class immediately. A student like you should never be standing around wasting time. You need all the time in class you can get." Jason says, "Ms. Wertz, my class is right here and we have another two minutes..." Before he can finish, Ms. Wertz interrupts, "Don't give me any excuses always have excuses." Again, Jason says, "Ms. Wertz, this isn't an excuse; this is my class." Ms. Wertz goes on, "Jason, you are nothing but trouble and someday you'll find out that you aren't such a big shot." Jason turns to Ms. Wertz and says, "I don't even have you for a teacher this year so why don't you get out of my face and leave me alone?" Ms. Wertz refers Jason to the office, and later that day he is given three days of detention.

some students in school are in a constant state of emotional arousal that makes it virtually impossible physiologically and psychologically for them to expend any cognitive energy focused on learning. For example, "If heading to the playground conjures up thoughts of survival for students, their ability to find math engaging is probably going to be compromised" (Glick 2011, p. 25). Bullying is an example of a student attempting to obtain social recognition through the faulty goals of power and revenge seeking and self-esteem through distorted significance and distorted power.

Bullying does not have a universally accepted definition, but there is consensus that three components are present in bullying behavior. These are (1) intentional "harm-doing" behavior by a person or a group (2) carried out repeatedly and over time and (3) targeted toward someone less powerful (Nansel et al., 2001).

The National Institute of Child Health and Human Development's 1998 nationally represented survey of more than 15,600 students in grades 6 through 10 indicated that 30 percent of the students were involved in bullying either as perpetrators, victims, or both. Expanding this to a nationwide population, 3.7 million students were bullies, 3.2 million were victims, and 1.2 million were both. Results indicate that bullying is present in all schools and rates are not significantly different among rural, urban, and suburban schools. Boys were more likely to be victims (21%) and bullies (26%) than girls (14% and 14%, respectively; Nansel et al., 2001). The great majority of bullying occurs in schools, with middle and junior high schools experiencing more bullying than elementary and high schools (Nolin, Davies, and Chandler, 1995; Sampson, 2002).

In school, several types of bullying behavior involve direct or physical action and/or indirect action such as verbal harassment (Quiroz, 2002). These are (1) direct and physical behavior (hitting, spitting, shoving), (2) verbal behavior (name calling, verbal threats, put-downs), (3) emotional behavior (making indecent gestures, rejecting, starting rumors, blackmailing); (4) sexual behavior (propositioning, physical touching, commenting about physical traits); and (5) hate-motivated behavior (taunting about sexual orientation, race, religion, culture). Boys tend to engage more in direct bullying, whereas girls bully using more indirect behavior (Nansel et al., 2001).

The negative impact on victims and bullies is both immediate and long-term. Students who are victims of bullying become fearful of going to school. Coy (2001) estimated that 160,000 students miss school each day because of fear of being bullied Other student behavior associated with being bullied includes avoiding certain places or people in school; exhibiting sudden changes in behavior, such as becoming withdrawn, fearful, or anxious; complaining about unexplained physical symptoms, such as headaches, stomach pains, or tiredness; and unexpected changes in academic performance resulting in lower grades (Pace, 2001). Students who were bullied were found to have lower self-esteem and higher levels of depression at age 23 when compared to adults who were not bullied in school (Nansel et al., 2001). After the shootings in Columbine High School in 1999, the U.S. Secret Service attempted to profile a school shooter. It found that of the 37 school shootings studied, almost three-quarters of the perpetrators were bullied prior to choosing to attack others in the school. Upon being interviewed, some of the shooters described bullying that in the workplace would meet the legal definition of harassment and/or assault (Vossekuil et al., 2002).

Approximately 60 percent of boys who were classified as bullies in grades 6 through 9 were convicted of at least one crime by age 24, and 40 percent had three or more convictions compared to 23 percent and 10 percent, respectively, of boys who were not bullies (Olweus, 1993).

Research focuses on three areas in trying to understand and predict which students will likely become bullies. These are the characteristics of the child, parental/home influences, and the out-of-home environment (Batsche and Knoff, 1994). To date, there are no definitive characteristics of children that predict future bullying behavior. At home, parents who fail to set behavioral limits for their children's behavior; who use controlling, aggressive, and coercive means to discipline; and who encourage their children to assert themselves in socially unacceptable ways increase the likelihood that their children may become bullies. In the larger environment, the media often glamorize bullies, and their actions frequently go without consequences and may actually be rewarded. One study showed a positive relationship between exposure to media violence and bullying behavior (Kaiser Family Foundation, 2003b). Society's attitude that bullying is transient and part of growing up and that "kids will be kids" leads adults and particularly teachers to pay little if any attention to the bullies or their victims. Finally, crowded school conditions and poorly supervised school locations such as locker rooms, cafeterias, playgrounds, and hallways increase the likelihood of bullying.

Because most bullies victimize "weaker" students, lack empathy for their victims, and seem to derive pleasure from the torment they inflict on others, it is only natural that the traditional school intervention is intended to "teach the bully a lesson" through some form of punishment. For all the reasons discussed in Chapter 6, punishments are limited in their effectiveness to prevent inappropriate behavior and encourage appropriate behavior. If punishments are aggressively delivered, there is an additional disadvantage because this models the bullying process. This time it's a bigger, stronger adult picking on the smaller, weaker bully.

Bullying should not be considered a stage in the normal development of young people. Bullying is a precursor of more serious future behavior, including violence and weapons and assault offences (Nansel et al., 2003). Given the fact that bullying occurs in a social context of schools where teachers and parents are unaware or believe that kids will be kids, observing students are afraid or reluctant to get involved; victims are usually scared and defenseless; and bullies are motivated by revenge, control, and power, effective intervention necessary to prevent bullying must involve the entire school community. A well-researched school-wide prevention program, Olweus Bullying Prevention Program, has consistently reduced bullying by 50 percent (Olweus, 2001; Olweus and Limber, 1999). Other comprehensive bullying prevention programs are described by Smith, Pepler, and Rigby (2004). Detailed coverage of bullying prevention is beyond the scope of this text. However, the text does offer many appropriate interventions to influence students to behave appropriately. The short-term strategies (Chapters 8 and 9) and particularly the longer-term strategies (Chapter 10) are quite relevant for influencing appropriate behavior when bullying is overt and visible to the teacher. Teaching appropriate behavior (Chapter 6), facilitating pro-social self-esteem (Chapter 3), and building positive relations with students (Chapters 7 and 10) are strategies that are critical in eradicating and preventing bullying in schools. These strategies are effective not because students fear punishments but because they understand the lifelong negative outcomes for both the bullies and those who are bullied and have learned new more appropriate behaviors.

Cyberbullying

A relatively new and particularly virulent form of bullying is online or cyberbullying. *Cyberbullying* is the willful and repeated harm to a person inflicted through electronic media. It enables bullies to post put-downs, nasty rumors, and humiliating pictures on e-mail, blogs, chat rooms, websites, instant messages, and cell phones. As noted previously, bullying behavior has three components: (1) intentional harm (2) carried out repeatedly over time and power differential. Power is usually physical or social with traditional bullying. With cyberbullying, power stems from the online proficiency of the bully (Patchin and Hinduja, 2006). Unlike traditional bullying that occurs in school, cyberbullying follows a student home where she can be victimized at any time.

The most recent comprehensive data indicate that 7 percent of students were victims of cyberbullying, and 15 percent were bullied online during the previous year. Boys and girls are equally likely to be targeted as well as to be bullies. Teens 14 years old and older are more likely to be victims than younger students (Ybarra and Mitchell, 2004).

Victims of cyberbullying exhibit the same effects as those who are victimized in person. These effects include lower grades, lower self-esteem, a loss of interests, depression, and—in extreme cases—suicide. In one study, more than 30 percent of cyberbullied victims reported being very or extremely upset and 19 percent very or extremely afraid (Finkelhor, Mitchell, and Wolak, 2000).

Sexting

A subset of cyberbullying is sexting. *Sexting* is the term used to describe the creation and transmission of sexual images using any digital media. The term is inclusive and refers to the transmission of sexual images of oneself as well as others. It has been commonly reported that 20 percent of teens, ages 13 to 19, have posted on the web or sent nude or seminude pictures of themselves via cell phone. More females, 22 percent, than males, 18 percent, were involved, with the majority sent to boyfriend or girlfriends. However, studies vary in definition, sample size and population, and the reliability of the estimate of its prevalence is uncertain (Lounsbury, Mitchell, and Finkelhor, 2011).

The outcomes of sexting include all the negative academic and psychological consequences discussed with bullying. Additionally, criminal charges related to child pornography may result, even when the student takes her own picture. Such charges can be problematic well into adulthood. Suicides related to sexting have been reported (Bowker and Sullivan, 2010).

STAGES OF COGNITIVE AND MORAL DEVELOPMENT

Not too long ago, it was believed that children thought exactly the same way as adults do. Jean Piaget's work in the area of cognitive development, however, has shown that children move through distinct stages of cognitive and moral development. At each stage, children think and interpret their environment differently from children at other stages. For this reason, a child's behavior varies as the child moves from one stage to another. An understanding of the stages of development enables a teacher to better understand student behavior patterns.

Cognitive Development

Throughout his life, Piaget studied how children interacted with their environment and how their intellect developed. To him, knowledge was the transformation of an individual's experience with the environment, not the accumulation of facts and pieces of information. His research resulted in the formulation of a four-stage age-related cognitive development theory (Piaget, 1970), which has significantly influenced the manner in which children are educated.

Piaget called the four stages of development the sensorimotor, the preoperational, the concrete operational, and the formal operational stages. The sensorimotor stage occurs from birth to approximately 2 years of age. It is characterized by the refinement of motor skills and the use of the five senses to explore the environment. This stage obviously has little importance for teachers working with school-age children.

The preoperational stage occurs from approximately ages 2 to 7 and is the stage most children have reached when they begin their school experience. Children at this stage are egocentric. They are unable to conceive that others may see things differently from the way they do. Although their ability to give some thought to decisions is developing, the great majority of the time they act only on perceptive impulses. Their short attention span interacts with their static thinking, resulting in an inability to think of a sequence of steps or operations. Their sense of time and space is limited to short duration and close proximity.

The concrete operational stage occurs from approximately ages 7 to 12. Children are able to order and classify objects and to consider several variables simultaneously as long as they have experiences with "concrete" content. These children need step-by-step instructions if they are expected to work through lengthy procedures. What can be frustrating to teachers who do not understand the characteristics of this stage is that these children do not attempt to check their conclusions, have difficulty thinking about thinking (how they arrived at certain conclusions), and seem unaware of and unconcerned with inconsistencies in their own reasoning.

At about age 12, at the earliest, children begin to move into the formal operational stage. They begin to develop independent critical thinking skills, to plan lengthy procedures, and to consider a number of possible answers to problems. They no longer are tied to concrete examples but instead are able to use symbols and verbal examples. These children, who are adolescents, begin to think about their own and others' thinking, which leads them to consider motives; the past, present, and future; the abstract; the remote; and the ideal. The methodological implications for teaching students at each stage are somewhat obvious and have been researched and written about extensively (Adler, 1966; Gorman, 1972; Karplus, 1977).

Moral Development

Piaget related his theory of a child's cognitive development directly to the child's moral development. Through his work, Piaget demonstrated that a child is close to or at the formal operational stage of cognitive development before she possesses the intellectual ability to evaluate, consider, and act on abstract moral dilemmas. Thus, what an elementary school child thinks is bad or wrong is vastly different from what an adolescent thinks is wrong (Piaget, 1965).

Using Piaget's work as his basis, Laurence Kohlberg proposed that moral development progresses through six levels of moral reasoning: punishment-obedience, exchange of favors, good boy–nice girl, law and order, social contract, and universal ethical principles (Kohlberg, 1969, 1975).

Between ages 4 and 6, children have a "punishment-obedience" orientation to moral reasoning. Their decisions are based on the physical consequences of an act; will they be punished or rewarded? Outcomes are paramount, and there is very little comprehension of a person's motive or intention. Children's egocentrism at this stage limits their ability to see other points of view or alternatives.

Between ages 6 and 9, children move into the "exchange of favors" orientation. At this level, judgments are made on the basis of reciprocal favors; you do this for me and I will do this for you. Fulfilling one's own needs comes first. Children are just beginning to understand the motives behind behaviors and outcomes.

Between ages 10 and 15, children move into the "good boy–nice girl" orientation. Conformity dictates behavior and reasoning ability. Peer review is strong, and judgments about how to behave are made on the basis of avoiding criticism and pleasing others. The drive to conform with peers is so strong that it is quite common to follow peers unquestioningly but, at the same time, continually to ask "why" when requests are made by adults.

The "law and order" orientation dominates moral reasoning between ages 15 and 18. Individuals at this stage of development are quite rigid. Judgments are made on the basis of obeying the law. Motives are understood but not wholeheartedly considered if the behavior has broken a law. At this stage, teenagers are quick to recognize and point out inconsistencies in expected behavior. It is quite common to hear them say to adults, "Why do I have to do this? You don't." At this stage, adolescents begin to recognize the consequences of their actions.

According to Kohlberg, few people reach the last two levels of moral reasoning. The "social contract" orientation is reached by some between ages 18 and 20. At this level, moral judgments are made on the basis of upholding individual rights and democratic principles. Those who reach this level recognize that individuals differ in their values and do not accept "because I said so" or "that's the way it is" as rationales for rules.

The highest level of moral reasoning is the "universal ethical" orientation. Judgments are based on respect for the dignity of human beings and on what is good for humanity, not on selfish interests or standards upheld by authority.

As in cognitive development, the ages of any moral development stage are approximations. Individuals continually move back and forth between stages, depending on the moral situation at hand, especially at transitional points between stages.

Behavior: The Interaction of Cognitive and Moral Development

To understand how children perceive what is right and wrong, what cognitive skills they are able to use, and what motivates their social and academic behavior, teachers must understand the stages of moral and cognitive growth. Teachers must also recognize common developmental behaviors that are a result of the interaction of the cognitive and moral stages through which the children pass. Although this interaction does not and cannot explain all disruptive classroom behaviors, it does provide a basis on which we can begin to understand many disruptive behaviors. Table 3.1 summarizes the cognitive and moral stages of development, their characteristics, and associated behaviors.

Some misbehavior can result when instruction is not matched with students' cognitive development stages.

At the beginning of elementary school, students are in the preoperational stage cognitively and the punishment-obedience stage morally. Their behavior is a result of the interplay of factors such as their egocentricity, limited sense of time and space, little comprehension of others' motives, and short attention span. At this stage, children become frustrated easily, have difficulty sharing, argue frequently, believe that they are right and their classmates wrong, and tattle a lot.

By middle to upper elementary school and beginning junior high or middle school, children are in the concrete operational stage cognitively and the exchange of favors to the good boy–nice girl stages morally. Early in this period, students form and re-form cliques, act on opinions based on a single or very few concrete characteristics, and tell secrets. They employ many annoying attention-seeking behaviors to please the teacher. Later in the period, the effects of peer conformity appear. Students are often off-task because they are constantly in conversation with their friends. Those who do not fit into the peer group are excluded and ridiculed, which may explain why cyberbullying begins to increase in junior and middle school (Ybarra and Mitchell, 2004).

Students still have little patience with long discussions and lengthy explanations. They are unaware

TABLE 3.1 Cognitive and Moral Development with Common Associated Behaviors

Cognitive Stage	Cognitive Abilities	Moral Stage	Moral Reasoning	Common Behaviors
Sensorimotor (0–2)	Use of senses to "know" environment			
Preoperational (2–7)	Difficulty with conceiving others' points of view (egocentric) Sense of time and space limited to short duration/close proximity Difficulty thinking through steps or decisions Acts impulsively	Punishment-obedience (4–6)	Actions based on physical outcome Little comprehension of motives Egocentric	Inattentiveness Easily frustrated Difficulty sharing Arguments during play
Concrete operational (7–12)	Limited ability to think about thinking Often will not check conclusions Unaware of and unconcerned with their own inconsistencies	Exchange of favors (6–9)	Actions based on reciprocal favors Fulfilling one's own needs comes first Beginning to understand motives	Cliques Attention-getting behavior Exclusion of certain classmates Inattentiveness during periods of discussion "Know-it-all" attitude
		Good boy-nice girl (10–15)	Actions based on peer conformity	
Formal operational (12–)	Able to think about thinking Can use independent critical thinking skills Can consider motives; the past, present, and future; the abstract; and the ideal	Law and order (15–18)	Rigid judgments based on following the law Motives and consequences recognized	Point out inconsistencies between behaviors and rules Challenge rules and policies Demand rationale behind rules Will not unquestioningly accept authority Argumentative
		Social contract (18–20)	Actions based on upholding individual rights and democratic principles	Refuse to change even in face of punishment
		Universal ethical (few people reach this level)	Actions based on respect for human dignity	

of, or unconcerned about, their inconsistencies. They are closed minded, often employing such phrases as, "I know!" "Do we have to discuss this?" or "I don't care!" with a tone that communicates a nonchalant lack of interest.

By the time students are leaving junior high school and entering high school, most of them are in the formal operational stage cognitively and moving from the good boy–nice girl to the law and order stage morally. By the end of high school, a few of them have reached the social contract level.

At this stage, students can deal with abstractness and conceive of many possibilities and ideals as well as the reality of their environment. Although peer pressure is still strong, they begin to see the need and rationale for rules and policies. They eventually see the need to protect rights and principles. They are now attempting to discover who they are, what they believe in, and what they are competent in.

Because students at this stage are searching for self-identity and are able to think abstractly, they often challenge the traditional values taught in school and home. They need to have a valid reason for why everything is the way it is. They will not accept "because I said so" as a legitimate reason to conform to a rule. Some hold to a particular behavior, explanation, or judgment, even in the face of punishment, if they feel that their individual rights have been challenged or violated. Unfortunately, many of these behaviors are carried out in an argumentative format.

A number of studies support the idea that normal developmental changes can lead to disruptive behavior. Jessor and Jessor (1977) found that the correlates of misbehavior in school are (1) growth in independence, (2) decline in traditional ideology, (3) increase in relativistic morality, (4) increase in peer orientation, and (5) increase in modeling problem behaviors. They concluded that the normal course of developmental change is in the direction of greater possibility of problems. However,

Age-specific behavior often is the result of the interaction of cognitive and moral development.

Clarizio and McCoy (1983) found that normal problem behaviors that occur as a developmental phenomenon have a high probability of being resolved with increasing age. A study of 400 famous twentieth-century men and women, which concluded that four out of five had experienced difficulties and problems related to school and schooling (Goertzel and Goertzel, 1962), appears to support the Clarizio and McCoy findings.

NEUROSCIENCE RESEARCH   Teenagers have been labeled moody, impulsive, indifferent, inconsistent, risk taking, and many other more colorful labels. In 1904, what was known about adolescents was detailed by G. Stanley Hall, a pioneer of psychology and education, in the text *Adolescents*. The teen years were summarized as a time replicating the early less civilized stages of human development. Similarly, Eric Erikson thought adolescence was always problematic, and Freud viewed it as a time of conflict. Thus, adolescence was considered to be a difficult if not downright impossible time that both teachers and parents dreaded. Such thinking prevailed into the late twentieth century when brain-imaging technology emerged. However, even today, in workshops led by the authors, we have heard comments such as "how do you do it" or "bless you" from elementary and high school teachers when participants introduce themselves as middle school teachers.

Images of hundreds of teenage brains studied in the late 1990s indicated that a human brain develops much more slowly than scientists had thought. By age 6, the brain has reached 90 percent of its size; however, what the research discovered was that human brains go through an extensive reorganization between ages 12 to 25. The brain's axon and neurons become more insulated with myelin, boosting transmission speed by 100 times. The dendrites become more branchlike and synapses that see lots of activity grow more efficient and those that see little activity begin to wither. This maturation period does not end in middle school as once thought, but instead lasts through late adolescence.

This progressing development of the brain eventually allows students to be able to balance impulses vs. long-term goals, self-interest vs. altruism, instant gratification vs. more intrinsic motivations, and risky behavior vs. consideration of the possible consequences. However, the development process is slow and uneven, which helps explain the inconsistent nature of adolescents. Simultaneous changes in the chemistry of the brain, particularly dopamine and oxytocin, help explain increased risk taking particularly in the presence of peers and the importance of fitting in and giving in to peer pressure. As we learn more about brain maturation, teachers can only imagine the impact this knowledge will have on instruction as well as how it will enlighten teachers in terms of influencing students to display appropriate behavior.

INSTRUCTIONAL COMPETENCE

At first glance, it would seem that the teacher has little or no control over the influences of misbehavior that have been discussed thus far. Although it is true that a teacher cannot significantly alter the course of most of these societal, familial, and developmental events, she can control her instructional competence. Excellent instructional competence can minimize the effects of these ongoing events, maximize the learning potential in the classroom, and prevent misbehavior caused by poor instructional methodology.

Why does Ms. Cook in Case 3.14, who is knowledgeable and enthusiastic about her subject matter and enjoys working with young people, have such discipline problems? Why do otherwise well-behaved students misbehave to such an extent in one particular class? The students' responses indicate a reasonable answer: the teacher's lack of skill in basic instructional methodology.

Because of Ms. Cook's instructional skill deficiencies, her students did not accord her *expert power,* the social authority and respect a teacher receives because she possesses special knowledge and expertise (French and Raven, 1960). (This and other authority bases are discussed in depth in Chapter 4.) Her inability to communicate content clearly, evaluate and remediate student misunderstandings, and explain the relevancy of the content to her students' lives caused her students to fail to recognize her expertise in the field of mathematics.

CASE 3.14
Not Being Able to Teach

Ms. Cook loves mathematics and enjoys working with young people, which she often does in camp and youth organizations. After graduating with a B.S. degree in mathematics, she goes on to earn a master's degree in mathematics and becomes certified to teach at the secondary level. She obtains a teaching position at a progressive suburban junior high school.

Ms. Cook conscientiously plans for all of her algebra and geometry classes and knows the material thoroughly. Within a few months, however, her classes are characterized by significant discipline problems. Most of her students are out of their seats, talking, throwing paper, and calling out jokes. They come in unprepared and, in a few instances, openly confront Ms. Cook's procedures and competence. Even though she is given assistance, supervision, and support from the administration, Ms. Cook decides not to return for her second year of teaching.

In an attempt to understand the class's behavior, the students are interviewed at the end of the school year. The following are the most common responses concerning Ms. Cook's methods:

1. Gave unclear explanations
2. Discussed topics having nothing or little to do with the subject at hand
3. Kept repeating understood material
4. Wrote things on the board but never explained them and her board work was sloppy
5. Would say, "We already did this" when asked for help
6. Did not involve the class and called on only the same people
7. Had difficulty giving clear answers to questions
8. Didn't explain how to use the material
9. Always used her note cards
10. Could not determine why the class was having difficulty understanding the material
11. Either gave the answers to the homework or didn't go over it, so no one had to do it

A teacher's ability to explain and clarify is foremost in developing authority. Kounin (1970) found that teachers who are liked are described by students as those who can explain the content well, whereas those who are disliked leave students in some state of confusion. Kounin also noted that when students like their teachers, they are more likely to behave appropriately and are more motivated to learn. As Tanner (1978) stated, "Teacher effectiveness, as perceived by pupils, invests the teacher with classroom authority" (p. 67). To students, teacher effectiveness translates to "explaining the material so that we can understand it." When this occurs, students regard the teacher as competent, and the teacher is invested with authority.

RESILIENCY

This chapter summarizes many of the ills of society and how such environments negatively affect students' behavior. These negative influences are often called risk signs. Research in identifying factors that put students at risk for developing problems later in life began in the 1970s. Most of these risks are beyond the control of teachers and schools and include exposure to social and economic disadvantages, dysfunctional child-rearing practices, family and marital discord, parental mental health problems, antisocial peer group, and trauma. These factors are cumulative; the risk for poor life outcome rises sharply as the number of risk factors increases (Resiliency Resource Centre, 2008). However, much qualitative and empirical evidence supports what most teachers already know: many children rise above the multiple and severe risks in their lives to become competent adolescents and adults. When this occurs it is said that the student possesses resiliency, or the student is resilient. In other words, *resiliency* is the capacity for children to adapt successfully and overcome severe stressors and risks (Werner and Smith, 1992).

Longitudinal studies consistently document that at least half to as many as two-thirds of children growing up in dysfunctional families, poverty, and drug- and violence-infested environments overcome these adversities and turn their life from one characterized by extreme risk to one of resilience or successful adaptation (Benard, 1995). What are the characteristics that differentiate those children who possess resiliency from those who succumb to the adversities they face?

Researchers have considered a wide range of individual, family, social, and environmental factors as discriminators. These factors seem to cluster into three broad categories: (1) cognitive and behavioral, (2) social and contextual, and (3) genetic. Cognitive and behavioral factors that enable a child to cope effectively with stress include social and emotional problem-solving abilities, a sense of optimism and autonomy, and self-esteem (Rutter, 1985). Social and contextual factors include quality relationships with parents, teachers, and other significant adults; access to community services; and regular attendance at schools where teachers have high behavioral and academic standards (Werner, 1993). Genetic factors include gender, temperament, intelligence, and physical health. Girls, individuals with an easygoing personality with above-average intelligence, and individuals in good health are more resilient.

Resiliency is not a finite characteristic of a student, with some students possessing it and some students not. Instead, resiliency is a complex dynamic process reflecting the interactions among cognitive, social, and genetic factors. Thus, it is probably more accurate to think in terms of children manifesting resilient behaviors and those who are not rather than describing a student as resilient or not resilient. Resiliency is dynamic and depends on context, age of the student, and the teacher. What may be considered resilient behavior in elementary school is likely not the same behavior in high school.

Researchers have analyzed the experiences of teachers and families working and living with at-risk youth. An outcome of this research is an understanding that there are characteristics of the family, school, and community that can aid students in circumventing risks and increase the likelihood of students' displaying resilient behaviors. The family, school, and community can serve as protective factors, which can be grouped into three major categories: (1) caring and supportive relationships, (2) positive and high expectations, and (3) opportunities for meaningful participation. Many of the protective factors are the reverse of risk factors. Thus, it is often helpful to consider risk factors and protective factors to be the opposite ends of a continuum. For example, a risk factor might be a pessimistic outlook toward the future, whereas a protective factor might be an optimistic orientation.

Caring, supportive teachers are the most frequently encountered positive role models outside the immediate family (Benard, 1995; Noddings, 1988). A meaningful student-teacher relationship built on a foundation of care, respect, and trust gives young people the motivation to try (Levin and Shanken-Kaye, 2002).

Teachers and schools that establish high academic and behavioral standards and provide students with the support needed to reach expectations have high rates of appropriate behavior and academic performance. The expectations and support

A teacher has total control over the use of effective teaching strategies.

are characterized by pedagogy and evaluations informed by what is known about how students learn and are not driven by high-risk standardized tests (Cotton, 2001). Providing young people with opportunities for meaningful involvement and responsibilities within the school and community, particularly in ways that provide students' with a sense of virtue, fosters resiliency (Benard, 1991).

To summarize, caring teachers who communicate high expectations, provide students with support, and encourage meaningful student involvement are positively addressing young people's basic needs and their self-esteem. When basic needs are met and young people feel good about themselves, they are likely to be more protected from their adverse environment and to display resilient behavior.

For teachers to be a catalyst for facilitating resilient behavior in their students, they must examine their beliefs. Teachers must genuinely believe their students are capable of succeeding; otherwise, teachers may experience the negative effects of a self-fulfilling prophecy (Rosenthal and Jacobson, 1968), that is, negative beliefs about students lead to negative feelings about students that lead to negative behaviors toward students (Levin and Shanken-Kaye, 2002). Thus, teachers need not master new strategies or specialized skills to encourage resilient student behavior. Instead, they must remain positive and encouraging and serve as a role model to their students (Howard and Johnson, 1998). The best outcomes for students are more likely when interventions are continuous and are implemented at an early age, before problematic behaviors become evident (Nastasi and Bernstein, 1998).

Summary

Although there are innumerable influences on students' behavior in schools, this chapter has focused on some of the major ones.

Societal changes, most notably the effects of the knowledge explosion and the media revolution, have created an environment that is vastly different from that in which children of previous generations grew up. More children now than ever before live in single-parent homes. Also, more children today are living at or below the poverty level than in previous generations. Additionally, schools are more diverse now than ever before, and the number of students changing schools for reasons other than grade promotion is increasing. Because of these and other factors, some children's basic needs, including the need for self-esteem, are not met the home. In-school bullying and cyberbullying are often overlooked and dismissed by teachers and administrators, even though it is widespread and has a significant negative physical and emotional impact on both the bully and the bullied. Out-of-school experiences are much more significant predictors of school behavior than children's in-school experiences. When a child's basic need for self-esteem is not met at home and/or is not met at school, discipline problems frequently result.

Throughout the school years, children's cognitive and moral development, as well as their continual need for social recognition, is reflected in their behavior. The implications of emerging neuroscience research concerning the maturation of the brain during adolescence have yet to be realized. A teacher has little or no control over many of these developments. What she can control is her own instructional competence. Excellent instruction can ameliorate the effects of outside influences and can be a catalyst for encouraging resiliency. Effective teaching can also prevent the misbehavior that occurs as a direct result of poor instruction. Effective teaching techniques are covered in more detail in Chapter 5.

Exercises

1. Look back on your own school experiences. What are some instructional techniques your teachers used that had the potential to discourage disruptive student behaviors?

2. What, if anything, can schools and classroom teachers do to help students meet the following basic human needs: (a) physiological, (b) safety and security, and (c) belonging and affection?

3. Self-esteem can be conceptualized mathematically as follows:

$$\text{Self-Esteem} = \text{Significance} + \text{Competence} + \text{Power} + \text{Virtue}$$

How does the self-esteem formula help explain why students behave disruptively inside and outside the classroom?

4. How does the self-esteem formula provide insight into the types of interventions that can lead to decreasing a student's disruptive behavior?

5. Research indicates that bullying prevention programs should be school wide to include parents, teachers, students, bullies, and victims. If you were designing a comprehensive prevention program, what would be some important objectives for each of the constituents?

6. Because cyberbullying usually occurs outside school, should schools intervene?

7. Even though they are beyond the school's control, changes in society can influence student behavior in school. What changes in society during the past 10 years do you believe have had negative influences on classroom behavior?

8. In your opinion, can media influence students to misbehave in the classroom? If so, list some specific examples to support your opinion. If not, explain why.

9. How might a lack of cultural synchronization between a teacher and students influence students' behavior?

10. What can a teacher do to improve cultural synchronization in a classroom?

11. Explain why some educational researchers believe that cognitive development is a prerequisite for moral development.

12. Considering students' cognitive development, how might a teacher teach the following concepts in the third, seventh, and eleventh grades?
    (a) Volume of a rectangular solid = $L \times W \times H$
    (b) Civil rights and equality
    (c) Subject-predicate agreement
    (d) Gravity

13. How might inappropriate teaching of these concepts for the cognitive level of the students contribute to classroom discipline problems?

14. Considering students' moral development, what can we expect as typical reactions to the following events at each of the following grade levels?

Event	First	Fourth	Seventh	Twelfth
a. A student from a poor family steals the lunch ticket of a student from a fairly wealthy family.				
b. A teacher keeps the entire class on a detention because of the disruptive behavior of a few.				
c. A student destroys school property and allows another student to be falsely accused and punished for the vandalism.				
d. A student has points subtracted from her test score for talking after her test paper was already turned in.				

15. What are some normal behaviors (considering their developmental level) for elementary students, junior high or middle school students, and senior high students that can be disruptive in a classroom?

16. What might a teacher do to allow the normal behaviors (listed in the answer to question 15) to be expressed while preventing them from disrupting learning?

17. Disruptive students often rationalize their inappropriate behavior by blaming it on the teacher: "I'll treat Mr. Lee with respect when he treats me with respect." Unfortunately, teachers often rationalize their negative behavior toward a student by blaming it on the student: "I'll respect Nicole when she respects me." Using the levels of moral cognitive development, explain why the student's rationalization is understandable but the teacher's is not.

18. Many resiliency researchers conceptualize risk signs and protective factors as opposite end points on a continuum. Provide a few examples that illustrate this.

19. What behaviors have you employed to successfully overcome stressors and adversities that you have experienced?

20. **Principles Of Teacher Behavior** After reading Chapter 3 and doing the exercises, use what you have learned to briefly describe your understanding of the implications of the principles listed at the beginning of the chapter for a classroom teacher.

PRINCIPLE 1:

PRINCIPLE 2

PRINCIPLE 3:

PRINCIPLE 4

PRINCIPLE 5:

Philosophical Approaches to Influencing Students

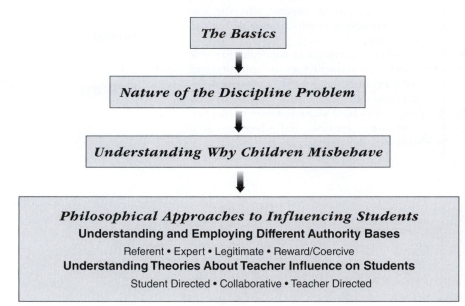

The Basics

Nature of the Discipline Problem

Understanding Why Children Misbehave

Philosophical Approaches to Influencing Students
Understanding and Employing Different Authority Bases
Referent • Expert • Legitimate • Reward/Coercive
Understanding Theories About Teacher Influence on Students
Student Directed • Collaborative • Teacher Directed

PRINCIPLES OF TEACHER BEHAVIOR THAT INFLUENCE APPROPRIATE STUDENT BEHAVIOR

1. Theoretical approaches to influencing students are useful to teachers because they offer a basis for analyzing, understanding, and influencing student and teacher behavior.

2. As social agents, teachers have access to a variety of authority bases that can be used to influence student behavior.

3. The techniques a teacher employs to influence student behavior should be consistent with the teacher's beliefs about how students learn and develop.

PREREADING ACTIVITY: UNDERSTANDING THE PRINCIPLES OF TEACHER BEHAVIOR

Before reading Chapter 4, briefly describe your understanding of the implications of the principles for a classroom teacher:

PRINCIPLE 1:

PRINCIPLE 2:

PRINCIPLE 3:

PREREADING QUESTIONS FOR REFLECTION AND JOURNALING

1. As you see it, is there a particular model or philosophy of teacher influence that is appropriate for all teachers and students? How would you justify your answer?

2. What tools do teachers have in their possession to influence students to choose appropriate behavior?

3. What are four or five of your key beliefs about influencing student behavior?

INTRODUCTION

Teaching can be a threatening and frustrating experience, and all of us at some time entertain doubts about our ability to maintain effective classroom learning environments. For many teachers, however, these normal self-doubts, which are especially common early in a teaching career, lead to a frantic search for gimmicks, techniques, or tricks that they hope will allow them to survive in the real classroom world. This is indeed unfortunate, as Case 4.1 illustrates. When classroom behavior problems are approached with a frenetically sought-after bag of tricks instead of a carefully developed systematic plan for decision making, teachers are likely to find themselves behaving in ways they regret later. The teachers who are most successful at creating a positive classroom atmosphere that enhances student learning are those who employ a carefully developed plan for influencing student behavior. Clearly, any such plan must be congruent with their basic beliefs about the nature of the teaching and learning process. When teachers use this type of plan, they avoid the dilemma that Ms. Knepp encountered.

There are multiple models or approaches and hundreds of techniques for promoting positive student behavior within these models. Most of these techniques are effective in some situations but not others, for some students but not others, and for some teachers but not others. What most of the experts fail to mention is that the efficacy of a technique is contextually dependent. Who the teacher teaches and who the teacher is dictate what technique will have the greatest potential for addressing the complex management problems evidenced in classrooms (Lasley, 1989). Because every technique is based implicitly or explicitly on some belief system concerning how human beings behave and why, the classroom teacher must find prototypes of teacher influence that are consistent with his beliefs and employ them under appropriate circumstances.

How can teachers ensure that their behavior in dealing with classroom discipline problems will be effective and will match their beliefs about students, teachers, and learning? First, they can understand their own basic beliefs about influencing student behavior. Second, they can develop, based on their beliefs, a systematic plan for promoting positive student behavior and dealing with inappropriate behavior. Chapters 8 through 11, which provide multiple options for dealing with any single classroom behavior problem, are designed to help teachers develop a systematic plan. Numerous options are provided to allow every teacher to develop a personal plan for encouraging appropriate student behavior and for dealing with unacceptable behavior in a manner congruent with his own basic beliefs. Because there are numerous options, the teacher can prioritize his options in a hierarchical format.

To help teachers and future teachers lay the philosophical foundation for their own classroom instructional plan, this chapter offers an overview of a variety of philosophical approaches to influencing student behavior. So that they may be considered in a more systematic and orderly fashion, the approaches are grouped under two major headings: teacher authority bases and theories of teacher influence. The first section discusses the various types of authority or influence that are available to teachers to promote appropriate student behavior. The second section explains three theories of teacher influence and their underlying beliefs and includes models and techniques for each of the theoretical approaches.

It is important to be aware of the inherent connection among the three theories and the four authority bases. Each of the three theories relies on the dominant use of one or two authority bases. Teachers can examine the foundations on which their own instructional plans rest by comparing their beliefs with those inherent in each of the various teacher authority bases and theories of teacher influence.

CASE 4.1

The Tricks-of-the-Trade Approach

Ms. Judy Knepp is a first-year teacher at Armstrong Middle School. Although most of her classes are going well, she is having a great deal of difficulty with her sixth-grade developmental reading class. Many of the students seem disinterested, lazy, immature, and rebellious. They perform poorly on state assessment tests. As a result of the class's continuous widespread chattering, Ms. Knepp spends the vast majority of her time yelling and reprimanding individual students. She has considered using detention to control students, but there are so many disruptive students that she doesn't know whom to give detention to first. The class has become such a battlefield that she finds herself hating to go to school in the morning.

After struggling on her own for a couple of long weeks, Ms. Knepp decides that she had better ask somebody for help. She is reluctant to go to any of the administrators because she thinks that revealing the problem will result in a low official evaluation for her first semester's work. Finally, she decides to go to Ms. Hoffman, a veteran teacher of 14 years with a reputation for striking fear into the hearts of her sixth-grade students.

After she tells Ms. Hoffman all about her horrendous class, Ms. Knepp waits anxiously for some words of wisdom that will help her get the class under control. Ms. Hoffman's advice is short and to the point: "I'd just keep the whole class in for detention. Keep them until about 4:30 just one day, and I guarantee you won't have any more trouble with them. These kids think they're tough, but when they see that you're just as mean and tough as they are, they'll melt pretty quickly."

Ms. Knepp is dismayed. She immediately thinks, "That's just not fair. What about those four or five kids who don't misbehave? Why should they have to stay in too?" She does not voice her objections to Ms. Hoffman, fearing Ms. Hoffman will see her as rude and ungrateful. She does ask, "What about parents who object to such punishment?" However, Ms. Hoffman assures her that she has never had any trouble from parents and that the principal, Dr. Kropa, will support the disciplinary action even if any parents do object.

Ms. Knepp feels trapped. She knows that Ms. Hoffman expects her to follow through, and she fears that Ms. Hoffman will tell the other veteran teachers if she doesn't take the advice. Like most newcomers, Ms. Knepp longs to be accepted.

Despite her misgivings, Ms. Knepp decides to follow the advice and to do so quickly before she loses her nerve. The next day, she announces that one more disruption—no matter who is the culprit—will bring detention for the entire class. For five minutes silence reigns, and the class actually accomplishes some work. Ms. Knepp has begun to breathe a long sigh of relief when suddenly she hears a loud "You pig" from the back right-hand corner of the room. She is positive that all the students have heard the epithet and knows that she cannot ignore it. She also fears that an unenforced threat will mean disaster.

"That does it. Everyone in this class has detention tomorrow after school." Immediately, the air is filled with "That ain't fair," "I didn't do nothing," "You wish," and "Don't hold your breath." Naturally, most of these complaints come from the biggest troublemakers. However, several students who never cause trouble also complain bitterly that the punishment is unfair. Deep down, Ms. Knepp agrees with them, but she feels compelled to dismiss their complaints with a fainthearted, "Well, life just isn't always fair, and you might as well learn that now." She stonewalls it through the rest of the class and is deeply relieved when the class is over.

When Ms. Knepp arrives at school the next morning, there is a note from Dr. Kropa in her box stating that Mr. and Mrs. Pennsi are coming in during her free period to talk about the detention of their son, Fred. Fred is one of the few students who rarely cause trouble. Ms. Knepp feels unable to defend her action. It contradicts her beliefs about fairness and how students should be treated. The conference is a disaster. Ms. Knepp begins by trying to convince the Pennsies that she is right but ends by admitting that she too feels that she has been unfair to Fred. After the conference, she discusses the punishment with Dr. Kropa, who suggests that it is best to call it off. Ms. Knepp drags herself, half in tears, to her class. She is going to back down and rescind the punishment. She believes that the kids will see this as a sign of weakness, and she is afraid of the consequences.

TEACHER AUTHORITY BASES

French and Raven (1960) identified four types of authority that teachers as social agents can use to influence student behavior. The effective teacher is aware of the type of authority he wants to use to influence student behavior and is also aware of the type of authority that is implicit in each of the techniques available. It cannot be emphasized enough that when teachers' beliefs and behaviors are consistent, they are more likely to be successful than when their beliefs and behaviors are not consistent. When beliefs and behaviors are congruent, the teacher usually follows through and is consistent in dealing with student behavior because he (unlike Ms. Knepp) believes that it is the right thing to do, and students usually perceive the teacher as a genuine person who practices what he preaches. When the teacher's beliefs and behaviors are not congruent, the mismatch between the two can actually influence students to behave inappropriately. For example, a teacher who really does not care about students and attempts to use referent authority to influence student behavior will be spotted by students as a phony. Students, especially adolescents, will view the teacher as manipulative and disingenuous. The result is likely to be increased disruptive behavior. As you read, ask yourself which type or types of authority fit your beliefs and which types you could use comfortably. Although every teacher probably uses each of the four types of authority at some time, each teacher has a dominant authority base or two that he uses most often.

The four teacher authority bases are presented in a hierarchical format, beginning with those more likely to engender student control over their own behavior and proceeding to those that foster increasing teacher control. If a teacher believes, as we do, that one of the important long-range goals of schooling is to foster student self-direction, using those authority bases at the top of the hierarchy as often as possible will be consistent with this belief. If a teacher does not share this belief, the hierarchical arrangement of authority bases is not as important for him. Whatever one's beliefs about the long-range goals of education, it is still necessary to understand the four teacher authority bases because no single one is effective for all students, all classrooms, or all teachers. Thus, effective teaching requires the use of a variety of authority bases.

Referent Authority

Consider Case 4.2. The type of authority Mr. Emig uses to influence student behavior has been termed *referent authority* by French and Raven (1960). When a teacher has referent authority, students behave as the teacher wishes because they enjoy a positive relationship with the teacher and like the teacher as a person. Students view the teacher as a good person who is concerned about them, cares about their learning, and demands a certain type of behavior because it is in their best interest. One of the benefits of the use of referent authority is the positive relationship that develops between the students and the teacher. Teachers who engage in more positive interactions with students are generally more effective teachers and create emotionally positive classroom climates in which students show more respect to the teacher and to peers (Glick, 2011).

There are two requirements for the effective use of referent authority: (1) the teacher must perceive that the students have a good relationship with him, and (2) the

CASE 4.2

The Involved Teacher

Administrators and teachers alike at Spring Grove Junior High envied Mr. Emig. Even though he taught eighth-grade English to all types of students, he never sent students to the office, rarely gave detentions, and never needed parent conferences to discuss student behavior. In fact, it seemed as if students never exhibited discipline problems in his class.

Mr. Karr, the principal, decided that other teachers might be able to learn some techniques from Mr. Emig and so asked some of Mr. Emig's students why his classes were so well behaved. Students said that they liked Mr. Emig because he was always involved in activities with them. He sponsored the school newspaper, went on ski club trips, went to athletic events, coached track, chaperoned dances, and advised the student council. Because of his heavy involvement with them, students got a chance to see him as a person, not just as a teacher, and they felt that he was a really good person who cared a lot about kids. As a result, nobody hassled him in class. In addition, Mr. Emig got to know the students very well. He knew about their activities and hobbies, their families, and their backgrounds and was able to connect classroom instruction to their individual interests.

teacher must communicate that he cares about and likes the students. He does this through positive nonverbal gestures; positive oral and written comments; extra time and attention; and displays of sincere interest in students' ideas, activities, and especially, learning. Teachers with referent authority are able to appeal directly to students to act a certain way. Examples of such direct appeals are "I'm really not feeling well today. Please keep the noise level at a minimum," and "It really makes me angry when you hand assignments in late. Please have your assignments ready on time." These teachers might handle Ms. Knepp's problem with a statement such as, "You disappoint me and make me very angry when you misbehave and disrupt class time. I spend a great deal of time planning activities that you will enjoy and that will help you to learn, but I must spend so much time on discipline that we don't get to them. I would really appreciate it if you would stop the misbehavior."

Referent authority must not be confused with the situation in which the teacher attempts to be the students' friend. A teacher who wants to be friends with students usually is dependent on students to fulfill his personal needs. This dependency creates an environment in which students are able to manipulate the teacher. Over time, the teacher and students become equals, and the teacher loses the ability to influence students to behave appropriately. In contrast, the teacher who uses referent authority is in an adult role and does make demands on students. Students carry out the teacher's wishes because they like the teacher as a teacher, not as a friend.

Although the use of referent authority is effective with all students, Lisa Delpit's (2012) powerful insights on successful teachers of African American students suggest that referent authority may be a particularly effective authority base for influencing the behavior and academic learning of students of color. Delpit suggests that teachers who are "warm demanders" are most effective in teaching students of color (we return to this concept in Chapter 5). Delpit suggests that it is the underlying positive relationship that allows these warm demanders to relentlessly push students to achieve more: "It is the quality of the relationship that allows a teacher's push for excellence. As I have previously written, many of our children of color do not learn from a teacher as much as for a teacher. They don't want to disappoint a teacher who believes in them" (Delpit, 2012, p. 86). Ms. Brubeck, the novice teacher in Case 4.3 unfertands the "demand" component of these ideas but missses the boat on the notion of "warmth."

Delpit also suggests that in order to use referent authority effectively, the teacher must get to know students' lives and cultures outside of the school context and that a lack of understanding of students' cultures and family lives interferes with the ability of many white, middle-class teachers to see students of color as just as capable and brilliant as white students. Thus, referent authority, grounded in deep knowledge about the students, may well be a powerful tool for learning to teach students whose cultures and family lives differ from those of the teacher.

It is neither possible nor wise to use referent authority all the time with all students. Indeed, using referent authority with students who genuinely dislike the teacher may result in disaster. To understand this caution, one need only consider the possible and probable response to direct appeals by students who see their primary

CASE 4.3

Demand without the Warmth

Linda Brubeck is a first-year middle school English teacher in an urban schol with students from a variety of cultural backgrounds. Many of the students come from poor families. Although she is from a white, middle-class background, Linda was quite confident as the year began that she would be able to teach her students effectively. She loves her subject, really enjoys middle school students, and discovered, in her 12-week student teaching experience in a high-powered suburban middle school, that she had the instructional competence to make reading and writing interesting and enjoyable for her students.

From her course on culturally relevant pedagogy, she understands clearly that effective teachers of students from poor families must hold high expectations for students and believe that all students are capable of learning. Ms. Brubeck expects all of her students to achieve. Unfortunately, the first six weeks

of the school year have been anything but enjoyable for Linda. Despite her high expectations and love for her subject, her students will simply not make any significant effort to complete the work that she asks them to do. A few students complete the work but don't seem to make much of an effort at it. Most students pretend that they will do the assignments but never seem to produce, whereas a few other students blantantly and publicly refuse to even try. Frustrated and in tears, she approaches Carrie Johnson, a veteran, African American colleague who is recognized as an amazing teacher by everyone in the school community. Linda pours out her heart to Carrie, who listens to her sympathetically and then asks a question that leaves Linda speechless. Ms. Johnson asks, "Linda, can you talk to me about some of the things that you have done to learn about your students' lives outside of school and about them as individuals?"

goal as making the teacher's life miserable. However, when students make it clear that they have a positive relationship with the teacher through their general reactions to him before, during, and after class, and when the teacher has communicated his caring and concern to students, the use of referent authority can make influencing student behavior much easier.

Expert Authority

Ms. Sanchez in Case 4.4 is a teacher who uses *expert authority* to influence student behavior. When a teacher enjoys expert authority, students behave as the teacher wishes because they view him as a good, knowledgeable teacher who can help them learn. This is the power of professional competence. To use expert authority effectively, two important conditions must be fulfilled: (1) the students must believe the teacher has both special knowledge and the teaching skills to help them acquire that knowledge, and (2) the students must value learning what the teacher is teaching. Students may value what they are learning for any number of reasons: the subject matter is inherently interesting, they can use it in the real world, they want good grades, or they want to reach some personal goal such as college or a job. The more that a teacher knows about the lives of his students, the more likely it is that the students will recognize the teacher's expertise in being able to connect the subject matter to their world. Knowledge of students' lives is always important, but it is particularly important when the teacher is teaching students who are culturally different from the teacher.

The teacher who uses expert authority successfully communicates his competence through mastery of content material, the use of motivating teaching techniques, clear explanations, and thorough class preparation. In other words, the teacher uses his professional knowledge to help students learn. When expert authority is employed successfully, students make comments similar to these: "I behave because he is a really good teacher," "She makes biology interesting," and "He makes you really want to learn." A teacher with an expert authority base might say to Ms. Knepp's disruptive class: "I'm sure you realize how important reading is. If you can't read, you will have a rough time being successful in our society. You know that I can help you learn to read and to read well, but I can't do that if you won't behave as I've asked you to behave."

CASE 4.4

Her Reputation Precedes Her

Ms. Sanchez is a chemistry teacher at Lakefront High School. Each year, Ms. Sanchez teaches an advanced placement (AP) chemistry course to college-bound seniors. For the past five years, none of her AP students has received less than a three on the AP exam. As a result, each student has received college credit for AP chemistry. Students in Ms. Sanchez's class recognize that she is knowledgeable about chemistry and knows how to teach. If an observer walks into Ms. Sanchez's AP class, even during April and May, he will find the students heavily involved in class activities, with little off-task behavior.

As is the case with referent authority, a teacher may be able to use expert authority with some classes and some students but not with others. A math teacher may be able to use expert authority with an advanced calculus group but not with a remedial general math group; an auto mechanics teacher may be able to use expert authority with the vocational-technical students but not with students who take auto mechanics to fill up their schedules.

One final caveat concerning this type of authority: whereas most primary school teachers are perceived as experts by their students, expert authority does not seem to be effective in motivating these students to behave appropriately. Thus, unlike the other three authority bases, which can be employed at all levels, the appropriate use of expert authority seems to be confined to students above the primary grades.

Legitimate Authority

The third type of authority identified by French and Raven and utilized by Mr. Davis in Case 4.5 is *legitimate authority*. The teacher who seeks to influence students through legitimate authority expects students to behave appropriately because the teacher has the legal and formal authority for maintaining appropriate behavior in the classroom. In other words, students behave because the teacher is the teacher, and inherent in that role are a certain legitimacy and authority.

Teachers who wish to use a legitimate authority base must demonstrate through their behavior that they accept the responsibilities, as well as the role status, inherent in the role of teacher. Students must view them as fitting the stereotypical image of teacher (e.g., in dress, speech, and mannerisms). Students must also believe that teachers and school administrators are working together. School administrators help teachers gain legitimate authority by making clear through words and actions that students are expected to treat teachers as legitimate authority figures. Teachers help themselves gain legitimate authority by following and enforcing school rules and by supporting school policies and administrators.

Students who behave because of legitimate authority make statements such as, "I behave because the teacher asked us to. You're supposed to do what the teacher

CASE 4.5

"School Is Your Job"

Mr. Davis looked at the fourth graders in front of him, many of whom were talking or staring into space instead of doing the seat work assignment. He said, "You are really disappointing me. You're sitting there wasting precious time. School is not a place for wasting time. School is your job, just like your parents have jobs, and it is my job to see that you work hard and learn during school. Your parents pay taxes so that you'll have the chance to come to school and learn. You and I both have the responsibility to do what we're supposed to do. Now, let's cut out the talking and the daydreaming, and do your math.

I will not put up with disrespectful behavior. I am responsible for making sure that you learn, and I'm going to do that. If that means using the principal and other school authorities to help me do my job, I'll do just that."

says." A teacher who employs legitimate authority might use a statement in Ms. Knepp's class such as, "I do not like the way you people are treating me. I am your teacher."

Because of the societal changes discussed in Chapter 3, most teachers rightly believe that today's students are less likely to be influenced by legitimate authority than students of 30 or 40 years ago were. However, it is still possible to use legitimate authority with some classes and some students. Groups of students who generally accept teacher-set rules and assignments without question or challenge are appropriate groups with whom to use legitimate authority.

Reward/Coercive Authority

Notice how the teacher in Case 4.6 is using *reward and coercive authority* to influence student behavior. Although they may be considered two separate types of teacher authority, reward and coercive authority are really two sides of the same coin. They are both based on behavioral notions of learning, foster teacher control over student behavior, and are governed by the same principles of application.

There are several requirements for the effective use of this authority base: (1) the teacher must be consistent in assigning and withholding rewards and punishments, (2) the teacher must ensure that students see the connection between their behavior and the reward or punishment, and (3) the rewards or punishments actually must be perceived as rewards or punishments by the student (many students view a three-day out-of-school suspension as a vacation, not a punishment).

Teachers employing this base use a variety of rewards, such as oral or written praise, gold stars, free time, "good news" notes to parents, and release from required assignments, as well as a variety of punishments, including verbal reprimands, loss of recess or free time, detention, in-school suspension, out-of-school suspension, and corporal punishment.

Students who behave appropriately because of reward/coercive authority are apt to say, "I behave because if I don't, I have to write out a stupid saying 50 times and get it signed by my parents." A teacher using reward/coercive authority to solve Ms. Knepp's problem might say, "I've decided that for every five minutes without a disruption, this class will earn one point. At the end of each week, for every ten points it has accumulated, the class may buy one night without homework during the

CASE 4.6

Going to Recess

"O.K., second graders, it's time to put your spelling books away and get ready for recess. Now, we all remember that we get ready by putting all books and supplies neatly and quietly in our desks and then folding our hands on top of the desk and looking at me quietly. Let's see which row can get ready first. I see that Tammy's row is ready. O.K., Tammy's row, you can walk quietly out to the playground. Oh, no, wait a minute. Where are you going, Joe? You're not allowed to go out to recess this week because of your misbehavior on the bus. You can go to Mr. Li's room and do your math assignment. I'll check it when I get back."

following week. Remember, if there are any disturbances at all, you will not receive a point for the five-minute period." This point system is an example of a behavior modification technique. More information on the use of behavior modification in the classroom may be obtained in Chapter 10 as well as from Alberto and Troutman (2012) or Martella et al. (2011).

As is true for the other three authority bases, reward/coercive authority cannot be used all the time. As students become older, they often resent obvious attempts to manipulate their behavior through rewards and punishments. In addition, older students are very sensitive to the setting in which praise is delivered. Students in middle and high school typically prefer to receive praise outside of the range of hearing of others (Dean et al., 2012). It is also difficult with older students to find rewards and punishments under the classroom teacher's control that are powerful enough to motivate them. (Still, some teachers have found their control of student time during school has allowed them to use reward/coercive authority successfully with some students and some classes at all levels of schooling.) It should be noted that there are some inherent dangers in the use of reward/coercive authority.

A great deal of controversy surrounds the effects of rewards on students' intrinsic motivation. Lepper and Green (1978) first noted that rewarding children for engaging in activities that had been initially intrinsically motivating resulted in decreased intrinsic motivation for those activities. After many years of research on the issue, four caveats seem particularly important in considering the use of extrinsic rewards. First, tangible external rewards (e.g., stickers, candy, free time) seem to undermine students' intrinsic motivation for engaging in the activities for which they received the rewards. The younger the child, the greater the negative impact seems to be (Deci, Koestner, and Ryan, 2001). Second, verbal rewards (e.g., praise) that are linked to success on a task or to obtaining or exceeding a performance standard do not seem to negatively affect intrinsic motivation (Cameron, 2001). Third, verbal rewards that are perceived as primarily conveying information about how well students have performed on a task are less likely to affect intrinsic motivation negatively. Verbal rewards, on the other hand, that are seen as tools for controlling students' behavior or for manipulating them to engage in a task that they would otherwise perceive as boring are likely to undermine intrinsic motivation for that activity. Fourth, in any situation in which one explanation for a person's behavior seems most powerful and salient, all other explanations are likely to be ignored or disregarded, both by the individual himself and by others. Stipek (2002) referred to this phenomenon as the *discounting principle*. This principle suggests that if powerful extrinsic rewards are provided to induce students to engage in a particular task, students will explain their engagement as being driven by the extrinsic reward and ignore or downplay any intrinsic value in the activity.

In making sense of this somewhat contested research, we suggest the following guidelines. Whenever possible, use intrinsic motivation and encouragement (see Chapter 5) rather than extrinsic tangible or verbal rewards. If you see extrinsic rewards as important in implementing your beliefs about teacher influence, use the most modest extrinsic rewards possible, that is, verbal rewards rather than tangible ones. Make the rewards contingent on the quality of task performance or on some prespecified standard as opposed to a reward for simply engaging in a task. For example, in praising students, it is important to provide praise that is specific and aligned with expected performance behaviors (Dean et al., 2012). Finally, remove the extrinsic rewards as quickly as possible and help the student recognize the intrinsic value of the activity through the use of encouragement.

It is important for a teacher to recognize what authority base he uses to influence students in a given situation and to recognize why that base is appropriate or inappropriate for the given students and situation. It is also important for the teacher to recognize the authority base he uses most frequently as well as the authority base he is comfortable with and would like to use. For some teachers, the two may be quite different. Examining your beliefs about teacher authority bases is one important step toward ensuring that your beliefs about teacher influence and your actions are compatible. Table 4.1 offers a brief comparison of the four authority bases on several significant dimensions.

Of course, most teachers use a combination of authority bases. They use one for one type of class and students and another for another type of class and students. They may even use a variety of authority bases with the same students. This may, indeed, be the most practical and effective approach, although combining certain authority bases—for example, coercive and referent—may be difficult to do.

TABLE 4.1   Teacher Authority Bases

	Referent	Expert	Legitimate	Reward/Coercive
Motivation to behave	Student likes teacher as a person	Teacher has special knowledge	Teacher has legal authority	Teacher can reward and punish
Need for teacher management of student behavior	Very low	Very low	Moderate	High
Requirements for use	Students must like the teacher as a person	Teacher expertise must be perceived and valued	Students must respect legal authority	Rewards and punishments must be effective
Key teacher behaviors	Building positive relationships	Demonstrates mastery of content and teaching skills	Acts as a teacher is expected to act	Has and uses knowledge of student likes and dislikes
Age limitations	Useful for all levels	Less useful at primary level	Useful at all levels	Useful at all levels but less useful at senior high level
Caveats	Teacher is not the student's friend	Heavily dependent on student values	Societal changes have lessened the usefulness of this authority base	Emphasizes extrinsic over intrinsic motivation

THEORIES OF TEACHER INFLUENCE

In this section, we describe three theories about how teachers can influence student behavior through the teaching decisions that they make. In order to make the differences among the three theories clear, we describe each theory as if it were completely independent of the others. In reality, however, the three theories are more like three points on a continuum moving from student-directed toward teacher-directed practices. On such a continuum, collaborative models represent a combination of the two end points. Of course, the classroom behavior of most teachers represents some blending of the three theories. As Bob Strachota (1966) noted, "Theories about how to best help children learn and change have to be broad enough to encompass the vitality and ambiguity that come with life in a classroom. If relied on too exclusively, behaviorism or constructivism end[s] up living awkwardly in school" (p. 133). Still, if a teacher's behavior is examined over time, it is usually possible to classify the teacher's general approach to working with students and influencing students into one of the theories on a fairly consistent basis.

Before reading the specific theories, determine your answers to the following nine basic questions about influencing student behavior. Inherent in each theory are answers, either implicit or explicit, to these questions. If you are aware of your own beliefs before you begin, you will be able to identify the theory that is aligned most closely with them.

1. Who has primary responsibility for influencing student behavior?
2. What are your primary goals in establishing your classroom's learning environment?
3. How do you view time spent on behavioral issues and problems?
4. How would you like students to relate to each other within your classroom?
5. How much choice will you give students within your classroom?
6. What is your primary goal in influencing students who are misbehaving?
7. What interventions will you use to influence students who choose to misbehave?
8. How important to you are individual differences among students?
9. What teacher authority bases are most compatible with your beliefs?

Because the student-directed approach is used less frequently in schools than the other two approaches and may be unfamiliar, more specific details are provided for it than for the other two. Additional information concerning these management theories can be found in Charles and Senter (2010) and Wolfgang (2008).

Student-Directed Theories

Advocates of student-directed teacher influence theories believe that the primary goal of schooling is to prepare students for life in a democracy, which requires citizens who are able to control their behavior, care for others, and make wise decisions. When the first two editions of this text were written, student-directed theories of "classroom management" (we used the term *classroom management* instead of *teacher influence* at that point in time) were drawn primarily from counseling models. Gordon's (1989) teacher effectiveness training, Berne's (1964) and Harris's (1969) transactional analysis, and Ginott's (1972) communication model relied almost exclusively on one-to-one conferencing between teacher and student to deal with behavior issues. Such models were difficult to implement in the reality of a classroom filled with 25 to 30 students, each with a variety of talents, needs, interests, and problems. As a result, teacher-directed influence models dominated most classrooms. Since the early 1990s, however, there has been considerable progress in developing student-directed theories that can be employed effectively within classrooms. Alfie Kohn (2006), Bob Strachota (1996), Ruth Charney (2002), Putnam and Burke (1992), and writers from the Developmental Studies Center and the Northeast Foundation for Children have provided a variety of practical strategies that classroom teachers can use effectively.

The student-directed theory of influence, which Ms. Koskowski in Case 4.7 uses to handle David's behavior, rests on two key beliefs: (1) students must have the primary responsibility for controlling their behavior, and (2) students are capable of controlling their behavior if given the opportunity to do so. Given these beliefs, student-directed theories advocate the establishment of classroom learning communities that are designed to help students become more self-directed, more responsible for their own behavior, more independent in making appropriate choices, and more caring toward fellow students and their teachers. The successful classroom learning environment is one in which students care for and collaborate successfully with each other, make good choices, and continuously strive to do high-quality work that is interesting and important to them.

Teachers often use punishment and rewards; however, they may not be the most effective means for influencing student behavior.

CASE 4.7

Handling Disruptive David

Ms. Koskowski, Ms. Sweely, and Mr. Green teach fourth grade at Longmeadow School. Although they work well together and like each other, they have very different approaches to classroom discipline. To illustrate their differing approaches, let's examine their behavior as each one deals with the same situation.

Three students are at the reading center in the far right-hand corner and two students are working quietly on insects at the science interest center near the chalkboard located in the front of the room. Five students are correcting math problems individually, and ten students are working with the teacher in a reading group. David, one of the students working alone, begins to mutter out loud, "I hate this math. It's too hard to do. I never get them right. Why do we have to learn about fractions anyway?" As his monologue

(Continued)

(Continued)

continues, David's voice begins to get louder and clearly becomes a disruption for the other students.

Ms. Koskowski

Ms. Koskowski recognizes that David, who is not strong in math, is really frustrated by the problems on fractions. She walks over to him and quietly says, "You know, David, the other night I was trying to learn to play tennis, and I was getting really frustrated. It helped me to take a break and get away from it for a minute, just to clear my head. How about if you do that now? Go get a drink of water, and when you come back, you can get a fresh start." When David returns to his seat and begins to work, Ms. Koskowski helps him think through the first problem and then watches and listens as he does the second one on his own.

Ms. Sweely

As soon as she sees that David is beginning to interrupt the other students, Ms. Sweely gives the reading group a question to think about and walks toward David's desk. She puts her hand gently on his shoulder, but the muttering continues. She says, "David, you are disrupting others; please stop talking and get back to math." David stops for about five seconds but then begins complaining loudly again. "David, since you can't work without disrupting other people, you will have to go back to the castle [a desk and rocking chair partitioned off from the rest of the class] and finish your math there. Tomorrow, if you believe that you can handle it, you may rejoin your math group."

Mr. Green

As soon as David's muttering becomes audible, Mr. Green says, "David, that behavior is against our class rules. Stop talking and concentrate on your math." David stops talking momentarily but begins again. Mr. Green walks calmly to David's desk and removes a small, round, blue chip. As he does, he says, "Well, David, you've lost them all now. That means no more recess today and no good-news note to your mom and dad."

When viewed from a student-directed perspective, time spent on behavior is seen as time well spent on equipping students with skills that will be important to them as adult citizens in a democracy. The responsive classroom approach to student-directed classroom environments points out five social skills that are exceptionally important for all healthy human beings to develop. The skills can be summed up in the acronym, CARES: C–cooperation, A–assertiveness, R–responsibility, E–empathy, and S–self-control (Denton and Kriete, 2000). In attempting to develop a student-directed learning environment in which students develop self-regulation skills, collaborative social skills, and decision-making skills, the teacher relies heavily on several major concepts: student ownership, student choice, community, and conflict resolution and problem solving.

Student ownership is established in several ways. Although the teacher takes responsibility for the arrangement of the classroom and for the safety of the environment, students are often responsible for deciding how the room should be decorated; for creating the posters, pictures, and other works that decorate the walls; and for maintaining the room. Throughout the year, students rotate through committees (the art supplies committee, the plants and animals committee, the cleanup committee, etc.) that are responsible for various aspects of the class's work. These committees are often structured so that students gain experience in planning, delegating, and evaluating their own work in a fair and equitable manner.

Students are also given a great deal of responsibility for determining classroom rules. Typically, a class meeting is held during which the teacher and students discuss how they want their classroom to be. Students are asked to think about the ways they are treated by others that make them feel good or bad. These experiences are then used as a springboard for a discussion about how the students want to treat each other in the classroom. The students' words become the guidelines for classroom behavior.

Choice plays a key role in student-directed learning environments because it is believed that a student can learn to make good choices only if he has the opportunity to make choices. In addition to making choices about the physical environment of the room and the expectations for behavior, students are given choices about classroom routines and procedures, topics and questions to be studied in curriculum units, learning activities, and the assessment of their learning including assessment options and criteria. Classroom meetings, which are viewed as important vehicles for establishing and maintaining a caring classroom community, provide more opportunities for choices. Agendas for the meetings, which may be planning and decision-making meetings, check-in meetings, or problem-solving and issues-oriented meetings, are often suggested by the students (Developmental Studies Center, 1996).

Through the physical arrangement of the room, class meetings, and planned learning activities, the teacher attempts to build a community of learners who know and care for each other and work together productively. A great deal of time is spent

Cooperative learning activities can help students realize that they have responsibilities to both themselves and the class.

at the beginning of the year helping students get to know each other through get-acquainted activities, meetings, and small-group activities. Throughout the year, cooperative learning activities stressing individual accountability, positive interdependence, face-to-face interaction, social skill development, and group processing are utilized (see Chapter 5). These types of activities are emphasized because student-directed theorists believe that students learn more in collaborative activities and that when they know and care for those in their classroom community, they are more likely to choose to behave in ways that are in everyone's best interest.

Interpersonal conflict is seen as a teachable moment (Crowe, 2009). Student-directed teachers realize that conflict is inevitable when individuals are asked to work closely together. In fact, the absence of conflict is probably a good indication that individuals are not working together very closely. Thus, these teachers believe that helping students deal with interpersonal conflict productively is an important goal of classroom management. Conflict resolution, peer mediation, and interpersonal problem-solving skills are taught just as academic content is taught. Students are encouraged to use the skills when conflicts arise. Issues that concern the class as a whole—conflicts concerning the sharing of equipment, class cliques, and relationship problems—become occasions for using group problem-solving skills during class meetings. Some teachers even use class meetings to involve the entire class in helping improve the behavior of a particular student. It is important to note that encouraging caring relationships and teaching ways to deal with conflict productively go hand-in-hand and demand ongoing effort and consistency on the part of the teacher. If students do not know or care about each other, conflict is hard to resolve. Conversely, if students do not acquire the ability to resolve conflict productively, they are unlikely to build caring relationships with each other.

Student misbehavior is seen not as an affront to the teacher's authority but rather as the student's attempt to meet needs that are not being met. In response to misbehavior, the teacher tries to determine what motivates the child and to find ways to meet the unmet needs. A student-directed teacher would view the behavior problems in Ms. Knepp's class, Case 4.1, as a clear indication that student needs were not being met by the learning activities and curriculum. He probably would hold a class meeting to address the problem behaviors in the classroom. He would articulate his feelings and reactions to the class and would elicit student feelings about the class as well. Through a discussion of their mutual needs and interests, the teacher and the class would develop a solution to the problem that would probably include some redesign of the tasks that students were asked to perform.

Kohn (2006) suggested that the two questions the teacher should ask when a child is off-task are (1) "What is the task?" and (2) "Is it really a task worth doing?" Many teachers try to identify with the child. Strachota (1996) called this "getting on their side." This strategy seems especially appropriate when coping with students who seem out of control and unable to behave appropriately. If a teacher can identify experiences in which he has felt out of control, he is usually more empathetic and helpful (see Chapter 10). In Case 4.7, Ms. Koskowski employs this strategy with David.

Student-directed teachers also believe in allowing students to experience the consequences of their behavior. Natural consequences (consequences that do not require teacher intervention) are the most helpful because they allow the student to experience the results of his behavior directly. However, sometimes the teacher must use logical consequences. The teacher's role in using consequences is neither to augment nor to alleviate the consequences but rather to support the child or the class as the consequences are experienced. This can be a difficult role for teachers and parents to play. Even when a teacher can predict that a given choice is going to lead to negative consequences, student-directed theorists argue, the student should experience the consequence unless that will bring great harm to the child. Students learn to make wise choices, according to student-directed theorists, by recognizing that their behavior inevitably has consequences for themselves and others.

Some student-directed theorists also believe that restitution is an important part of dealing with misbehavior when a behavior has hurt other students. In order to emphasize that the classroom is a caring community and that individual behavior has consequences for others, a student whose behavior has hurt others is required to make amends to those harmed. One strategy used by some teachers is called "an apology of action" (Forton, 1998). The student who has been hurt is allowed to decide what the offending student must do to make restitution. The strategy not only helps students recognize that inappropriate behavior hurts others but also can be a powerful way to mend broken relationships.

Referent and expert teacher authority bases seem most compatible with student-directed influence theories. Each authority base emphasizes students' control over their own behavior. At the same time, the student-directed perspective adds a new dimension to the notion of expert authority. Students must recognize the teacher's specialized knowledge and his ability to build a caring classroom community in which students are given the opportunity to make choices and take responsibility for directing their own behavior. Putting this philosophy into practice demands highly competent and committed teachers who truly believe that enabling students to become better decision makers who are able to control their own behavior is an important goal of schooling. These teachers must be committed to establishing more democratic classrooms that are true caring communities. A teacher who is not committed to these beliefs will be unwilling to invest the time and effort needed to establish a student-directed learning environment. Long-term commitment is one key to success.

It is important to note that student-directed classrooms are not laissez-faire situations or classrooms without standards. In fact, the standards for student behavior in most of these classrooms are exceptionally high. When student efforts fall short of meeting agreed-upon standards for behavior and work, the teacher plays the role of encourager, helping students identify ways to improve. The teacher's role is not to punish the student with behavior or academic problems but rather to find ways to help the student overcome the problems.

Although potentially applicable at all grade levels, student-directed strategies seem most well suited for self-contained early childhood and elementary settings for several reasons. First, students and teachers in these settings typically spend a large portion of the day together, which gives them the opportunity to build close relationships. Second, because the classes are self-contained, it is possible to build a community in which students really know and care about each other. Finally, teachers in these settings have greater control over the allocation of time during the day than do most secondary teachers. Because they are not "bell bound," they are free to spend more time dealing with classroom behavior issues with individual students or the class as a whole. The current practice of teacher looping in which teachers stay with one group of students for two or three years (e.g., from first through second or third grade) provides an outstanding opportunity to create a student-directed environment because teachers and students work together for an extended period of time. Secondary schools would seem to be well served by adopting similar structures to personalize the environment and make it more student directed, for example, by instituting block scheduling. At present, in many secondary schools, students and teachers spend only 45 minutes together per day, and an individual teacher may teach 150 students or more per day. In such environments, it is difficult, if not impossible, for students and teachers to get to know each other personally, to understand each other's needs, and to establish a caring community. Teachers who can do so are truly remarkable.

Collaborative Theories

Collaborative theories of teacher influence are based on the belief that influencing student behavior is the joint responsibility of the student and the teacher. Although those who adopt the collaborative approaches often believe in many of the tenets of student-directed theories, they also believe that the number of students in a class and the size of most schools make it impractical to put a student-directed philosophy into practice. Many secondary teachers, in particular, believe that the size of their classes and the limited time they have with students make it imperative for them to place the needs of the group above the needs of any individual student. Following the collaborative theories, then, students must be given some opportunity to control their own behavior because a long-range goal of schooling is to enable students to become mature adults who can control their own behavior, but the teacher, as a professional, retains primary responsibility for influencing student behavior because the classroom is a group learning situation.

In Case 4.7, Ms. Sweely represents collaborative theory in action. Note that she tries to protect the reading group activity and, at the same time, deal with David. While the group is occupied, she uses touch interference (see Chapter 8) to signal David that he should control his behavior. When he cannot, she emphasizes the effect of his behavior on others and separates him from the rest of the group to help him recognize the logical consequences of being disruptive in a group situation. Thus, the teacher oriented toward collaborative theories promotes individual control over behavior but sometimes subordinates this goal to the right of all students to learn.

When viewed from the collaborative perspective, the goal of establishing a learning environment is to develop a well-organized classroom in which students are (1) engaged in learning activities, (2) usually successful, (3) respectful of the teacher and fellow students, and (4) cooperative in following classroom guidelines because they understand the rationale for the guidelines and see them as appropriate for the learning situation. From the collaborative point of view, students become capable of controlling their own behavior not by simply following rules but rather by understanding why rules exist and then choosing to follow them because they make sense. Neither blind obedience to rules nor complete freedom in deciding what rules should exist is seen as the best route toward self-regulated behavior.

In collaborative classrooms, the teacher and students develop rules and procedures jointly. Some teachers begin with a minimum list of rules—those that are most essential—and allow students to develop additional ones. Other teachers give students the opportunity to suggest rules but retain the right to add rules or veto suggested rules. Both of these techniques are intended to help the teacher maintain the ability to use his professional judgment to protect the rights of the group as a whole.

Teachers who adopt a collaborative approach to teacher influence often give students choices in other matters as well. Typically, the choices are not as open ended as those provided by student-directed advocates. For example, instead of allowing students to develop the criteria for judging the quality of their work, a collaborative teacher might present a list of ten potential criteria and allow students to choose the five criteria that will be used. Thus, the students are provided with choices, but the choices are confined to some degree by the teacher's professional judgment. This same system of providing choice within a given set of options may be followed in arranging and decorating the classroom or selecting topics to be pursued during academic units.

Advocates of a collaborative approach see time spent on behavior issues as potentially productive for the individual but not for the class as a whole unless there is a major problem interfering with the learning of a large number of students. Thus, collaborative teachers, whenever possible, do not take time away from group learning to focus on the behavior of an individual or a few students. Interpersonal conflicts are treated in a similar way. They are not dismissed, but collaborative teachers usually do not use classroom time to deal with them unless they involve many students. When an interpersonal conflict arises, the teacher deals with the individuals involved when there is a window of time to do so. Class meetings are used to deal with issues or conflicts involving large numbers of students. Collaborative teachers tend to view a class meeting as a means for solving problems rather than as an integral process for maintaining the classroom community.

While collaborative influence advocates believe that outward behavior must be managed to protect the rights of the group, they also believe the individual's thoughts and feelings must be explored to get at the heart of the behavior. Therefore, collaborative teachers often use deliberate interventions (see Chapter 8) to influence student behavior in a group situation and then follow up with a conference with the student. Because collaborative theorists believe that relating behavior to its natural or logical consequences helps students learn to anticipate the consequences of their behavior and thus become more self-regulating (see Chapters 6 and 9 for discussions of consequences), they advocate consequences linked as closely as possible to the misbehavior itself. A student who comes to school five minutes late, for example, might be required to remain five minutes after school to make up work.

The teacher authority bases most compatible with collaborative theories are the expert and legitimate bases. Each of these authority bases rests on the belief that the primary purpose of schools is to help students learn important information and processes. Therefore, the teacher must protect the rights of the group while still nurturing the learning of individual students. A collaborative teacher in Ms. Knepp's class might decide to hold a class meeting to review the classroom expectations and the rationale for them, to answer any questions or concerns regarding those expectations, and to remind students that the expectations will be enforced through the use of logical consequences. The teacher might also allow the class to make some choices concerning upcoming activities and events from a list of options that he has presented. Four well-known collaborative models come from the work of Dreikurs (2004), Glasser (1992), Curwin and Mendler (1999; 2008), and Nelson (2006).

Teacher-Directed Theories

Advocates of teacher-directed theories believe that students become good decision makers by internalizing the rules and guidelines for behavior that are given to them by responsible and caring adults. The teacher's task, then, is to develop a set of guidelines and rules that will create a productive learning environment, to be sure that the students understand the rules, and to develop a consistent system of rewards and punishments that make it likely that students will follow the guidelines and rules. The goal of teacher-directed theories is to create a learning environment in which behavior issues and concerns play a minimal role, to discourage misbehavior, and to deal with it as swiftly as possible when it does occur. Using these theories, the teacher assumes primary responsibility for influencing student behavior. Time spent on behavior issues is not seen as productive time because it reduces time for teaching and learning. The well-managed classroom is seen as one in which the learning environment operates efficiently and students are cooperative and consistently engaged in learning activities. The primary emphasis in teacher-directed classrooms is on academic content and processes.

In teacher-directed environments, the teacher makes almost all of the major decisions, including room arrangement, seating assignments, classroom decorations, academic content, assessment devices and criteria, and decisions concerning the day-to-day operation of the classroom. Students may be given a role to play in implementing teacher decisions—for example, they may be asked to create a poster—but they are usually restricted to implementing the teacher's decisions. Advocates of teacher-directed theories view the teacher as a trained professional who understands students, teaching, and the learning process and therefore is in the best position to make such choices.

Usually the teacher presents his rules and a system of consequences or punishments for breaking them to students on the first or second day of school. Students are often asked to sign a commitment to obeying the rules, and frequently their parents or guardians are asked to sign a statement declaring that they are aware of the rules. Consequences for misbehavior are not always directly related to the misbehavior itself but rather are universal consequences that can be applied to a variety of transgressions. For example, the student's name may be written on the board, a check mark may be made in the grade book, or a call may be made to the student's family. Many teachers also establish a set of rewards that are provided to the class as a whole if everyone follows the rules consistently. Punishments and rewards are applied consistently to ensure that the procedures and rules are internalized by all.

Although teachers who follow teacher-directed approaches do use cooperative learning strategies, their influence strategies are not usually focused on the creation of a caring classroom community in which caring is a primary motivator for choosing to behave appropriately. In a teacher-directed classroom, the primary relationship is usually that between the teacher and individual students. Students tend to be seen as a collection of individuals who should not interfere with each other's right to learn or with the teacher's right to teach. Self-control is often viewed as a matter of will. If students want to control their own behavior, they can.

Given this, conflict is seen as threatening, nonproductive, and disruptive of the learning process. The teacher deals swiftly with any outward manifestations of a conflict but usually not with the thoughts and feelings that have resulted in conflict. Students have a right to feel upset, it is argued, but not to act in inappropriate ways. Using the predetermined list of punishments or consequences, the teacher influences the misbehaving student toward more appropriate behavior by applying the appropriate consequence. For the most part, punishments are sequenced so that second or third offenses bring more stringent consequences than first offenses. Although individual differences may play an important part in the academic aspects of classroom work, they do not play a major role in the behavior intervention process. Consider the actions of Mr. Green in Case 4.7. As an advocate of teacher-directed influence, he moves quickly to stop the misbehavior, emphasizes classroom rules, employs blue chips as rewards, and uses punishments in the form of loss of recess privileges and good-news notes.

Clearly reward and coercive authority are most compatible with the teacher-directed theories. Advocates use clear, direct, explicit communication; behavior contracting; behavior modification; token economy systems; consistent reinforcement of appropriate behavior; and group rewards and punishments. A teacher following this approach might handle Ms. Knepp's dilemma by setting up a group intervention plan in which the group earned points for appropriate behavior. The points could then be exchanged for meaningful rewards. At the same time, the teacher uses a predetermined set of punishments for any students who misbehaved.

The teacher who wants to use a teacher-directed approach should be aware of some important considerations. A thorough understanding of the principles of behavioral psychology is necessary in order to apply behavior modification appropriately. Individual student differences do play a role in the intervention system because they must be considered in developing rewards and punishments. After all, what is a reward to some individuals may be a punishment to others. Thus, most teacher-directed theorists are concerned with students' thoughts and emotions; however, the primary goal in dealing with misbehavior is redirection of the students' outward behavior, not inner feelings. Therefore, individual differences do not play a role in determining what behaviors are acceptable. Finally, the effective use of behavior modification with secondary students tends to be much more difficult for several reasons: (1) the reactions of other students are more powerful than those of the teacher, (2) students have reached a higher stage of moral reasoning, and (3) in-school rewards are not as powerful as out-of-school rewards. Some well-known authors of teacher-directed systems derived from the teacher-directed perspective are Alberto and Troutman (2012), Canter and Canter (2007), Cangelosi (2008), and Nelson, Marchand-Martella, and O'Reilly (2011).

Table 4.2 provides a summary of the three theories of influence in terms of their answers to the nine basic questions introduced at the beginning of this section.

TABLE 4.2 Theories of Teacher Influence

Question	Student Directed	Collaborative	Teacher Directed
Primary responsibility for influence	Student	Joint	Teacher
Goal of environment	Caring community focus and self-direction	Respectful relationships, academic focus	Well-organized, efficient, academic focus
Time spent on behavior	Valuable and productive	Valuable for individual but not for group	Wasted time
Relationships within classroom	Caring, personal relationships	Respect for each other	Noninterference with each other's rights
Provision of student choice	Wide latitude and freedom	Choices within teacher-defined options	Very limited
Primary goal in handling misbehavior	Unmet needs to be explored	Minimize in group; pursue individually	Minimize disruption, redirect
Interventions used	Individual conference, group problem solving, restitution, natural consequences	Coping skills, natural and logical consequences, anecdotal record keeping	Clear communication, rewards and punishments, behavior contracting
Individual differences	Extremely important	Somewhat important	Minor importance
Teacher authority bases	Referent, expert	Expert, legitimate	Reward/coercive, legitimate
Theorists	Charney, Crowe, Faber and Mazlish, Gordon, Kohn, Strachota	Curwin, Mendler and Mendler, Dreikurs, Erwin, Glasser, Fay and Funk, Nelson	Alberto and Troutman, Cangelosi, Canter and Canter, Martella et al., Kerr and Nelson

Summary

The first section of the chapter provided an explanation of the four teacher authority bases: referent, expert, legitimate, and reward/coercive. Each base was presented in terms of the underlying assumptions about student motivation to behave, the assumed need for teacher control over student behavior, the requirements for employing the base effectively, the key teacher behaviors in using the base, and limitations and caveats concerning its use.

The second section discussed nine basic questions that are useful for articulating beliefs about teacher influence:

1. Who has primary responsibility for managing student behavior?
2. What is your primary goal in establishing a classroom learning environment?
3. How do you view time spent on behavior issues and problems?

4. How would you like students to relate to each other within your classroom?
5. How much choice will you give students within your classroom?
6. What is your primary goal in handling misbehavior?
7. What interventions will you use to deal with misbehavior?
8. How important to you are individual differences among students?
9. What teacher authority bases are most compatible with your beliefs?

Articulating one's beliefs is the initial step toward developing a systematic plan for influencing student behavior. These nine basic questions were used to analyze three theories of teacher influence: student directed, collaborative, and teacher directed.

The information and questions provided in this chapter may be used by teachers to develop a plan for preventing behavior problems and for dealing with disruptive student behavior that is congruent with their basic beliefs about teaching and learning.

Influence Theories on the Web

You can visit the websites listed here to get more information about the various models of classroom management that were discussed in the chapter.

Student-Directed Theories

http://www.responsiveclassroom.org—Northeast Foundation for Children
http://www.gordontraining.com—Thomas Gordon's model
http://eqi.org/ginott.htm—Haim Ginott's ideas
http://www.alfiekohn.org—Alfie Kohn's model

Collaborative Theories

http://www.wglasser.com—William Glasser's ideas
http://tlc-sems.com/—Curwin and Mendler's model

Teacher-Directed Theories

http://www.canter.net—Canter's model

Teacher Authority Bases on the Web

http://changingminds.org/explanations/power/french_and_raven.htm

Exercises

1. If one of the long-term goals of teaching is for students to gain control over their own behavior, what are some advantages and disadvantages of using each of the four teacher authority bases to help students achieve that goal?
2. Do you think there is any relationship between teacher job satisfaction and the authority base the teacher uses most frequently to influence student behavior? Why or why not?
3. What specific teacher behaviors would indicate to you that a teacher was trying to use (a) referent authority and (b) expert authority?
4. Using referent authority successfully requires the teacher to communicate caring to students.

(a) How can a teacher communicate caring without initiating personal friendships? (b) As you see it, is there a danger in initiating personal friendships with students?
5. What are some strategies that you would use as a teacher to gain a better understanding of your students' family lives and cultural backgrounds?
6. If one of the long-range goals of teaching is to help students gain control over their own behavior, what are the advantages and disadvantages of each of the three theories of teacher influence in helping students meet that goal?

7. Think of the best teacher that you have ever had. What authority base and influence model was this teacher using the majority of the time?

8. Think of the worst teacher you have ever had. What authority base and influence model was this teacher using the majority of the time?

9. Beliefs About Teacher Influence—Forced Choice Activity

    Directions: You will see several groups of three statements about teacher influence. Read each statement and think about how much you agree or disagree with each. Place the numbers of the statements in one of three boxes corresponding to the degree that you agree with each statement. Place the statement you agree with most in the top choice box, the one you agree with second most in the middle choice box, and the one you agree with least in the lowest choice box. For a given group of statements, you might agree or disagree strongly with all three, but you must still place each statement in one box.

    Group 1: Responsibility for Controlling Behavior

    a. As an adult, the teacher has primary responsibility for controlling student behavior.
    b. Responsibility for controlling student behavior is a shared responsibility of student and teacher.
    c. The student alone has primary responsibility for controlling his or her behavior.

    Place the letter of each statement in one of these three boxes:

Top Choice	Middle Choice	Lowest Choice

    Group 2: Goal of Classroom Learning Environment

    d. The goal is the development of a caring community of self-directed learners.
    e. The goal is an efficiently run classroom in which academic learning is maximized.
    f. The goal is the development of an environment in which students feel respected and academic learning is the focus.

Place the letter of each statement in one of these three boxes:

Top Choice	Middle Choice	Lowest Choice

Group 3: Goal in Dealing with Misbehavior

g. The goal in dealing with misbehavior is to minimize the loss of learning time.
h. The goal in dealing with misbehavior is to find a way to help the misbehaving student while minimizing the loss of learning time for others.
i. The goal in dealing with misbehavior is to identify the unmet need that led the student to misbehave and to find a productive way to get that need met.

Place the letter of each statement in one of these three boxes:

Top Choice	Middle Choice	Lowest Choice

Group 4: Students' Relationships with Each Other

j. Above all, students must learn to really care about each other as people.
k. Above all, students must learn not to interfere with each other's right to learn.
l. Above all, students should learn to respect each other as well as the teacher.

Place the letter of each statement in one of these three boxes:

Top Choice	Middle Choice	Lowest Choice

Group 5: Choices and Freedom

m. Students should be given freedom and choices about classroom activities within options defined by the teacher.
n. Students should be given lots of freedom and choices about classroom activities.
o. Given their limited experience, students should not be given much freedom and choice. The teacher must make the decisions.

Place the letter of each statement in one of these three boxes:

Top Choice	Middle Choice	Lowest Choice

Group 6: Consistency and Individual Needs

p. Because students are different in terms of their needs, it is okay for teachers to handle discipline problems in different ways for different individuals.

q. Consistency is crucial. Misbehavior must be dealt with in the same way for all individuals.

r. In dealing with individual differences, the teacher must find a way to balance the need for consistency with the need to meet individual needs.

Place the letter of each statement in one of these three boxes:

Top Choice	Middle Choice	Lowest Choice

10. **Beliefs About Teacher Influence—Forced Choice Activity: Connections to Management Philosophies and Theories**

   Directions: Give each top choice 3 points, each middle choice 2 points, and each lowest choice 1 point in the blank in the chart that follows that corresponds to that item's number and letter. Then add up the total points in each column to see how your choices match the three philosophies.

Teacher Directed	Collaborative	Student Directed
1a	1b	1c
2e	2f	2d
3g	3h	3i
4k	4l	4j
5o	5m	5n
6q	6r	6p
Total	**Total**	**Total**

11. **Principles of Teacher Behavior** After reading Chapter 4 and doing the exercises, use what you have learned to briefly describe your understanding of the implications of the principles listed at the beginning of the chapter for classroom teachers.

   PRINCIPLE 1:

   PRINCIPLE 2:

   PRINCIPLE 3:

Iterative Case Study Analyses

Second Analysis

Considering the concepts discussed in the Foundation section, Chapters 1 through 4, reanalyze your first analysis. What has changed and what has stayed the same since your first analysis? Once again, consider why the students may be choosing to behave inappropriately and how you might intervene to influence them to stop the disruptive behavior and resume appropriate on-task behavior.

Elementary School Case Studies

"I don't remember"   During silent reading time in my fourth-grade class, I have built in opportunities to work individually with students. During this time, the students read to me and practice word work with flash cards. One student has refused to read to me but, instead, only wants to work with the flash cards. After a few times, I suggested we work with flash cards this time and begin reading next time. He agreed. The next time we met, I reminded him of our plan, and he screamed, "I don't remember. I want to do word cards." At this point, I tried to find out why he didn't like reading, and he said, "There's a reason, I just can't tell you," and he threw the word cards across the room, some of them hitting other students. What should I do?

"Let's do it again"   Cathy is in my third-grade class. Whenever I ask the class to line up for recess, lunch, or to change classes, Cathy is always the last to get in line. When she does, she pushes, shoves, and touches the other students. When this happens, I usually demand that all the children return to their seats, and we repeatedly line up again and again until Cathy lines up properly. I thought that peer pressure would cause Cathy to change her behavior, but, instead, it has resulted in my students being late to "specials" and having less time for recess and lunch.

Middle School Case Studies

"It makes me look cool"   I can't stop thinking about a problem I'm having in class with a group of 12-year-old boys. They consistently use vulgar language to one another and some of the shy kids in the class, especially the girls. In addition, they are always pushing and shoving one another. I've tried talking to them about why they keep using bad language when they know it's inappropriate.

The response I get is that "it makes me look cool and funny in front of my friends." I have asked them to please use more appropriate language in the classroom, but that has not worked. I haven't even started to deal with the pushing and shoving. What should I do?

"My parents will be gone all weekend"   One of my seventh-grade girls was passing notes to a boy two rows over. After the second note, I made eye contact with her and it stopped for about half an hour. When I saw her getting ready to pass another note, I went over to her desk and asked her to give me the note and told her that that the note passing had to stop. She looked very upset, but she did give me the note. I folded it and put it in my desk drawer. When class ended, she ran out of the room crying. My personal policy is not to read students' notes but, instead, give it back to the student at the end of class or throw it away. However, this time, maybe because of her reaction, something told me to read the note. It said "Mike, my parents will be away Saturday night. Why don't you and John sleep over? It will be fun. I promise I'll do whatever you want me to do and that you and John can do anything you want to me." What should I as the teacher do?

High School Case Studies

"Homo"   This past week I had a student approach me about a problem he was experiencing in our class. This eleventh-grade student had recently "come out" as a homosexual. He said he was tired and upset with the three boys who sit near him. These boys frequently call him a "homo" and a "fag" every time they see him, both in and out of class.

"Why don't you get out of my face?"   A twelfth-grade student came up to me the first day of class and said, "My name is Ted. I don't want to be here, so just leave me alone and we'll get along just fine." I did not react to his comment but, instead, said "After you see what we will be learning, I think you will find the class interesting." Ted walked away and took a seat in the back of the room. Later that week, I noticed Ted was reading a magazine while everyone else was working on an in-class assignment. Without making it obvious, I walked by Ted's desk and quietly asked him to put away the magazine and to begin working on the assignment. Ted turned to me and said, "Maybe you don't understand; I asked you not to bother me. I'm not bothering you, so why don't you get out of my face?"

The Professional Teacher

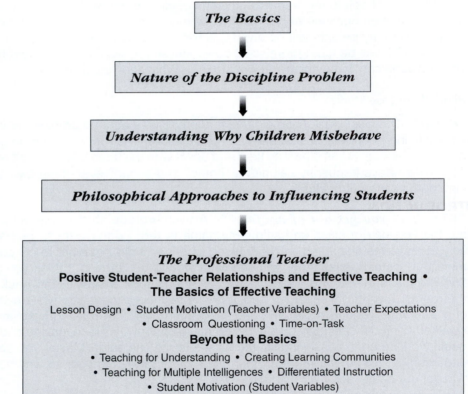

The Basics

Nature of the Discipline Problem

Understanding Why Children Misbehave

Philosophical Approaches to Influencing Students

The Professional Teacher
Positive Student-Teacher Relationships and Effective Teaching •
The Basics of Effective Teaching
Lesson Design • Student Motivation (Teacher Variables) • Teacher Expectations
• Classroom Questioning • Time-on-Task
Beyond the Basics
• Teaching for Understanding • Creating Learning Communities
• Teaching for Multiple Intelligences • Differentiated Instruction
• Student Motivation (Student Variables)

PRINCIPLES OF TEACHER BEHAVIOR THAT INFLUENCE APPROPRIATE STUDENT BEHAVIOR

1. Developing positive relationships with students will enhance the teacher's instructional effectiveness and exert a great influence on student learning.

2. Student learning and on-task behavior are maximized when teaching strategies are based on what educators know about student development, how people learn, and what constitutes effective teaching.

**PREREADING ACTIVITY: UNDERSTANDING THE PRINCIPLES
OF TEACHER BEHAVIOR**

Before reading Chapter 5, briefly describe your understanding of the implications
of the principles for a classroom teacher:

Principle 1:

Principle 2:

PREREADING QUESTIONS FOR REFLECTION AND JOURNALING

1. What role does relationship building with students and learning about them as
   individuals play in effective teaching?
2. As you think about what good teaching looks like, make a list of key instructional
   behaviors that teachers can use to maximize their instructional effectiveness.
3. What can teachers do to motivate students to choose to be actively engaged in
   learning activities?
4. How do cultural differences between the teacher and students impact effective
   teaching?

INTRODUCTION

Classroom management is frequently conceptualized as a matter of control
rather than as a dimension of curriculum, instruction, and overall school climate
(Duke, 1982). In reality, classroom management is closely intertwined with effective instruction: "Research findings converge on the conclusion that teachers who
approach classroom management as a process of establishing and maintaining
effective learning environments tend to be more successful than teachers who place
more emphasis on their roles as authority figures or disciplinarians" (Brophy, 1988a,
p. 1). An integral aspect of creating an appropriate learning environment is making
ongoing efforts to get to know students well and build supportive relationships
with them. In the hierarchical decision-making model of classroom management
presented in this text, the teacher must ensure that she has done all she can to prevent problems from occurring before using intervention techniques. This means that
the teacher's classroom instructional behavior must match the behaviors defined as
best professional practice—that is, those behaviors most likely to maximize student
learning and influence appropriate student behavior. If they do not, employing techniques to remediate misbehavior is likely to prove fruitless because the misbehavior
will inevitably recur.

Unfortunately, one of the problems that has long plagued classroom teachers
has been identifying the yardstick that should be used to measure their teaching
behavior against best professional practice. Fortunately, there is a growing knowledge base, which when used as input for professional decision making as opposed

to a checklist of behaviors, can help teachers ensure that their practice will enhance student learning and appropriate behavior.

This chapter presents a synopsis of that knowledge base. The chapter is divided into three parts. The first section, Positive Student-Teacher Relationships and Effective Teaching, focuses on the key role that the teacher-student relationship plays in how students perceive both the classroom learning environment and the teacher's instructional competence. Section two, The Basics of Effective Teaching, explains research that emphasizes teacher behaviors that promote student achievement as measured by most standardized, paper-and-pencil tests. The third section of the chapter, Beyond the Basics, examines conceptualizations of teaching that focus primarily on student cognition and student performance on higher-level cognitive tasks.

One of the major differences between sections two and three of this chapter concerns the emphasis placed on teacher versus student behavior. Early research on effective teaching was based primarily on the premise that the teacher is the most important factor in the classroom. Thus, this research focused on the overt behavior of the teacher during instruction. In the mid-1980s, however, researchers began to see the student as the most important variable and the student's thought processes as the key elements during instruction. As a result, the focus of the research switched from the overt behavior of the teacher to the covert behavior of the learner during instruction. This change in focus is most obvious in the research on student motivation. Indeed, it has led to the two sections on student motivation in this chapter. In the second section of the chapter, the explanation focuses on student motivation as influenced by teacher behavior. In the final section, the explanation focuses on student motivation as influenced by student cognition.

POSITIVE STUDENT-TEACHER RELATIONSHIPS AND EFFECTIVE TEACHING

The reader will note that the concept of positive student-teacher relationships is discussed in almost every chapter of this text. Although it is true that many chapters discuss relationship building, the framing of the discussion varies from chapter to chapter. For example, in Chapter 4, we focused on the connection to referent authority. In Chapter 7, the focus is on professional knowledge that teachers can use to control their behavior so that it maximizes positive relationships with students and families. In Chapters 10 and 11, the focus is on the importance of relationship building in influencing students who exhibit chronic behavior problems. In this chapter, the concept of positive relationships is framed in terms of its importance in enhancing teacher instructional competence and effectiveness. The repeated attention to the importance of relationship building attests to the central role that positive relationships play in enabling the teacher to influence student behavior more positively and consistently.

More than 40 years ago, Aspy and Roebuck (1977) published a popular text entitled *Students Do Not Learn from Teachers They Don't Like.* Although we might not agree completely with the premise of that text, many researchers and theorists, as well as practicing teachers, would argue that teachers who work hard at getting to know their students as individuals and who work at building positive relationships with them are more likely to positively influence student academic success and appropriate behavior and be perceived as effective teachers. Recently, one of the authors attended the retirement party for a beloved elementary principal who had been a teacher, a curriculum coach, and then a very successful building principal. In her remarks that evening, the principal, Linda Colangelo said, "I spent literally hundreds of hours during my career interviewing teachers. I made it a habit of asking them challenging academic questions, but as I asked those challenging questions, what I was really trying to figure out was how they would make my children feel."

Relationship building is not only an important component of developing the use of referent authority as noted in Chapter 4, it is also an important aspect of general teaching effectiveness. Learning about students and building supportive relationships with them appear to be important for all students, but recent research (Delpit, 2012) suggests that these teacher behaviors may be even more critical when teachers are teaching students who are culturally different from the teacher and in working with students who underachieve.

Relationship building is not *apart from* skilled teaching; rather it is *a part of* skilled teaching. Relationship-building strategies permeate every aspect of effective teaching practice. Effective teachers build positive relationships as they engage in the process of establishing rules and routines, as they explain content, when they ask questions, when they allow students to experience the consequences of their choices, and as they work with students to solve long-term learning and behavior problems. As noted in Chapter 3, a sense of significance or belonging is a critical component of self-esteem. Research suggests that developing a sense of significance has both short-term and long-term positive impacts on the academic and behavioral outcomes of schooling and that the failure to establish a sense of significance is connected with severe long-term negative effects, including poor academic performance, dropping out of school, and engagement in antisocial behavior (Osterman, 2000). When students feel a sense of belonging and comfort in a positive classroom climate, they are able to focus their energies on learning. When students feel that they are in an environment that is hostile or negative, they are so preoccupied emotionally with dealing with the negative climate, that little energy is left for cognition (Glick, 2011).

In addressing the question of why so many boys seem to be lagging behind in school achievement, Kathleen Palmer Cleveland identified the failure to develop a sense of significance as a possible explanation for poor performance among boys:

> It was evident that what was alternately valued or reviled by many boys had much to do with the experience of school. The types and qualities of their interactions with peers and teachers seemed to affect boys' perspectives about school in general.... I wondered how much a sense of belonging had to do with an underachieving boy's ability to engage in academic learning and if an absence of this feeling might negatively affect his behavior, his attitudes about school in general, and his perceptions about himself as a capable learner. (2010, p.12)

Cleveland goes on to suggest that belonging is a primary motivator for the in-school behavior of most boys. Belonging is, in fact, so important that some boys will do almost anything, endure almost anything, and inflict on one another almost anything in order to be part of the group.

Typically, most teachers conceptualize a sense of belonging or significance as referring to a student's relationship with peers. Although it is true that a sense of belonging is intimately connected to peer relationships (especially as students grow into adolescence), Osterman's (2000) research synthesis suggests that the teacher's feelings about and behavior toward individual students exert tremendous influence on student-student relationships. This is particularly true in elementary school.

The importance of developing positive teacher-student relationships is also affirmed by the research that focuses on effective teachers of African American students. One of the concepts that has been derived from that research to describe effective teachers is the notion of "warm demanders" (Delpit, 2012). The "demand" component refers to teachers who make it clear that they have high expectations for student learning, hold students accountable for meeting those high expectations, and also are willing to provide students whatever assistance they need to achieve those goals. The "warm" element refers to teachers who establish strong relationships with students that communicate a sense of trust and confidence in them and create an atmosphere of psychological safety that allows students to take risks and make mistakes: "Warm demanders expect a great deal from students, convince them of their own brilliance, and help them to reach their potential in a disciplined and structured environment" (Delpit, 2012, p. 71).

All students, but especially those students who struggle academically or behaviorally, need to believe that the teacher has confidence in their ability to be successful and is willing to provide the support the student needs (Cleveland, 2010). Teachers can consciously employ some specific strategies and behaviors over time to create the trusting relationships with students that will help all students feel believed in and supported. We briefly discuss some of those strategies here, but they will make more sense and be more useful when they are placed into the context of professional knowledge about relationship building that is addressed in Chapter 7. Among the important teacher behaviors that help build such relationhsips are (1) gaining an understanding of students' interests and backgrounds (e.g., through informal conversations as well as observing what students talk about and do); (2) paying attention to how students learn and tailoring instruction to meet student learning styles; (3) seeking to understand the student's cultural background and family life and incorporating that knowledge into curriculum and instruction; (4) using teaching behaviors that indicate affection for students such as humor, smiles, compliments, gratitude, respect, and so on; (5) making affirming statements that acknowledge effort and affirm growth; (6) noticing improvements in knowledge, skills, and behavior; (7) taking an interest in students' activities outside of school; (8) not taking inappropriate behavior personally; (9) not holding grudges; (10) giving students second chances when they are not successful or make inappropriate behavior choices; and (11) not disparaging or criticizing students in front of others (Cleveland, 2010; Marzano, Frontier, and Livingston, 2011; Rothstein-Fisch and Trumbull, 2008). As you read Case 5.1, try to identify what Carol Rose, the student teacher, who was supervised by one of the authors of this text, did to create a positive reationship that eventually influenced the academic performance of Jennifer Fowler.

CASE 5.1

Relating to Jennifer

Carol Rose was a student teacher in a high school chemistry class during the spring semester of the school year. Carol was not slated to take over this section of chemistry until the sixth week of the semester, so she had plenty of opportunities to observe the students in the class. One of the most perplexing students was Jennifer Fowler. Jennifer was an obese and withdrawn young lady who did not appear to have any friends in her third period class. Each day Carol watched as Jennifer came into class early, sat in the back by herself, and stared out the window. When class started, Jennifer sometimes opened her notebook and sometimes did not. In either case, she typically continued to stare out the window. Carol's cooperating teacher did not seem to care whether or not Jennifer opened her notebook. She told Carol that whether or not her book was open really didn't matter because Jennifer's mind was clearly somewhere else. She explained that Jennifer had failed every quiz and test for the entire year and, as a result, had failed chemistry for the first two marking periods before Carol came to student teach. The cooperating teacher's advice was to not worry about Jennifer too much because she probably shouldn't have been placed in chemistry anyway.

Carol Rose decided that influencing Jennifer's behavior in a positive way would become her goal. She began by walking back to Jennifer every day before class started, greeting her, and trying to begin a conversation to get to know Jennifer better. For 10 days straight, Jennifer responded with a cursory, "Hi," answered all questions with one-word answers, and initiated no interaction on her own. Carol, though discouraged, was determined not to give up. Then one day, she noticed Jennifer reading the school newspaper before class. She asked Jennifer if she worked on the paper. Jennifer replied that she did not but that she would like to become a journalist some day.

Seizing on that opening, Carol explained to Jennifer that she drove to the school from campus every day and would be happy to pick up a copy of the collegiate newspaper and bring it to Jennifer if she would like that. Jennifer actually smiled! For two weeks, Carol faithfully produced the college newspaper for Jennifer. Each day, she would also ask Jennifer what she had read in the paper that she found interesting. Jennifer always had something to share. At the end of that second week of newspaper delivery, Jennifer was coming home from school one afternoon and spotted Carol coming out of a local grocery store. She literally ran across the street and offered to help Carol carry the heavy grocery bags.

Carol used that chance meeting to ask Jennifer what she did typically after school. Usually Jennifer just walked home and watched TV. Carol offered to stay after school with Jennifer three days a week and tutor her in chemistry. From the time that Carol Rose took over the teaching of her chemistry class, Jennifer Fowler passed every quiz and every test and eventually passed chemistry for the year by a very slim margin.

THE BASICS OF EFFECTIVE TEACHING

Most of the research findings discussed here were derived from studies of teacher behaviors that were effective in promoting student achievement as defined by lower-level cognitive objectives, which are efficiently measured by paper-and-pencil tests (Brophy, 1988b). It appears that general principles for teaching behavior derived from these studies apply to "instruction in any body of knowledge or set of skills that has been sufficiently well organized and analyzed so that: (1) it can be presented systematically, and then (2) practiced or applied during activities that call for student performance that (3) can be evaluated for quality and (4) can be given corrective feedback (where incorrect or imperfect)" (Rosenshine and Stevens, 1986, p. 49).

The research findings from which general principles have been drawn are the result of various long-term research projects that usually followed a three-step process, called process-product research. In step one of the process, teams of researchers observed classroom teachers who were considered to be either very effective or very ineffective. Effectiveness was most often defined as enhanced student achievement on paper-and-pencil tests. From the observations, it was possible to develop a list of teaching behaviors that were used frequently by the effective teachers but not by the ineffective ones. Researchers hypothesized that at least some of these teaching behaviors were responsible for the success of the effective teachers.

In step two, correlational studies were conducted to find positive relationships between the use of these effective teaching behaviors and student behavior or student learning as measured by paper-and-pencil achievement test scores. The correlational studies indicated that some of the effective teaching behaviors were positively related to student behavior and achievement, whereas others were not. Thus, the result of step two was to narrow the list of effective teaching behaviors to those that were used by effective teachers and had a positive relationship with student behavior or student achievement test scores.

In step three, experimental studies were conducted. The researchers trained an experimental group of teachers to use the narrowed-down list of effective teaching behaviors consistently in their teaching. The achievement scores and classroom behavior of their students were then compared with the achievement scores and behavior of students taught by a control group of teachers, who had not been trained to use the effective teaching behaviors. The results of these experimental comparison studies showed that students of the experimental teachers had significantly higher achievement scores or significantly better classroom behavior. The renewed emphasis on performance-based measures of student attainment of standards makes this body of research especially timely now.

Lesson Design

During the 1970s and 1980s, Madeline Hunter (1982), Barak Rosenshine (Rosenshine and Stevens, 1986), and other researchers spent a great deal of time trying to identify the type of lesson structure that was most effective for student learning. Robert Marzano (2007) has continued that tradition by providing excellent summaries of that research. Marzano's own work has been further refined and reframed in recent years as well (Dean et al., 2012, Marzano, Frontier, and Livingston, 2011;). Although the various researchers tend to use their own specialized vocabulary, they agree that lessons that include the following components are the most effective in helping students learn new material: a lesson introduction, clear explanations of the content, checks for student understanding, a period of coached practice, a lesson summary or closure, a period of solitary practice, and periodic reviews. As you read the discussion of these components that follows, remember that a lesson does not equal a class period. A *lesson* is defined as the amount of instructional time required for students to achieve a specific learning objective. Because a lesson may extend over several class periods, it is not essential to have all of these components in each class period. On the other hand, if one class period contains two lessons, one would expect the components to be repeated twice.

1. *Lesson introduction.* A good introduction makes students aware of what they are supposed to learn, activates their prior knowledge of the topic, focuses their attention on the main elements of the lesson to come, motivates them to be interested in the lesson, and actively involves them in introductory activities. Establishing and communicating learning goals are the starting place. Making sure that students are clear about the learning objectives is a critical component of creating an appropriate learning environment (Dean et al., 2012). After all, for learning to be effective, clear targets in terms of information and skill must be established (Marzano, 2007, p. 9).

2. *Clarity.* Clear explanations of the content of the lesson proceed in step-by-step fashion, illustrate the content by using concrete examples familiar to the students, and are interspersed with questions that monitor student understanding: "Lessons in which learners perceive links among the main ideas are more likely to contribute to content learning than are lessons in which links among the main ideas are less easily perceived by learners" (Anderson, 1989, p. 102). Well-organized presentations help learners process linking ideas by telling them what prior knowledge should be activated and by pointing out what pieces of information are important in using activated prior knowledge (Anderson, 1989). Techniques for ensuring that presentations are well organized include (a) using structured overviews, advance organizers, and statements of objectives near the beginning of the presentation; (b) outlining the content, signaling transitions between ideas, calling attention to main ideas, and summarizing subsections of the lesson during the presentation; and (c) summarizing main ideas near the end of the presentation. Using nonlinguistic representations of content in the form of pictures, diagrams, concept webs, and other graphic organizers also increases content clarity (Marzano et al., 2011). The use of metaphors, similes, and analogies also helps make content more understandable by linking it with students' prior knowledge (Dean et al., 2012). Marzano (2007) suggests a variety of instructional tactics that a teacher can use to enhance clarity of instruction, including previewing content, presenting information in small chunks, and organizing students in groups to enhance information processing. Marzano also suggests a variety of macro strategies that can be used to enhance active student processing of information. These strategies include involving students in summarizing and note taking, developing nonlinguistic representations of the content, asking inferential questions to force elaboration of content, asking students to reflect on their learning and identify any areas of confusion, and using cooperative learning as an information-processing strategy.

3. *Checking for understanding and adjusting.* Effective teachers do not take for granted that students understand the content of the lesson. They periodically ask specific questions or engage students in focused activities (e.g., a writing task) to assess comprehension. In designing such activities or in asking questions, effective teachers attempt to have as many students as possible overtly engaged in demonstrating their understanding so that the teacher can observe their degree of comprehension directly. Instead of asking questions and obtaining only one student's response, effective teachers ask several students for responses before commenting on the accuracy of any response. They ask students to comment on other students' responses. They employ choral responses to engage multiple students overtly. In addition, many teachers use small whiteboards or chalkboards to have all students respond quickly in writing and show their responses to the teacher so that the teacher can quickly scan the level of understanding of the class as a whole. Electronic clickers and cell phones are now being used in many classrooms to ask students to respond electronically to multiple choice or true/false questions that can be used to assess whole group understanding. If a large number of students appear to be having difficulty, effective teachers reteach the material in a different way. If only a few students are having problems, they do not reteach the entire class; instead, they work with those students individually.

4. *Coached practice.*   Effective lessons include a period of coached or guided practice during which students practice using the skill or knowledge, through written exercises, oral questions and answers, or some type of group work. The teacher closely monitors this initial practice so that students receive frequent feedback and correction. Feedback and correction can occur as frequently as after every two or three problems. Students should experience high amounts of success (more than 75 percent) with the coached practice exercises before moving on to solitary practice. Otherwise, they may spend a large portion of the solitary practice period practicing and learning the wrong information or skill.

Wang and Palinscar (1989) cited "scaffolding" as an additional important aspect of the coached practice portion of lessons designed to help students acquire cognitive strategies (e.g., study skills, problem-solving skills, and critical thinking skills). They cited scaffolding as a process that underlies all the elements of lesson design: "Scaffolding occurs when the teacher supports students' attempts to use a cognitive strategy; adjusts that support according to learner characteristics, the nature of the material, and the nature of the task; and treats the support as temporary, removing it as students show increased competence in using the cognitive strategy" (p. 79). In other words, the teacher plans instruction to move from modeling and instruction to feedback and coaching and increasingly transfers control to students.

5. *Closure.*   A good lesson summary or closure asks students to become actively involved in summarizing the key ideas that have been learned in the lesson and gives students some ideas about where future lessons will take them. Teaching students how to summarize written material to enhance understanding and retention is a critical metacognitive skill that teachers can help students acquire. Dean et al. (2012) suggest the following rules for summarizing material: (a) take out material that is not important, (b) take out any words that repeat information, (c) replace lists with a category name (e.g., replace Washington, Lincoln, Obama with "presidents"), and (d) find or create a topic sentence if one is missing. One very useful strategy for bringing closure to a lesson with upper elementary, middle, or high school students is the use of an exit slip. In using this strategy, each student is asked to supply specific information in writing (e.g., explain what an isosceles triangle is or identify two problems with the Treaty of Versailles) on a half sheet of paper. This paper then becomes the ticket or exit slip that allows the student to exit the class. The exit slip strategy can serve as a synthesizing activity as well as an additional check for understanding.

6. *Solitary practice.* Effective lessons also include a period of solitary or independent practice during which students practice the skill on their own and experience significant amounts of success (more than 75 percent). This practice often takes the form of independent seat work or homework. The effectiveness of homework as a tool for promoting learning is enhanced when the purpose of the assignment is clear, the homework is checked, and feedback is provided to students (Dean et al., 2012).

7. *Review.* Finally, periodic reviews conducted on a weekly and monthly basis help students consolidate their learning, distribute practice over time, and provide additional reinforcement.

These seven research-based components, which are especially effective in lessons designed to impart basic information or specific skills and procedures, should not be viewed as constraints on the teacher's creativity and individuality. Each component may be embellished and tailored to fit the unique teaching situations that confront every teacher. Together, however, the components provide a basic framework that lessens student confusion about what is to be learned and ensures that learning proceeds in an orderly sequence of steps. When students try to learn more difficult content before they have mastered prerequisites and when they are not given sufficient practice to master skills, they become confused, disinterested, and much more likely to exhibit disruptive behavior in the classroom.

Student Motivation: Teacher Variables

Motivation refers to an inner drive that focuses behavior on a particular goal or task and causes the individual to be persistent in trying to achieve the goal or complete the task successfully. Fostering motivation in students is undoubtedly one of the most powerful tools the teacher has in preventing classroom discipline problems. When students are motivated to learn, they usually pay attention to the lesson, become actively involved in learning, and direct their energies to the task. When students are not motivated to learn, they lose interest in lessons quickly, look for sources of entertainment, and may direct their energies at amusing themselves and disrupting the learning process of others. A professional teacher can manipulate many variables to increase student motivation to learn. According to a review of research on student motivation (Brophy, 1987), some of the most powerful variables are the following:

1. *Student interest.* Teachers can increase student motivation by relating subject content to life outside school. For example, an English teacher can relate poetry to the lyrics of popular music, and a chemistry teacher can allow students to analyze the chemical composition of products they use. Although there is no subject in which every topic can be related to the real world, games, simulations, videos, group work, and allowing students to plan or select activities can increase interest. Although these strategies can't be used effectively every day, all teachers can employ them at some time.

2. *Student needs.* Motivation to learn is increased when students perceive that learning activities provide an opportunity to meet some of their basic human needs as identified by Maslow (see Chapter 3). For example, simply providing elementary students with the opportunity to talk while the whole group listens can be an easy way to help meet students' needs for belonging. At the secondary level, allowing students to work together with peers on learning activities helps meet their needs for a sense of belonging and acceptance by others. At the most basic level, providing a pleasant, task-oriented climate in which expectations are clear helps meet students' needs for psychological safety and security.

3. *Novelty and variety.* When the teacher has designed learning activities that include novel events, situations, and materials, students are likely to be motivated to learn. The popcorn lesson in Case 5.2 is an excellent example of the use of novelty to gain students' attention. Once students' attention has been captured, a variety of short learning activities will help keep it focused on the lesson.

Human attention spans can be remarkably long when people are involved in an activity that they find fascinating. Most students, however, do not find typical school activities fascinating. Therefore, their attention spans tend to be rather short. For this reason, the professional teacher plans activities that last no longer than 15 to 20 minutes. A teacher who gives a lecture in two 15-minute halves with a 5-minute oral exercise interspersed is much more likely to maintain student interest than a teacher who gives a 30-minute lecture followed by the 5-minute oral exercise. Reality TV shows are an excellent example of how changing the focus of activity every 5 to 10 minutes can hold an audience's attention.

4. *Success.* When students are successful at tasks they perceive to be somewhat challenging because they have made a strong effort, their motivation for future learning is greatly enhanced. It is unreasonable to expect students who fail constantly to have any motivation to participate positively in future learning activities. Thus, it is especially important for teachers to create success for students who are not normally successful. Teachers help ensure that all students experience some success by making goals and objectives clear, by teaching content clearly in small steps, and by checking to see that students understand each step. Teachers can also encourage success by helping students acquire the study skills they need when they must work on their own—outlining, note taking, and using textbooks correctly. Still, the most powerful technique for helping students succeed is to ensure that the material is at the appropriate level of difficulty, given the students' prior learning in that subject.

CASE 5.2

The Popcorn Popper

As Mr. Smith's students walk into tenth-grade creative writing class, they hear an unusual noise. On the teacher's desk, a microwave filled with popcorn is running. Soon the room is filled with the aroma of fresh popcorn. When the popping is finished, the teacher passes a bowl of popcorn around for everyone to eat. After the students finish eating, Mr. Smith asks them to describe out loud the sights, sounds, smells, taste, and feel of the popcorn. Mr. Smith then uses their accounts as an introduction to a writing exercise on the five senses.

5. *Tension.* In teaching, *tension* refers to a feeling of concern or anxiety on the part of the student because she knows that she will be required to demonstrate her learning. A moderate amount of tension increases student learning. When there is no tension in the learning situation, students may be so relaxed that no learning occurs. On the other hand, if the amount of tension is overwhelming, students may expend more energy in dealing with the tension than they do in learning. Creating a moderate amount of tension results in motivation without tension overload.

When a learning task is inherently interesting and challenging for students, there is little need for the teacher to add tension to the situation. When the learning task is routine and uninteresting for students, a moderate amount of tension created by the teacher enhances motivation and learning. Teacher behaviors that raise the level of tension include moving around the room, calling on volunteers and non-volunteers to answer questions in a random pattern, giving quizzes on class material, checking homework and seat work, and reminding students that they will be assessed on the material they are learning.

6. *Feeling tone.* Feeling tone refers to the emotional atmosphere or climate in the classroom. According to Madeline Hunter (1982), classroom feeling tone can be extremely positive, moderately positive, neutral, moderately negative, and extremely negative. An extremely positive feeling tone can be so sweet that it actually directs student attention away from learning, a neutral feeling tone is bland and non-stimulating, and an extremely negative feeling tone is threatening and may produce a tension overload. The most effective feeling tone is a moderately positive one in which the atmosphere is pleasant and friendly but clearly focused on the learning task at hand. The teacher can help create such a feeling tone by creating a room that is comfortable and pleasantly decorated, by treating students in a courteous and friendly manner, by expressing sincere interest in students as individuals, and by communicating positively with students both verbally and nonverbally. See how one teacher expresses his interest in students in Case 5.3.

Although a moderately positive feeling tone is the most motivating one, it is sometimes necessary to create, temporarily, a moderately negative feeling tone. If students are not doing their work and not living up to their responsibilities, it is necessary to shake them out of their complacency with some well-chosen, corrective comments. The wise teacher understands that undesirable consequences may result from

CASE 5.3
Talking Between Classes

Mr. Dailey, the eighth-grade social studies teacher, does not spend the time between classes standing out in the hallway or visiting with friends. Instead, he uses the three minutes to chat with individual students. During these chats, he talks about their out-of-school activities, their hobbies, their feelings about school and his class in particular, their plans and aspirations, and everyday school events. He believes that these three-minute chats promote a more positive feeling tone in his classroom and allow him to relate to his students as individuals.

a classroom feeling tone that is continuously negative and, therefore, works to create a moderately positive classroom climate most of the time.

7. *Assessment and feedback.* Assessment of student learning is a primary responsibility of every teacher and, when implemented effectively, can have a dramatic impact on student learning, motivation, and behavior: "Major reviews of the research on the effects of formative assessment indicate that it might be one of the more powerful tools in a teacher's arsenal" (Marzano, 2007, p. 13). Formative assessment, effectively implemented, can do as much or more to improve student achievement than any of the most powerful instructional innovations, intensive reading instruction, one-on-one tutoring, or the like (Shepard et al., 2005, p. 277). The potentially powerful impact of formative assessment on students is dramatically illustrated in a story taken from Shepard et al. (2005).

Akeem, a third-grade student in New York City, was placed in the classroom of Susan Gordon after he was expelled from another school for throwing a desk. Initially, he had frequent outbursts, disrupted classroom meetings, and was aggressive and surly. Susan made a concerted effort to assess both his strengths and his weaknesses. She documented his progress in literacy and math. She noted the conditions that seemed to trigger outbursts as well as moments when he seemed at ease and comfortable. She designed learning activities that focused on his strengths and allowed him to feel comfortable emotionally. Akeem began to experience greater success and eventually learned to read and write. Based on his success, he began a track record of achievement that led to admission to a high school for the arts.

Well-designed formative assessment begins with preinstructional diagnostic assessment designed to identify both what students know and what misconceptions they bring with them. It continues throughout the learning process. Formative assessment tools may take a variety of forms, including but not limited to KWL (Know, Want to Know, Learned) charts, paper-and-pencil diagnostic tests, homework assignments and other projects, science talks or other small- and large-group discussions, individual conferences with students, and daily checking for understanding by listening to what students say and watching what they do. Teachers can maximize the potential of formative assessment as a motivational tool by helping students understand that, through assessment, the teacher is trying to help each student understand three things: (a) where the teacher wants the student to go, (b) where the student is now, and (c) how the student might get from where she is now to where the teacher wants her to be (Shepard et al., 2005).

Making the assessment process and the criteria by which the student's learning will be judged as transparent as possible facilitates the student's understand of where the teacher wants her to go. Marzano (2007) suggests making a rubric for each important learning goal. Well-designed rubrics, exemplars of work from former students, and allowing students to help develop criteria for assessing work are all useful strategies for making goals and assessment criteria clear. Another powerful strategy for helping students understand the goals toward which they are progressing is the use of student self-assessment or self-evaluation as discussed in Chapter 6. Self-assessment serves cognitive and motivational purposes, leads to self-monitoring of performance, and helps students understand and make sense of what the criteria mean and develop metacognitive abilities (Shepard et al., 2005).

Once the student has a clear understanding of the learning goals and assessment criteria, the teacher must turn her attention to helping the learner understand where she is right now in relation to those goals. Clearly, teacher feedback to the student is the most important mechanism for accomplishing this task. Feedback is most effective when it focuses on particular qualities of a student's work in relation to established criteria, identifies strengths as well as weaknesses, and provides guidance about what to do to improve. Feedback should focus on what the students is doing correctly as well as elaborating on what the student needs to do next (Dean et al., 2012). In addition, teachers must establish a classroom climate of trust and norms that enable constructive criticism. This means that feedback must occur throughout the learning process (not at the end, when teaching on the topic is finished); teacher and students must have a shared understanding that the purpose of feedback is to facilitate learning; it may mean that grading should be suspended during the formative stage (Shepard et al., 2005, p. 288). Clear, constructive feedback in a classroom context marked by this type of shared understanding is a powerful strategy for enhancing student motivation. One of the more powerful strategies for developing shared understanding of both assessment and feedback is engaging students in assessing their own work and the work of peers under the guidance of the teacher (Dean et al., 2012). The final aspect of assessment and feedback focuses on helping the student get from where she is now to where she wants to be. This process involves both (a) designing specific learning tasks that will fill in the gaps between the current and desired level of performance and (b) providing the emotional support and encouragement that the student needs to persist in achieving the desired outcomes.

8. *Encouragement.* Encouragement is a great motivator. It emphasizes the positive aspects of behavior; recognizes and validates real effort; communicates positive expectations for future behavior; and communicates that the teacher trusts, respects, and believes in the child. All too frequently, teachers and parents point out how children have failed to meet expectations. Pointing out shortcomings and focusing on past transgressions erode children's self-esteem, whereas encouraging communication, as defined by Sweeney (1981), enhances self-esteem. It emphasizes present and future behavior rather than past transgressions and what is being learned and done correctly rather than what has not been learned.

Ms. Johnson in Case 5.4 would have had a far more positive impact on Heidi's motivation if she had pointed out the positive aspects of Heidi's work as well as the

CASE 5.4

Nonconstructive Feedback

Ms. Johnson was handing back the seventh graders' reports on their library books. Heidi waited anxiously to get her report back. She had read a book on archaeology and had really gotten into it. She spent quite a bit of time explaining in her report how neat it must be to be able to relive the past by examining the artifacts people left behind.

When she received her book report, Heidi was dejected. The word *artifact*—Heidi had spelled it *artafact*—was circled twice on her paper with *sp* written above it. At the bottom of the paper, Ms. Johnson had written, "spelling errors are careless and are not acceptable." The only other mark Ms. Johnson had made on the paper was a grade of C.

error in spelling. Have you ever thought about the fact that a child who gets a 68 on an exam has learned twice as much as she has failed to learn? Does the feedback provided to a student who earns a 68 usually convey that message? For more on encouragement, see Dreikurs (2004).

How can you use these research findings to improve student motivation in your own classroom? Ask yourself the following questions as you plan classroom activities for your students:

1. How can I make use of natural student interests in this learning activity?
2. How can I help students meet their basic human needs in this activity?
3. How can I use novel events and/or materials in this activity?
4. How can I provide for variety in these learning activities?
5. How can I ensure that my students will be successful?
6. How can I create an appropriate level of tension for this learning task?
7. How can I create a moderately pleasant feeling tone for this activity?
8. How can I provide feedback to students and help them recognize their progress in learning?
9. How can I encourage my students?

This list of nine questions is also an important resource when discipline problems occur. By answering the questions, the teacher may find ways to increase the motivation to learn and decrease the motivation to misbehave.

Teacher Expectations

Teacher expectations influence both student learning and student motivation. The initial line of inquiry into expectations began with Robert Rosenthal's doctoral dissertation in 1956 that asserted that an experimenter could have an effect on the outcome of an experiment (Weinstein, 2002). Marzano (2007) discusses this idea's entry into the educational scene when an elementary school principal named Lenore Jacobson contacted Rosenthal and encouraged him to examine the application of his theory to the effect that teachers' perceptions might have on student achievement. In a famous study entitled *Pygmalion in the Classroom* (1968), Rosenthal and Jacobson began a line of inquiry that still continues and has yielded powerful insights concerning the effects of teacher behavior on student achievement. For their study, Rosenthal and Jacobson told teachers in an inner-city elementary school that they had developed an intelligence test designed to identify "intellectual bloomers," that is, students who were on the verge of taking a tremendous leap in their ability to learn. They also told these teachers that certain students in their classes had been so identified. This was a total fabrication. There was no such test. However, when Rosenthal and Jacobson checked student achievement test scores at the end of the year, the students identified as intellectual bloomers had actually bloomed. Compared to a matched group of their peers, the researcher-identified bloomers had made much greater gains in achievement. As a result, Rosenthal and Jacobson assumed that the teachers must have treated the bloomers differently in some way in the classroom, but they had no observational data to support this assumption. Although still considered controversial (Wineburg, 1987), the study provided the impetus for further research (Good, 1987).

Beginning in the 1970s, researchers such as Thomas Good and Jere Brophy conducted observational studies of teacher behavior toward students whom the teachers perceived as high achievers and those they perceived as low achievers. Multiple research studies (e.g., Good and Brophy, 2008) found that teachers often unintentionally communicate low expectations toward students whom they perceive as low achievers. These lower expectations are communicated by behaviors such as the following:

1. Calling on low achievers less often to answer questions.
2. Giving low achievers less think time when they are called on.
3. Providing fewer clues and hints to low achievers when they have initial difficulty in answering questions.
4. Praising correct answers from low achievers less often.
5. Criticizing wrong answers from low achievers more often.
6. Praising marginal answers from low achievers but demanding more precise answers from high achievers.
7. Staying farther away physically and psychologically from low achievers.
8. Rarely expressing personal interest in low achievers.
9. Smiling less frequently at low achievers.
10. Making eye contact less frequently with low achievers.
11. Complimenting low achievers less often.

Some of these behaviors may be motivated by good intentions on the part of the teacher, who, for example, may give low achievers less think time to avoid embarrassing them if they don't know an answer. However, the cumulative effect is the communication of a powerful message: "I don't expect you to be able to do much." This message triggers a vicious cycle. Students begin to expect less of themselves, produce less, and confirm the teacher's original perception of them. In many cases, the teacher may have a legitimate reason to expect less from some students; however, communicating low expectations produces only negative effects.

Good and Brophy (2008) have identified two types of lowered expectations that teachers sometimes hold for their students:

> The first is the self-fulfilling prophecy effect, in which an originally unfounded expectation nevertheless leads to behavior that causes the expectation to become true.… The second type of expectation effect is the sustaining expectation effect. Here, the expectations are better founded, in that teachers expect students to sustain previously demonstrated patterns. However, the teachers take these patterns for granted to the point that they fail to see and capitalize on changes in students' potential.… Self-fulfilling prophecies are more powerful than sustaining expectation effects because they introduce significant change in student behavior instead of merely minimizing such change by sustaining established patterns. However, subtle sustaining expectation effects occur more frequently than powerful self-fulfilling prophecy effects. (pp. 49–50)

The debilitating effects of low teacher expectations have also been noted as a critical issue in relation to cultural differences within the classroom. Lisa Delpit (2012) argues that Americans have been unconsciously influenced by our society's deeply ingrained practice of equating blackness with inferiority. Delpit uses a powerful analogy to make her point. She suggests that people who live in Los Angeles continually breathe smog without being aware of it. They have become unconscious smog breathers. She asserts that racism in America is akin to the smog in LA. We all breathe racism unconsciously: "We don't try to be. We are not conscious of the racism we breathe. We just go about our everyday lives" (2012, p. 38). All teachers must be deliberate in communicating high expectations to all learners, but Delpit argues that the conscious use of behaviors that communicate high expectations coupled with bringing to consciousness and changing our previously unconscious attitudes toward culturally different learners can help us exert powerful influences on the motivation of all children to be successful:

> When we educators look at a classroom of black faces, we must understand that we are looking at children as least as brilliant as those from any well-to-do white community. If we do not recognize the brilliance before us, we cannot help but carry on the stereotypic societal views that these children are somehow damaged goods and that they cannot be expected to succeed. (Delpit, 2012, p. 5)

Researchers have demonstrated that when teachers equalize response opportunities, feedback, and personal involvement, student learning can improve. The message is clear: communicating high expectations to all learners appears to influence low achievers to learn more, whereas communicating low expectations, no matter how justified, has a debilitating effect.

Good and Brophy (2008) provide an excellent and comprehensive overview of the research on teacher expectation effects and suggest that teachers take three specific steps to ensure that they are communicating high levels of expectations for all students: (1) in developing expectations for students, consider the full range of the students' abilities, including all of the multiple intelligences discussed later in this chapter; (2) keep expectations flexible and current, basing your decisions about students on what each one can do today, not what she was unable to do yesterday; and (3) emphasize the positive while still being realistic.

Although empirical research in this area has been limited to the effects of teacher expectations on achievement, we believe that the generalizations hold true for student behavior as well. Communicating high expectations for student behavior is likely to bring about increased positive behaviors; communicating low expectations for student behavior is likely to bring about increased negative behavior. A teacher who says, "I am sure that all of you will complete all of your homework assignments carefully because you realize that doing homework is an important way of practicing what you are learning" is more likely to have students complete homework assignments than a teacher who says, "I know you probably don't like to do homework, but if you fail to complete homework assignments, it will definitely lower your grades." As Brophy (1988a) noted:

> Consistent projection of positive expectations, attributions, and social labels to the students is important in fostering positive self-concepts and related motives

that orient them toward pro-social behavior. In short, students who are consistently treated as if they are well-intentioned individuals who respect themselves and others and desire to act responsibly, morally, and pro-socially are more likely to live up to those expectations and acquire those qualities than students who are treated as if they had the opposite qualities. (p. 11)

Given the powerful research results in this area, all teachers should step back and reflect on the expectations they communicate to students through their verbal and nonverbal classroom behavior.

Classroom Questioning

Of all the instructional tools and techniques classroom teachers possess, questioning is perhaps the most versatile. Ester Fusco (2012) suggests that questions can provoke student curiosity, engage students more actively in learning, improve critical thinking skills, and help students become better listeners. According to Good and Brophy (2008), effective questions are clear, purposeful, brief, naturally sequenced, and thought provoking. When a teacher's questions have these characteristics, they may be used to assess readiness for new learning, create interest and motivation in learning, make concepts more precise, check student understanding of the material, redirect off-task students to more positive behavior, and create the moderate amount of tension that enhances learning. The use of good questioning techniques is a potent means of keeping students actively involved in lessons and thereby minimizing disruptive behavior. Wilen (1986) compiled a good summary of the research done on teacher questioning. Findings on classroom questioning indicate that the following behaviors help promote student learning:

1. Ask questions at a variety of cognitive levels. Asking questions in a hierarchy that proceeds from knowledge and comprehension to application, analysis, synthesis, and evaluation promotes both critical thinking and better retention of basic information (Good and Brophy, 2008). Marzano (2007) suggests using a questioning strategy called "elaborative interrogation." The teacher begins with an inferential question such as, "What led the Germans to accept an evil individual such as Adolf Hitler as their leader?" When a student provides an answer, the teacher responds by asking why the student believes this to be true or asking the student to explain how she arrived at this conclusion: "This strategy requires some skillful interaction with students, in that the teacher tries to make explicit the thinking the student is using to generate her answer" (p. 49).

2. Call on volunteers and non-volunteers to answer questions in a random rather than predictable order. (*Note:* In working with first and second graders, research [e.g., Brophy and Good, 1986] indicates that the use of a predictable order in selecting students to answer questions is more effective than the use of a random order.)

3. After asking a question, allow students three to five seconds of "wait time 1" before calling on someone to answer. This time is especially important when asking higher-level questions that require students to make inferences, connections, and judgments.

Effective questioning techniques increase student participation.

4. Have many students respond to a question before giving feedback. This may be done through a variety of strategies as noted in the previous section such as asking questions and requiring overt student participation.

5. After a student answers a question, wait three to five seconds before you respond. This planned silence, or "wait time 2," tends to increase the number of students who respond, increase the length of student answers, increase the amount of student-student interaction, and increase the diversity of student responses.

6. Vary the type of positive reinforcement you give and make it clear why student answers are worthy of positive reinforcement.

7. Ask follow-up or probing questions to extend student thinking after correct and incorrect responses. Some sample types of follow-up questions are (a) asking for clarification, (b) asking students to re-create the thought process they used to arrive at an answer, (c) asking for specific examples to support a statement, (d) asking for elaboration or expansion of an answer, and (e) asking students to relate their answers to previous answers or questions.

Teachers who employ these techniques, which may be adapted to fit their own classroom context, are likely to improve student learning and to increase student involvement in the learning activities, thereby minimizing disruptive student behavior. Fusco (2012) suggests the use of a questioning cycle that includes planning questions to match the lesson objectives, asking the questions, using wait time 1 before calling on responders, listening carefully to student responses, assessing the response privately, using wait time 2 before responding, then using a follow-up question to probe student reasoning.

Maximizing Learning Time

One of the variables that affects how much students learn is the amount of time they spend learning. As Lieberman and Denham (1980) found, there is a statistically positive relationship between time devoted to learning and scores on achievement tests. This is not, however, a simple relationship. Other factors, such as the quality of instruction and the kinds of learning tasks, must be considered in assessing the potential impact of increased time spent on learning. In other words, spending more instructional time with a poor teacher or on poorly devised learning tasks will not increase student learning.

Assuming that the teacher is competent and the learning tasks are appropriate, students who spend more time learning will probably learn more and create fewer management problems because they are occupied by the learning activities. Two areas that teachers can control or influence in order to increase the amount of time students spend learning are the time allocated to instruction and the rate of student engagement in the learning tasks.

ALLOCATED TIME   *Allocated time* refers to the amount of time that the teacher makes available for students to learn a subject. Studies have found that the amount of time allocated to various subjects in elementary schools differs widely even among teachers in the same district at the same grade level (e.g., Karweit, 1984). For example, some teachers at the fourth-grade level allocate 12 hours per week to reading and language arts, whereas other fourth-grade teachers allocate 5 hours per week. Some fourth-grade teachers allocate 10 hours per week to math, and others allocate 4. Other factors being equal, the student who spends 12 hours per week in learning reading and language arts is going to learn a great deal more than the student who spends 5 hours per week.

In secondary schools, the amount of time actually allocated to instruction also varies widely among teachers. The need to deal with routine attendance and housekeeping chores (e.g., "Who still owes lab reports?" "Who needs to make up Friday's test?") as well as the need to deal with disruptions that can range from student behavior problems to public address announcements can steal large chunks of time from learning activities (see Chapter 2). Both elementary and secondary school teachers need to examine how much time they make available for students to learn the various subjects they teach. Elementary teachers should investigate how they allocate time to their various subjects. Secondary school teachers should investigate how to handle routine duties more efficiently and how to minimize disruptions.

TIME-ON-TASK (ENGAGED TIME)   In addition to increasing allocated time, teachers need to maximize student *time-on-task*:

> Research on teaching has established that the key to successful management (and to successful instruction as well) is the teacher's ability to maximize the time students spend actively engaged in worthwhile academic assignments and to minimize the time they spend waiting for activities to get started, making transitions between activities, sitting with nothing to do, or engaging in misconduct. (Brophy, 1988a, p. 3)

Brophy's statement refers to the percentage of the total time allocated for learning that the student spends actually engaged in learning activities. Once again, research has provided some guidelines to increase student time-on-task:

1. The use of substantive interaction—a teaching mode in which the teacher presents information, asks questions to assess comprehension, provides feedback, and monitors student work—usually leads to higher student engagement than independent or small-group work that is not led by the teacher.

2. Teacher monitoring of the entire class during the beginning and ending portions of a seat work activity as well as at regular intervals during the activity leads to higher engagement rates. Periodically scanning the room during any activity to ascertain the level of engagement is also critical (Marzano et al., 2011).

3. Making sure that students understand what the activity directs them to do, that they have the skills necessary to complete the task successfully, that each student has access to all needed materials, and that each student is protected from disruption by others leads to greater student time-on-task during seat work.

4. Giving students oral directions as well as written directions concerning how to do a seat work activity and what to do when they have finished the activity also leads to greater time-on-task during seat work.

5. Communicating teacher awareness of student behavior seems to lead to greater student involvement during seat work activities.

6. "Providing a variety of seat work activities with concern for students' attention spans helps keep students on task and allows the teacher more uninterrupted small-group instruction" (Evertson, 1989, p. 64).

7. Using physical movement appropriately can enhance student energy and engagement: "Oxygen is essential for brain function, and enhanced blood flow increases the amount of oxygen transported to the brain. Physical activity is a reliable way to increase blood flow, and hence oxygen, to the brain" (Jensen, 2005, p. 62). Strategies such as asking students to stand up and stretch periodically, acting out concepts when appropriate, and standing up and chatting with a partner for a few seconds are suggested by Marzano (2007) as ways to incorporate physical movement.

8. Using games that focus on academic content and that also involve low-stakes competition will often lead to greater engagement (Marzano, 2007).

9. Teacher modeling of enthusiasm, high energy, and high intensity focused on academic content, is also likely to increase student interest and engagement in learning (Marzano, 2007).

When students are on task, they are engaged in learning and less apt to disrupt the learning of others. The effective teacher uses these guidelines to increase student learning and to minimize disruptive student behavior.

BEYOND THE BASICS

By the late 1980s—in the educational period between the process-product research and the current high-stakes testing movement—many educational researchers were beginning to express great dissatisfaction with the research that had been done on effective teaching. They were dissatisfied because it focused almost exclusively on low-level outcomes and generic teaching and learning strategies, paying little attention to contextual variables and to the subject matter being taught. Lee Shulman (1987) and his associates at Stanford began a line of research focused not on generic questions concerning good teaching but rather on good teaching of particular content in particular contexts. Their work was one of the major forces to give rise to the notions of teaching described in this section. As you will discover, these notions focus primarily on student cognition.

A second major impetus for a change in the focus of the research on effective teaching came from conceptual change research in science (Pintrich, Marx, and Boyle, 1993). This line of research focused on the difficulty science teachers face in attempting to change the misconceptions that students bring to the classroom. For example, most students come to the classroom believing that the explanation for warmer weather in the summer is the fact that the sun is closer to the earth in the summer. Obviously, this is not true. The sun is actually closer to the earth in the winter. However, research indicates that even after they hear the correct explanation, which they are able to reproduce for the test, most students leave the classroom believing that the sun is closer to the earth in the summer. Researchers have studied student learning of a number of scientific concepts including photosynthesis, electricity, gravity, and density with similar results—that is, students enter the classroom with misconceptions, learn the correct explanations for the test, and leave the classroom with their basic misconceptions completely unchanged. It is clear from these studies that we need to pay much closer attention than we have to date to the prior knowledge that students bring with them to the classroom as well as to the actual thought processes that take place during instruction.

The third major impetus for the current models of teaching and learning is the rise in popularity of *constructivism* as a set of philosophical beliefs to explain learning. Until recently, educational thinking and research have been dominated by behaviorist and information-processing views of learning, which, although different in many respects, share a conception of the learner as a rather passive processor of information received from the external environment. In contrast, constructivism places its greatest emphasis on active construction of knowledge by the learner. Thus, constructivism places the learner squarely in the center of the learning paradigm and sees the role of the teacher as one of coaching, guiding, and supporting the learner when necessary. Indeed, among the tenets of constructivism are the following five: (1) knowledge is actively constructed, (2) knowledge should be structured around a few powerful ideas, (3) prior knowledge exerts a powerful influence on new learning, (4) restructuring of prior knowledge and conceptual change are key elements of new learning, and (5) knowledge is socially constructed (Good and Brophy, 2008). Given this view, it is not surprising that constructivism emphasizes conceptual-change teaching and the need to link new learning with prior knowledge. Using the constructivist paradigm, teachers must provide opportunities for students to make knowledge their own through question, discussion, debate, and other appropriate activities (Brophy, 1993).

The research on student cognition, constructivism, conceptual-change teaching, and subject-specific teaching has led to several changes in our thinking about instructional practice. Indeed, it has led to a new paradigm for learning that rests on the following: (1) teaching for understanding as the major goal for teaching, (2) moving from individual learning to the creation of learning communities, (3) teaching for multiple types of intelligence, (4) differentiating instruction to meet individual student needs, and (5) emphasizing student cognitive variables rather than overt teacher behavior as the key aspect of student motivation in the classroom. In this section of the chapter, these concepts will be described individually even though they are interwoven and closely related to one another.

Teaching for Understanding

For much of the history of education in the United States, the goals for classroom learning have focused on the acquisition of factual information and routine skills and procedures. Although still important to some degree, these goals have become increasingly less sufficient for enabling students to function competently in today's technologically sophisticated, information-rich society. To function effectively in a global, interactive society, students need to go beyond memorization and routine skills to much deeper levels of understanding. Howard Gardner (Brandt, 1993) asserted that our schools have never really taught for deep understanding. Instead, they have settled for what Gardner called the "correct answer compromise"; that is, students give agreed-upon answers that are counted as correct, but their real-world behavior indicates that they have failed to really understand the material. Gardner believes that we need to enable students to achieve a deep understanding of the material that they encounter in school. Deep understanding means being able to do a variety of thought-demanding tasks such as explaining a topic in one's own words, making predictions, finding exemplars in new contexts, and applying concepts to explain new situations (Blythe, 1998; Wiggins and McTighe, 1998).

The first step in making deep understanding one of our goals for student learning involves the teacher coming to grips with the "content coverage" dilemma. Teaching for understanding involves time. Learners do not develop deep understandings of content overnight. They need opportunities to become engaged with the content in different contexts. They need the opportunity to see many examples, to ask many questions, to discuss ideas with peers and with the teacher, and to practice demonstrating their understanding in a variety of situations. As a result, it is simply not possible to cover the same amount of material that can be covered in a classroom in which student memorization is the goal. The teacher who wants to teach for understanding must be willing to take the time to allow students to become deeply involved with the material.

Teachers who struggle with the task of deciding what content to focus on in teaching for in-depth understanding are advised by Wiggins and McTighe (1998) to use the following guidelines: choose content that (1) has enduring value beyond the classroom, (2) is important to the discipline being studied, (3) is a topic students are likely to have preconceived misconceptions about, (4) has the potential to be enjoyable for students, and (5) will naturally reoccur at several points throughout the learner's study of the subject area. Wiggins and McTighe suggested that teachers develop curriculum around essential questions that meet those five guidelines. Examples of such enduring questions are, "What factors lead nations to choose war over peaceful conflict resolution?" "What does it mean to divide fractions?" "What does it mean to say that, in biology, structure follows function?"

For those teachers who are willing to cover less material at deeper levels of student understanding, Wiske (1998) offered a four-part framework to focus classroom learning on creating deep understanding. The first part of the framework calls for the teacher to use "generative topics" as the focus for classroom learning. For a topic to qualify as generative, it must meet three criteria: (1) it must be an important topic in the discipline, (2) it must be able to be reasonably conveyed to learners at their particular developmental level, and (3) it must be able to be related to learners' lives and interests outside school. The second part of the framework asks the teacher to set learning goals that require students to demonstrate their understanding. For example, students might identify examples of Newton's laws of motion in everyday sports events. The third part of the framework requires students to demonstrate their understanding through classroom performances such as discussions, debates, experiments, problem solving, and so forth. The final part of the framework calls for ongoing assessment of student progress using publicly shared criteria for success, frequent feedback by the teacher, and periodic opportunities for students to reflect on their own progress toward demonstrating a deep understanding of the particular topic.

Creating Communities of Learners

One of the most dramatic changes that has taken place in our thinking about teaching since the early 1990s is the emphasis we now place on the importance of building learning communities in the classroom. In the past, we emphasized individual student learning and interaction between individual students and the teacher. Note that the research on effective teaching described in the first section of this chapter focuses almost exclusively on individual student-teacher interaction. Early research on effective teaching viewed peers as superfluous to the learning process. However, because of the work on cooperative learning conducted by Johnson, Johnson, and Holubec (1993), Robert Slavin (1989–90), Spencer Kagan (1994), and others, we now believe that peers can play a tremendously important role in enhancing student learning and in developing positive classroom environments. For this reason, we now believe that the creation of a classroom learning community in which learners engage in dialogue with each other and the teacher is a critical step toward making classrooms productive learning environments (Dean et al., 2012; Prawat, 1993). "Several studies have found that cooperative learning typically results in achievement levels that are equal to or greater than individualistic or competitive classroom teaching methods. Results for other kinds of outcomes such as motivation, attitudes, and behavior often favor cooperative group methods as well" (Emmer, Evertson, and Worsham, 2003, p. 112).

The creation of communities of learners often begins with lessons designed to involve students in cooperative learning activities. Cooperative learning should not be equated to simply putting students into groups. Cooperative learning activities share a set of common characteristics. Although the number of specific elements in cooperative learning differs among theorists (Johnson et al., 1993, favored five elements whereas Slavin, 1989–90, favored three), at least three elements are critical to its success (Slavin, 1989–90): face-to-face interaction, a feeling of positive interdependence, and a feeling of individual accountability. Face-to-face interaction requires placing students in close physical proximity and ensuring that they are required to talk to each other in order to complete the assigned tasks. If students can complete the task without interacting, they have been engaged in an individual learning activity rather than a cooperative learning activity. Given the explosion in networking technologies, the concept of face-to-face interaction may be a bit outmoded in a literal sense. However, its conceptual underpinning—that students must interact to complete the learning task successfully—remains true no matter what technology is used.

Establishing a feeling of positive interdependence means that students believe each individual can achieve the particular learning goal only if all the learners in the group achieve the learning goal. Johnson et al. (1993), who referred to this as sinking or swimming together, identified several types of interdependence that the teacher can work to create. *Positive reward interdependence* occurs when everyone is rewarded or no one is rewarded, and everyone gets the same reward. *Positive resource interdependence* occurs when each member of the group has only a portion of the information or materials needed to complete the task. A teacher is employing positive resource interdependence when each student has only one piece of the puzzle or one section of the required reading. *Positive task interdependence* occurs when a task is broken into a series of steps and is then completed in assembly-line fashion, with each group member completing only one section of the total task. *Positive role interdependence* is the practice of assigning roles to individual group members, for example, consensus checker, writer, reader, time keeper, and so on. Obviously, each role must be important to the completion of the task. Finally, *positive identity interdependence* is established by allowing the group to form its own identity by creating a group name, decorating a group folder or flag, or developing a group motto or some other symbol that describes the group. The Johnsons and Holubec suggested that the teacher build as many of these types of positive interdependence into cooperative learning lessons as possible in order to increase the likelihood of creating feelings of positive interdependence.

Individual accountability refers to each group member's feeling that she is responsible for completing the task and cannot rest on the laurels of the group or allow other members to do the work for her. Feelings of individual accountability can be established in a variety of ways, including assigning individual grades; giving individual tests, worksheets, and quizzes; or structuring tasks so that they must be completed by the group while making it clear that individual group members will be called on at random to answer questions about the task.

In addition to face-to-face interaction, positive interdependence, and individual accountability, the Johnsons believed two more elements—teaching social skills and processing group functioning—are crucial for the creation of cooperative learning activities. These two elements are described at length in Chapter 7 under the topic of using group norms to structure the classroom environment. As Case 5.5 illustrates, cooperative learning activities can have a positive impact on student motivation and behavior at the secondary level.

Teaching Toward Multiple Intelligences

As a result of the work of Howard Gardner (2004) and his colleagues, many educators have come to realize that success in school has been unnecessarily restricted to those individuals who have talents in the areas of mathematical and verbal intelligence. Many of the tasks and learning activities performed in schools require learners to use verbal and mathematical reasoning while ignoring other avenues of expressing talent. One need only look at standardized achievement tests, traditional IQ tests, and the

CASE 5.5

Cooperative Learning in Biology

As I walked into Mr. Higgins's seventh-period biology class, which was filled primarily with vocational-technical students, I was surprised to see a variety of specimen samples lying on the lab tables. Mr. Higgins began class informing his students that they would be having a lab quiz—which he referred to as a "practical"—the next day that would constitute a major grade for the marking period. The students who were busily engaged in their own private conversations met this news with shrugs of indifference. Mr. Higgins continued speaking:

> The practical will also be a cooperative learning team activity. Each of your individual scores on the quiz will be added together and averaged to form a team score. Your team score will be counted as part of the scores for our team competition. Just to review team standings so far, we have the Plumbers in first place with 93 points, followed by the Body Fixers with 88 points, the Hair Choppers with 87, and the Live Wires in last place with 86 points. Don't

> forget that we have all agreed that the winning team will be treated to a pizza party by the rest of the class. Now, you may go ahead and get started studying in teams for tomorrow's practical.

For a brief moment, the room fell completely silent. This was followed by the scrape of chairs and scuffling of feet as students moved into cooperative learning teams. Within minutes, the students were busy looking at the specimens and relating them to the diagrams in their textbook. Students were clearly engaged in helping one another memorize the various specimen parts that they would need to know for the quiz. Suddenly, one of the students from the Plumbers sat down and began to read a comic book. Within a few minutes, however, the other members of the team informed him that he was not going to sit there and do nothing. They assured him that they would help him obtain a passing grade on the quiz whether he liked it or not. The student got to his feet with a look of resignation and resumed looking at the specimens.

Scholastic Aptitude Tests (SATs) to recognize our overdependence on verbal and mathematical ability. Fortunately, Gardner's theory of multiple intelligences and its application have helped us recognize how other types of talent can be tapped. Callahan, Clark, and Kellough (2006) suggest that Gardner's (1996, 2004) theory asserts that there are many types of human intelligence and it is possible to group the various types into eight comprehensive categories: linguistic, logical-mathematical, spatial, bodily-kinesthetic, musical, interpersonal, intrapersonal, and naturalist. Every one of us, according to Gardner (1996), possesses each of these types of intelligence to some degree. He also asserted that intelligence is not fixed or static. It can be learned and taught. Those who exhibit high degrees of linguistic intelligence are able to use oral and written language effectively. They are often individuals who succeed in areas such as politics, sales, advertising, and writing. Individuals with strengths in the area of logical-mathematical ability use numbers effectively and tend to use reason and logical arguments well. They are accountants, lawyers, scientists, and so on. Some individuals, for example, artists, architects, and interior designers, excel at tasks that require them to perceive and transform graphic and visual representations of reality. Athletes, dancers, and craftspeople such as mechanics fall into the category of bodily-kinesthetic intelligence. They are able to use their bodies to express feelings and ideas and are able to use their hands to produce things. Musicians, conductors, music critics, and composers have a special capacity to perceive and express musical form. Thus, they have a high degree of musical intelligence. Individuals who are very sensitive to the feelings, moods, and intentions of others display interpersonal intelligence. They are often quite successful in people-oriented occupations such as teaching, counseling, and psychology. Certain individuals seem to possess a high degree of self-knowledge and awareness. They understand themselves well and are able to act on that knowledge. Although it is difficult to pinpoint specific careers that are connected to intrapersonal intelligence, such individuals are drawn to and successful in occupations that require self-direction and the ability to recognize one's own strengths and weaknesses. Finally, those who possess naturalist intelligence are able to draw on materials and features of the natural environment to solve problems and fashion products. Farmers, national park rangers, environmentalists, and wilderness guides draw heavily on this type of intelligence.

Although good teachers have always been aware of the variety of ways in which students demonstrate high ability, standard classroom practices and assessment devices have not allowed students to demonstrate their knowledge in ways compatible with their strengths. Thomas Armstrong (1994) and others (e.g., Callahan et al., 2006) have begun to help teachers figure out how to structure classroom activities and assessments to take full advantage of the range of intelligences that learners possess. According to Armstrong, learners who are linguistically talented benefit from activities such as storytelling, listening to and giving lectures, journal writing, and participating in classroom discussions. Students who have high aptitudes in mathematical-logical ability usually enjoy activities such as problem solving, observing and classifying, Socratic questioning, and experiments. Students who have strengths in spatial reasoning often profit from visual displays, color coding and color cues, and graphic representations such as semantic maps and webs. Students who are talented in the bodily-kinesthetic area profit from learning activities that include body movement, such as acting out stories and concepts and using manipulatives. Learners who exhibit high degrees of musical ability usually learn more effectively when learning activities include songs, raps, chants, and the use of music as either a teaching tool or a background environment. Learners who are strong in interpersonal intelligence perform best when they are engaged in collegial interactions such as peer tutoring, cooperative learning, simulations, and board games. Finally, students who possess a high degree of intrapersonal intelligence learn best when provided opportunities for personal goal setting, for connecting school work to their personal lives, for making choices about learning activities, and for individual reflection on their own learning. These students often are exceptionally good at self-assessment.

Armstrong (1994) suggested that teachers ask themselves the following questions when planning a unit of instruction:

1. How will I use the spoken or written word in this unit?
2. How can I bring numbers, calculations, and logic into the unit?
3. How can I use visual aids, color, and symbolism in the unit?

4. How can I involve movement and create hands-on activities?
5. How can I use music or environmental sounds?
6. How can I involve students in peer tutoring, cooperative learning, and sharing?
7. How can I evoke personal feelings and connections and provide students with the opportunity to make individual choices about the unit?
8. How can I use students' interest in nature and the world around them?

Differentiating Instruction

Gardner's theory of multiple intelligences represents only one dimension of difference among the learners in any given classroom. Anyone who has spent any time in a first-grade classroom understands that children are not the same when they begin compulsory schooling, and anyone who has spent any time working with seniors in high school recognizes that students are not all the same when they graduate from high school. Even students who are grouped homogeneously for instruction differ in significant ways. Students differ on readiness to learn, prior subject matter understanding, motivation, thinking ability, metacognitive understanding, interest in the subject, self-regulation ability, cultural background, and learning style. We could certainly generate a much longer list, but we hope the point is clear. There is no possibility of pretending that we can effectively teach all learners in exactly the same way.

It would be wonderful if our schools were all structured so that each student had access to a skilled individual tutor who could adjust instruction to meet her needs, but this is simply not the case. The burden for differentiating instruction to meet the needs of every student lies squarely on the shoulders of the classroom teacher. The need for differentiation is especially obvious today with the demands of No Child Left Behind (NCLB) that all students be proficient in reading and mathematics by 2014. Although there is talk about replacing this requirement with a focus on common core standards, the legislation that requires 100 percent proficiency still stands as of this writing. Some doubt that this goal can ever be reached. Everyone should realize that even attempting to reach it will require highly skilled teachers who are adept at differentiating instruction so that each student can be successful.

Research on effective differentiated instruction reveals the following key points: (1) differentiation uses small, flexible instructional groups to meet learner needs; (2) differentiation employs a wide variety of materials to address learner needs; (3) differentiation allows learners to proceed at different paces; (4) differentiating instruction demands a knowledgeable teacher who understands what the essential learnings of each unit of instruction are; and (5) differentiation is learner centered; that is, the teacher studies individual learners to identify their needs (Tomlinson, 2005). It is important to note that differentiation is not a dichotomous concept; that is, it is not a question of whether a teacher differentiates or does not differentiate. Almost all teachers differentiate instruction to some degree. Differentiation is most appropriately conceived of as a continuum of instructional practices ranging from very little attention to individual differences at the low end to great attention to individual differences at the high end. The amount of differentiation can be assessed by the answers to three key questions, (1) "To what degree do students have the opportunity to work in small groups and individually both with classmates and with the teacher?" (2) "To what degree do students have the opportunity to spend different amounts of time on the same learning task in order to learn it well?" (3) "To what degree do students have the opportunity to work with different materials to learn the same content?" (Tomlinson and Imbeau, 2010).

Tomlinson and Edison (2003) suggested that teachers pay attention to three types of student characteristics in attempting to differentiate instruction: readiness, interest level, and learning style. *Readiness* refers to the current understandings, prior knowledge, attitudes, and skills that a student possesses in relation to particular content to be learned. *Interest* refers to what the student enjoys learning and thinking about. *Learning style* refers to the way in which learners like to learn (e.g., visually, aurally, kinesthetically) as well as the manner in which they process information (e.g., globally, analytically, concretely, abstractly).

Once the teacher has an understanding of the student's readiness to learn, interest in learning, and learning style, Tomlinson and Edison (2003) suggested that there are five elements of instruction that teachers can modify to meet students' needs. First, teachers can modify the content of instruction. Most learners should be expected to master the knowledge and skills that are most essential to a given unit of instruction, especially in light of NCLB and high-stakes testing. However, some students may need a great deal of time, scaffolding, and support to master these basic concepts, whereas others may be able to master the basics fairly independently and be given the opportunity to expand and enrich their understandings through related activities. They may be asked to go beyond the essential knowledge and skills and to acquire information or abilities that might be of particular interest to them.

Second, teachers can differentiate process; that is, they can provide different types of learning activities or different ways of acquiring information. Some students may prefer learning individually, whereas others prefer learning in groups. Some enjoy writing to learn, whereas others enjoy physical movement. Some need very concrete experiences to understand material, whereas others are able to think abstractly and hypothetically. This is not to say that students should experience only those types of activities and thinking processes that they enjoy and are good at. The teacher's role is to expand the repertoire of learning capabilities that each student has. Therefore, all students should have the opportunity to learn in a variety of ways. However, each learner should also have multiple opportunities to learn in ways that are most comfortable and preferable to her.

Third, teachers may differentiate the products that result from learning activities to provide evidence that the learner has gained the essential understandings. Some students may demonstrate their understanding through speeches and oral presentations; others may create models, collages, and posters; still others may prefer creating musical performances or written projects. As was the case with learning activities, each student should have both the opportunity to demonstrate understandings in a variety of ways as well as multiple opportunities to demonstrate understandings in ways that are most comfortable.

Fourth, the teacher might also modify the learning environment to accommodate different student needs. The physical environment can be manipulated in many ways to create individual work stations or desks, sets of desks where students work in close proximity to one another, learning centers, and special spaces around the room where different types of learning activities take place (e.g., the computer table or the reading nook). The temporal environment can also be adjusted to meet students' needs. The teacher can structure the day or the class period so that students are given choices about how time is used, how much time is spent on different activities, and the sequence in which events occur. Obviously, elementary teachers have more flexibility than secondary teachers in this regard because they spend most of the day with their children. Secondary teachers, though limited by a strict schedule, can still provide choices about length and sequence of activities.

Finally, the teacher can also modify the classroom climate to meet student needs. Creating work situations that also allow students to meet their social needs, engaging in morning meeting or other routines that make students feel welcomed each day, and using class time for a class meeting when tensions and disagreements arise are all good examples of teachers' differentiating the affective climate to help students be more successful.

Teachers who want to differentiate instruction to better meet their students' needs should be cognizant of several principles that underlie the differentiation process:

1. Good curriculum comes first. If the curriculum is poorly designed and unengaging, differentiation will make little difference.
2. When in doubt, teach up. Ask students to stretch rather than teach at a lower level.
3. Ongoing assessment is crucial. Both informal and formal assessment tools should be used to assess student learning as well as to adjust the differentiation strategies.
4. Flexible grouping is a critical factor. Students must have the opportunity to move easily from one group to another to better meet their needs.
5. The emphasis should be on student strengths. Make sure that students have multiple opportunities to learn in preferred ways and to demonstrate their understanding in ways that are comfortable for them.
6. Make your expectations for student learning clear. Students should have a clear picture of what they are supposed to learn as well as an understanding of the criteria that will guide assessment of their understanding. (Lewis and Batts, 2005; Tomlinson, 2005)

Case 5.6 illustrates the use of technology by a novice teacher to differentiate instruction with her fifth-grade students.

CASE 5.6

Differentiation Through Technology

Ms. Flanagan, a novice teacher in a fifth-grade classroom had a dilemma. She needed to teach the elements of story—plot, characterization, point of view, and so on—to her fifth-grade students. The curriculum called for using two chapter books to teach these story elements to all of the students. Ms. Flanagan, however, knew that these two books would interest a handful of her students but would be of little interest to the majority of the class. She was not sure how to differentiate her instruction to meet the curriculum goals and also to engage her students with a variety of books that would relate to individual student interests. She decided to use technology to help resolve the dilemma.

(Continued)

(Continued)

Ms. Flanagan used Google Docs to create story element documents for each of the three reading groups in her classroom. Each student was able to read a story of her choice and then use a laptop from the shared laptop cart to work on the group Google Docs to fill in the setting, the key elements of plot, the character traits for the main characters in the story, and also a descriptions of the point of view from which the story was told. The use of Google Docs allowed each student to be working on a similar goal using different materials while seated in different parts of the room. This strategy allowed each student to learn about story elements as they were exemplified in multiple stories and also introduced each student to other stories that she might like to read.

The technology offered one other advantage that Ms. Flanagan had not expected. As the students were working on the Google Docs, one student found the chat function on the document and began chatting with another student by typing questions about her work. Ms. Flanagan noted the use of chatting and asked the students if they wanted to "talk" with each other that way. When they replied enthusiastically that they did, Ms. Flanagan said she would allow them to do so if they promised not to use verbal talk as well. The students kept their promise. This tool allowed the students to "talk" with each other without disturbing anyone else, and at the end of the activity, Ms. Flanagan had a typed transcript of the student conversations that had taken place.

Student Motivation: Student Cognition

In the second section of this chapter, we discussed theories and models of motivation that emphasized factors external to the student. Indeed, the focus of that section was on overt teacher behaviors that affect student motivation. In this section, we will look at motivation from a different perspective, that of student cognition and its impact on motivation to learn. Social learning theory, self-efficacy, attribution theory, and expectancy value theory provide important information concerning the relationship between student cognition and motivation.

The primary developer of the *social learning theory* of student motivation was Albert Bandura (1997). Bandura took issue with the behavioral notions of motivation that emphasized external reinforcers. He asserted that the individual's thoughts play a central role not only in determining the individual's motivational level but also how the individual will perceive variables that are intended to be reinforcers. Bandura's research demonstrated that personal evaluation and self-satisfaction are potent reinforcers of behavior, in fact probably more potent than reinforcers provided by others. Bandura's research findings showed that involving students in personal goal setting and providing frequent opportunities for them to monitor and reflect on their progress toward these goals could increase student learning efforts. In fact, according to Bandura, external praise can diminish self-evaluation and create dependency on others, thereby reducing an individual's intrinsic motivation to succeed.

Bandura's work on personal evaluation and self-satisfaction led to a related concept that he called *self-efficacy*, which refers to an individual's expectation of success at a particular task. When feelings of self-efficacy are high, individuals are much more likely to set higher goals and exert effort toward task completion because they believe they have the potential to be successful. When feelings of self-efficacy are low, efforts are diminished. Feelings of self-efficacy develop from judgments about past performance as well as from vicarious observations of others in similar situations (Stipek, 2002). The greater the perceived similarity between the person we are observing (the model) and ourselves, the greater the impact their fate will have on our own feelings of self-efficacy.

Teachers can use social learning theory in the classroom by focusing students' attention on the improvement of individual effort and achievement over time. Teachers who wish to use this theory should begin by engaging students in setting personal goals that are concrete, specific, and realistic. Teachers then involve students in monitoring their own performance toward the achievement of these goals. When students are successful, teachers encourage them to engage in self-reinforcement so that they will build positive feelings of self-efficacy toward the accomplishment of future tasks.

Attribution theory deals with student-perceived causes of success and failure in school tasks. Clearly, student perceptions of why they succeed or fail at school tasks have a direct impact on their motivation to perform (Stipek, 2002). Research has identified five factors to which students are likely to attribute success or failure: ability, effort, task difficulty, luck, and other people such as the teacher. The only factor that can be controlled directly by the student is effort. When students attribute success to effort and failure to lack of effort or inappropriate types of effort, they are likely to exert additional effort in the future. Students who believe that their personal efforts influence their learning are more likely to learn than those who believe that learning depends on teachers or other factors such as task difficulty or luck (Wang and Palinscar, 1989).

When students attribute failure to lack of ability, the impact on future performance is devastating. Negative feelings of self-efficacy develop, and students see little value in making any effort because they believe that they are not likely to be successful. As negative judgments of ability become more internalized and self-worth more damaged, students stop making any effort as a defense mechanism. Not making the effort allows them to protect their self-concept from further damage. They can simply shrug their shoulders and claim, "I could have done it if I wanted to, but I really didn't think it was worth it." This face-saving device prevents the further ego damage that would result from additional negative ability attributions. To avoid setting up the vicious cycle of failure and lack of future effort, teachers need to recognize the danger of placing students in competitive situations in which they do not have the ability to compete, or of asking students to complete tasks that are too difficult for them.

The implications of attribution theory for classroom teaching are clear. Students need to be assigned tasks that are moderately challenging but within their capability. This may mean that the teacher has to break complex tasks into subtasks that the student can handle and provide a great deal of scaffolding for the student, especially early in the learning process. The teacher should encourage students to make the right kind of effort in completing classroom tasks, and this may require teaching students explicitly what it means to expend effort to be successful (Dean et al., 2012). When students are successful, the teacher can help them attribute their success to this effort.

When students are not successful, the teacher may want to focus their attention on the lack of effort or on using inappropriate strategies. Research has demonstrated that teacher statements concerning attributions for success or failure are the key variable in influencing students to attribute success or failure to one variable rather than another. Another strategy that seems to have real merit is asking students to document over time both the effort they make at learning particular concepts and the progress that they make in learning the concepts as demonstrated by assessments and teacher feedback (Dean et al., 2012). Case 5.7 illustrates the impact of changing attributions in influencing student effort.

The *expectancy value theory* of motivation proposes that the effort that an individual is willing to put forth in any task is directly related to the product of two factors: the belief that she will be successful and the value of the outcomes that will be gained through successful completion of the task (Feathers, 1982). A multiplication sign is used to indicate the interaction between the two factors. Note that

CASE 5.7
Three Years of History Rolled into One

Mark was a senior who had failed tenth-grade history and eleventh-grade history and was now taking tenth-grade history, eleventh-grade history, and twelfth-grade history in order to graduate on time. The school counselor, who was working with him to improve his study skills, began by helping Mark prepare for a test on the Egyptians. When the counselor asked what material seemed important for the test, Mark replied, "Well, I know that one thing he is going to ask is what the Egyptians used for cleaning instead of soap—sand." With this response it became clear to the counselor that Mark was not good at distinguishing important from unimportant material. Over the next couple of weeks, they spent a great deal of time looking at Mark's notes and his textbook, practicing how to separate important from unimportant material.

Two days before the test, Mark had a list of important material to study and did a reasonably good job learning that material. Immediately after taking the test, Mark went to the counselor's office and announced, "You know what? I noticed something on the test." "What did you notice?" asked the counselor. "I noticed that the stuff I studied for, I knew, and the stuff I didn't study, I didn't know."

At first, the counselor thought that Mark was putting him on. However, as the conversation continued, it became clear that Mark was serious. Until this point in his life, Mark had felt that success on tests was simply a matter of luck. If you happened to be paying attention to the right things in class, you did well on tests. If you were unfortunate enough to be daydreaming during key information, you did poorly. It was all a matter of luck in terms of when you were paying attention.

Armed with this information, the counselor now had a two-pronged approach to working with Mark. Not only did they work on identifying important information but also on attributing both success and failure to personal effort rather than to chance. As a result of this work, Mark managed to pass (albeit barely) all three histories and graduate on time.

if either of the two factors is zero, no effort will be put forth. Thus, if a student believes that she has the potential to be successful in academic work and values good grades and the other outcomes that accompany academic success, she will be highly motivated to put forth a strong effort. On the other hand, if the student doubts her ability to perform the academic tasks successfully or does not value good grades and the other outcomes attached to academic success, she is likely to put forth a limited effort. Teachers can increase a student's effort at success either by encouraging the learner to believe that she can be successful or by increasing the value of the outcomes.

Good and Brophy (2008) suggested that teachers should take the following steps to take advantage of the expectancy × value theory in the classroom: (1) establish a supportive classroom climate, (2) structure activities so that they are at the appropriate level of difficulty, (3) develop learning objectives that have personal meaning and relevance for the students, and (4) engage students in personal goal setting and self-appraisal. Finally, for the expectancy × value theory to succeed, the teacher needs to help students recognize the link between effort and outcome suggested by attribution theory. We will return to these concepts of expectancy, value, and attribution in Chapter 7 and demonstrate how they apply to positive relationship building.

Summary

The first section of this chapter presented an argument for the importance of building positive student-teacher relationships to enhance the instructional effectiveness of the teacher; the second section provided an overview of the research on teaching that, as we see it, constitutes the basics of effective teaching. The final section of the chapter presented descriptions of several conceptualizations of teaching that have influenced our current understanding of best teaching practice. These conceptualizations focus on student cognition, community building, and higher-order thinking and understanding. Taken together, these two sections of the chapter provide the reader with a comprehensive understanding of current thinking concerning best teaching practice. All teachers have a professional obligation to examine their teaching behavior to ensure that it reflects best practice. This is a critical step toward making sure that the teacher has done all that can be done to prevent classroom management problems from occurring. Among the questions teachers should ask in assessing the congruence between their own teaching and best practice are the following:

Do I work at getting to know my students individually and building positive relationships with them?

Do the lessons I design include an introduction, clear presentation of content, checks for student understanding, guided practice, independent practice, closure or summary, and periodic reviews?

Have I used each of the following factors in trying to increase my students' motivation to learn: student interests, student needs, novelty and variety, success, student attributions, tension, feeling tone, assessment and feedback, and encouragement?

Have I communicated high expectations for learning and behavior to all students by equalizing response opportunities, providing prompt and constructive feedback on performance, and treating all students with personal regard?

Have I used classroom questioning to involve students actively in the learning process by asking questions at a variety of cognitive levels, using questions to increase student participation and to probe for and extend student thinking?

Have I maximized student learning by allocating as much time as possible for student learning and by increasing the percentage of student engagement in learning activities?

Am I teaching to enable students to develop a deep understanding of content rather than a surface-level knowledge?

Am I building communities of learners through cooperative learning and other strategies?

Am I teaching so that students can demonstrate their learning by using a variety of intelligences?

Am I differentiating instruction to meet student needs?

Am I using student cognition to increase student motivation to learn?

The teacher who can answer yes honestly to each of these questions has made giant strides toward ensuring that the classroom will be a learning place for students in which discipline problems are kept to a minimum.

Exercises

1. Think of the five most effective teachers in terms of instructional competence whom you have experienced as a learner. What role did your relationship with the teacher have in your perception of that teacher's effectiveness?

2. Select a concept from any discipline with which you are familiar.
   a. Write a series of questions on the concept at each of the following levels: knowledge, comprehension, application, analysis, synthesis, and evaluation.
   b. Would there be any difference in the use of wait time in asking the six questions you wrote? Why?
   c. Why is a hierarchical ordering of questions important in classroom management?

3. Why is it better to ask the question first and then call on someone to answer it? Would there be any justification for doing it the other way around?

4. What specifically can teachers do to communicate high expectations for learning and behavior to students?

5. What are some things teachers can do to ensure that their explanation of content is clear?

6. If you were observing a teacher, what specific behaviors would you look for to indicate that the teacher was attempting to maximize student time-on-task during a (a) lecture, (b) discussion, and (c) seat work activity?

7. How might secondary teachers handle routine chores such as taking attendance and receiving slips for excuses or early dismissals to maximize the time allocated for learning? What might elementary teachers do to ensure that all subjects receive the appropriate amount of allocated time?

8. Make a list of the topics taught in a given unit of instruction and identify those topics that can be considered generative topics to be taught at a deeper level of understanding.

9. Take a lesson you have taught using an individual lesson structure and redesign it as a cooperative learning lesson with all three critical elements of cooperative learning. Include as many types of positive interdependence as possible in the lesson.

10. Choose an assignment that you or a colleague has used in the past to assess student learning of a concept or topic. Identify how many types

of intelligence were tapped by this assessment. Now, redesign the assignment to include all seven types of intelligence.

11. Carefully review the two bodies of knowledge on teaching presented in the final two sections of this chapter (The Basics of Effective Teaching and Beyond the Basics) and answer the following questions:

    a. In what ways are the two similar?

    b. In what ways are the two different?

    c. Can the two be used compatibly in the same classroom?

12. **Principles of Teacher Behavior** After reading Chapter 5, briefly describe your understanding of the implications of the principles listed at the beginning of the chapter for a classroom teacher.

    Principle 1:

    Principle 2:

Structuring the Environment

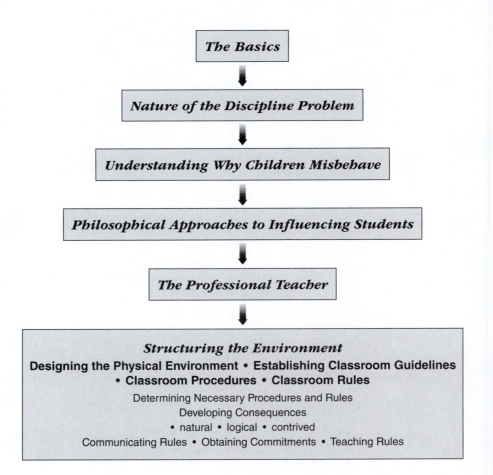

The Basics

⬇

Nature of the Discipline Problem

⬇

Understanding Why Children Misbehave

⬇

Philosophical Approaches to Influencing Students

⬇

The Professional Teacher

⬇

Structuring the Environment
**Designing the Physical Environment • Establishing Classroom Guidelines
• Classroom Procedures • Classroom Rules**
Determining Necessary Procedures and Rules
Developing Consequences
• natural • logical • contrived
Communicating Rules • Obtaining Commitments • Teaching Rules

PRINCIPLES OF TEACHER BEHAVIOR THAT INFLUENCE APPROPRIATE STUDENT BEHAVIOR

1. When environmental conditions are appropriate for learning, the likelihood of disruptive behavior is minimized.

2. Students are more likely to follow classroom guidelines if the teacher models appropriate behavior; explains the relationship of the guidelines to learning, mutual student-teacher respect, and protection and safety of property and individuals; and obtains student commitment to follow them.

3. Teaching students appropriate behavior increases the likelihood that disruptive behavior will be prevented.

4. Enforcing teacher expectations by using natural and logical consequences helps students learn that they are responsible for the consequences of their behavior and thus are responsible for controlling their own behavior.

PREREADING ACTIVITY: UNDERSTANDING THE PRINCIPLES OF TEACHER BEHAVIOR

Before reading Chapter 6, briefly describe your understanding of the implications of the principles for a classroom teacher.

Principle 1:

Principle 2:

Principle 3:

Principle 4:

PREREADING QUESTIONS FOR REFLECTION AND JOURNALING

1. If you were asked to go to a school and judge the appropriateness of a classroom's physical environment, what criteria would you use in making your judgment?

2. What classroom rules do you or will you establish in your classroom?

3. Do you think that rules should be jointly decided upon by the teacher and students or just by the teacher? Why?

INTRODUCTION

Misbehavior does not occur in a vacuum. Psychologists have long believed that behavior is influenced by the events and conditions (antecedents) that precede it as well as by the events and conditions (consequences) that follow it.

Antecedents may increase the likelihood that appropriate behavior will take place, or they may set the stage for the occurrence of misbehavior. Therefore, when teachers act to prevent or modify inappropriate behavior, they must examine antecedents carefully before resorting to the delivery of consequences. The start of the school year and the introduction of novel learning activities are two critical times when antecedent variables must be carefully considered. Unfortunately, because their workload is heavy and planning time is limited, teachers often give only cursory attention to antecedent variables at these times. Although it is understandable that many teachers decide to spend this time on designing learning activities, it must be stressed that learning activities are more successful when teachers have preplanned seating arrangements, supplies, and rules and procedures (Brophy, 1988a).

Because of the impact of antecedent variables on student behavior, teachers should take time to examine the two most crucial variables—the physical environment and classroom guidelines—if they do not take time to examine all of them. In this chapter, the importance of classroom furniture arrangements and the design of classroom procedures and rules are examined.

DESIGNING THE PHYSICAL CLASSROOM ENVIRONMENT

Environmental Conditions

Inadequate heating and lighting, poor ventilation, peeling paint, crumbling plaster, and inoperable toilets affect student learning, student behavior, teacher morale, and student and teacher health (Hopkins, 1998; Lewis et al., 2000; Schneider, 2002). In some schools, the air quality is so poor that students' ability to concentrate is significantly impacted.

This is particularly problematic for the estimated 14 million students who attend schools in need of extensive repairs or replacement or the 46 million students who attend schools that have unsatisfactory environmental conditions. It is estimated that 60 percent to 75 percent of public schools need at least one major building feature repaired or replaced (Hansen, 1992; Hopkins, 1998). Although teachers cannot install new lighting or remodel inefficient heating systems, they can ensure that the physical environment of the classroom is the most appropriate one for learning, given what is available. For instance, teachers can control lighting intensity. Dim lights, a flickering ceiling light, or inadequate darkening of the room for media and technology use causes frustration, disinterest, and off-task behavior among students. Always checking on appropriate lighting before the start of a lesson can avoid these problems. Because many schools are on predetermined heating schedules, there are usually some days in every season when rooms may be uncomfortably hot or cold. Whereas a teacher may not be able to adjust the thermostat, he can open windows to let in fresh air, turn off unnecessary lights to cool the room, and remind students to bring sweaters or dress in layers.

Depending on the school's location, outside noise may be uncontrollable, but inside noise is often manageable. As a group, teachers should insist that noisy repairs be completed either before or after school when possible. Teachers should also insist on predetermined times for public address announcements. Finally, school policy should dictate and enforce quiet hallway use by both teachers and students when classes are in session.

The importance of doing as much as possible to create environmental conditions conducive to learning cannot be stressed too much, as humans must be physically comfortable before their attention is voluntarily given to learning.

Use of Space

Although teachers have no control over the size of their classrooms, they usually can decide (except possibly in shops and labs) how best to utilize their space. Careful use of physical space makes a considerable difference in classroom behavior (Clayton and Forton, 2001; Evans and Lovell, 1979).

SEATING ARRANGEMENTS A teacher's first concern should be the arrangement of seating. No matter what basic seating arrangement is used, it should be flexible enough to accommodate and facilitate the various learning activities that occur in the classroom. If a teacher's primary instructional strategy involves a lot of group work, the teacher may put three or four desks together to facilitate these activities. On the other hand, if a teacher emphasizes teacher-directed lecture and discussion followed by individual seat work, the traditional rows of desks separated by aisles may be the appropriate seating arrangement. It is quite acceptable and often warranted for the teacher to change the primary seating arrangement to accommodate changing instructional activities. Seating arrangements in which higher- and lower-achieving students are interspersed throughout the room can increase involvement and participation. Also, when lower-ability students are seated closer to the front of the room, their achievement may improve (Jones and Jones, 2012).

An effective seating arrangement allows the teacher to be in close proximity to all students. This type of arrangement allows the teacher to reach any student in the class with minimal disturbance to other students and enables all students to see instructional presentations. An effort should be made to avoid having students face distractions, such as windows or hallways. Finally, seating should not interfere with high-usage areas, those areas with pencil sharpeners, sinks, closets, or wastepaper cans. Many interactive web-based tools allow teachers to explore different seating arrangements for various instructional models along with the advantages and limitations for both the teacher and learners of each arrangement (e.g., Training Room Design, Seating Chart Maker, Super Teacher Tools). Online tools for teachers whose classes include students with special needs or students who are prone to inattentiveness such as those with attention deficit disorder (ADD) or attention deficit hyperactivity disorder (ADHD) are also available. For these students, an appropriate seating arrangement is very important in meeting their special needs as well as influencing appropriate behavior by reducing distractions.

Besides planning the location of seats and desks, which occupy most of the classroom space, the teacher must decide where learning centers, computers, storage cabinets, and large worktables are to be placed. Appropriate placement helps make the classroom an exciting environment where a variety of different learning styles are accommodated. Because many people find a cluttered area an uncomfortable environment in which to work and learn, classrooms should be neat and uncluttered. A cluttered, sloppy, unorganized classroom suggests to students that disorganization and sloppiness are acceptable, which may lead to behavior problems. In designing the classroom environment, it is also important to make sure that the size of the classroom furniture matches the physical developmental level of the students. When high school students are asked to squeeze into desks that are too short or kindergarten students are asked to put supplies away on shelves that are too high, the likelihood of inappropriate student behavior increases significantly. Teachers should also think carefully about how much equipment and furniture is really necessary to support instructional activities and learning. It is important that storage space for equipment and supplies be sufficient, but too much furniture can result in cluttered walkways that impede student movement, obstruct student views of learning displays, crowd seating, and become potential safety hazards (Clayton and Forton, 2001).

BULLETIN BOARDS AND DISPLAY AREAS   The bulletin boards in Mr. Jaffee's room in Case 6.1 serve two purposes: they publicly recognize students' efforts and they provide an opportunity for students to enrich their mathematics learning through their own efforts and ideas. This is in striking contrast to bulletin boards that are packed away unchanged at the end of each school year only to reappear again in September or bulletin boards that have only a few yellowed notices dated a few months earlier pinned to them.

The more bulletin boards are used to recognize students, as Ms. White does in Case 6.2, or to provide students with opportunities for active participation, the more likely they are to facilitate and enhance appropriate student behavior. Bulletin boards and display areas may also be used to post local or school newspaper articles mentioning students' names and to display students' work. A part of a bulletin board or

CASE 6.1

Fourteen to Ten, Music Wins

Each of Mr. Jaffee's five classes has a bulletin board committee, which is responsible for the design of one bulletin board during the year. The only criterion is that the topic has to be mathematically related or its design has to use some mathematical skill.

The fifth-period bulletin board committee is ready to present three ideas to the class. Before the presentation, Mr. Jaffee reminds his students that they can vote for only one idea. Dana presents the first idea: "We would like to make a graph showing popular music sales of 2012." Tina presents the second idea: "I propose that we make bar graphs that

compare the 2012 Olympic track and field outcomes to the world records." Jamie presents the third idea: "It would be interesting to have a display showing the many careers there are in mathematics."

After the class asks the presenting students questions about each idea, Mr. Jaffee calls for a vote. The popular music graph receives 14 votes; the Olympics 10; and not surprisingly, mathematics careers only 4. The committee immediately begins its research on popular music sales so that the bulletin board will be completed before parents' back-to-school night.

CASE 6.2

Having Your Name Placed on the Board Isn't Always Bad

One by one the seventh-grade students enter Ms. White's room and cluster around the bulletin board. Today is the day after the test and the new "Commendable Improvements" list goes up. Cathy hollers, "Great, I made it!" Jimmy says, "Me too!" The list notes those students who have made improvements from one test to another regardless of test grade. Names appear on it in alphabetical order and do not reflect a grade ranking. The enthusiasm with which students greet this bulletin board surprises even Ms. White.

other wall space may be set aside for a list of classroom guidelines. Remember that decisions about the use of classroom space and decorations may be shared with students to create a more student-directed learning environment, in which students feel ownership, pride, and a sense of community.

ESTABLISHING CLASSROOM GUIDELINES

There is at least one antecedent variable over which the teacher has major control and that is the development of classroom guidelines. Classroom guidelines are necessary for the efficient and effective running of a classroom. After all, a classroom is a complex interaction of students, teachers, and materials. Guidelines help increase the likelihood that these interactions are orderly and the environment is conducive to learning. Properly designed guidelines should support teaching and learning and provide students with clear expectations and well-defined norms, which in turn will give them feelings of safety, security, and direction. A safe, secure atmosphere often provides students with the motivation and rationale to compete with those peer pressures that oppose behaviors conducive to learning (Jones and Jones, 2012).

Classroom Procedures

There are two types of classroom guidelines: procedures and rules. *Procedures* are routines that call for specified behaviors at particular times or during particular activities. Procedures are directed at accomplishing something, usually logistical, not at discouraging disruptive behavior. In contrast to classroom rules that govern behavior generally and are always in effect no matter what the activity, classroom procedures are designed to have students accomplish specific tasks and are usually activity specific. Examples of procedures include standard ways of passing out and turning in materials, entering and leaving the room, and taking attendance. Procedures reflect behaviors necessary for the smooth operation of the classroom and soon become an integral part of the running of the classroom.

Procedures are deliberately taught to students through examples and demonstrations, typically the first time that the procedure will be used. Properly designed and learned, procedures maximize on-task student behavior by minimizing the need for students to ask for directions and the need for teachers to give instructions for

Classroom procedures have to be taught to students.

everyday classroom events. Certain important procedures, for example, steps to be followed during fire drills and appropriate heading information for tests and assignments, may be prominently displayed for students' reference.

Because students often do not learn and use a teacher's procedures immediately, feedback and practice must be provided. However, the time spent on teaching the procedures is well invested and eventually leads to a successful management system (Brophy, 1988b). Often in art, science, and elementary classes, which are quite procedurally oriented, teachers have students practice the required procedures. In classrooms in which procedures are directly related to safety or skill development (such as equipment handling in industrial arts, technology education, or science laboratory techniques), instructional objectives involving the procedures are used in addition to subject matter objectives. In these situations, the procedures become an integral part of the classroom instruction. Note how Ms. Hersh uses an analogy to provide feedback on procedures to her third-grade students in Case 6.3.

After teaching the procedures and making sure that students can carry them out, many skilled teachers, especially at the elementary level, make sure to remind students about the appropriate procedure every time the procedure is used during the first few weeks of school. After a few weeks, these teachers will begin to have students share with each other what the appropriate procedure should be for a few weeks after that, just to ensure that the procedures have been internalized and have become automatic for students.

The use of natural and logical consequences is quite appropriate for students who fail to follow procedural guidelines. *Natural consequences* are outcomes of behavior that occur without teacher intervention. Examples of natural consequences

CASE 6.3

Hitting the Bull's-eye

Karen Hersh, a third-grade teacher, has a drawing on one corner of the whiteboard in her classroom that depicts a target consisting of several concentric circles with a bull's-eye in the middle. The first time each year that Karen uses writers' workshop with her students, she teaches them the procedure for peer conferencing about each other's writing. For the procedure to work well, the noise level in the classroom must be at an appropriately low level. Karen begins by teaching what a "one-foot" voice sounds like, that is, a voice level that can be heard at no farther away than one foot. She tells her students that a one-foot voice is the appropriate volume for peer conferencing. Immediately after teaching the one-foot voice concept, Ms. Hersh has her students pair up and practice one-foot conversations. After a few seconds, Karen goes to the target on her board and uses a suction cup dart to show her students visually how close the volume level of the class came to the target level. Typically, the initial practice volume dart is placed somewhere in the concentric circle that is most removed from the bull's-eye. Karen has her students practice one-foot voices several times, each time depicting on the target how well the volume matches the target. Finally, when the class volume is at the level that Karen wants, she puts the dart right on the bull's-eye.

are the inability of a teacher to record a student's grade if an assignment is handed in without a name and the incorrect results that occur because of inappropriate laboratory procedures (if not a safety hazard).

The use of logical consequences is much more common and has wider applicability in school settings than the use of natural ones. *Logical consequences* are outcomes that are directly related to the behavior but require teacher intervention to occur. Examples of logical consequences are students having less time for recess because they did not line up correctly to leave the room and students having to pay for the damage to their textbooks because of careless use.

Natural and logical consequences are powerful learning experiences because the consequences that students experience are directly related to their behavior. Students quickly learn that if they do not want to experience the same consequence in the future, they need to change their behavior. Therefore, anything the teacher does that removes students' attention from himself decreases the learning effectiveness of natural and logical consequences and in effect turns the teacher into the punisher. This is illustrated in Case 6.4. It is quite obvious to Tess why she fell and got angry with Ms. Blanco after the teacher's first response (a). When Ms. Blanco does not explain the cause-and-effect relationship, Tess continues to focus on herself ("it really hurts") as in the second response (b). In many situations, the best thing a teacher can do is to say is nothing.

Classroom Rules

In contrast to procedures, *rules* focus on appropriate behavior in general. They provide the guidelines for those behaviors that are required if teaching and learning are

CASE 6.4

Leave Me Alone

For more times than Ms. Blanco would like to recall, Tess, her fourth-grade student, is running down the ramp that leads to the playground for recess. On numerous occasions, Ms. Blanco has called Tess back to have her walk down the ramp, but it does not seem to work. However, this time, Tess trips and falls. Crying loudly, she is holding her knee, which is bleeding. Ms. Blanco rushes over to see if Tess is all right.

a: She says: "See, I told you that if you kept running that someday you would fall and get hurt well today it finally happened." Tess screamed at her "No kidding, just leave me alone!"

b: Alternatively, Ms. Blanco rushes over to see if Tess is all right. She says: "Tess, please go to the restroom wash your knee then come back I have some Band-Aids." Tess responds, "O.K., it really hurts."

to take place. Because they cover a wider spectrum of behavior than procedures, the development of rules is usually a more complex and time-consuming task.

THE NEED FOR RULES Schools in general and classrooms in particular are dynamic places. Within almost any given classroom, learning activities vary widely and may range from individual seat work to large-group projects that necessitate cooperative working arrangements among students. Although this dynamism helps motivate student learning, human behavior is highly sensitive to differing conditions across situations as well as to changing conditions within situations (Walker, 1979). Evidence indicates that children in general and children who exhibit disruptive behavior in particular are highly sensitive to changing situations and conditions (Johnson, Bolstad, and Lobitz, 1976; Kazdin and Bootzin, 1972). Given this, the need for rules is apparent.

Rules should be directed at organizing the learning environment to ensure the continuity and quality of teaching and learning and not at exerting control over students (Brophy, 1988a). Appropriately designed rules increase on-task student behavior and result in improved learning.

DETERMINING NECESSARY RULES A long list of do's and don'ts is one sure way to reduce the likelihood that rules will be effective. Teachers who attempt to cover every conceivable classroom behavior with a rule place themselves in the untenable position of having to observe and monitor the most minute and insignificant student behaviors. This leaves little time for teaching. Students, especially in upper elementary and secondary grades, view a long list of do's and don'ts as picky and impossible to follow. They regard teachers who monitor and correct every behavior as nagging, unreasonable, and controlling.

Teachers must develop individually or with students a list of rules that is fair and realistic and can be rationalized as necessary for the development of an appropriate classroom environment (Emmer and Evertson, 2008). Before meeting a class for the first time, a teacher must seriously consider the question, "What are the necessary student behaviors that I need in my classroom so that discipline problems will not occur?"

To assist in answering this question, keep in mind the definition of a discipline problem from Chapter 2: *A discipline problem is any behavior that interferes with the teaching act, interferes with the rights of others to learn, is psychologically or physically unsafe, or destroys property.* Thus, any rule that is developed by the teacher or by the teacher and students jointly must be able to be rationalized as necessary to ensure that (1) the teacher's right to teach is protected, (2) the students' rights to learning are protected, (3) the students' psychological and physical safety are protected, and (4) property is protected. Rules that are so developed and rationalized make sense to students because they are not arbitrary. Such rules also lend themselves to the use of natural and logical consequences when students do not follow them.

Teachers who develop a more student-directed approach to creating a classroom learning environment (see Chapter 4) may prefer to provide students with the opportunity to develop rules with the guidance of the teacher. Brady et al. (2003, p. 22) suggested a four-part process for carrying out this task: (1) begin by having the teacher and students discuss their hopes, dreams, and goals for the year; (2) generate an initial list of rules by discussing the types of classroom conditions and behaviors that will be necessary to help both teacher and students achieve their goals and dreams; (3) reframe the list of rules in positive terms, that is, what to do instead of what not to do; and finally, (4) trim the list down to a small number (four or five) of global rules.

The reframing of rules in positive terms, in other words, what is allowed, rather in negative terms, what is not allowed, increases the likelihood that students will abide by the rules. Let's look at a nonschool example. A park allows only dogs that are leashed. This can be communicated by signs. One sign reads, "No dogs allowed without leashes." The other sign reads, "Dogs allowed with leashes." Which sign is friendlier? How do you feel when you read the two signs? Which sign are you more likely to follow? Similarly in classrooms, if every rule is stated as what you cannot do, students are more likely to view the classroom and the teacher as controlling. If rules are worded as what you can do, the teacher is viewed as less controlling. Almost every rule can be rephrased. For example, "Do not call out answers" can be rephrased as "Please raise your hand when you want to answer."

Of course, rules are dynamic and should be reviewed periodically during the school year. Regardless of how the rules were initially developed, the review should be a shared activity with students and the teacher. The teacher should pose questions such as, "Are these the rules we still need?" "Do we have too many rules?" "Are there rules that we need but we do not have?" In answering these questions, the teacher should remind students often that the decision to remove, keep, or add rules must be based on providing a safe environment in which the teacher's right to teach and the students' right to learn are protected. When rules are removed, the class should be recognized as moving toward achieving the ultimate goal of self-control.

DEVELOPING CONSEQUENCES   When students choose not to follow classroom rules, they should experience consequences (Canter, 1989). The type of consequences and how they are applied may determine whether or not students follow rules and respect the teacher. Therefore, the development of appropriate consequences is as important as the development of the rules themselves.

Unfortunately, teachers usually give considerably more thought to the design of rules than they do to the design of consequences. When a rule is not followed, teachers often simply determine the consequence on the spot. Such an approach may lead to inconsistent, irrational consequences that are interpreted by students as unfair, unreasonable, and unrelated to their behavior. This view of the teacher's behavior eventually undermines the teacher's effectiveness as an influencer of appropriate behavior and leads to more disruptive student behavior.

Although the teacher should plan consequences in advance, there is some debate about whether or not students should know in advance what the consequences will be. Some teachers believe that sharing potential consequences helps students live up to teacher expectations and avoids later complaints about the fairness of the consequences. Although this may be true, if consequences are known, some students may do a risk analysis and determine that engaging in the disruptive behavior is worth more than the consequences that follow (Kamii, 1991). Other teachers believe that announcing consequences in advance gives students the impression that the teacher expects students not to live up to expectations. They prefer to act as if they have no need to think about consequences because they know that all the students will be successful in meeting both behavioral and academic expectations. There is no empirical answer to this debate. It is a matter of teacher beliefs and preference.

There is another reason that a teacher may not want to communicate the consequences of not following each rule. The teacher may not know at the time of the infraction what the consequence will be, if any at all. This has to do with the idea that we teach appropriate behavior like we teach academics. If you tried once or twice to teach a student ratios and proportions in math and he still has not mastered this content, do you give up or try something different? Of course you keep trying. In Chapter 8, the hierarchy of teacher interventions will be introduced, and the hierarchy will be expanded in Chapters 9 and 10. Basically, the hierarchy of interventions is an ordered listing of nonverbal and verbal teacher interventions that follow a few continua such as starting with interventions that student control to interventions that have minimum student control and from interventions that are least disruptive to the learning environment to interventions that are most disruptive. The delivery of consequences is listed 17th out if a list of approximately 20 interventions. So in most cases of a student violating a rule, the consequence is that the teacher now intervenes to influence the student to choose appropriate behavior. Thus, there may be no consequence at all.

As we have already noted in the discussion of procedures, the two types of consequences are natural and logical. Natural consequences, which occur without anyone's intervention and are the result of a behavior, are powerful modifiers of behavior. After all, have you ever

Had an accident because you ran a red light or a stop sign?

Injured your foot while walking barefoot?

Locked yourself out of your house because you forgot your key?

Lost or broken something because of carelessness?

Missed a bus or train because of lateness?

All of these events usually lead to a change in behavior, and they all have certain common characteristics. Each is an undesirable consequence all persons experience each equally regardless of who they are, and it comes about without the intervention of anyone else. Dreikurs (2004) emphasized that children are provided with an honest and real learning situation when they are allowed to experience the natural consequences of their behavior.

Although students are more likely to experience natural consequences at home or in the general society than in school, allowing them to experience the natural consequences of their behavior, if at all possible, in classroom situations is a very effective learning technique. It clearly communicates a cause-and-effect relationship between a student's chosen behavior and the experienced consequence, and it removes the teacher from negative involvement with the students. Some examples of natural consequences in schools follow:

Obtaining a low test grade because of failure to study.

Losing assignments or books because of carelessness.

Ruining a shop project as a result of the inappropriate use of tools.

Losing a ball on a roof or over a school fence because of playing with it inappropriately.

Of course, inherent ethical, moral, and legal restraints prohibit a teacher from allowing some natural consequences to happen. For instance, the natural consequence of failing to follow safety precautions in science laboratories or technology education classes may be serious bodily injury or even death. Obviously, such a consequence must be avoided. Other natural consequences take a long time to occur. For example, the natural consequence of a student refusing to join a reading group may be a failure to gain necessary reading skills, which may eventually result in the student failing to get into college or to find meaningful employment. Consequences like these are not evident to the student at the time of the behavior.

When natural consequences are not appropriate or do not closely follow a given behavior, the teacher needs to intervene and apply a logical consequence. Have you ever

Been subjected to a finance charge because you were late paying a bill?

Received a ticket for a traffic violation?

Had a check returned for insufficient funds because you didn't balance your checkbook?

These are logical consequences. They are directly and rationally related to the behavior, but they are usually the result of the purposeful intervention of another person. In school, that person is usually the teacher, who optimally administers logical consequences in a calm, matter-of-fact manner. If logical consequences are imposed in anger, they cease to be consequences and tend to become punishments. Children are likely to respond favorably or positively to logical consequences because they do not consider them mean or unfair, whereas they often argue, fight back, or retaliate when punished (Dreikurs, 1964). Logical consequences may be applied in two ways. In the first way, the teacher prescribes the logical consequence without giving the student a choice:

"Morrisa, if you keep pushing, I will have you hold my hand as we walk."

"Heidi, if you keep bothering Joey, I will change your seat."

"Mike, when you raise your hand, I will call on you."

In the second way, the teacher offers the student a choice of changing his behavior or experiencing the logical consequence. The use of this technique places the responsibility for appropriate behavior where it belongs, on the student. If the student chooses to continue the disruptive behavior, the logical consequence is forthcoming. If the student chooses to cease the disruptive behavior, there is no negative consequence:

> "Morrisa, you have a choice to walk down the hall without pushing or hold my hand."
>
> "Heidi, you have the choice to stop disturbing Joey or change your seat."
>
> "Mike, you have a choice to raise your hand or not be called on."

Notice that the phrasing for all the choices clearly identifies the student being addressed and the desired behavior as well as the logical consequence if the behavior does not change. Using the words "*you* have a choice" communicates to the student that the teacher is in a neutral position and thus serves to remove the teacher from arguments and power struggles with the student. This is crucial, especially in highly explosive situations. Natural or logical consequences are not often readily apparent to an extremely angry and upset student who has spewed vulgarities at his teacher during class. If, in response to this behavior, the teacher says, "Your behavior is unacceptable. If this occurs again, your parents will be contacted immediately," the student is made aware of exactly what will happen if he chooses to continue his behavior. Furthermore, the teacher remains neutral in the eyes of not only the student but also the rest of the class.

A third form of consequence is *contrived consequence*, more commonly known as punishment. The strict definition of *punishment* is any adverse consequence of a targeted behavior that suppresses the behavior. However, in day-to-day school practice, punishment takes on two forms: removal of privileges and painful—physical or psychological—experiences. Either form may or may not suppress misbehavior.

If appropriately planned and logically related to the misbehavior, the removal of privileges becomes a logical consequence. For example, taking away a student's recess time because he has to complete classwork that was missed while daydreaming is a logical consequence. However, if the teacher cancels the student's participation in a trip to the zoo scheduled for the following week, it is a punishment and not a logical consequence because it is not directly related to helping the student complete his work. Additionally, a logical consequence can be perceived as a punishment if the teacher delivers the consequence in an aggressive, hostile, or demeaning tone of voice. Rather than the student focusing on his inappropriate behavior, he focuses on the teacher's behavior, attempting to avoid the verbal attack (Levin and Shanken-Kaye, 2002).

Painful punishments may be physical (shaking, hitting, or pulling) or psychological (yelling, sarcasm, or threats) or take the form of extra assignments (extra homework or writing something 100 times). Such punishments are often designed only to cause discomfort and get even. The use of painful punishment has been and remains a highly controversial issue on the grounds of morality, ethics, law, and proven ineffectiveness (Hyman and Snook, 1999; Jones and Jones, 2012; Kohn, 1999).

Research has indicated consistently that painful punishment suppresses undesirable behavior for short periods of time without effecting lasting behavioral change (Clarizio, 1980; Curwin and Mendler, 1999). Because avoidance or escape behavior is often a side effect of painful experiences, frequent punishment may teach a child only how to be "better at misbehaving." In other words, the child may continue to misbehave but find ways to avoid detection and thus punishment. Because punishment seldom is logically related to the behavior and does not point to alternative acceptable behavior, punishment deprives the student of the opportunity to learn prosocial, acceptable behavior. In addition, punishment reinforces a low level of moral development because it models undesirable behaviors. Students come to believe that it is appropriate to act in punishing ways toward others when one is in a position of authority (Clarizio, 1980; Curwin and Mendler, 1999; Jones and Jones, 2012).

Because it focuses the child's concern on the immediate effect, punishment does not help the child examine the motivation behind the behavior and the consequences of the behavior for himself and others, which is important for him to do as he learns to control his disruptive behavior (Jones and Jones, 2012). It also limits the teacher's ability to help the child in this examination process because the child frequently does not associate the punishment with his actions but with the punisher. This often leads to rage, resentment, hostility, and an urge to get even (Dreikurs, Grunwald, and Pepper, 1982; Jones and Jones, 2012).

Although there has been an ever-increasing opposition to its use in schools, physical or corporal punishment is still used in many classrooms. More than three decades ago, Epstein (1979) stated, "There is no pedagogical justification for inflicting pain.... It does not merit any serious discussion of pros and cons" (pp. 229–230). Similarly, Canter (1989) stated, "[C]onsequences should never be psychologically or physically harmful to the students...corporal punishment should never be administered" (p. 58). Clarizio (1980) stated, "[T]here is very little in the way of evidence to suggest the benefit of physical punishment in the schools but there is a substantial body of research to suggest that this method can have undesirable long-term side effects" (p. 141). Hyman and Snook (1999) stated that "there is absolutely no legitimate pedagogical justification for corporal punishment" (p. 51) and that "the major decision to use corporal punishment...has nothing to do with its effectiveness to deter misbehavior" (p. 49). Both Clarizio (1980) and Epstein (1979) noted that some of the side effects of physical punishment are dislike and distrust of the teacher and school. Kamii (1991) noted that students may develop a feeling of powerlessness, with predictable negative effects on their motivation to learn. To regain a sense of power (see Chapter 3), students are likely to develop escape and avoidance behaviors that may take the form of lying, skipping class, daydreaming, the calculation of risks, blind conformity, revolt, or additional disruptive behavior. Given the wealth of evidence opposing the use of corporal punishment over such a long period of time, one may ask why its use is still an issue.

Those who advocate the use of physical punishment usually cite one of two myths (Clarizio, 1980). The first myth is that it is a tried-and-true method that aids students in developing a sense of personal responsibility, self-discipline, and moral character. The reality, however, is that studies have consistently indicated that physical punishment correlates with delinquency and decreased conscience development. The second myth is that it is the only form of discipline some children understand. This has never been shown to be true. Perhaps it is a case of projection on the part of the teacher. One study showed that teachers who relied heavily on physical punishment did not know other means of solving classroom management problems (Dayton Public Schools, 1973). Teachers must understand that if a technique has not worked in the past, more of the same technique will not produce desirable results.

Indeed, the unproven effectiveness of physical punishment and the risk of harmful side effects have caused some of the largest school districts in the country to prohibit corporal punishment (e.g., Philadelphia; Washington, D.C.; and Chicago), even though many of these school districts are plagued with discipline problems. In addition, 27 states prohibit corporal punishment in their public schools. The National Education Association, the American Federation of Teachers, the National Association of School Psychologists, and the American School Counselor Association have also consistently supported the abolition of physical punishment.

For teachers who occasionally use mild forms of nonphysical punishment, guidelines for minimizing possible harmful side effects are discussed by Clarizio (1980) and Heitzman (1983). Table 6.1 compares natural and logical consequences with punishment.

COMMUNICATING RULES   If the teacher decides to develop classroom rules by himself, he must communicate the rules clearly to the students (Canter and Canter, 1992; Evertson and Emmer, 1982; Jones and Jones, 2012). Clear communication entails a discussion of what the rules are and a rationale for each and every one (Good and Brophy, 1997). When students understand the purpose of rules, they are likely to view them as reasonable and fair, which increases the likelihood of appropriate behavior.

TABLE 6.1   Comparison of Consequences versus Punishment

Natural/Logical Consequence	Punishment
Expresses the reality of a situation	Expresses the power of authority
Logically related to misbehavior	Contrived and arbitrary connection with misbehavior
Illustrates cause and effect	Does not illustrate cause and effect
Involves no moral judgment about person—You are O.K.; your behavior isn't	Often involves moral judgments
Concerned with the present	Concerned with the past
Administered without anger	Anger is often present
Helps develop self-discipline	Depends on extrinsic control
Choices often given	Alternatives are not given
Thoughtful, deliberate	Often impulsive
Does not develop escape and avoidance behaviors	Develops escape and avoidance behaviors
Does not produce resentment	Produces resentment
Teacher is removed from negative involvement with student	Teacher involvement is negative
Based on the concept of equality	Based on superior-inferior relationship
Communicates the expectation that the student is capable of controlling his own behavior	Communicates that the teacher must control the student's behavior
Facilitates growth in moral development	Maintains students in lower levels of moral development (reward/punishment) stage

Source: Dreikurs et al., 1998; Sweeney, 1981.

The manner in which rules are phrased is important. Certain rules need to be stated so that it is clear that they apply to both the teacher and the students. This is accomplished by using the phrase "We all need to" followed by the behavioral expectation and the rationale. For example, the teacher might say, "We all need to pay attention and not interrupt when someone is speaking because it is important to respect each other's right to participate and voice his or her views." Such phrasing incorporates the principle that teachers must model the behaviors they expect (Brophy, 1988a).

Although it is essential for the teacher to communicate behavioral expectations and the rationales behind them, in many cases, this does not ensure student understanding and acceptance of the rules. A final critical strategy, then, is to obtain from each student a strong indication that he understands the rules as well as a commitment to attempt to abide by them (Jones and Jones, 2012).

OBTAINING COMMITMENTS When two or more people reach an agreement, they often finalize it with a handshake or a signed contract to indicate that the individuals intend to comply with the terms of the agreement. Although agreements are often violated, a handshake, verbal promise, or written contract increases the probability that the agreement will be kept. With this idea in mind, it is a wise teacher who has his students express their understanding of the rules and their intent to abide by them. Both Mr. Merit and Ms. Loy in Cases 6.5 and 6.6 are attempting to get their students to understand and agree to follow the classroom rules. However, notice that they use different methods because the developmental level of their students is different. Unlike Mr. Merit, Ms. Loy asks her students only to confirm that they understand the rules, not that they will abide by them. This is an important distinction that should be made

CASE 6.5

"I Don't Know If I Can Remember"

At the beginning of the school year, Mr. Merit has a discussion of class rules with his second-grade class. He explains each rule and gives examples. Members of the class are asked to give the reason for each rule. The class as a whole is encouraged to ask questions about the rules, and Mr. Merit in turn asks questions to assess their understanding of the rules.

After the discussion, Mr. Merit says, "All those who understand the rules, please raise your hand." Next he says, "All those who will attempt to follow the rules, please raise your hands." He notices that Helen and Gary do not raise their hands and asks them why. Helen says, "I'm not sure if I'll always

remember the rules, and if I can't remember, I can't promise to follow the rules." Mr. Merit replies, "Helen, I understand your concern, but I have written these rules on a poster, which I am going to place on the front bulletin board. Do you think that this will help you?" Helen answers, "Yes," and both Helen and Gary then raise their hands.

Mr. Merit shows the class the poster of rules, which is entitled "I Will Try to Follow Our Classroom Rules." One by one, each student comes up and signs his or her name at the bottom of the poster. When all the students have signed it, Mr. Merit asks Helen to staple the poster to the front bulletin board.

CASE 6.6

"I'm Not Promising Anything"

On the first day of class, Ms. Loy explains the classroom rules to her tenth-grade mathematics classes. She discusses with the class why these rules are necessary for the teaching and learning of mathematics.

Ms. Loy then says to the class, "I am going to pass out two copies of the rules that we just discussed. You'll notice that at the bottom is the statement, 'I am aware of these rules and understand them,' followed by a place for your signature. Please sign one copy

and pass it up front so I can collect them. Place the other copy in your notebook."

Alex raises his hand and says, "I can't make any promises about my future behavior in this class. I'm not sure what the class is even going to be like." Ms. Loy replies, "Please read what you are signing." Alex reads, "I am aware of these rules and understand them" and says out loud "Oh, I see; I'm not promising anything." Alex then signs the sheet and passes it to the front.

when working with older students because it reduces the potential of a student confrontation during a time when the development of teacher-student rapport is critical.

Although many experts recommend having classroom rules on display or available for quick reference (Evertson and Emmer, 1982; Jones and Jones, 2012), it should be noted that merely displaying them has little effect on maintaining appropriate student behavior (Madsen, Becker, and Thomas, 1968). Teachers must refer to and use the displayed rules to assist individual students in learning the rules and developing self-control. Mr. Martinez in Case 6.7 understands this. He not only displays and teaches the rule to Lowyn but also reinforces the behavior when she finally does raise her hand. He understands that noting appropriate behavior and positively encouraging it enhances the likelihood of appropriate behavior in the future (Clarizio, 1980; Evertson and Emmer, 1982; Madsen et al., 1968).

Teachers may also employ student self-analyses to remind students of appropriate behavior and to help enhance their self-control. Indeed, any student can use self-analysis of his own behavior, although the actual manner of employment of the technique varies. Whereas Mr. Hite's smiley faces in Case 6.8 are appropriate for younger elementary students (see Figure 6.1), older students evaluate their behavior better by using rating continua. As with younger students, self-analysis is requested of all students or individual students as the need arises. Figure 6.2 is an example of a continuum rating scale that was successfully used to influence appropriate behavior in a seventh-grade art class.

TEACHING AND EVALUATING   Teachers do not expect students to learn a mathematical skill on its first presentation because they know students need practice and feedback. Frequently, however, teachers forget this when it comes to rules. They expect students to follow classroom rules immediately (Evertson and Emmer, 1982). But rules, like academic skills, must be taught (Brophy, 1988a; Canter and Canter, 1992; Evertson and Emmer, 1982; Jones and Jones, 2012). This entails practice and feedback. The amount of practice and feedback depends on the grade level and the novelty of the procedures

CASE 6.7

Calling Out Correct Answers

Mr. Martinez, a fourth-grade teacher, posts his classroom rules on the front bulletin board. One by one, the students sign the poster, thus agreeing to follow the rules.

Mr. Martinez soon notices that Lowyn is having a difficult time remembering to raise her hand before answering questions. Instead, Lowyn just calls out the answers. At first, Mr. Martinez ignores her answer. The next time she calls out, he makes eye contact with her and shakes his head in a disapproving fashion. Finally, he moves close to Lowyn and quietly says, "Lowyn, you have great answers, but you must raise your hand so that everyone has an equal chance to answer."

The next lesson begins, and Mr. Martinez asks the class, "Who can summarize what we learned about magnets yesterday?" Enthusiastically, Lowyn calls out, "Every magnet has a north and south pole."

Because Mr. Martinez has half expected that Lowyn will continue to call out answers, he is prepared for the situation and says, "Class, please, put down your hands. Lowyn, please look at the rules on the bulletin board and find the one that you are not obeying." Lowyn answers, "Number four. It says we need to raise our hands to answer a question." Mr. Martinez responds, "Yes it does, and why do we need such a rule?" "So that everyone in the class has a chance to answer questions," she replies. Mr. Martinez then asks, "Lowyn, did you agree to follow these rules when you signed the poster?" "Yes," Lowyn says.

Mr. Martinez asks her to try harder in the future and tells her that he will help her by pointing to the rules if she calls out again. The first time Lowyn raises her hand, Mr. Martinez calls on her, and says, "Lowyn, that was a great answer and thank you for raising your hand."

CASE 6.8

The Smiley Face Self-Analysis

Mr. Hite teaches first grade. After analyzing the types of behaviors he believes are necessary for the proper running of his class, he shares the rules with the children and explains what he calls the Smiley Face Procedure: "We all know what smiley faces are, and we are going to use smiley faces to help us learn and obey the classroom rules." Holding up a sheet of paper (see Figure 6.1), he continues, "As you can see, this sheet has faces next to each rule for every day of the week. At the end of class each day, you will receive one of these sheets and you will circle the faces that are most like your behavior for the day."

Each day, Mr. Hite collects the sheets and reviews them. When a pattern of frowns is observed or when he disagrees with a student's rating, he is quick to work with the student in a positive, supportive manner.

After a few weeks, Mr. Hite discontinues the self-analysis sheets on a regular basis. They are, however, brought back into use whenever the class's behavior warrants it. Mr. Hite also uses the sheets for individual students who need assistance in self-control. When outdoor activities or new activities such as field trips occur throughout the year, Mr. Hite develops new sheets for the students.

CIRCLE SMILEY FACES THAT IS MOST LIKE YOUR BEHAVIOR TODAY

	MONDAY			TUESDAY			WEDNESDAY			THURSDAY			FRIDAY		
Shared with Others	😊	😐	🙁	😊	😐	🙁	😊	😐	🙁	😊	😐	🙁	😊	😐	🙁
Listened to the Teacher	😊	😐	🙁	😊	😐	🙁	😊	😐	🙁	😊	😐	🙁	😊	😐	🙁
Listened while Others Talked	😊	😐	🙁	😊	😐	🙁	😊	😐	🙁	😊	😐	🙁	😊	😐	🙁
Was Friendly to Others	😊	😐	🙁	😊	😐	🙁	😊	😐	🙁	😊	😐	🙁	😊	😐	🙁
Worked Quietly	😊	😐	🙁	😊	😐	🙁	😊	😐	🙁	😊	😐	🙁	😊	😐	🙁
Joined in Activities	😊	😐	🙁	😊	😐	🙁	😊	😐	🙁	😊	😐	🙁	😊	😐	🙁
Stayed in My Seat	😊	😐	🙁	😊	😐	🙁	😊	😐	🙁	😊	😐	🙁	😊	😐	🙁
Followed Directions	😊	😐	🙁	😊	😐	🙁	😊	😐	🙁	😊	😐	🙁	😊	😐	🙁
Cleaned My Area	😊	😐	🙁	😊	😐	🙁	😊	😐	🙁	😊	😐	🙁	😊	😐	🙁
Helped Put Away Materials	😊	😐	🙁	😊	😐	🙁	😊	😐	🙁	😊	😐	🙁	😊	😐	🙁

FIGURE 6.1 Smiley Face Self-Analysis.

Name _____ Date _____

Class _____

Teacher-Student Evaluation
Class Behavior

1. Have you worked successfully with minimum supervision during the class period?

0% of the time		50% of the time		All the time
1	2	3	4	5

2. Have you been respectful and considerate to other students and their property?

0% of the time		50% of the time		All the time
1	2	3	4	5

3. Have you been cooperative with your teacher?

0% of the time		50% of the time		All the time
1	2	3	4	5

4. Have you used art materials properly?

0% of the time		50% of the time		All the time
1	2	3	4	5

5. Have you shown a high degree of maturity and responsibility through proper class behavior?

0% of the time		50% of the time		All the time
1	2	3	4	5

6. Have you been considerate of your classmates and teacher by talking softly, remaining in your seat, and helping classmates if help is needed?

0% of the time		50% of the time		All the time
1	2	3	4	5

7. Have you cleaned your area and put your materials away?

0% of the time		50% of the time		All the time
1	2	3	4	5

FIGURE 6.2   Behavior Self-Analysis for Art Class.

and rules. Rules that students have not encountered before, such as rules for a science lab, take longer to learn than rules that are traditionally part of classroom settings.

New activities often require new procedures and rules. Because learning is not instantaneous, students will learn, understand, and abide by classroom rules only over time. It is not uncommon for teachers to spend entire lessons on how to conduct a debate, cooperatively work on a group project, safely operate machinery, set up and care for science apparatus, or behave on field trips or outdoor activities. In such cases, specific objectives directed toward the procedures and rules are formulated and incorporated into the lesson plans. In these situations, they become an integral part of the course content; therefore, their evaluation and consideration in grading decisions are warranted.

Some teachers, particularly those in the elementary grades, evaluate their students' understanding of rules through the use of written exams or student demonstrations (Curwin and Mendler, 1999). Secondary science and industrial arts teachers often insist that students pass safety exams and demonstrate the appropriate use of equipment before being given permission to progress with the learning activities. There are no limits to the number of ways teachers have taught and assessed classroom guidelines. Jones and Jones (2012) provide an extensive list of creative, fun ways for teachers to teach and assess students' understanding of procedures and rules.

Teaching Appropriate Behavior

The previous section on teaching and evaluating mentioned that it takes time to learn mathematics or any academic subject, so why should learning rules and appropriate behavior be any different? In other words, if teachers expect to teach and reteach academic objectives, why shouldn't this also be expected for behavioral objectives? Teachers who believe learning academics and learning behavior are similar processes approach their working with students who exhibit disruptive behavior differently from teachers who believe the two processes are different. For example, if a student demonstrated that he did not know how to multiply a two-digit number by a two-digit number, the teacher would go through a process that is congruent with the definition of teaching (Chapter 1). The teacher would ask the question, "How can I change my behavior to increase the likelihood that students will learn to multiply any two 2-digit numbers?" Similarly, if students demonstrated they did not know what respect is, the teacher would ask the question, "How can I change my behavior to increase the likelihood that students will learn to demonstrate respect?"

Next, the teacher would design a lesson plan to reteach multiplication that might involve (1) task analyzing the terminal objective (two-digit x two-digit multiplication) into enabling objectives, what the student needs to know in order to meet the terminal objective; (2) ordering of the enabling objectives, from the least complex to most complex; (3) designing a teaching strategy for each objective; and (4) evaluating.

This same process can be used to teach appropriate behavior starting with a lesson on designing classroom rules. The terminal objective might be "Students will develop a set of classroom rules that are necessary for teaching and learning to occur in a safe learning environment. Some of the enabling objectives might be

Why rules are necessary.

What is required for a safe environment.

How to determine which are the necessary rules.

Next, a teaching strategy would be designed for each objective, which may include brainstorming, looking at samples of rules from other classes, cooperative teamwork, and so on. Many of the creative ideas in Jones and Jones (2012) would be appropriate. As with all instruction, the objectives and strategies must be developmentally appropriate.

One of the most frequently mentioned concerns that teachers have is that students are disrespectful or do not know what respect is. An appropriate terminal objective might be "Students will respect all members of the school community." Some enabling objectives could be

> Students will define respect.
>
> Students will define disrespect.
>
> Students will explain why respect to important.
>
> Students will define the school community.

Strategies might involve role-playing, analyzing media, debates, designing posters, or designing PowerPoint® presentations.

Other terminal objectives, as the need arises, might be

> Students will recognize bullying and know what to do when it is observed.
>
> Students will resolve conflicts through peer mediation.
>
> Students will behave appropriately in the lunchroom.

As with all instruction, lesson must be developmentally sound and culturally sensitive.

Some teachers believe that teaching respect and appropriate behavior is a parent's job and responsibility. It is also the parents' job to encourage reading and provide their children with breakfast, but parents often do not or cannot meet these responsibilities. So the school steps in and provides intensive remedial reading and breakfast for students meeting certain financial criteria. Others say it takes too much time to teach behavior. Given that it is going to take time, when would it be best to spend that time—up front at the beginning of classes or everyday throughout the semester?

To summarize, teachers must communicate to students the importance of the rules for learning and teaching. This is best accomplished through a no-nonsense approach that involves

1. Analyzing the classroom environment to determine the necessary rules and procedures needed to protect teaching, learning, safety, and property, preferably cooperatively with the students.
2. Clearly communicating the rules and their rationales to students.
3. When appropriate, phrasing rules so as to indicate that they are for both the teacher and the students.
4. Obtaining students' commitments to abide by the rules.
5. Teaching and evaluating students' understanding of the rules.
6. Enforcing each rule with natural or logical consequences.

Summary

This chapter first examined two of the critical variables that influence behavior in the classroom: the physical environment and classroom guidelines. Although teachers have no control over the size or the environmental condition of their classrooms, they can control the seating arrangements within their classrooms and the use of bulletin boards and can ensure that the available environmental conditions are optimal for learning to occur. The seating arrangement should accommodate the learning activity. It must also permit all students to see instructional presentations and allow the teacher to be close to all students. Bulletin boards should reflect and add to the learning excitement occurring in the classroom. Properly used, they can provide students with the opportunity to enrich and actively participate in their learning and allow the teacher to recognize and display students' work and achievements.

Classroom guidelines are needed for routine activities (procedures) and for general classroom behavior (rules). When they are well designed, guidelines provide students with clear expectations. The teacher can increase the effectiveness of guidelines by (1) analyzing the classroom environment to determine what guidelines are needed to protect teaching, learning, safety, and property; (2) communicating the guidelines and their rationales to students; (3) obtaining student commitments to abide by the rules; (4) teaching and evaluating student understanding of the rules; and (5) enforcing each guideline with natural or logical consequences.

Teachers who believe that teaching academics and teaching appropriate behavior are similar processes design lessons that involve stating terminal objectives, task analyzing them into enabling objectives, ordering the enabling objective from least to most complex, and designing teaching strategies congruent with the objectives.

Exercises

1. For each of the following activities, design a seating arrangement for 24 students that maximizes on-task behavior and minimizes disruptions:
   a. Teacher lecture
   b. Small-group work (four students per group)
   c. Open discussion
   d. Individual seat work
   e. Class project to design a bulletin board
   f. Teacher-led group work and simultaneous individual seatwork
   g. Student group debate
   h. Teacher demonstration

2. Give examples of how a teacher can use the classroom environment (bulletin boards, shelves, walls, chalkboard, etc.) to create a pleasant atmosphere that increases the likelihood of appropriate student behavior.

3. With your present or future classroom in mind, determine the common activities that do or will regularly occur. Design appropriate procedures to accomplish those activities. How would you teach these procedures to the class?

4. a. With your present or future classroom in mind, determine which general student behaviors are necessary to ensure that learning and teaching take place and that students and property are safe.
   b. State a positive rule for each of the behaviors you previously listed.
   c. For each behavior, give a rationale you can explain to students that is consistent with the definition of a discipline problem and appropriate for the age of the students you do or will teach.
   d. For each behavior, determine a natural or logical consequence that will occur when the rule is broken.
   e. How will you communicate these rules to students?
   f. How will you obtain student commitment to these rules?

5. Determine a natural, logical, and contrived consequence for each of the following misbehaviors:
   a. Fourth-grade student who interrupts small-group work
   b. Eleventh-grade student who continually gets out of his seat
   c. Seventh-grade student who makes noises during class
   d. Tenth-grade student who makes noises during class
   e. Twelfth-grade student who refuses to change his seat when requested to do so by the teacher
   f. First-grade student who interrupts reading group to tattle on a student who is not doing his seat work

g. A group of sixth-grade students who drop their pencils in unison at a given time

h. Ninth-grade student who threatens to beat up another student after class

i. Eighth-grade student who continually pushes the chair of the student in front of him

j. Tenth-grade student who does not wear goggles while operating power equipment

6. The following are examples of some rules developed for an eighth-grade science class. Identify and correct any problems in the rule, rationale, or consequences.

Rule	Rationale	Consequences
a. Don't be late to class	Because we have a lot of material to cover and we need the whole class period	**a.** Reminder by teacher **b.** Student required to get a note **c.** Student writes 100 times "I will not be late"
b. We all need to work without disrupting others	Because everyone has a right to learn and no one has a right to interfere with the learning of others	**a.** Reminder by teacher **b.** Student moved where he cannot disrupt others **c.** Student removed from class **d.** Student fails
c. We all have to raise our hands to answer questions or contribute to a discussion	Because I do not like to be interrupted	**a.** Student ignored **b.** Reminder by teacher **c.** Parents notified
d. We must use lab equipment properly and safely	Because it is expensive to replace	**a.** Pay for broken equipment **b.** Pay for equipment and additional fine

8. Given the terminal objective "All students will respect all members of the school community," task analyze the objective into enabling objectives, order the enabling objectives from least to most complex, and design teaching strategies for each objective for grades 4, 7, and 11.

9. **Principles of Teacher Behavior** After reading Chapter 6 and doing the exercises, use what you have learned to briefly describe your understanding of the implications of the principles listed at the beginning of the chapter for a classroom teacher.

Principle 1:

Principle 2:

Principle 3:

Principle 4:

7

Building Relationships

The Basics

Nature of the Discipline Problem

Understanding Why Children Misbehave

Philosophical Approaches to Influencing Students

The Professional Teacher

Structuring the Environment

Building Relationships
The Cultural Embeddedness of Rules and Guidelines • Creating Group
Norms to Structure Appropriate Behavior • Relationships • Student-Teacher
Relationships • Family-Teacher Relationships

PRINCIPLES OF TEACHER BEHAVIOR THAT INFLUENCE APPROPRIATE STUDENT BEHAVIOR

1. When classroom guidelines and rules match the culture of the students' home community, the likelihood that students will behave appropriately is increased.

2. When the teacher creates group norms that are supportive of engagement in learning activities, the likelihood that students will behave appropriately is increased.

3. When teachers use their professional knowledge base to build positive student-teacher relationships, the likelihood that students will behave appropriately and demonstrate higher academic achievement is increased.

4. When teachers proactively build relationships with parents that communicate that home support for school endeavors is important, parents have the ability to help, and the school welcomes and encourages their involvement, the likelihood that students will behave appropriately and demonstrate higher academic achievement is increased.

PREREADING ACTIVITY: UNDERSTANDING THE PRINCIPLES OF TEACHER BEHAVIOR

Before reading Chapter 7, briefly describe your understanding of the implications of the principles for a classroom teacher.

Principle 1

Principle 2

Principle 3

Principle 4

PREREADING QUESTIONS FOR REFLECTION AND JOURNALING

1. Do you see any relationship between student culture, school culture, and student behavior in the classroom?

2. What might a teacher do to increase her knowledge of different cultures?

3. What power bases are best for building positive student-teacher relationships?

4. What can teachers do so that parents are cooperative and supportive when notified of an academic or behavior problem exhibited by their child?

INTRODUCTION

Although deliberately designing the physical environment, as noted in Chapter 6, is important, the human environment, that is, the relationship that exists among the teacher, the students, and the students' families is probably an even more powerful variable in influencing appropriate student behavior and academic learning. Students achieve at higher academic levels and exhibit less disruptive behavior when they have positive relationships with teachers, yet the building of student-teacher relationships has been relatively absent from the literature on classroom management. This chapter details the importance of student-teacher relationships and proposes a model that uses a teacher's professional knowledge base to build positive relationships with students. Creating a supportive human environment is a complex undertaking. Students and teachers are not one-dimensional. They are multifaceted. Each student is a unique individual, a member of a particular classroom group with its own norms, and also a member of distinct family and cultural groups that bring values, norms, beliefs, and customs to the school setting. Thus, relating to individual students is only one aspect of relationship building. In this chapter, teachers encounter ideas for examining the congruence between the culture of the classroom and the culture of students for creating classroom group norms that are supportive of student engagement in learning activities and for relating to students as individuals. The chapter concludes with a discussion of the benefits to students and teachers of good family-teacher relationships. It discusses why some teachers are reluctant to interact with parents and suggests ideas that can facilitate a team approach. It is stressed several times that building this relationship is proactive.

THE CULTURAL EMBEDDEDNESS OF RULES AND GUIDELINES

When teachers are establishing and teaching classroom rules and procedures, they need to remember that their students come from a variety of cultural backgrounds. *Culture* refers to the knowledge, customs, rituals, emotions, traditions, values, and norms shared by members of a population and embodied in a set of behaviors designed for survival in a particular environment. Because students come to the classroom from different cultural backgrounds, they bring with them different values, norms, and behavioral expectations. Traditionally, teachers have acted as if everyone shared the same cultural expectations and have ignored cultural differences. However, this does not appear to be a wise strategy. Schools and classrooms are not culturally neutral or culture free. Most schools follow the values, norms, and behavioral patterns of middle-class, white, European cultures. As Irvine (1990) pointed out, however, these values and norms differ in significant ways from the values, norms, and behavioral expectations found in nondominant cultural groups such as African Americans, Hispanic Americans, and Native Americans: "If the norms and values that pertain in a student's home or community diverge significantly from those that pertain in school, the student experiences conflict, and the way this conflict is resolved by both the student and the school has much to do with whether the student experiences success" (Banks et al., 2005, p. 240).

Irvine (1990) has pointed out several specific differences in value orientation. Middle-class European American culture, which is the typical school culture, tends to

Surface behaviors are the most common type of disruptive behaviors that teachers must manage on a day-to-day basis.

value mastery over nature rather than living in harmony with nature, impulse control rather than expressive movement and demonstrative behavior, rugged individualism and standing on your own two feet rather than interconnectedness and helping others, the use of reason rather than emotion during discussions and argumentation, print-based communication over oral communication, sedateness and passivity over verve and panache, and personal conformity rather than demonstrations of personal uniqueness. As a result of these differences in values and norms, the typical behavior patterns displayed by youngsters who come from a nondominant culture, although acceptable at home and in the community, are not acceptable in schools. Indeed, cultural differences in what is regarded as appropriate occur in many areas, including language patterns, nonverbal behavior, amount and freedom of movement, use of personal space, expression of emotions, and dress.

Because of these cultural differences, many children from underrepresented groups experience cultural dissonance or lack of cultural synchronization in school; that is, teachers and students are out of step with each other when it comes to their expectations for appropriate behavior. Cultural synchronization is an extremely important factor in the establishment of positive relationships between teachers and students. According to Jeanette Abi-Nader (1993), one of the most solidly substantiated principles in communication theory is that of *homophily*, which holds that the more two people are alike in background, attitudes, perceptions, and values, the more effectively they will communicate with each other and the more similar they will become. A lack of cultural synchronization leads to misunderstandings between teachers and students that can and often do result in conflict, distrust, hostility, and possibly school failure (Irvine, 1990). According to Ladson-Billings (1994, p. 138),

> The typical experience in the school is a denigration of African and African American culture. Indeed there is a denial of its very existence. The language that students bring with them to school is seen to be deficient—a corruption of English. The familial organization is considered pathological. And the historical, cultural, and scientific contributions of African Americans are ignored or trivialized.

Case 7.1 illustrates how stereotyping and a lack of cultural synchronization interfere with a teacher's ability to positively interact with a minority student as well as to find anything positive about the student.

The lack of cultural synchronization or so-called cultural discontinuity has been viewed as a major factor that contributes to the well-documented disproportional rate of disciplinary actions taken against African American children (Townsend, 2000). The differential administration of disciplinary actions is particularly evident with the use of corporal punishment, suspensions, and expulsions of African American males. The U.S. Department of Education, Office for Civil Rights (1993) reported that nationally African American males received corporal punishment and suspension at a rate

CASE 7.1
Believing What You Want To

Beth is a white, middle-class teacher who is in her fifth year of teaching elementary school at a predominantly white middle-class school. As a result of redistricting, the school now enrolls students from a nearby public housing project. These children are mostly poor and black. Beth is faced with teaching students with whom she is completely unfamiliar.

Nicole is a 7-year-old African American student. The teacher has described Nicole as a little girl with academic, behavioral, and language deficiencies and problems. The teacher requested that the school psychologist observe Nicole in Beth's classroom so that the problems can be documented and eventually be the basis for obtaining special services for Nicole. The following excerpts are taken from a post-observation meeting with the teacher (Delpit, 1995):

SCHOOL PSYCHOLOGIST: Nicole told me that she liked school and that her favorite thing in class was group time.

TEACHER: That's amazing because she can't sit still. She just says anything sometimes. In the morning she's O.K.; after nap she's impossible.

SCHOOL PSYCHOLOGIST: She's really talking more.

TEACHER: She's probably never allowed to talk at home. She needs communicative experience. I was thinking of referring her to a speech therapist.

SCHOOL PSYCHOLOGIST: She told me about her cousin she plays with after school. It seems she really does have things to talk about.

TEACHER: It's unfortunate, but I don't think she even knows what family means. Some of these kids don't know who their cousins are and who their brothers and sisters are.

more than three times their percentage in the school population. One explanation for the disproportional use of disciplinary actions against minority students is how teachers explain the reasons for disruptive behavior of majority and minority children. One study found that teachers tended to explain the disruptive behavior of European American students as a function of situational or environmental factors, such as the home or community environment. On the other hand, the explanation given for African American and Hispanic American students was dispositional factors or personal characteristics (Jackson, 2001). In other words, for European American students, inappropriate behavior was viewed as a result of the environment, which is viewed as excusable, whereas for African American and Hispanic American students, it was viewed as a result of the makeup of the individual, which is viewed as inexcusable.

To illustrate her discussion of the importance of cultural synchronization, Irvine (1990) has pointed out several differences in cultural style between whites and African Americans. We use these differences in the following discussion simply as an illustration of the influence of culture on values, norms, and expectations. We recognize, as does Irvine, that these attributes are neither representative of all African Americans nor all white Americans. It would, of course, be possible to use any other nondominant cultural group to illustrate such differences. With these caveats in mind, we now turn to some of the differences in style identified by Irvine.

African Americans tend to be higher keyed, more animated, more intense, and more confrontational than whites. African Americans tend to appreciate social contexts in which overlapping speech and participatory dialogue are used rather than turn taking in which only one person is free to speak at any given time. African Americans tend to favor passionate, emotional argumentation in defense of beliefs as opposed to the nonemotional, uninvolved, logical argumentation preferred by whites. African Americans tend to have a relational, field-dependent learning style as opposed to the analytical, field-independent style of learning characteristic of most whites. Whereas whites prefer confined or restricted movement, African Americans tend to learn better through freedom of movement. Finally, African Americans tend to have a much greater people focus than whites during learning activities and tend to favor modes of learning in which they interact with others. As a result of these differences in cultural style, African Americans often find their expressive behavior style criticized in contexts in which white standards of behavior prevail (Kochman, 1981).

Townsend (2000) suggested another aspect of behavior in which African American students and teachers often interpret events differently:

> African American students' task orientations may conflict with mainstream school culture. African American students have a propensity for "stage setting" behaviors before actually beginning tasks. Toward this end, they may execute ritual behaviors to prepare for tasks (e.g., sharpening pencils, straightening out papers, socializing with others, going to the bathroom) before beginning the task at hand. Yet methods to prepare for tasks that differ from those of the teacher provide further opportunities for misinterpretation. Teachers may mistakenly interpret those behaviors as signs of avoidance and assume that students are being noncompliant. (p. 383)

In situations in which white teachers find themselves teaching students from a nondominant culture, the reactions of teachers and students to differences in cultural style tend to be quite different and not understood by the other party. Teachers sometimes revert to what Irvine calls *cultural aversion*; that is, they pretend not to notice that their students have a different racial and ethnic identity and act as if there were no cultural differences. This behavior tends to increase conflict because the teachers fail to attempt to understand reasons for the students' behavior. Students also engage in behavior that tends to exacerbate the problem. They decide that certain behaviors are characteristic of white culture and therefore are not appropriate for blacks (Ogbu, 1988). They view cultural differences as symbols of cultural identity that must be maintained rather than as obstacles to communication that can be overcome. Seen from this perspective, failure to conform to teacher expectations and lack of effort toward achieving teacher-valued goals can be regarded as a form of resistance against cultural assimilation: "Somehow they have come to equate exemplary performance in school with a loss of their African American identity; that is, doing well in school is seen as 'acting white.' The only option, many believe, is to refuse to do well in school" (Ladson-Billings, 1994, p. 11). Although some students' desire to resist cultural assimilation explains their rejection of the white, middle-class culture's value of academic achievement, other minority students may be attempting to protect their self-esteem. Case 7.2 illustrates what can happen when minority students are placed in unfamiliar and uncomfortable educational settings.

Differences in values, norms, and expectations resulting from cultural differences have several implications for teachers. First, teachers must understand that schools are culturally situated institutions. The values, norms, and behaviors promoted by schools are never culturally neutral. They are always influenced by some particular cultural mind-set. Therefore, school and classroom rules and guidelines must be seen as culturally derived. Second, teachers should strive to learn more about the cultural

CASE 7.2

No One Looks Like Me

Maria is a black ninth-grade student whose family just recently immigrated from the Dominican Republic to the United States. Her schooling in her country was barely adequate and when compared to U.S. standards, she is reading and doing math at the fifth-grade level. She is now attending a predominately white middle-class school in a blue-collar, working-class community. In other words, she is now expected to learn and achieve in an environment that is significantly different from any previous educational setting she has experienced. At best, Maria is woefully unprepared to compete for grades as well as friends. Such an environment tends to diminish Maria's self-esteem; she does not feel significant, competent, or virtuous or that she has much power. In an attempt to raise her self-esteem, she seeks out and bonds with other minority students, behaves aggressively toward white classmates, rejects white values, and refuses to learn from her white teachers.

backgrounds of the students they teach. This can be accomplished by observing how students behave in other contexts, by talking to students about their behavior and allowing them to teach about their behavior, by involving parents and community members in the classroom, and by participating in community events and learning more about the institutions in the students' home community: "Students are less likely to fail in school settings where they feel positive about both their own culture and the majority culture and are not alienated from their own cultural values" (Cummins, 1986, quoted in Ladson-Billings, 1994, p. 11). Third, teachers should acknowledge and intentionally incorporate students' cultural backgrounds and expectations into their classrooms. When teacher rules and expectations conflict with student cultural expectations, it may be appropriate to reexamine and renegotiate rules and procedures. In a variety of studies in different settings and contexts and with students from different cultural groups (Native American, Hawaiian, Latino, African American), the findings are remarkably similar. When teachers incorporate language and participation patterns from the home and community into the classroom, relationships and academic learning improve significantly (Banks et al., 2005). At the very least, students need a clear rationale for why the rules and procedures are important. It goes without saying that the rationale for the rules should be in keeping with the four guidelines articulated earlier in the chapter. Finally, when students behave inappropriately, teachers should step back and examine the behavior in terms of the students' cultural background. Racial and cultural differences in the definition of good behavior, along with miscommunication, lead to inequitable punishment of students of color by school personnel who do not respect or understand the students' style of participation (Gathercoal, 1998). Using a different set of cultural lenses to view behavior may shed a very different light on the teacher's perceptions of individual students. Obviously, misbehavior that results from differences in cultural background and expectations should be handled quite differently from misbehavior that signifies intentional disruption on the part of the student.

CREATING GROUP NORMS TO STRUCTURE APPROPRIATE BEHAVIOR

Although students and teachers bring their own cultural backgrounds with them, each classroom tends to develop its own culture; that is, certain norms develop over time that exert a great influence on student behavior. During the early years of schooling, it is the teacher's wishes and behavior that create the norms for student behavior. However, as students grow older, they become the dominant influence in establishing the cultural norms within the given classroom. According to Johnson, Johnson, and Holubec (1993), the relationships that develop among peers in the classroom exert a tremendous influence on social and cognitive development and student socialization. In their interactions with peers, children and adolescents learn attitudes, values, skills, and information that are unobtainable from adults. Interaction with peers provides support, opportunities, and models for personal behavior. Through peer relationships, a frame of reference for perceiving oneself is developed. In both educational and work settings, peers influence productivity. Finally, students' educational aspirations are influenced more by peers than by any other social influence (Johnson et al., 1993).

Traditionally, teachers have ignored the notion of peer culture and group norms in the classroom. They have focused their attention on individual learners and have viewed influencing students to behave appropriately as an issue between the teacher and the individual student. As a result, the development of group norms among students has been left almost completely up to chance. However, evidence is growing that teachers can intervene to create group norms that will promote prosocial behavior as well as lead to peer relationships that will enhance the four components of self-esteem identified earlier: significance, power, competence, and virtue. Group norms can be facilitated early in the year when the teacher involves students in designing classroom guidelines. In addition, cooperative learning lessons (see Chapter 5) that include face-to-face interaction, positive interdependence, and individual accountability can help establish positive group norms. When teachers make a concentrated effort to help students develop the social skills necessary to function effectively as group members during cooperative learning activities, they enhance the power of these activities to create positive group norms.

Johnson et al. (1993) identified four sets of skills—forming skills, functioning skills, formulating skills, and fermenting skills—that students need to develop over time in order to function most effectively as a group. When these skills are in place and groups function successfully, group norms develop that lead students to (1) be engaged in learning activities, (2) strive toward learning and achievement, and (3) interact with each other in ways that will facilitate the development of positive self-esteem.

Forming skills are an initial set of management skills that are helpful in getting groups up and running smoothly and effectively. These skills include moving into groups quietly without bothering others, staying with the group rather than moving around the room, using quiet voices that can be heard by members of the group but not by others, and encouraging all group members to participate.

Functioning skills are group-management skills aimed at influencing the types of interactions that occur among group members. These skills include staying focused on the task, expressing support and acceptance of others, asking for help or clarification, offering to explain or clarify, and paraphrasing or summarizing what others have said.

Formulating skills refer to a set of behaviors that help students process material mentally. These skills include summarizing key points, connecting ideas to each other, seeking elaboration of ideas, finding ways to remember information more effectively, and checking explanations and ideas through articulation.

Finally, *fermenting skills* are needed to resolve cognitive conflicts that arise within the group. These skills include criticizing ideas without criticizing people, synthesizing diverse ideas, asking for justification, extending other people's ideas, and probing for more information.

Johnson et al. (1993) suggested that teachers teach these social skills just as they teach academic content. Therefore, when teachers plan a cooperative learning activity, they must plan social skill objectives as well as the academic objectives. Making the social skills explicit as lesson objectives helps focus both student and teacher attention on them. To do this, the teacher should explain the skill before the activity begins and make sure students know what the skill looks like and sounds like as it is expressed in behavior. Once the teacher is convinced that students understand the meaning of the skill, students may practice the skill during the cooperative learning activity. While the students are practicing, the teacher moves from group to group monitoring the use of the skill. When the activity has been completed, the teacher engages each group in reflecting on how successfully the skill was used and in setting goals for improving their use of the skill in the future. Although teaching social skills in addition to academic content takes time, the time is well spent for two reasons. First, many of these skills are exactly the kinds of skills students will need to help them succeed as adults. Second, when students are skilled at interacting with each other in positive ways, group norms develop in the classroom that are supportive of prosocial behavior and of engagement in appropriate learning activities.

RELATIONSHIPS

Student-Teacher Relationships

Student-teacher relationships are introduced now but will be covered in more detail in Chapters 10 and 11, in which it will be framed in terms of working with students who display chronic disruptive behavior. The good news is that if teachers can build positive relationships with all students early in the school year, the need for interventions for chronic discipline problems will be greatly reduced. The dictionary definition of *relationship* is the connection between two or more people and their involvement with one another, particularly in regard to how they feel about and behave toward one another. Student-teacher relationships involve teachers building positive relationships with students whereby students feel respected, supported, and cared about. Two questions arise: "How do teachers build such relationships?" and "Why are these relationships important?"

There are two ways to address the first question. We can hypothesize a list of teacher behaviors that produce positive student-teacher relationships (similar to the behaviors identified in Chapter 5). Next, train teachers to use these behaviors and then assess students' feelings and record their interactions with the teacher. The alternative approach is to identify situations in which students already have positive relationships with teachers and then observe and record the behaviors of their teachers. We will use a modification of the second method. Following are descriptions of four teachers and what they believe about students' abilities and motivation to control their behavior, what they do to prevent discipline problems and how they intervene when discipline problems arise.

Carefully read each teacher's description, keeping in mind how you would answer the following questions:

1. In which teacher's room would you most want to be?
2. With which teacher would you learn the most?
3. With which teacher would you most willingly cooperate?
4. Which teacher would you most likely seek help from for an academic problem?
5. Which teacher would you most likely seek help from for a personal problem?
6. With which teacher would you most willingly be best behaved?
7. If the teacher gave you a consequence for inappropriate behavior, with which teacher would you most likely blame yourself for the consequence rather than blame the teacher?

TEACHER A believes that students have the ability and responsibility to behave appropriately in the classroom. She believes that students will use their ability and accept responsibility for self-control when they are in environments in which the teacher shows sincere interest in students and shows respect for students' competence and opinions.

She displays the following behaviors in order to **prevent** discipline problems. She demonstrates that she is sincerely interested in the individual student as a unique and valuable person, shows respect for student opinions, and trusts the student to make appropriate choices. She cooperatively plans classroom guidelines with the class and seeks understanding of the guidelines and works on obtaining student consensus to follow the guidelines. Differences among students are recognized and respected in all student-teacher interactions.

When disruptive behavior occurs, she uses techniques, often nonverbal, that do not embarrass or draw undue attention to the student. She speaks to the student privately, uses empathy to understand the student's frame of mind, and encourages the student to problem solve in order to reassert self-control. She provides students many opportunities to correct their own behavior and when consequences are warranted, they are logically related to the inappropriate behavior, are intended to teach the student appropriate behavior, and are delivered in a respectful tone by giving students choices.

TEACHER B believes that students have the ability and responsibility to behave appropriately in the classroom. Further, she believes that students use their ability and accept responsibility for self-control when they are in classrooms in which the teacher designs exciting and meaningful learning environments.

She **prevents** discipline problems by using instructional techniques and planning instructional activities that increase the likelihood of student success and by making on-task behavior more interesting and meaningful than disruptive behavior. Differences among students are considered and respected because this is inherent in effective instruction. She most likely cooperatively plans classroom guidelines with the class and seeks understanding of the guidelines and works on obtaining student consensus to follow the guidelines.

When disruptive behavior occurs, as a result of her emphasis on effective instruction, she most likely uses techniques that redirect student interest to the lesson. When necessary, she uses a hierarchy of intervention that gives students many opportunities for correcting their own behavior. When consequences are warranted they are logically related to the inappropriate behavior, are intended to teach the student appropriate behavior, and are delivered in a respectful tone by giving students choices.

TEACHER C believes that students have the ability and responsibility to behave appropriately in the classroom. She believes students use their ability and accept responsibility for self-control when they are in environments in which the guidelines have been clearly explained and in which they clearly understand that the teacher is in charge.

She **prevents** discipline problems by clearly communicating to the students what her roles are as the teacher and what their roles are as students. In addition, she prepares a predetermined set of classroom guidelines that students are to follow. She is less likely to take individual student differences into account when formulating expectations for student behavior because individual differences are not mitigating circumstances when it comes to what is and what is not appropriate classroom behavior.

When disruptive behavior occurs, she likely uses techniques that remind the student that she, the teacher, is in charge, indicates which classroom guideline has been violated and shows the exact behavior that is required in the classroom. If the behavior does not change in a reasonable amount of time, punishments (usually removal of privileges, referral to administrators, or calling parents) are administered.

TEACHER D believes that students have the ability and responsibility to behave appropriately in the classroom. She believes that students use their ability and accept responsibility for self-control primarily when they are in environments in which the teacher uses reward and punishment (behavioral contingency plans) to influence student behavior.

She **prevents** disruptive behavior by designing a system of rewards and incentives for appropriate behavior and a system of increasingly unpleasant punishments for inappropriate behavior. She is not likely to take individual student differences into account when attempting to understand student behavior. In addition, she prepares a predetermined set of classroom guidelines that students are to follow along with predetermined consequences.

When disruptive behavior occurs, she may give a verbal reminder and then communicate to the student that a punishment is imminent if the behavior continues. If the student does not comply in a timely manner, the teacher administers the punishment.

The authors have taught many classes and lead many workshops where this activity was conducted for students, parents, teachers, and administrators. THE RESULTS ARE ALWAYS THE SAME:

1. In which teacher's room would you most want to be? The great majority of respondents select teacher A, followed by teacher B. Teachers C and D are never selected.
2. With which teacher would you learn the most? The majority select teacher B followed closely by teacher A. Teachers C and D are never selected.

3. With which teacher would you most willingly cooperate? The great majority of respondents select teacher A, followed by teacher B. Teachers C and D are never selected.

4. Which teacher would you most likely seek help from for an academic problem? The great majority of respondents select teacher B, followed by teacher A. Teachers C and D are never selected.

5. Which teacher would you most likely seek help from for a personal problem? The great majority of respondents select teacher A, followed by teacher B. Teachers C and D are never selected.

6. With which teacher would you most willingly be best behaved? Teachers A and B are usually equally divided. Teachers C and D are never selected.

7. If the teacher gave you a consequence for inappropriate behavior, with which teacher would you most likely blame yourself for the consequence rather than blame the teacher? The majority of respondents select teacher A, followed by teacher B. Teacher C sometimes is selected, but teacher D has never been chosen.

To summarize, given this set of questions, teachers A and B are always selected. Teachers C and D are never selected (except for question 7). Without much extrapolation, it is fairly safe to say that teachers A and B would enjoy positive relationships with their students. If you recall from Chapter 4 the four power or authority bases, it is obvious that teacher A believes in and practices referent authority. Teacher A attempts to influence students through building meaningful relationships based on trust, respect, care, and support. Teacher B believes in and practices expert authority. Teacher B attempts to influence students through her knowledge of her subject area

A teacher can redirect students to on-task behavior by the use of interest-boosting techniques.

and the use of excellent pedagogy. Teacher C believes in and uses legitimate authority. Teacher C attempts to influence her students by clearly delineating roles and rules that students must follow. Teacher D illustrates, believes in, and uses coercive authority. Teacher D attempts to influence students using behavioral contingency strategies. In other words, students are rewarded for doing what they are told and are punished for not obeying.

Probably the combination of referent and expert authority would maximize the outcomes of positive student-teacher relationships. Stipek (2006) substantiates this combination: "The key to raising achievement is connecting students with teachers who support them not just as learners [expert authority] but also as people [referent authority]" (p. 46).

Research indicates that effort is the key to learning, and one of the best predictors of effort is the relationship the student has with the teacher (Osterman, 2000). When students are asked "How do you know if a teacher cares about you"? younger students reply, "She says hi to me and smiles when I come in the room." "She saves a snack for me if I miss snack time." "When I get on the bus go home she says 'see you tomorrow.'" Older students perceive that the teacher cares when she expresses an interest in their out-of-school personal lives, treats them as individuals, treats them with respect, and is fair. Respect and trust are facilitated by teachers who give students autonomy and choices in designing classroom rules and choosing assignments and allow students to express their opinions in classroom discussions (Stipek, 2006).

Student-teacher relationships have also been examined as a factor related to students dropping out of school (Davis and Dupper, 2004). When students are asked why they left school, a common response is "no one cared." However, when students decide to stay in school, they often cite a meaningful relationship with a teacher, administrator, or staff member "who cared about the student as an individual" (National Research Council, 2004). Disruptive behavior has been mitigated by teachers who are perceived by students as being trustworthy and caring (Gregory and Ripski, 2008). After all, it is very difficult for a student to continue to disrupt classes and/or continue to be disrespectful toward teachers who in turn continually show students respect, care, and trust.

Building Student-Teacher Relationships

Most educators agree that positive student-teacher relations are important and result in positive academic gains with a reduction of discipline problems. Some teachers think that positive student-teacher relations refer to a teacher who treats students well but does not have high expectations. Nothing is further from the truth. Teachers who maintain good student-teacher relationships have high expectations and hold students accountable for meeting them. As noted in Chapter 5, teachers who are "warm demanders" demonstrate a sense of confidence and belief in student ability by communicating high expectations. But along with student accountability comes teacher accountability and the continual support of students' efforts. This section outlines a process that can be used by teachers to begin to build and maintain positive relationships with students. In Chapter 1, teaching was defined as a profession, which infers that there is a specialized body of knowledge that informs the practice of the profession. If teaching is a profession, which we believe it is, then teachers (professionals) use a specialized body of knowledge when making decisions about teaching

Touch is an effective intervention skill but one that can also produce student reactions.

and learning and designing instruction. Therefore, the often sought after list of "10 ways to get students to like and trust the teacher" is professionally inappropriate and inadequate for building positive student-teacher relationships. It is inappropriate because the teacher has not used any of her own professional knowledge to generate the list or to connect it to her knowledge and experience. Furthermore, the teacher is rarely afforded the opportunity to learn about the underlying bodies of knowledge and philosophical orientations from which the strategies are derived. So if an administrator or a parent asks in-depth questions regarding the use of the strategies on the list, the teacher is not prepared to reply.

A list of do's and don'ts is also inadequate because the strategies are assumed to be a one-size-fits-all model. The list does not consider the individual nature of students in a given classroom context. Additionally, it does not take into account the teacher's experience, philosophical orientation, or the knowledge the teacher has regarding each student. Lastly, what happens if the teacher reaches strategy 10 and some students are still not experiencing a positive relationship with the teacher, must the teacher search for the second list of "10 more ways to get students to like and trust the teacher"? Teachers who use a list of 10 behaviors are like bakers who can bake a cake only by following one specific recipe. If some ingredients on the list are missing, it is not possible to bake the cake. In contrast, those bakers who have in-depth knowledge about cake baking are able to use a variety of ingredients to bake many kinds of delicious cakes. Our goal then is to provide a deeper rather than a superficial understanding of relationship building. The end result will not be a list of answers provided for a one-size-fits-all application mentality, but rather a list of essential questions, informed by concepts from the professional knowledge base, that the teacher can use as a starting point to develop powerful strategies for building relationships. Unlike techniques that are context specific, the questions are applicable across contexts.

Building that deeper knowledge base requires a review of some previously discussed concepts that are powerful tools in thinking about relationship building. The body of knowledge that is relevant for building positive student-teacher relationships includes the power bases, motivation, and self-esteem.

Authority or power bases (see Chapter 4) refer to the different ways that teachers can influence students. To review, the four power bases are referent, expert, legitimate, and coercive. Referent power is influencing students by the teacher demonstrating respect, care, trust, and support of students. Expert power is influencing students by professional competency, meaning that the teacher knows her subject matter and knows how to teach it. Legitimate power is influencing students by using titles ("I'm your teacher"), and coercive power is influencing students through the use of rewards and punishments. For the purpose of building positive relationships with students, referent and expert power are emphasized because of the findings of the previous activity describing four teachers and the unanimous selection of the teachers who employed either the referent or expert power base.

Motivation (see Chapter 5) is conceptualized as student willingness to put forth effort to achieve a certain goal. Motivation (M) can be conceptualized as the product of expectation of success (E) times the value (V) of the desired outcome ($M = E \times V$). The expectation of success is highly influenced by the factors to which the students attribute success. If students perceive that success is attributable to the effort they put forth (e.g., studying well, time management) as opposed to other factors, students will believe that they have great control over their own success. This is referred to as an *internal locus of control* regarding expectations for success, and it increases student effort and motivation. On the other hand, if students attribute success to factors they cannot control such as the teacher is easy or it's my lucky day, then the students have an *external locus of control* regarding expectations for success that decreases effort and motivation.

Value refers to the importance the student places on the outcomes of successful efforts. Outcomes that are highly valued tend to increase motivation, but the full story is a bit more complicated. If students value the outcome because it satisfies their own goals (e.g., because they are interested in the activity or because they want to learn), they possess an *internal value structure*. On the other hand, if the students value the outcome primarily because it satisfies the goals of others (e.g., parents who want them to get good grades), they possess an *external value structure*. For the task of building positive relationships with students, fostering an expectation of success due to an internal locus of control and a high value due to an internal value structure is appropriate because these outcomes are congruent with the goal of student self-control. Referent and expert power bases are much more appropriate for developing an internal locus of control and an internal value structure than the other power bases, which tend to focus much more heavily on teacher control and rewards provided by the teacher.

Self-esteem refers to how one feels about oneself. It is the sum of significance, competence, virtue, and power. Significance is feeling a sense of belonging because of being liked, respected, and trusted by people who are important to the student.

Competence is feeling good because of being successful at tasks that are important to the student. Virtue is feeling good because the student is able and willing to help others. Power is feeling good because of having some control over the outcomes and goals of one's life. Referent authority clearly contributes to the students' sense of significance because of the positive nature of the relationship, the sense of power because of the focus on student self-control, and the sense of virtue by modeling caring behavior toward others. Expert authority clearly contributes to the sense of competence by emphasizing the role of teacher expertise in enhancing student academic success.

Having reviewed these key concepts, it is now time to begin developing and answering the essential questions that can be used to generate professional knowledge about building relationships. In keeping with our central theme of influencing student behavior by deliberately controlling teacher behavior, the essential questions and answers relate factors that are under the teacher's control (i.e., choice of authority bases) to achieve desired student outcomes. Tables 7.1 and 7.2 are used in that process. Table 7.1 analyzes the relationship-building process and generates questions about it, whereas the matching Table 7.2 generates teacher answers to the questions in the form of strategies that the teacher can employ.

Table 7.1 is a matrix composed of rows that represent teacher authority bases and columns that represent desired student outcomes in terms of both higher levels of intrinsic motivation (i.e., internal locus of control and internal value structure) and higher levels of the four components of self-esteem. The matrix can be used to analyze the relationship-building process and to generate the key questions that a professional teacher needs to answer in developing positive relationships with students. Using the plain language definition for each component, any given cell can be written as a question. Let's focus on cell A1 to illustrate the process. Cell A1 is the interaction between teacher use of referent authority and the development of expectations of success through an internal locus of control on the part of the student. To frame the question: (1) review the definition of referent authority, (2) review the definition of expectation of success by an internal locus of control, and (3) write a question using the two definitions.

1. Referent power = influencing students by the teacher demonstrating respect, care, and trust.
2. Expectation of success by internal locus of control = being successful using factors that are within the students' control.
3. Combining the two definitions the question is, "How can the teacher use respect, care, and trust to emphasize that students control the factors that lead to success?"

As is the case with all of the questions that can be framed using the various cells in the matrix, many answers to the question are possible. One specific answer in relation to cell A1 is that the teacher can teach a lesson on what expending effort to learn really means, list various ways that effort can be applied to learning and then begin to recognize students' effort and improvement rather than just giving a final grade for academic performance. This is referred to as *redefining success*. Rather than only the final grade being the measure of success, effort and resulting improvement are now seen as indicators of success. It's not that the grade is no longer important, because it is, but what the teacher is doing is tracing and recognizing the path to success; more

TABLE 7.1 Analysis of Student-Teacher Relationships: Authority Base by Student Outcomes

Authority Bases	Student Outcomes					
	Intrinsic motivation		Pro-social self-esteem			
	(1) Expectation of success: internal locus of control	**(2) Value:** internal value structure	**(3) Significance:** pro-social	**(4) Competence:** pro-social	**(5) Virtue** pro-social	**(6) Power:** pro-social
	Students control the factors leading to success	Students put forth effort to satisfy interests and enjoyment of learning	Feeling good because people like, respect, and support you	Feeling good because you are successful at a task important to you	Feeling good because you are able and willing to help others	Feeling good because you can control important aspects of your life
(A) Referent: influencing others by respect, care, support, etc.	How can the teacher use respect, care, and trust to emphasize that students control the factors that lead to success?					
(B) Expert: influencing others by using best professional pedagogy		How can the teacher use pedagogy to increase students' interests and enjoyment of learning?				How can a teacher use pedagogy to enable students to control certain aspects of the learning environment?

TABLE 7.2 Strategies to Build Positive Student-Teacher Relationships: Authority Base by Student Outcomes

Authority Bases	Student Outcomes					
	Intrinsic motivation		Pro-social self-esteem			
	(1) Expectation of success: internal locus of control	**(2) Value:** internal value structure	**(3) Significance:** pro-social	**(4) Competence:** pro-social	**(5) Virtue:** pro-social	**(6) Power:** pro-social
	Students control the factors leading to success	Students put forth effort to satisfy interests and enjoyment of learning	Feeling good because people like, respect, and support you	Feeling good because you are successful at a task important to you	Feeling good because you are able and willing to help others	Feeling good because you can control important aspects of your life
(A) Referent: influencing others by respect, care, support, etc.	The teacher can teach a lesson on effort and then begin to recognize effort and improvement rather than just the final grade for academic performance, which is what is typically recognized					
(B) Expert: influencing others by using best professional pedagogy						The teacher can design parallel assignments that accommodate different learning styles and allow students to choose which assignment they would like to use.

effort leads to improvement that is reflected in the grade. This strategy would be placed in the appropriate cell in Table 7.2. For a second illustration, let's turn to cell B6, which represents the interaction between expert authority and increasing student feelings of power. First, review the definition of expert authority. Second, review the definition of power. Third, write a question using the two definitions.

1. Expert authority = influencing students by use of expertise of content and pedagogy.
2. Power = having control over the goals and outcomes of one's life.
3. Combining the two definitions, the question is, "How can a teacher use pedagogy to enable students to control certain aspects of the learning environment?"

Again, there are many approaches. Because individualizing instruction requires expert authority, the teacher can design parallel assignments that accommodate different learning styles and allow students to choose which assignment they would like to use. Table 7.2 is used to record this strategy. Placing the strategy within the concepts in Table 7.2 clearly illustrates both the authority base and the desired student outcome that the strategy is meant to address. It is extremely helpful in talking with parents, teachers, or administrators or if you are looking to revise the strategies. Finally, it keeps teachers from falling back into a legitimate/coercive approach.

Some readers maybe wondering why the legitimate and coercive power bases have not been employed. There are two reasons. The first is that both bases employ extrinsic means to influence students. Legitimate authority uses titles and organizational hierarchies, and coercive authority employs rewards and punishments, which are antithetical to learning self-control and to the development of an internal locus of control and an internal value structure. Second, try designing strategies using the process outlined previously and illustrated with Tables 7.1 and 7.2. It becomes difficult at best and in some cases absurd. How can you build supportive, respectful, and trustworthy relationships by being the boss or by rewarding and punishing? For example, might one strategy be that the student will serve increasingly longer detentions until she believes that the teacher respects and supports her? Basically, legitimate and coercive power bases are not appropriate to obtain the outcomes of intrinsic motivation and prosocial self-esteem.

To wrap up this section, let's consider a relevant question that is commonly asked by students and workshop participants. Why go to all this trouble when you can go to the web and find many strategies that others have designed or follow the 10-item cookbook approach? The answer is multifaceted and has to do with the appropriateness and adequacy discussed earlier in this section. When designing complex strategies and interactions, the professional has to thoroughly understand the conceptualizations from which the strategies were derived. This is needed so that it can be explained to students, parents, and other professional educators. Strong student-teacher relationships do not occur overnight; working at developing them requires patience and a strong desire to succeed, which come only from ownership of the designed strategy. Additionally, the use of the concepts represented in Tables 7.1 and 7.2 is generative, that is, their use allows the professional teacher to generate new ideas and strategies independently or in collaboration with others as opposed to being dependent on some external authority to suggest the strategies. Like students, teachers also need an expectation of success, value, and a feeling of prosocial self-esteem. These outcomes are brought about by not copying others but by improving upon the ideas of others and also creating positive student-teacher relationships on your own.

Finally, some teachers may ask why they should put all this effort into building positive student-teacher relationships. They have some students so hardened that no one could get through to them. In education, no approach is 100 percent effective. We look for methodologies that impact more students than before. Don't make the mistake of doing nothing because all you could do was a little. This brings to mind a famous quote attributed to Helen Keller, "I am only one, but I am one! I can't do everything, but I can do something! Because I cannot do everything, I will not refuse to do what I can do" (***http://thinkexist.com/***).

Family-Teacher Relationships

BENEFITS Family-teacher relationships are introduced now and will be revisited in more detail in Chapter 11, in which this relationship is examined in the context of working with students who display chronic disruptive behavior. The good news is that if teachers can be proactive and build positive relations with all families early in the school year, the need for interventions for chronic discipline problems will be greatly reduced.

A growing body of research indicates that when families are involved in their children's education, the children earn higher grades, have better attendance, have higher rates of homework completion, are more motivated, and have more positive attitudes about school. There is also a decrease in students exhibiting behavior (e.g., substance abuse, violence) that is predictive of later serious antisocial behavior as parent involvement increases (Darsch, Miao, and Shippen, 2004). The benefits afforded students when parents and teachers have positive working relationships, when parents are welcomed as a team member, and when parents get involved in their child's education crosses both racial and socioeconomic status lines. Indeed, the most accurate predictor of a student's achievement in school is the extent that parents become involved in their children's education, not racial background, marital status, PARENTS education, and so on (Henderson and Berla, 1997).

Teachers also benefit from a positive relationship with parents. The benefits include improved behavior in the classroom, greater job satisfaction, and higher ratings from parents and administrators (American Federation of Teachers, 2007).

Reluctance to Contact Parents

Given all the benefits and few if any downsides, teachers are still reluctant to contact parents for a number of reasons, including the following:

1. *Lack of training* Very few, if any, teacher education programs cover in any significant depth how to work effectively with families. Therefore, it is understandable that the newer teacher would be anxious about making contact with parents.

2. *Age difference* It is not uncommon especially with newer teachers that the parents are older than they are. Coming from a culture in which younger people typically defer to older people out of respect, the younger teacher may feel particularly uncomfortable, especially if the teacher is called upon to suggest actions that the parents should take at home.

3. Time   Teachers are busy planning before and after class and also during their prep time. Interacting with parents can be time consuming, especially if the parents are working and message after message goes unanswered.

4. Legacies   Some families have attended the same schools for generations and over that time developed a legacy, which could be positive or negative. Teachers are disconcerted by those families with a negative legacy of disruptive behavior. A teacher could hear the following in the teachers' lounge:

> I had Tom Sr. and was he ever a challenge, at least I though he was till Tom Jr. showed up on my class list. You talk about seeds not falling far from the tree. Did you know that Tom Jr. hooked up with Sally, who is a story in herself and now we have little Billy about to run havoc in the middle school.

Billy's mom and dad and grandfather all had problems in the same school. How cooperative do you think they will be when a teacher calls to discuss Billy's poor grades and unacceptable behavior? How motivated do you think teachers will be to make the contact?

5. Cultural differences   The majority of teachers continue to be white, middle-class women. Although this is changing, the change is not as rapid as the changes occurring in our students. It is not uncommon that in a class of 25 students, more than half are from different races or economic backgrounds. Rothstein–Fisch and Trumbull (2008) suggest that reaching out to parents can be a culture-bridging activity. They report several strategies that have proven effective in encouraging parents from diverse cultural backgrounds to become more involved in activities at school: (a) reaching out to talk informally with parents at the school door, (b) having the children write letters inviting their parents to school events, and (c) using back-to-school nights as an opportunity to take family photos. Language barriers may also exist that make communications with the parents more difficult. For example, in Case 7.3, both the teacher and the counselor thought that the mother fully understood the situation only to find out that there seemed to be a total lack of understanding.

CASE 7.3
The Doctor Said He Was OK

A fifth-grade teacher had a student from Cambodia. She requested a meeting with his mother to discuss what the teacher and counselor thought might be a learning disability that interfered with his reading skills. After explaining the problem, they agreed that the reading specialist would be consulted, recommendations would be made, and another meeting would be held with the mother before any final decisions were made. The mother left and thanked the teacher and counselor. The teacher and counselor felt good about the meeting, and they thought that the mother fully understood the problem, the upcoming consultation with the reading specialist, and the follow-up meeting. What a surprise when the mother called a few days later and left a message that she took her son to the doctor for a checkup, and he is not sick, so there is no need for another meeting.

Building Parent-Teacher Relationships

Because of the many benefits of having positive parent-teacher relationships and the necessity of having positive proactive interactions with parents before any contacts are made regarding disruptive behavior, it is in everyone's best interest to overcome the challenges noted earlier. The need to be proactive in regard to working effectively with students who pose chronic problems cannot be stressed enough. Unfortunately, when parents are contacted by the school or by a teacher, it is usually with bad news. If it's the nurse, your child is sick. If it's the vice-principal, your child was removed from class, usually because of disruptive behavior. If it's the teacher, it is because of discipline problems or poor grades. At one workshop's break, the authors overheard two attendees speaking, "I'm even a teacher and when I get a call from my child's school, I get so nervous, my mind starts racing—what did my kid do now?"

Needless to say that when the time arrives that we are requesting parents' assistance with a chronic problem, most parents would be unreceptive if all they have ever heard from the school are negative complaints about their child. On the other hand, if teachers are proactive and positive, then most parents would willingly help out or at leas be supportive of the teacher's efforts because they view the school in a positive light and the teacher is perceived as trying to help their child.

A review of research on parental involvement in schools by Hoover-Dempsey and Sandler (1997) suggested that three major factors influence parents' decisions about whether or not to become involved in their child's education. The first factor is role construction, that is, parents' beliefs about their role as parents as it relates to providing home support for school endeavors. A second key factor is parents' sense of efficacy concerning their ability to help their child be successful in school. The third key factor is the parents' perceptions of the general invitation for parental involvement in the school and classroom. Schools can influence parental choice of involvement by engaging in activities that affect these three perceptions. Consistently advocating that parental involvement is a critical factor in school success can affect parental role perception. Conducting workshops, classes, and courses on parental effectiveness can increase parents' sense of efficacy. Finally, making sure that both the general school climate and individual classroom climate welcome parental involvement can influence parents to become more actively involved in their child's education. Even the most well-designed program for parents will not reach its potential impact unless it clearly addresses these three factors: role construction, sense of efficacy, and general invitation.

The foundation upon which a family-teacher relationship is built should be laid even before classes start in the fall and should continue throughout the school year. Following are a few of the hundreds of different efforts that can be made to build positive family-teacher relationships. These are mostly teacher initiated, but a school can also develop special programs that encompass the whole school (cyberbullying), subject areas (a new mathematics curriculum), or grade levels (preparing for middle school).

Before school starts and once the teacher receives a class list, she can write a letter of introduction to both students and parents. The letter should introduce the teacher summarize the class and curriculum and express optimism about what a great year it will be. Some teachers arrive at school a few days early to get their room ready and set up bulletin boards. If your school allows it, invite parents and students to stop by and introduce themselves.

Once school starts, send "good news" notes home to recognize real effort, achievement, and improvement. Another excellent strategy is to set up a website where the teacher can list homework, rules, curriculum, study skills, and so on and also how parents can initiate contact with the teacher. It is important to enthusiastically encourage families to attend back-to-school programs. In elementary school, birthday greetings to your students are warmly received by both students and parents. Unsolicited phone calls to parents recognizing a student accomplishment or good deed or just communicating your enjoyment in working with their child takes only a few minutes but means a lot to parents. Throughout the year, provide opportunities for those parents who wish to volunteer to help in the classroom or to share their special expertise. All correspondence with parents should be professionally written with no spelling or grammatical errors. If the correspondence addresses a problem, it should be positive, encouraging, and optimistic about the future. Finally, the problem being addressed should not be of a trivial nature. The correspondence should engender in parents a desire to help; however, all too often parents read it and are puzzled as to why the teacher has sent this letter home. They believe that she should be able to manage this behavior herself. Case 7.4 is a letter sent home by a sixth-grade teacher who was starting to experience problems with homework completion and inattentiveness in the classroom.

If you were a parent and received the letter shown in Case 7.4, how would you feel? Would you be motivated to support this teacher? Would you be glad that your child was in this teacher's classroom? How convinced are you the teacher's statement "I will do what is needed to help your child be successful academically"? Who does it seem the teacher is blaming for incomplete homework? Is it clear to you what exactly the teacher is concerned about?

CASE 7.4

Not Doing Homework

Talking in the classroom and off-task behavior have started to interfere with our making progress with the curriculum. I am encouraging you to speak to your child about the importance of being focused during the school day and when completing home assignments. Handing in quality work and meeting requirements are a strong focus in both homework and class work now that students have gained and practiced study skills. If your child chooses to interfere with learning, I will be calling you to meet with your child and me. I will do what is needed to help your child be successful academically.

There will be daily homework assignments. The homework policy will be strictly enforced. I will be taking time each day to individually check assignments. If your child has chosen not to complete the homework on the due date, the student has chosen to reduce the highest possible grade to be earned.

Homework at this time of the year is a prerequisite activity for the next day's content work in the classroom. Be assured that I will give your child the needed materials and background knowledge and model the thinking and working process to allow the student to independently complete work.

A cautionary note: be proactive in developing family-teacher relationships before there are any problems. Having a proactive relationship will be beneficial if a student becomes disruptive later in the school year. The model supports the notion of student self-control. Therefore, unlike many of the models used today, we disagree with the advice of that the teacher should contact parents at the first sign of a discipline problem. Instead, as we see it, building a proactive relationship comes first and contacting parents about problems comes much later after a number of teacher interactions that will be discussed in Chapters 8–11. Remember that we build these relationships to be proactive. The authors find the sending of the letter in Case 7.4 and its content and tone inappropriate; do you see why?

Summary

Classrooms and schools are never culturally neutral or value free; they are always situated within a particular cultural context. When the culture of the school and the culture of the students are synchronized, positive behavior increases and positive relationships are established between teachers and students. However, when teachers and students hold differing values, norms, and behavioral expectations, the potential for misunderstanding, conflict, and mistrust are greatly enhanced.

Each classroom also develops its own culture with its own set of group norms and values. Traditionally, teachers have ignored the communal aspects of classroom life, focusing instead on individual relationships. Evidence now indicates that the use of cooperative learning activities that contain all essential elements combined with the teaching of pro-social skills will lead to the establishment of group norms that are supportive of appropriate student behavior.

The benefits to students when the teacher builds positive relations with students and their parents include better academic achievement and better behavior. A model derived from power bases, motivation, and self-esteem is a valuable planning tool when designing student-teacher relationships.

Having a positive working relationship with parents that emphasizes home support for school endeavors is important. When parents have the ability to help and the school welcomes and encourages their involvement, the likelihood increases that parents will be cooperative and supportive if discipline problems arise in the future.

Exercises

1. How do differences in cultural values, norms, and behavioral expectations influence the development of teacher expectations for student achievement?
2. What are some traditional teacher behavioral expectations that may conflict with the cultural norms of some students?
3. For each of the following social skills, develop an explanation of what the social skill means for students at the third-grade level, at the seventh-grade level, and at the eleventh-grade level:

   a. Encouraging everyone to participate
   b. Paraphrasing what others have said
   c. Seeking elaboration
   d. Asking for justification for ideas

4. Using the definitions of the authority bases, motivation, and self-esteem, complete Table 7.1 by writing appropriate sentence for each vacant cell.
5. Using the questions for each cell from the completed Table 7.1, design an instructional strategy for each vacant cell and complete Table 7.2.

6. Critically analyze the letter in Case 7.4 using what you have learned about building positive parent-teacher relationships.

7. Rewrite the letter in Case 7.4 using what you have learned about building positive parent-teacher relationships.

8. Using what you have learned about building positive parent-teacher relationships, complete the table that follows by listing possible efforts that met the criteria and the timeline:

Criteria	Before School Begins	During the School Year
Role Construction: home support for school endeavors		
Efficacy: parents are capable of helping child be successful in school		
General Invitation: schools welcome parental involvement		

9. **Principles of Teacher Behavior** After reading Chapter 7 and doing the exercises, use what you have learned to briefly describe your understanding of the implications of the principles listed at the beginning of the chapter for a classroom teacher.

Principle 1:

Principle 2:

Principle 3:

Principle 4:

Using the concepts from Chapters 5–7, complete the third analysis of the iterative case studies on the next page.

Iterative Case Study Analyses

Third Analysis

Considering the concepts discussed in the Prevention section, Chapters 4–7, review your second analysis. What has changed and what has stayed the same since your last analysis? Once again, consider why the students may be choosing to behave inappropriately and how you might intervene to influence the students to stop the disruptive behavior and resume appropriate on-task behavior.

Elementary School Case Studies

"I don't remember"   During silent reading time in my fourth-grade class, I have built in opportunities to work individually with students. During this time, the students read to me and practice word work with flash cards. One student has refused to read to me but instead only wants to work with the flash cards. After a few times I suggested we work with flash cards this time and begin reading next time. He agreed. The next time we met, I reminded him of our plan, and he screamed, "I don't remember. I want to do word cards." At this point, I tried to find out why he didn't like reading and he said, "There's a reason, I just can't tell you," and he threw the word cards across the room, some of them hitting other students. What should I do?

"Let's do it again"   Cathy is in my third-grade class. Whenever I ask the class to line up for recess, lunch, or to change classes, Cathy is always the last to get in line. When she does, she pushes, shoves and touches the other students. When this happens, I usually demand that all the children return to their seats, and we repeatedly line up again and again until Cathy lines up properly. I thought that peer pressure would cause Cathy to change her behavior, but, instead, it has resulted in my students being late to "specials" and having less time for recess and lunch.

Middle School Case Studies

"It makes me look cool"   I can't stop thinking about a problem I'm having in class with a group of 12-year-old boys. They consistently use vulgar language toward one another and some of the shy kids in the class, especially the girls. In addition, they are always pushing and shoving one another. I've tried talking to them about why they keep using bad language when they know it's inappropriate.

The response I get is that "it makes me look cool and funny in front of my friends." I have asked them to please use more appropriate language in the classroom, but that has not worked. I haven't even started to deal with the pushing and shoving. What should I do?

"My parents will be gone all weekend"   One of my seventh-grade girls was passing notes to a boy two rows over. After the second note, I made eye contact with her and it stopped for about half an hour. When I saw her getting ready to pass another note, I went over to her desk and asked her to give me the note and told her that that the note passing had to stop. She looked very upset, but she did give me the note. I folded it and put it in my desk drawer. When class ended, she ran out of the room crying. My personal policy is not to read students' notes but, instead, to give it back to the student at the end of class or throw it away. However, this time, maybe because of her reaction, something told me to read the note. It said, "Mike my parents will be away Saturday night don't you and John sleep over will be fun. I promise I'll do whatever you want me to do and that you and John can do anything you want to me." What should I as the teacher do?

High School Case Studies

"Homo"   This past week I had a student approach me about a problem he was experiencing in our class. This eleventh-grade student had recently "come out" as a homosexual. He said he was tired and upset with the three boys who sit near him. These boys frequently call him a "homo" and a "fag" every time they see him, both in and out of class.

"Why don't you get out of my face?"   A twelfth-grade student came up to me the first day of class and said, "My name is Ted. I don't want to be here, so just leave me alone and we'll get along just fine." I did not react to his comment but, instead, said, "After you see what we will be learning, I think you will find the class interesting." Ted walked away and took a seat in the back of the room. Later that week, I noticed Ted was reading a magazine while everyone else was working on an in-class assignment. Without making it obvious I walked by Ted's desk and quietly asked him to put away the magazine and to begin working on the assignment. Ted turned to me and said, "Maybe you don't understand; I asked you not to bother me. I'm not bothering you so why don't you get out of my face."

8

Using Nonverbal Interventions to Influence Students to Behave Appropriately

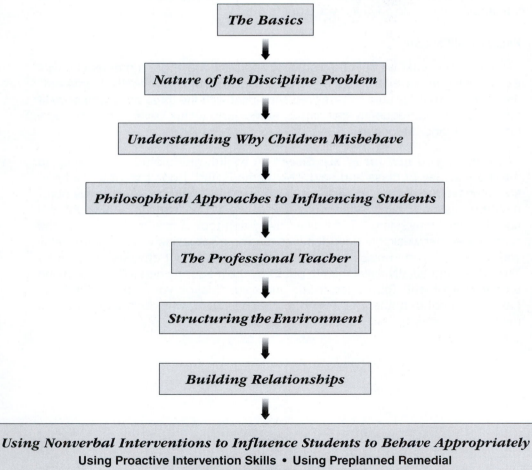

The Basics

Nature of the Discipline Problem

Understanding Why Children Misbehave

Philosophical Approaches to Influencing Students

The Professional Teacher

Structuring the Environment

Building Relationships

Using Nonverbal Interventions to Influence Students to Behave Appropriately
**Using Proactive Intervention Skills • Using Preplanned Remedial
Nonverbal Intervention**
• Planned Ignoring • Signal Interference • Proximity Interference • Touch Interference

PRINCIPLES OF TEACHER BEHAVIOR THAT INFLUENCE APPROPRIATE STUDENT BEHAVIOR

1. Classroom intervention techniques need to be consistent with the goal of helping students become self-directing individuals.

2. Use of a preplanned hierarchy of remedial interventions skills improves the teacher's ability to influence students exhibiting common behavior problems to behave appropriately.

3. The use of a hierarchy that starts with nonintrusive, nonverbal teacher behaviors gives students the opportunity to exercise self-control, minimizes disruption to the teaching/learning process, reduces the likelihood of student confrontation, protects students' safety, and maximizes the teacher's alternative interventions.

PREREADING ACTIVITY: UNDERSTANDING THE PRINCIPLES OF TEACHER BEHAVIOR

Before reading Chapter 8, briefly describe your understanding of the implications of the principles for a classroom teacher.

Principle 1:

Principle 2:

Principle 3:

PREREADING QUESTIONS FOR REFLECTION AND JOURNALING

1. In the middle of a lesson you are teaching, you notice student engagement waning. What would you do?

2. What are the advantages and disadvantages of using nonverbal interventions to deal with disruptive behavior?

3. How would you judge whether a teacher has handled inappropriate student behavior effectively?

INTRODUCTION

In most classrooms, the majority of student misbehaviors are verbal interruptions, off-task behavior, and disruptive physical movements. These behaviors, which are sometimes called *surface behaviors*, are present in every classroom in every school almost every day. With proper planning, instructional strategies, and human and physical environmental structuring, the frequency of surface behaviors is reduced greatly. However, no matter how much time and energy the teacher directs toward prevention, surface behaviors do not disappear and to some extent are an ever-present, continuing fact of life for all teachers.

The successful teacher can use many intervention skills to deal with surface behaviors in a manner that is effective, expedient, and least disruptive to the teaching/learning process. These skills are organized in a decision-making hierarchy of three tiers: (1) nonverbal behaviors, (2) verbal behaviors, and (3) consequences. Each tier consists of individual skills, which are themselves hierarchically ordered. The dimensions on which these sub-hierarchies are developed are the degree of intrusiveness and the potential for disruption to the teaching/learning environment. When these intervention skills are applied in a preplanned, systematic manner, they have been shown to be quite effective (Shrigley, 1980, 1985).

This chapter discusses nonverbal skills, the first tier in the decision-making hierarchy. This group of skills is the least intrusive and has the least potential for disrupting the teaching/learning process while leaving the teacher with the maximum number of intervention alternatives for future use.

PREREQUISITES TO INTERVENTION

All too often, teachers are quick to place total responsibility for inappropriate behavior on their students without carefully analyzing their own behavior. It is quite common to hear teachers say, "There's nothing I can do; all they want to do is fool around" or "These kids are impossible; why even try!" Such comments clearly indicate that teachers have assigned all blame for student misbehavior to the students themselves. However, effective teaching and maximum learning occur in classrooms when teachers and students understand that teaching/learning is the responsibility of both the student and the teacher.

The responsibilities of the students are obvious. Students must prepare for class, study, ask questions to enhance their understanding, and remain on task. Many of the preventive techniques discussed in previous chapters, as well as the intervention techniques to be discussed in this chapter, assist students in accepting responsibility for their learning. However, students more readily accept their responsibilities when it is clear to them that the teacher is fulfilling his responsibilities. These professional responsibilities, which have been discussed in previous chapters, are the basic minimum competencies that all teachers must possess. They are the prerequisites to appropriate teacher interventions:

1. The teacher is well prepared to teach. Prior to class, he has designed specific learning objectives and effective teaching strategies based on accepted principles of learning.
2. The teacher provides clear directions and explanations of the learning material.
3. The teacher clearly explains the importance of the material to be learned, ideally as to how it relates to students' lives.
4. The teacher ensures that students understand evaluation criteria.
5. The teacher clearly communicates, rationalizes, and consistently enforces behavioral expectations.
6. The teacher demonstrates enthusiasm and encouragement and models the behaviors expected from students.
7. The teacher builds positive, caring relationships with students.

Martin Haberman (1995) described competent and effective teachers as those who accept "their responsibility to find ways of engaging their students in learning….[and their responsibility for]…the continuous generation and maintenance of student interests and involvement" (p. 22).

When teachers reinforce the concept of shared responsibility for teaching and learning through their behavior, intervention techniques, if needed, are more likely to be effective in encouraging appropriate student behavior.

SURFACE BEHAVIORS

The most common day-to-day disruptive behaviors are verbal interruptions (talking, humming, laughing, calling out, whispering), off-task behaviors (daydreaming, sleeping, combing hair, playing with something, doodling), physical movement intended to disrupt (visiting, passing notes, sitting on the desk or on two legs of the chair, throwing paper), and disrespect (arguing, teasing, vulgarity, talking back) (Huber, 1984; Levin, 1980; Shrigley, 1980; Thomas et al., 1983; Weber and Sloan, 1986). These disruptive behaviors, which are usually readily observable to an experienced teacher, are called *surface behaviors* because they usually are not a result of any deep-seated personal problem but are normal developmental behaviors of children.

Some teachers are able to intervene appropriately, almost intuitively, with surface behaviors. They have usually referred to it as multitasking in everyday language, which is attending to two matters at the same time, and "with-it-ness," a subtle nonverbal communication to students that the teachers are aware of all activities within the classroom (Kounin, 1970). Other teachers acquire these skills through hard work and experience. Teachers who do not have or do not develop these skills have to deal with abnormally high frequencies of surface behaviors, and in some instances, as in Case 8.1, the absence of these skills actually causes disruptive behavior.

CASE 8.1

"… 3, 2, 1, Blast Off"

The students in Mr. Berk's seventh-grade English class have science before English. Today, their science teacher illustrated the concept of propulsion by folding a piece of tin foil around the tip of a match. When he heated the tin foil, the match was ignited and accelerated forward.

During English class, Mickey, seated in the back row, decides to try the propulsion experiment. It is not long before many students are aware of Mickey's activity and are sneaking glances at him. Mickey is enjoying the attention and continues to propel matches across his desk.

It does not take Mr. Berk long to become aware that many of his students are not paying attention. Instead of attempting to determine what the distraction is, he reacts impulsively. He sees Terri turn around to look at Mickey and says, "Terri, turn around and pay attention!" Terri immediately fires back, "I'm not doing anything." The class begins to laugh because only Mr. Berk is unaware of the propulsion activity in the back of the room.

PROACTIVE INTERVENTION SKILLS

Effective teachers are experts in the matter-of-fact use of not only multitasking and with-it-ness skills but also other more specific and narrower proactive intervention skills. Their expertise can be seen in the way they employ these skills with little, if any, disruption in the teaching/learning process. Developing expertise in the use of the following proactive skills should lessen the need for more intrusive intervention techniques:

1. ***Changing the pace of classroom activities.*** Rubbing eyes, yawning, stretching, and staring out the window are clear signs that a change of pace is needed. This is the time for the teacher to restructure the situation and involve students in games, stories, or other favorite activities that require active student participation and help refocus student interests. On the other hand, if students are getting too noisy or too off-task during a particular interactive learning situation, the teacher might decide to change the pace to a more individual seat work activity. To reduce the need for on-the-spot, change-of-pace activities, lesson plans should provide for a variety of learning experiences that accommodate the attention spans and interests of the students both in time and in type.

2. ***Removing seductive objects.*** This skill may be used with little, if any, pause in the teaching act. However, there should be an agreement that the objects will be returned after class. Teachers who find themselves competing with cell phones, magazines, or combs may simply walk over to the student, collect the object, and quietly inform the student that it will be available after class.

3. ***Interest boosting of a student who shows signs of off-task behavior.*** Rather than using other, less-positive techniques, the teacher shows interest in the student's work, thereby bringing the student back on task. Interest boosting is often called for when students are required to do individual or small-group class work. During these times, the potential for chatter, daydreaming, or other off-task behaviors is high. If the teacher observes a student engaging in activities other than the assigned math problems, for example, he can boost the interest of the student by walking over to the student and asking how the work is going or checking the answers of the completed problems. Asking the student to place correct problems on the board is also effective. Whatever technique is decided on, it must be employed in a matter-of-fact supportive manner to boost the student's interest in the learning activity.

4. ***Redirecting the behavior of off-task students.*** This skill helps refocus the student's attention. Students who are passing notes, talking, or daydreaming may be asked to read, do a problem, or answer a question. When this technique is used, it is important to treat the student as if he were paying attention. For instance, if you call on the off-task student to answer a question and the student answers correctly, give positive feedback. If he doesn't answer or answers incorrectly, reformulate the question or call on someone else. A teacher who causes the student embarrassment or ridicule by stating "You would know where we were if you were paying attention" invites further misbehavior, and this is, in fact, a punishment with all the accompanying negative effects. The "get back on task" message the teacher is sending is clearly received by the off-task student whether or not he answers the question or finds the proper reading place and does not require any negative comments.

5. *Nonpunitive time-out.* This skill should be used for students who show signs of encountering a provoking, painful, frustrating, or fatiguing situation. The teacher quietly asks the student if he would like to get a drink or invites him to run an errand or do a chore. The change in activity gives the student time to regain his control before reentering the learning environment. Teachers must be alert to the signs of frustration so they can act in a timely fashion to help students.

6. *Encouraging the appropriate behavior of other students.* A statement such as "I'm glad to see that most of you have your books open" reminds off-task students of the behavior that is expected of them.

7. *Providing cues for expected behaviors.* Cues can be quite effective in obtaining the desired behavior, but the teacher must be sure that all students understand the cue. For example, a teacher who expects students to be in their seats and prepared for class when the bell rings must make sure that everyone understands that the bell signals the start of class. In schools without bells or other indicators, closing the door is an appropriate cue. Some teachers flick the lights to cue a class that the noise has reached unacceptable levels. Using the same cues consistently usually results in quick student response.

REMEDIAL INTERVENTION SKILLS

The masterful use of proactive skills diffuses many surface behaviors and causes minimal disruptions to the teaching act. However, there will always be classroom situations that induce misbehavior or students who continue to display disruptive behaviors.

These behaviors may range from mildly off-task to very disruptive. Mastering the delivery of the intervention skills discussed here and in Chapters 9 and 10 should help produce an exceptional classroom in which misbehavior is minimized and teachers are free to teach and children are free to learn.

Before any intervention may be used, the teacher must have a basis on which to make decisions concerning common inappropriate behaviors in the classroom. To avoid inconsistency and arbitrariness, teachers must also have a systematic intervention plan of predetermined behaviors that clearly communicates disapproval to the student who calls out, throws paper, walks around, passes notes, or in any way interferes with the teaching or learning act (Canter, 1989; Lasley, 1989). This follows our definition of teaching presented in Chapter 1: *the conscious use of predetermined behaviors that increase the likelihood of changing student behaviors.*

The intervention decision-making approach is a sequence of hierarchically ordered teacher behaviors. Because we believe that students must learn to control their own behavior, the initial interventions are subtle, nonintrusive, and student centered. Although these behaviors communicate disapproval, they are designed to provide students with the opportunity to control their own behavior. If the misbehaviors are not curbed, the interventions become increasingly more intrusive and teacher centered; that is, the teacher takes more responsibility for managing the students' behavior.

Because we also believe that intervention techniques should not in themselves disrupt the teaching and learning act (Brophy, 1988), early intervention behaviors are almost a private communication between the teacher and the off-task student. It alerts the student to his inappropriate behavior but causes little, if any, noticeable disruption to either teaching or learning. If these nonverbal interventions, which make up the first tier of the decision-making hierarchy, are not successful, the second and third tiers follow: teacher verbal behaviors and consequences. These tiers are increasingly more teacher centered and more intrusive and may cause some interruption to the teaching/learning act. (These techniques are discussed in Chapters 9 and 10.)

The decision-making hierarchy described here and in the following two chapters is intended to be a dynamic model, not one that binds a teacher into a lock-step, sequential, cookbook intervention approach. Instead, the model requires the teacher to make a decision as to which intervention in the hierarchy to employ first. The decision should depend on the type and frequency of the disruptive behavior and should be congruent with the five implementation guidelines that follow. These guidelines should help ensure that any beginning intervention, as well as those that may follow, meets the two foundational precepts of the hierarchy: increasing student self-control and decreasing disruptions to the teaching and learning environment.

1. The intervention provides a student with opportunities for the self-control of the disruptive behaviors. Self-control is not developed to its fullest in classrooms where teachers immediately intervene with teacher-centered techniques to influence student behavior. Because we believe individuals make conscious choices to behave in certain ways and that individuals cannot be forced to learn or exhibit appropriate behavior, early interventions should not force students but rather influence them to manage themselves. Students must be given responsibility in order to learn responsibility.

2. The intervention does not cause more disruption to the teaching and learning environment than the student's disruptive behavior itself. We have all witnessed teacher interventions that were more disruptive to the class than the off-task student behavior. This usually occurs when the teacher uses an intervention too far up the decision-making hierarchy. For example, the teacher chooses to use a public verbal technique when a private nonverbal intervention would be more effective and less disruptive. When this happens, the teacher becomes more of a disruptive factor than the student.

3. The intervention lessens the probability that the student will become more disruptive or confrontational. Interventions should lessen and defuse confrontational situations. When teachers choose to employ public, aggressive, or humiliating techniques, they increase the likelihood of escalating confrontations and power struggles. Again, deciding where in the decision-making hierarchy to begin has a significant effect on whether or not a disruptive student will be brought back on task or will become confrontational.

4. The intervention protects students from and does not cause physical and psychological harm. When a teacher observes behaviors that could be harmful to any student, intervention should be swift and teacher centered. In such situations, nonverbal techniques are usually bypassed for the assertive delivery of verbal interventions. In all cases, we must be careful that the interventions are not in themselves a source of harm to students or to the teacher.

5. The choice of the specific intervention maximizes the number of alternatives left for the teacher to use if it becomes necessary. Every teacher knows that it often takes more than one intervention to influence student behavior. It is rare that disruptive behavior is noted, a teacher intervention occurs, and the student is back on-task forever. It is the unwise teacher who sends a student out of the classroom for the first occurrence of a disruptive behavior. Such an intervention leaves few options available to the teacher if the student continues to misbehave when he returns. By using the decision-making hierarchy of intervention skills, the teacher reserves many alternative interventions.

It is important to remember that the teacher's goal in employing any remedial intervention skill is to redirect the student to appropriate behavior. Stopping the misbehavior may be the initial step in the process, but it is not sufficient. The teacher's goal is not reached until the student becomes reengaged in learning activities. Thus, whenever the teacher is introduced to a new technique for dealing with disruptive behavior, one of the questions he should ask in determining whether to employ the technique is, "Is this technique likely to redirect the student to appropriate behavior?"

The first tier of the hierarchy of remedial intervention skills, nonverbal skills, consists of four techniques: planned ignoring, signal interference, proximity interference, and touch interference. Redl and Wineman (1952) first identified these body-language interventions. When they are used randomly, effective redirection of minor disruptions is not fully achieved. However, when they are consciously employed in a predetermined logical sequence, they serve to curb milder forms of off-task behavior (Shrigley, 1985).

Planned Ignoring

Planned ignoring is based on the reinforcement theory that if you ignore a behavior, it will lessen and eventually disappear. Although this sounds simple, it is difficult to ignore a behavior completely. That is why *planned* is stressed. When a student whistles, interrupts the teacher, or calls out, the teacher instinctively looks in the direction of the student, thereby giving the student attention and reinforcing the behavior. In contrast, planned ignoring intentionally and completely ignores the behavior. This takes practice.

This intervention has limitations. First, according to reinforcement theory, when a behavior has been reinforced previously, removal of the reinforcement causes a short-term increase in the behavior in the hope of again receiving reinforcement. Thus, when planned ignoring is first used, the off-task behavior will probably increase. Therefore, this technique should be used to manage only the behaviors that cause little interference to the teaching/learning act (Brophy, 1988). Second, other students who attend to the misbehaving student are often reinforcing the disruptive behavior. If this happens, planned ignoring by the teacher has little effect.

The behaviors that are usually influenced by planned ignoring are not having materials ready for the start of class, calling out answers rather than raising a hand, mild or infrequent whispering, interrupting the teacher, and daydreaming. Obviously, the type of learning activity has much to do with the behaviors that can or cannot be ignored. If, after a reasonable period of time of ignoring the off-task behavior, the behavior does not decrease or the point is reached at which others are distracted by it, the teacher has to move quickly and confidently to the next step in the hierarchy, signal interference.

Signal Interference

Signal interference is any type of nonverbal behavior that communicates to the student that the behavior is not appropriate without disturbing others. Signal interference must be clearly directed at the off-task student. There should be no doubt in the student's mind that the teacher is aware of what is going on and that the student is responsible for the behavior. The teacher's expression should be businesslike. It is ineffective for the teacher to make eye contact with a student and smile. Smiling sends a double message, which confuses students and may be interpreted as a lack of seriousness by the teacher.

Examples of signal interference behaviors are making eye contact with the student who is talking to a neighbor, pointing to a seat when a student is wandering around, head shaking to indicate "no" to a student who is about to throw a paper airplane, and holding up an open hand to stop a student's calling out. Like all intervention skills, signal interference behaviors may be hierarchically ordered, depending on the type, duration, and frequency of off-task behavior. A simple hand motion may serve to deal with calling out the first time, whereas direct eye contact with a disapproving look may be needed the next time the student calls out.

For disruptive behaviors that continue or for disturbances that more seriously affect others' learning, the teacher moves to the next intervention skill in the hierarchy, proximity interference.

Proximity Interference

Proximity interference is any movement toward the disruptive student. When signal interference doesn't work, or the teacher is unable to gain a student's attention long enough to send a signal because the student is so engrossed in the off-task behavior, proximity interference is warranted.

Often just walking toward the student while conducting the lesson is enough to bring the student back on task. If the student continues to be off-task, the teacher may want to conduct the lesson in close proximity to the student's desk, which is usually quite effective. This technique works well during question-and-answer periods.

Proximity interference combined with signal interference results in an effective nonverbal intervention technique. It's the rare student who is not brought back on-task by a teacher who makes eye contact and begins walking toward his desk. Like signal interference, proximity interference techniques may be hierarchically ordered from nonchalant movement in the direction of the student to an obvious standing behind or next to the student during class. If proximity does not bring about the desired behavioral change, the teacher is in a position to implement the next step in the hierarchy, touch interference.

Touch Interference

When a teacher takes a child's hand and escorts the child back to his seat or when a teacher places a hand on a student's shoulder, he is using touch interference. *Touch interference* is a light, nonaggressive physical contact with the student. Without any verbal exchange, touch interference communicates to the student that the teacher disapproves of the disruptive behavior. When possible, the technique also ought to direct the student to the appropriate behavior, such as when a student is escorted to a seat or the student's hand is moved from a neighbor's desk and back to his own paper.

When using touch interference, it is important to be aware of its limitations and possible negative outcomes. Certain students construe any touch by the teacher as an aggressive act and react with aggressive behavior. On one occasion, we saw a teacher calmly walk up to a student who was standing at her seat and place her hand on the student's shoulder. The student turned around and confronted the teacher, angrily yelling, "Don't you ever put your hands on me!" To lessen the chance of such an occurrence, teachers need to be sensitive to using touch interference when working with visibly angry or upset students and older students, especially those of the opposite sex. As with all techniques, the teacher must be cognizant of the situational variables as well as the student characteristics.

EFFECTIVENESS OF NONVERBAL INTERVENTION SKILLS

The use of these four remedial nonverbal intervention skills is considered successful if any one or any combination in the hierarchy leads the student to resume appropriate classroom behavior. Notice how Mr. Rotman in Case 8.2 skillfully uses the four nonverbal remedial intervention techniques in combination with the proactive skills of removing seductive objects, interest boosting, and redirecting the behavior to stop

CASE 8.2

Notes versus Math

Mr. Rotman asks each student to write one math problem from the assignment on the board. As two students write their problems, he notices out of the corner of his eye that Jerry is passing a note to Ben. Mr. Rotman decides to ignore the behavior, waiting to see if it is simply a single occurrence. When all the problems are on the board, Mr. Rotman asks questions about the solutions. During this questioning period, he notices Ben returning a note to Jerry. After a few attempts, Mr. Rotman makes eye contact with Jerry while questioning Ben about one of the problems. This technique stops the note passing for the remainder of the questioning activity.

The next activity calls for the use of calculators, and he asks Jerry to please pass one calculator to each predetermined pair of students. Jerry and Ben are partners, and Mr. Rotman monitors their behavior from a distance. As he circulates around the room helping students with the class work, he makes sure that he stops to look over Jerry and Ben's work, encouraging them on its accuracy. Throughout the activity, both boys are on task.

Following the group work, the students separate their desks, and Mr. Rotman begins to review the answers to the problems. He immediately notices that the two boys have begun to pass notes again. He quickly takes a position next to the boys, taps Jerry on the shoulder, and holds out his hand for the note. Jerry hands Mr. Rotman the note and he puts it in his pocket. Mr. Rotman stands near the boys for the rest of the period, asking questions of the class and reviewing the problems. Both Ben and Jerry volunteer and participate for the remainder of the class.

Humor can be a powerful tool in establishing relationships and defusing confrontations.

the note passing between Jerry and Ben without noticeably disrupting the teaching/learning act. He is able to do this because the intervention skills are not randomly and haphazardly applied. Mr. Rotman has a mental flowchart of the hierarchical sequence so that movement from one behavior to the next is accomplished quickly, calmly, and confidently. This does not happen overnight. Teachers must preplan and practice proactive and remedial intervention techniques before having to implement them.

Shrigley (1985) studied the efficiency of nonverbal proactive and remedial intervention skills when used in a hierarchical sequence. He found that after a few hours of in-service training, 53 teachers were able to curb 40 percent of 523 off-task surface behaviors without having to utter a word or cause any interruption to either teaching or learning. Five percent of the behaviors were corrected by the use of planned ignoring. Signal interference was the most effective technique, rectifying 14 percent of the behaviors. Twelve percent and 9 percent were stopped by proximity and touch interference, respectively. To manage the remaining 60 percent of unresolved behavior problems, the teachers needed to implement verbal intervention, the group of intervention skills covered in the next chapter.

Remember, however, the hierarchy is a decision-making model. Depending on the type, frequency, and distracting potential of the behavior, the teacher may decide to bypass the initial intervention skills in favor of a later technique. Certain behaviors need immediate attention; they can neither be ignored nor allowed to continue. This is demonstrated in Case 8.3, in which Ms. Niaz decides to bypass planned ignoring and signal interference in favor of proximity interference to manage a disruption during a test.

No matter which technique eventually brings the student back on task, efforts need to be directed toward maintaining the appropriate behavior. The teacher who encourages and attends to the student's new behavior most easily accomplishes this

CASE 8.3

Let Your Fingers Do the Walking

Ms. Niaz explains the test-taking procedures to her class and then passes out the tests. She walks around the room, answering questions and keeping students aware of her presence. As she does, she notices that Danny is walking his fingers up Tonya's back. Tonya turns around and says, "Stop it!" As soon as she turns back to her test, Danny again bothers her. Ms. Niaz immediately walks toward Danny and spends the next 10 minutes standing in close proximity to him.

task. The student must realize that he can obtain the same or even more attention and recognition for appropriate behavior than he did for disruptive behavior. The student who is ignored when calling out answers should be called on immediately when he raises his hand. The student who ceases walking around the room should be told at the end of the period that it was a pleasure having him in the class. These simple efforts of recognizing appropriate behavior are often overlooked by teachers, but they are a necessary supplement for the teacher who wants to maximize the effectiveness of proactive and remedial intervention skills.

Summary

This chapter began by stressing the fact that teaching/learning is the joint responsibility of the teacher and the students. Students are more willing to accept their responsibilities when it is clear to them that the teacher is fulfilling his responsibilities. These responsibilities include being well prepared to teach by developing learning objectives and using effective teaching strategies, providing clear directions and explanations, ensuring that students understand evaluation criteria, communicating and consistently enforcing behavioral expectations, demonstrating enthusiasm and encouragement, and modeling expected behavior. These behaviors are minimum competencies that all teachers must possess and are considered not only preventive in nature but also prerequisites to effectively intervening with disruptive behaviors.

Teachers proficient in curbing disruptive behavior are experts in the use of a variety of proactive intervention skills. Techniques such as changing the pace, removing seductive objects, interest boosting, redirecting behavior, nonpunitive time-out, encouraging appropriate behavior, and providing cues are employed to bring students back on task while causing little, if any, disruption to the teaching/learning process.

A three-tiered, decision-making hierarchy of remedial intervention skills provides a means to manage the inappropriate surface behaviors that are not brought on task through proactive intervention skills. The structure of the hierarchy ranges from nonintrusive techniques that cause little disruption and provide students with the opportunity to control their own behavior to intrusive techniques that potentially disrupt teaching and learning. The first tier of nonverbal remedial intervention consists of four nonverbal behaviors: planned ignoring, signal interference, proximity interference, and touch interference. When systematically employed, these techniques have been shown to be effective when working with students who exhibit surface behaviors.

Exercises

1. Seven teacher behaviors were listed as prerequisites to appropriate student behavior. Should these teacher behaviors be considered prerequisite? Why or why not?

2. Predict what type of student behavior may result if the teacher does not meet each of the seven prerequisite teacher behaviors.

3. What, if any, deletions or additions would you make to the seven prerequisite teacher behaviors? Explain any modification you suggest.

4. Suggest specific techniques a teacher can use that demonstrate each of the following proactive intervention skills:
   a. Changing the pace
   b. Interest boosting
   c. Redirecting behavior
   d. Encouraging appropriate behavior
   e. Providing cues

5. The hierarchy of remedial intervention skills is presented as a decision-making model, not as an action model. Explain why.

6. Two effective remedial intervention skills are signal interference and proximity interference. Suggest specific techniques a teacher could use that would demonstrate their use.

7. What types of student behaviors would cause you to decide to bypass initial remedial nonverbal intervention skills and enter the hierarchy at the proximity or touch-interference level?

8. Explain why you agree or disagree with the premise that intervention techniques should be employed in a manner that provides students with the greatest opportunity to control their own behavior.

9. Some teachers consider the hierarchical use of remedial intervention skills a waste of time. They say, "Why spend all this time and effort when you can just tell the student to stop messing around and get back to work?" Explain why you agree or disagree with this point of view.

10. **Principles of Teacher Behavior** After reading Chapter 8 and doing the exercises, use what you have learned to briefly describe your understanding of the implications of the principles listed at the beginning of the chapter for a classroom teacher.

    Principle 1:

    Principle 2:

    Principle 3:

9

Using Verbal Interventions and Logical Consequences to Influence Students to Behave Appropriately

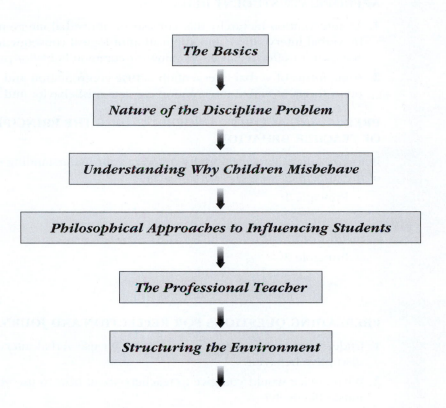

The Basics

Nature of the Discipline Problem

Understanding Why Children Misbehave

Philosophical Approaches to Influencing Students

The Professional Teacher

Structuring the Environment

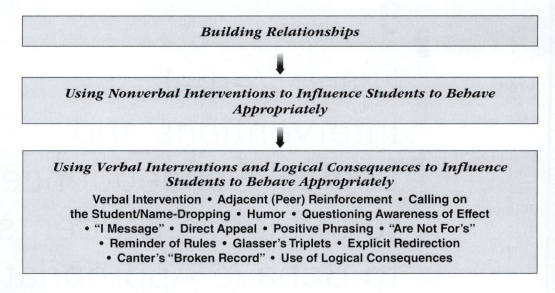

PRINCIPLES OF TEACHER BEHAVIOR THAT INFLUENCE APPROPRIATE STUDENT BEHAVIOR

1. An intervention hierarchy that consists of nonverbal intervention, followed by verbal intervention, and application of logical consequences, when necessary, seems most effective in intervening for common behavior problems.

2. Some forms of verbal intervention defuse confrontation and reduce misbehavior; other forms of verbal intervention escalate misbehavior and confrontation.

PREREADING ACTIVITY: UNDERSTANDING THE PRINCIPLES OF TEACHER BEHAVIOR

Before reading Chapter 9, briefly describe your understanding of the implications of the principles for a classroom teacher.

Principle 1:

Principle 2:

PREREADING QUESTIONS FOR REFLECTION AND JOURNALING

1. Under what circumstances should a teacher use verbal intervention to deal with disruptive behavior?

2. What advice would you give to teachers about how to use verbal interventions most effectively?

3. Is it ever acceptable or appropriate for a teacher to yell at a student or a group of students? If so, under what circumstances? If not, why not?

INTRODUCTION

It is probably correct to assume that John in Case 9.1 has caused many problems for Mr. Rodriguez and other students. By this point in the text, the diligent reader and hopefully Mr. Rodriguez should be thinking about the dynamics of this interaction with John, which has to do with authority bases, self-esteem, parallel processes, and building positive student-teacher relationships. With experience, the veteran professional would use this knowledge base to arrive at an understanding of the dynamics of what was occurring and plan interactions that would de-escalate rather than escalate the confrontation. Instead, Mr. Rodriguez decides to go public by saying, "John, you are one of the most obnoxious students I have ever had the misfortune to deal with." What do you think Mr. Rodriguez's goal was or what did he hope to accomplish? Although he does get his long-suppressed feelings off his chest, Mr. Rodriguez does more harm than good. He disrupts any learning that is taking place, he forces the other students to concentrate on John's behavior rather than on the content of the lesson, and he extends the off-task time by prolonging the reprimand. Thus, Mr. Rodriguez is now a discipline problem (Chapter 2). He is continuing to use distorted power to protect his self-esteem, which strengthens an existing negative parallel process (Chapter 3). This means that the student, John, who already dislikes him, is probably now more determined than ever to "get Rodriguez's goat." Finally, by overreacting to a minor incident, Mr. Rodriguez has probably created some sympathy for John among the other students.

Although we know Mr. Rodriguez has overreacted, we also know that he is not alone. Many teachers find themselves in Mr. Rodriguez's position at one time or another. They allow many incidents of relatively minor misbehavior to build up until one day they just can't take it anymore, and they explode. In letting loose their pent-up

---

CASE 9.1

Blowing His Stack

"John, you are one of the most obnoxious students I have ever had the misfortune to deal with. How many times have I asked you not to call out answers? If you want to answer a question, raise your hand. It shouldn't tax your tiny brain too much to remember that. I'm sick and tired of your mistaken idea that the rules of this classroom apply to everyone but you. It's because of people like you that we need rules in the first place. They apply especially to you. I will not allow you to deprive other students of the chance to answer questions. Anyway, half of your answers are totally off the wall. I'm in charge here, not you. If you don't like it, you can tell your troubles to the principal. Now sit here and be quiet."

When Mr. Rodriguez finished his lecture and turned to walk to the front of the room, John discreetly flipped him the "finger" and laughed with his friends. John spent the rest of the period drawing pictures on the corner of his desk. The other students spent the remainder of the period in either uncomfortable silence or invisible laughter. Mr. Rodriguez spent the rest of the class trying to calm down and get his mind back on the lesson.

feelings, these teachers make the situation worse rather than better. Teachers can avoid this by understanding the concepts discussed in this text such as authority bases, self-esteem, and parallel processes, and using the remedial intervention skills hierarchy first presented in Chapter 8 to contend with classroom behavior problems. This hierarchy consists of three major tiers of intervention: (1) nonverbal intervention skills, (2) verbal intervention, and (3) use of logical consequences. When teachers use this hierarchy to guide their thinking about classroom discipline problems, they are able to select interventions that influence the student to behave appropriately and stop the misbehavior swiftly and effectively. This chapter presents the second and third tiers of the hierarchy.

Verbal intervention is one of the most powerful and versatile tools the teacher has for influencing student behavior. When used effectively, verbal intervention makes classroom management relatively easy and less stressful. When used poorly and thoughtlessly, it may create new behavior problems, make existing problems worse, or turn temporary problems into chronic ones.

This chapter presents 12 verbal intervention techniques in a systematic, hierarchical format. As did the nonverbal intervention skills sub-hierarchy presented in Chapter 8, the verbal intervention sub-hierarchy begins with techniques designed to foster students' control over their own behavior and proceeds to those that foster greater teacher influence over student behavior. Because, as we noted in Chapter 8, this is a decision-making hierarchy, the teacher must decide which particular verbal intervention technique to use with a student who is misbehaving after determining that nonverbal intervention is not appropriate or has not worked.

The final section of the chapter discusses the third and last tier of the intervention hierarchy, the use of logical consequences to influence student behavior.

CLASSROOM VERBAL INTERVENTION

As explained in Chapter 8, there are four advantages to using nonverbal intervention whenever possible: (1) disruption to the learning process is less likely to occur, (2) hostile confrontation with the student is less apt to happen, (3) the student is provided the opportunity to correct her own behavior before more teacher-centered, public interventions are employed, and (4) a maximum number of remaining alternative interventions are preserved. However, nonverbal intervention is not always possible. When misbehavior is potentially harmful to any student or potentially disruptive for a large number of students, it should be stopped quickly, and often verbal intervention is the quickest way to do so. Before discussing specific techniques, teachers should keep in mind the following guidelines when using verbal intervention:

1. Whenever possible, use nonverbal interventions first.
2. Keep verbal intervention as private as possible. This minimizes the risk of having the student become defensive and hostile to avoid losing face in front of peers. Brophy (1988) suggested that this is one of the most important general principles for disciplinary intervention.
3. Make the verbal intervention as brief as possible. Your goal is to stop the misbehavior *and* redirect the student to appropriate behavior. Prolonging the verbal interaction extends the disruption of learning and enhances the likelihood of a hostile confrontation.

4. As Haim Ginott (1972) suggested, speak to the situation, not the person. In other words, label the behavior, not the person, as bad or inappropriate. If, for example, a student interrupts a teacher, "Interrupting others is rude" is a more appropriate response than "You interrupted me. You are rude." Labeling the behavior helps the student see the distinction between herself and her behavior, which in turn helps her understand that it is possible for the teacher to like her but not her behavior. If the student is labeled, she may feel compelled to defend herself and, perhaps, even to seek revenge against the teacher. Furthermore, the student may accept the label as part of her self-concept and match the label with inappropriate behavior in the future. This is exactly what Marcus Green decides to do in Case 9.2.

5. As Ginott urged, set limits on behavior, not on feelings. For instance, tell the student, "It is O.K. to be angry, but it's not O.K. to show your anger by hitting." "It is O.K. to feel disappointed, but it's not O.K. to show that disappointment by ripping up your test paper in front of this class and throwing it in the basket." Students need to recognize, trust, and understand their feelings. When teachers and parents tell students not to be angry or disappointed, they are telling them to distrust and deny their genuine and often justified feelings. The appropriate message for teachers and parents to communicate and understand is that there are appropriate and inappropriate ways for expressing feelings.

6. Avoid sarcasm and other verbal behaviors that belittle or demean the student. Using verbal reprimands to belittle a student lowers the student's self-esteem. A student may in turn raise her self-esteem by using distorted power often displayed as continued disruptive behavior. Additionally, demeaning teacher behavior toward a student often fosters sympathy and support for the student by onlooking classmates.

7. Begin by using a technique that fits the student and the problem and is as close as possible to the student-control end of the decision-making hierarchy.

CASE 9.2

Marcus, the Little Sneak

Marcus Green is in the sixth grade at Shortfellow School. His teacher, Mr. Gramble, has had a long history of difficulty in dealing with classroom discipline. Marcus is a fine student who rarely misbehaves. One day, as his back is partially turned to the class, Mr. Gramble notices Marcus talking to a neighbor. In a flash, Mr. Gramble turns and pounces on Marcus, who was only asking Craig Rutler for an eraser to correct a mistake in his homework. "So, you're the one who's been causing all the trouble," Mr. Gramble snaps. "You little sneak, and all the time I thought you were one of the few people who never caused trouble in here. Well, Buster, you can bet from now on I'll keep an eagle eye on you. You won't be getting away with any more sneaky behavior in here."

For a week or so, Marcus goes back to his typical good behavior, but every time something goes wrong or someone misbehaves, Mr. Gramble blames Marcus. After a week or so of unjust blame, Marcus decides that he may as well start causing some trouble because he is going to get blamed for it anyway. In a very short time, Marcus truly is a great sneak who causes all sorts of havoc and rarely gets caught in the act.

8. If the first verbal intervention does not result in a return to appropriate behavior, use a second technique that is closer to the teacher-influence end of the hierarchy.

9. If more than one verbal intervention technique has been used unsuccessfully, it is time to move to the next step of the intervention hierarchy, the use of logical consequences.

Equally as important as these guidelines on how to use verbal interventions is an awareness of commonly used ineffective verbal interventions. Many of these are instantaneous teacher reactions to students who exhibit disruptive behavior rather than systematic, preplanned, professional decisions enhanced by the use and understanding of the hierarchy of remedial intervention skills. Whereas there are many ineffective verbal interventions, they all share the common characteristics of not speaking directly to the disruptive behavior and not directing the student toward the appropriate behavior (Valentine, 1987).

Some ineffective verbal interventions encourage inappropriate behavior. For instance, "I dare you to do that again" actually increases the likelihood that a student will accept the dare and engage in further disruptions. Other verbal interventions focus on irrelevant behavior. "Aren't you sorry for what you did?" and "Why don't you just admit you have a problem?" address issues that are tangential to the real problem, the student's inappropriate behavior. Still other inappropriate interventions give abstract, meaningless directions or predictions, such as, "Grow up!" or "You'll never amount to anything." These do not address the disruptive behavior and are derogatory and humiliating. They increase the possibility of further confrontation when the student attempts to "save face" and also increase the desire for revenge on the part of the student or other displays of distorted power.

With the guidelines in mind and a cognizance of ineffective verbal reactions, let's turn our attention to the hierarchy of effective verbal intervention. Remember that this is a hierarchy of decision making that begins with verbal interventions that foster student control over student behavior and gradually progresses to interventions that foster greater teacher influence over student behavior. The teacher uses the hierarchy as a range of options to consider, not as a series of techniques to be tried in rapid succession. The teacher should begin the intervention at the point on the hierarchy that is likely to correct the misbehavior and still allow the student as much control and responsibility as possible. It is entirely appropriate to begin with a teacher-centered technique if the teacher believes that it is important to stop the misbehavior quickly and that only a teacher-centered intervention will do so. It is also important to remember that not all of these interventions are appropriate for all types of misbehavior or for all students. Lasley (1989) suggested that teacher-centered interventions are more appropriate for younger, developmentally immature children, and student-centered interventions are more appropriate for older, developmentally mature learners. Therefore, the effective use of this verbal intervention hierarchy requires the teacher to decide which particular intervention techniques are appropriate for both her students and the particular types of misbehaviors that are occurring.

As Figure 9.1 indicates, the verbal intervention hierarchy has been broken into three major categories: hints, questions, and requests or demands. *Hints* are indirect

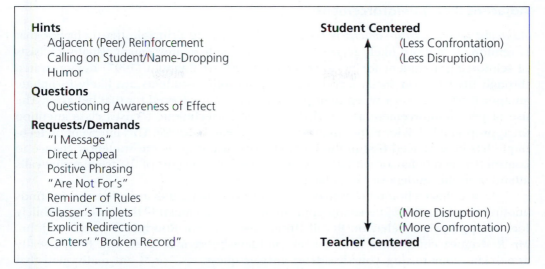

Hints	**Student Centered**
Adjacent (Peer) Reinforcement	(Less Confrontation)
Calling on Student/Name-Dropping	(Less Disruption)
Humor	
Questions	
Questioning Awareness of Effect	
Requests/Demands	
"I Message"	
Direct Appeal	
Positive Phrasing	
"Are Not For's"	
Reminder of Rules	
Glasser's Triplets	(More Disruption)
Explicit Redirection	(More Confrontation)
Canters' "Broken Record"	**Teacher Centered**

FIGURE 9.1 Hierarchy of Classroom Verbal Intervention Techniques.

means of letting the student know that her behavior is inappropriate. They do not directly address the behavior itself. Thus, of all the verbal interventions, they provide the greatest student control over behavior and are the least likely to result in further disruption or confrontation. Specific techniques that are classified as hints include adjacent or peer reinforcement, calling on students or name-dropping, and humor.

In using *questions* as an intervention strategy, the teacher asks the student if she is aware of how she is behaving and how that behavior is affecting other people. Questions are more direct than hints but provide greater student control and less likelihood of confrontation than demands. The only questioning technique that is illustrated as such is questioning awareness of effect. However, almost any request or demand can be utilized as a question. For example, "Pencils are not for drumming" can be rephrased as "What are pencils for?" When using questions, the teacher must make sure that the question is not said sarcastically.

The third level of verbal intervention is labeled as *requests/demands*. These are teacher statements explicitly directed at a misbehavior that make clear that the teacher wants the inappropriate behavior stopped. Such interventions must be delivered assertively, but not aggressively. The final section of the chapter distinguishes assertive from aggressive responses. The major differences between the two are depicted in Table 9.1, provided later in this chapter. Requests and demands exert greater teacher influence over student behavior and have the potential to be disruptive and confrontational. Despite their disadvantages, it is sometimes necessary for teachers to use these interventions when lower-level interventions have proved unsuccessful. The potential for confrontation can be minimized if the demands are delivered calmly and privately.

No matter which interventions a teacher employs, they must be used with full awareness of their limitations and of the implicit message about influencing student behavior that each one conveys.

Adjacent (Peer) Reinforcement

Adjacent (peer) reinforcement is based on the learning principle that behavior that is reinforced is more likely to be repeated. Although reinforcement usually consists of reinforcing a student for her own behavior, Albert Bandura (1997) demonstrated through his work on social learning theory that other students are likely to imitate an appropriate behavior when their peers have been reinforced for that behavior. The use of peer reinforcement as a verbal intervention technique focuses class attention on appropriate behavior rather than on inappropriate behavior. This intervention technique has been placed first in the hierarchy because it gives the student a chance to control her own behavior without any intervention on the part of the teacher that calls attention to the student or her behavior.

To use this technique effectively, a teacher who notes a disruptive behavior finds another student who is behaving appropriately and commends that student publicly for the appropriate behavior. Recall (from Case 9.1) Mr. Rodriguez's anger at John. Mr. Rodriguez could have handled the problem by saying, "Fred and Bob, I really appreciate your raising your hands to answer questions," or "I am really glad that most of us remember the rule that we must raise our hands before speaking."

This particular verbal intervention technique is more useful at the elementary level than at the secondary level. Younger students are usually more interested in pleasing the teacher than older students and often vie for the teacher's attention. Thus, public praise by the teacher is a powerful reinforcer of appropriate behavior. At the secondary level, peer approval is more highly valued than teacher approval; thus, public praise by the teacher is not a powerful reinforcer and indeed may not be a reinforcer at all. For these reasons, it is best to use public praise of individuals sparingly. Public reinforcement of the group as a whole, however, may be an appropriate intervention at the secondary level.

The authors are aware that some who write about classroom management argue that the use of adjacent reinforcement is problematic because the teacher is using praise disingenuously. These theorists argue that the intent is not really to praise the student who is behaving appropriately but rather to admonish those students who are not. We, the authors, are aware of the danger of disingenuous praise and certainly do not promote its frequent use. However, we would argue that when using peer reinforcement, the praise for the student who is behaving appropriately is genuine praise that has a twofold purpose, to recognize appropriate behavior and to provide an opportunity for those who are not behaving appropriately to recognize how they should be behaving.

Calling on the Student/Name-Dropping

To use the *calling on the student/name-dropping* technique, the teacher redirects the student to appropriate behavior by calling on the student to answer a question or by inserting the student's name in an example or in the middle of a lecture if asking a question is not appropriate. Rinne (1984) labeled the technique of inserting the student's name within the content of a lecture name-dropping. Hearing her name is a good reminder to a student that her attention should be focused on the lesson. This technique may be used to redirect students who are off-task but are not disrupting the learning of others (see Chapter 8), as well as students who are overtly disrupting the learning process.

Calling on a student who is misbehaving is a subtle yet effective technique for recapturing the student's attention without interrupting the flow of the lesson or risking confrontation with the student. There are two possible formats for calling on students exhibiting disruptive behavior. Some teachers state the student's name first and then ask a question; others ask the question and then call on the student. The latter technique invariably results in the student being startled and unable to answer the question because she did not hear it. Often, the teacher who uses this technique follows the period of embarrassed silence with a comment on why the student can't answer and why it is important to pay attention. Although this procedure may satisfy the teacher's need to say, "I gotcha," it is preferable to call on the student first and then ask the question. Using the name first achieves the goal of redirecting the student's attention without embarrassing her.

In Case 9.1, calling on John to answer or saying John's name is not an appropriate technique for Mr. Rodriguez to use in dealing with the situation because each encourages John's calling out by giving him recognition. Although not appropriate in this particular case, calling on the student and name-dropping are appropriate in a wide range of situations with learners of all ages.

Humor

Humor that is directed at the teacher or at the situation rather than at the student can defuse tension in the classroom and redirect students to appropriate behavior. The use of humor tends to depersonalize situations and can help establish positive relationships with students (Saphier and Gower, 2008).

If Mr. Rodriguez wished to use humor to handle John's calling out, he might say something like this: "I must be hallucinating or something. I'd swear I heard somebody say something if I didn't know for sure that I haven't called on anyone yet." In using this technique, teachers need to be very careful not to turn humor into sarcasm. There is a fine line between humor and sarcasm. Used as a verbal intervention, humor is directed at or makes fun of the teacher or the situation, whereas sarcasm is directed at or makes fun of the student. It is important to keep this distinction in mind to ensure that what is intended as humor does not turn into sarcasm.

Questioning Awareness of Effect

Sometimes students who disrupt learning are genuinely not aware of the effect their behavior has on other people. Our research (Levin et al., 1985) indicates that even students who exhibit chronic disruptive behavior learn to control their behavior when they are forced to acknowledge both its positive and negative effects. Given this, making disruptive students aware of how their behavior affects other people can be a powerful technique for getting them to control their own behavior. A teacher can usually make a student aware of the impact of her behavior through the use of a rhetorical question, which requires no response from the student. The teacher who wants to handle Mr. Rodriguez's problem by questioning the student's awareness of the behavior's effect might say something like this: "John, are you aware that your calling out answers without raising your hand robs other students of the chance to answer the question?" As soon as the question was asked, the teacher would continue with the lesson without giving John an opportunity to respond.

The informal question not only makes the student aware of the impact of the behavior but also communicates to other students the teacher's desire to protect their right to learn and may build peer support for appropriate behavior. In using this intervention, however, especially with students at the junior high level or above, the teacher must be prepared for the possibility that the student will respond to the question. If the student does respond and does so in a negative way, the teacher may choose to ignore the answer, thereby sending the message that she will not use class time to discuss the issue, or the teacher may respond, "Your behavior is having a negative impact on other people, and so I will not permit you to continue calling out answers." This option sends the message that the teacher is in charge of the classroom and will not tolerate the misbehavior. In dealing with a possible negative response from the student, it is important to remember that the teacher's goal is to stop the misbehavior and redirect the student to appropriate behavior as quickly as possible. Prolonged confrontations frustrate that goal. If, on the other hand, it seems clear from the student's nonverbal behavior that she is truly unaware of the impact of her behavior on others, the teacher can talk privately to explain how the behavior in question has a negative impact on other students, the teacher, and the student herself.

Sending an "I Message"

Thomas Gordon (1989), the author of *Teaching Children Self-Discipline at Home and in School,* developed a useful technique for dealing with misbehavior verbally. He termed the intervention an "I message." The *I message* is a three-part message that is intended to help the disruptive student recognize the negative impact of her behavior on the teacher. The underlying assumption of the technique is the same as the assumption underlying the previously discussed questioning awareness of effect: once a student recognizes the negative impact of her behavior on others, she will be motivated to stop the misbehavior. The three parts of an I message are (1) a simple description of the disruptive behavior, (2) a description of its tangible effect on the teacher and/or other students, and (3) a description of the teacher's feelings about the effects of the misbehavior. Using I messages models for students the important behavior of taking responsibility for and owning one's actions and feelings. There is one important caveat in the use of this technique. Just as the teacher expects students to respect the feelings that are expressed in an I message, the teacher must respect feelings expressed by students.

To use an I message to stop John from calling out, Mr. Rodriguez might say, "John, when you call out answers without raising your hand (part 1), I can't call on any other student to answer the question (part 2). This disturbs me because I would like to give everyone a chance to answer the questions (part 3)." Teachers who enjoy a positive relationship with students, which gives them referent authority (see Chapter 4), are usually successful in using I messages. When students genuinely like the teacher, they are motivated to stop behavior that has a negative impact on the teacher. On the other hand, if the teacher has a poor relationship with students, she should avoid the use of I messages. Allowing students who dislike you to know that a particular behavior is annoying or disturbing may result in an increase in that particular behavior.

Direct Appeal

Another technique that is useful when a teacher enjoys a referent or expert authority base is direct appeal. *Direct appeal* means courteously requesting that a student stop the disruptive behavior. For example, Mr. Rodriguez could say, "John, please stop calling out answers so that everyone will have a chance to answer." The direct appeal leans more toward an assertive delivery mode; it is not made in any sort of pleading or begging way.

Teachers must not use direct appeal in a classroom in which students seem to doubt the teacher's ability to be in charge. In this situation, the appeal may be perceived as a plea rather than as a straightforward assertive request.

Positive Phrasing

Many times, parents and teachers fall into the trap of emphasizing the negative outcomes of misbehavior more than the positive outcomes of appropriate behavior. We tell children and students far more frequently what will happen if they don't finish their homework than we tell them the good things that will occur if they do finish. Of course, it is often easier to identify the short-range negative outcomes of misbehavior than it is to predict the short-range positive impact of appropriate behavior. Still, when the positive outcomes of appropriate behavior are easily identifiable, simply stating what the positive outcomes are can redirect students from disruptive to proper behavior. Shrigley (1985) called this technique *positive phrasing*. It usually takes the form of "as soon as you do X (behave appropriately), we can do Y (a positive outcome)."

In using positive phrasing to correct John's calling out, Mr. Rodriguez might say, "John, when you raise your hand, you will be called on." The long-term advantage of using positive phrasing whenever possible is that students begin to believe that appropriate behavior leads to positive outcomes. As a result, they are more likely to develop internalized control over their behavior.

"Are Not For's"

Of all the verbal interventions discussed in this chapter, the phrase *are not for* (Shrigley, 1985) is the most limited in use. It is implemented primarily when elementary or preschool children misuse property or materials. For example, if a student is drumming on a desk with a pencil, the teacher may say, "Pencils *aren't for* drumming on desks; pencils *are for* writing." Although it is usually effective in redirecting behavior positively at the elementary or preschool level, most secondary students perceive this intervention as insulting. Using "are not for" is not an appropriate technique for Mr. Rodriguez because John is a secondary student and is not misusing property or material.

Reminder of the Rules

When a teacher has established clear guidelines or rules early in the year (see Chapter 6) and has received student commitment to them, merely reminding students of the rules may curb misbehavior. This approach is even more effective if past transgressions have been followed by a reminder and a negative logical consequence if the misbehavior continued. Notice that at this point on the hierarchy, the teacher is no longer relying solely on the student's ability to control her own behavior but instead is using external rules to influence behavior as well as the student's past commitment to follow the rules.

In using this technique, Mr. Rodriguez might say, "John, the classroom rules state that students must raise their hands before speaking," or "John, calling out answers without raising your hand is against our classroom rules that you agreed to follow." The technique is particularly effective for elementary and middle school students. Although it may be used at the senior high level, at this level many students resent the feeling that they are being governed by too many rules. It is important to note that when a reminder of the rules does not redirect the misbehavior, the application of consequences must follow. If this does not occur, the effectiveness of rule reminders will be diminished because students will not see the link between breaking classroom rules and negative consequences.

Glasser's Triplets

In his system for establishing suitable student behavior, William Glasser (1969, 1992) proposed that teachers direct students to appropriate behavior through the use of three questions: (1) What are you doing? (2) Is it against the rules? (3) What should you be doing? These questions, always used privately but not publicly, are known as *Glasser's triplets*. They obviously require a classroom in which the rules have been firmly established in students' minds. To stop John from calling out answers, Mr. Rodriguez would simply ask Glasser's triplets. The expectation underlying Glasser's triplets is that the student will answer the questions honestly and will then return to the appropriate behavior. Unfortunately, not all students answer the triplets honestly, and therein lies the intervention's inherent weakness. Asking open-ended questions may result in student responses that are dishonest, improper, or unexpected.

If a student chooses to answer the questions dishonestly or not to reply at all, the teacher responds by saying (in John's case), "No, John, you were calling out answers. That is against our classroom rules. You must raise your hand to answer questions." To minimize the likelihood of an extended, negative confrontation ensuing from the use of Glasser's triplets, it is suggested that teachers use three statements instead of questions: "John, you are calling out. It is against the rules. You should raise your hand if you want to answer." Some teachers may want to recognize the positive component of the student's behavior, that is the desire to participate. This can be done by adding a short phase to the triplets: "John you are calling out. It is against the rules. I like that you want to participate, but you should raise your hand if you want to answer."

Explicit Redirection

Explicit redirection consists of an assertive order to stop the misbehavior *and* return to acceptable behavior. The redirection is a teacher command and leaves no room for student rebuttal. If Mr. Rodriguez used explicit redirection with John, he might say, "John, stop calling out answers and raise your hand if you want to answer a question." Notice the contrast between this technique and those discussed in the earlier stages of the hierarchy in terms of the amount of responsibility the teacher assumes for influencing student behavior.

The advantages of this technique are its simplicity; clarity; and closed format, which does not allow for student rebuttal. Its disadvantage lies in the fact that the teacher openly confronts the student, who either behaves or defies the teacher in front of peers. The demand should be made as privately as possible for that reason. Obviously, if the student chooses to defy the teacher's command, the teacher must be prepared to proceed to the next step in the hierarchy and enforce the command with appropriate consequences.

Canter's "Broken Record"

Canter and Canter (2001) developed a strategy for clearly communicating to the student that the teacher will not engage in verbal bantering and intends to make sure that the student resumes appropriate behavior. They labeled their strategy the *broken record* because the teacher's behavior sounds like a broken record. The teacher begins by giving the student an explicit redirection statement. If the student doesn't comply or if the student tries to defend or explain her behavior, the teacher repeats the redirection. The teacher may repeat it two or three times if the student continues to argue or fails to comply. If the student tries to excuse or defend her behavior, some teachers add the phrase "that's not the point" at the beginning of the first and second repetitions. The following is an example of this technique as applied by Mr. Rodriguez:

RODRIGUEZ: John, stop calling out answers and raise your hand if you want to answer questions.

JOHN: But I really do know the answer.

RODRIGUEZ: That's not the point. Stop calling out answers and raise your hand if you want to answer questions.

JOHN: You let Mabel call out answers yesterday.

RODRIGUEZ: That's not the point. Stop calling out answers and raise your hand if you want to answer questions.
            Return to lesson.

We have found the broken record technique to be effective for avoiding verbal battles with students. If, however, the statement has been repeated three times without any result, it is probably time to move to a stronger measure, such as the application of logical consequences.

COMPLY OR FACE THE LOGICAL CONSEQUENCES: "YOU HAVE A CHOICE"

Although nonverbal and verbal interventions often stop misbehavior, sometimes the misbehavior remains unchecked. When this occurs, the teacher needs to use more overt techniques. The final tier on the decision-making management hierarchy is the use of logical consequences to influence student behavior.

As the reader will recall from Chapter 6, there are three types of consequences: natural, logical, and contrived (Dreikurs, Grunwald, and Pepper, 1998). Natural consequences result directly from student misbehavior without any intervention by the teacher; although not usually necessary, the teacher may point out the link between the behavior and the consequence. Doing so may actually lessen the impact on the student because it is usually not necessary. If a student runs down the hall and falls, no one needs to tell the student she fell because she was running; the student is quite aware of why she fell. By doing so, the teacher becomes the focus of the student's attention rather than her fall. The use of natural consequences is an intervention strategy because the teacher decides whether or not to let the natural consequences occur. That is, the teacher decides not to take any action to stop the consequence.

Unlike natural consequences, logical consequences require teacher intervention and are related as closely as possible to the behavior; for example, a student who comes to class five minutes late is required to remain five minutes after school to make up the work.

Contrived consequences are imposed on the student by the teacher and either are unrelated to student behavior or involve a penalty beyond what is fitting for the misbehavior. Requiring a student who writes on her desk to write 1000 times "I will not write on my desk" and sentencing a student who comes once to class five minutes late to two weeks of detention are contrived consequences. Because contrived consequences fail to help students see the connection between a behavior and its consequence and place the teacher in the role of punisher, we do not advocate their use. Consequently, contrived consequences are not part of the decision-making hierarchy.

When nonverbal and verbal interventions have not led to appropriate behavior, the teacher should use logical consequences to impact student behavior. To do so, the teacher applies logical consequences calmly and thoughtfully in a forceful but not punitive manner.

Brophy (1988) suggested that the teacher who uses logical consequences should emphasize the student changing her behavior rather than retribution. When this is

Talking to students one-on-one is the first step in establishing relationships and solving long-term problems.

done, the teacher makes sure that the student understands that the misbehavior must stop immediately or negative consequences will result. Often, it is effective to give the student a choice of either complying with the request or facing the consequence. This technique is called *you have a choice*. For example, if John continued to call out answers after Mr. Rodriguez had tried several nonverbal and verbal interventions, Mr. Rodriguez would say, "John, you have a choice. Stop calling out answers immediately and begin raising your hand to answer or move your seat to the back of the room, and you and I will have a private discussion later. You decide." Phrasing the intervention in this way helps the student realize that they are responsible for the positive as well as the negative consequences of the behavior and that the choice is theirs. It also places the teacher in a neutral rather than punitive role. Remember, students do, in fact, choose how to behave. Teachers can't control student behavior; they can only influence it.

Once the teacher moves to this final level of the hierarchy, the dialogue is over. Either the student returns to appropriate behavior or the teacher takes action. The manner in which the consequences are delivered is important and provides the teacher another opportunity to reinforce the idea that the student is in control of her behavior, that the choice to behave or misbehave is hers to make, and that her choice has consequences. In Mr. Rodriguez's case, if John chose to continue to call out, Mr. Rodriguez would say, "John, you have chosen to move to the back of the room; please move." There are no excuses, no postponements. The teachers intentions are clear. Because consistency is crucial, it is imperative that the teacher is ready to enforce the consequences that have been specified before moving to this final tier on the hierarchy.

Obviously, the exact consequence to be applied varies with the student misbehavior. However, one principle is always involved in the formulation of consequences: the consequence should be as directly related to the offense as possible. Consistent application of this principle helps students recognize that their behavior has consequences and helps them learn to control their own behavior in the future by predicting its consequences beforehand.

Because it can be difficult to come up with directly related logical consequences on the spur of the moment (Canter and Canter, 2001), teachers should consider logical consequences for common types of misbehavior before the misbehaviors occur. Developing one or two logical consequences for each of the classroom rules developed in Chapter 6 is a good way to begin. When misbehavior occurs for which there is no preplanned logical consequence, a teacher should ask the following questions to help formulate a consequence directly related to the misbehavior:

1. What would be the logical result if this misbehavior went unchecked?
2. What are the direct effects of this behavior on the teacher, other students, and the misbehaving student?
3. What can be done to minimize these effects?
4. What lesson will the consequences help the student learn?

The answers to these four questions will usually help a teacher identify a logical consequence. In Case 9.3, notice how Ms. Ramonda used the first of the four questions to formulate the logical consequences for Doug's behavior.

CASE 9.3

"Doing Nothin'"

Doug is a seventh-grade student with a learning disability who has serious reading problems and poses behavioral problems for many teachers. At the beginning of the year, he is assigned to Ms. Ramonda's seventh-period remedial reading class. Because Doug hates reading, he is determined to get out of the class and causes all sorts of problems for Ms. Ramonda and the other students. Ms. Ramonda's first reaction is to have Doug removed from her class to protect the other students; however, after talking to Doug's counselor and his resource room teacher, she comes to believe that it is important for Doug not to get his way and that he desperately needs to develop the reading skills that she can teach him.

Ms. Ramonda decides to try to use Doug's personal interests to motivate him. The next day she asks, "Doug, what would you like to do?" Doug answers, "Nothin'. I don't want to do nothin' in here. Just leave me alone." For the next two days, Doug sits in the back of the room and doodles as Ms. Ramonda tries to determine what the next step should be. Finally, Ms. Ramonda asks

herself what the logical result of doing nothing is. She decides that the logical result is boredom and resolves to use that to motivate Doug.

On the following day, she announces to Doug that he will get his wish. From then on, he can do nothing as long as he wants to. She explains that he will no longer need books or papers or pencils because books are for reading, and papers and pencils are for writing, and doing nothing means doing none of those things. He will not be allowed to talk to her or to his friends, she explains, because that too would be doing something and he wants to do nothing. "From now on, Doug, you will be allowed to sit in the back corner of the room and do nothing, just as you wish."

For one full week, Doug sits in the back corner and does nothing. Finally, he asks Ms. Ramonda if he can do something. She replies that he can do some reading but nothing else. Doug agrees to try some reading. That breaks the ice. Ms. Ramonda carefully selects some low-difficulty, high-interest material for Doug and gradually pulls him into the regular classroom situation.

It must be pointed out that Ms. Ramonda would have to speak to the school principal and obtain approval before allowing Doug to do nothing. Still, although most classroom behavior problems do not warrant the drastic measures that Ms. Ramonda took, the case does illustrate a successful use of logical consequences to deal with a difficult classroom situation. Ms. Ramonda's application of logical consequences in a firm but neutral manner helped redirect Doug to more appropriate behavior and, at the same time, helped him recognize the direct connection between his behavior and its consequences.

WHEN "YOU HAVE A CHOICE" DOESN'T WORK

At this point, almost all readers are probably thinking, what if "you have a choice" doesn't work? Some teachers confuse "not working" with a student choosing the negative consequences rather than changing her behavior. Remember, teachers cannot

Students need to believe that you are there to help them work through problems and issues.

force students to behave appropriately, but they can deliver the logical consequences when students choose them. Beyond this point, teachers can only hope that if they are consistent and follow the guidelines for verbal interventions, students will internalize the relationship between behavior and its consequences and choose to behave appropriately the next time.

Teachers can increase the likelihood of a student choosing appropriate behavior by using an assertive response style when employing "you have a choice." Assertiveness is communicated to others by the congruent use of certain verbal and nonverbal behaviors. Do not confuse assertiveness with aggressiveness, which leads to unwanted student outcomes. An aggressive response is one in which a teacher communicates what is expected but in a manner that abuses the rights and feelings of the student. When this happens, students perceive the stated consequences as threats. An aggressive delivery of "you have a choice," with the emphasis on *you* as opposed to on *choice*, would probably be viewed by students as "fighting words" and escalate both hostility and confrontation, leading to further disruptive behaviors. When a teacher uses an assertive response style, the teacher clearly communicates what is expected in a manner that respects a student's rights and feelings. An assertive style tells the student that the teacher is prepared to back up the request for behavioral change with appropriately stated consequences but is not threatening. The authors like to describe assertiveness as a style that communicates to the student a *promise* of action if appropriate behavior is not forthcoming. Table 9.1 compares the verbal and nonverbal behaviors that differentiate assertive response styles from aggressive ones.

TABLE 9.1 Comparisons of Assertive and Aggressive Response Styles

	Assertive	Aggressive
Audience	Private only to student	Public to entire class
How student is addressed	Student's name	"You. Hey, you"
Voice	Firm, neutral, soft, slow	Tense, loud, fast
Eyes	Eye contact only	Narrowed, frowning eyes
Stance	Close to student without violating personal space	Hands on hips, violating personal space
Hands	Gently touch student or student's desk	Sharp, abrupt gestures

Of course, some students will always choose not to behave appropriately. When the teacher assertively delivers the consequence, these students argue or openly refuse to accept and comply with the consequence. If this happens, the teacher must not be sidetracked by the student and enter into a public power struggle with the student. Instead, the teacher should integrate the use of the Canters' broken record (Canter and Canter, 2001) and a final "you have a choice" in a calm, firm assertive manner. The following example between Mr. Rodriguez and John illustrates integration of these verbal interventions:

1. Mr. Rodriguez gives John a choice of raising his hand or moving to the back of the room. John calls out again. Mr. Rodriguez says, "John, you called out; therefore, you have decided to move to the back of the class. Please move."
2. John begins to argue. At this point Mr. Rodriguez uses the Canters' broken record and, if necessary, a final "you have a choice."

JOHN: You know Tom calls out all the time and you never do anything to him.

RODRIGUEZ: That's not the point. Please move to the back of the room.

JOHN: I get the right answers.

RODRIGUEZ: That's not the point. Please move to the back of the room.

JOHN: This is really unfair.

RODRIGUEZ: That's not the point. Move to the back of the room.

JOHN: I'm not moving and don't try to make me.

RODRIGUEZ: John, you have a choice. Move to the back of the room now, or I will be in touch with your parents. You decide.

As this interaction illustrates, after two or three broken records, the teacher issues a final "you have a choice," and then disengages from the student. Some teachers will have the student removed from the classroom by an administrator as the consequence for the final "you have a choice." Whatever the consequence, the teacher must be willing and able to follow through. Thus, teachers must be sure the consequence can be carried out. Because interaction between a student and teacher at this level is likely to be of great interest to the other students in the class, it is imperative for the teacher to remain calm, firm, and assertive. This is a time for the teacher to show the rest of the class that she is in control of her behavior and means what she says. A teacher who remains in control, even if the student refuses to comply, will garner more respect from onlooking students than the teacher who becomes humiliating, harsh, or out of control.

Summary

This chapter presented the final two tiers of the hierarchy introduced in Chapter 8: verbal intervention and use of logical consequences. The following guidelines for verbal intervention were developed: (1) use verbal intervention when nonverbal is inappropriate or ineffective; (2) keep verbal intervention private, if possible; (3) make it as brief as possible; (4) speak to the situation, not the person; (5) set limits on behavior, not feelings; (6) avoid sarcasm; (7) begin with a verbal intervention close to the student-centered end of the hierarchy; (8) if necessary, move to a second verbal intervention technique closer to the teacher-centered end of the hierarchy; and (9) if two verbal interventions have been used unsuccessfully, move to the application of consequences.

In addition to the nine guidelines, three types of ineffective verbal communication patterns were reviewed: (1) encouraging inappropriate behavior; (2) focusing on irrelevant behaviors; and (3) abstract, meaningless directions and predictions.

Twelve specific intervention techniques were presented in a hierarchical format ranging from techniques that foster greater student control over behavior to those that foster greater teacher management over student behavior. The verbal interventions were divided into three categories: hints, questions, and requests/demands. Hints include (1) adjacent or peer reinforcement, (2) calling on the student or name-dropping, and (3) humor. The sole questioning intervention that was presented is (4) questioning awareness of effect. It was noted that many interventions could be used in a question format. The interventions classified as requests/demands include (5) I message, (6) direct appeal, (7) positive phrasing, (8) are not for's, (9) reminder of rules, (10) Glasser's triplets, (11) explicit redirection, and (12) the Canters' broken record.

The last section of the chapter discussed the final tier of the hierarchy: use of logical consequences. It was suggested that this intervention should be phrased in terms of student choice, and the consequences should be related as directly as possible to the misbehavior. Four questions were proposed to help teachers formulate logical consequences for those misbehaviors for which the teacher has not developed a consequence hierarchy. The use of an assertive response style and the integration of "you have a choice" with the Canters' broken record were presented as a means to increase the likelihood that a student chooses to behave appropriately.

When taken together with the information presented in Chapter 8, the ideas presented in this chapter constitute a complete hierarchy that teachers can use to guide their thinking and decision making concerning how best to intervene to influence students who exhibit disruptive behavior. The hierarchy is presented in its complete format in Figure 9.2.

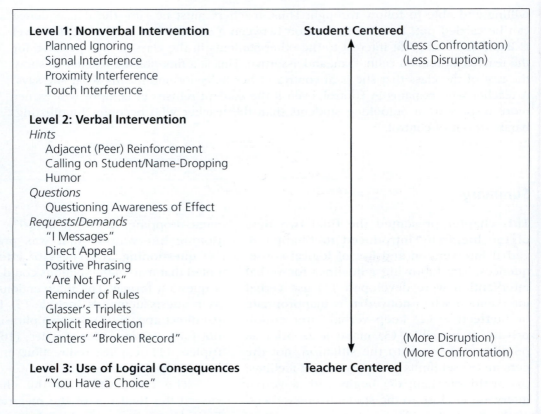

FIGURE 9.2   Hierarchy for Management Intervention.

Exercises

1. What types of student misbehavior might lead a teacher to use verbal intervention without first trying nonverbal techniques? Justify your answer.

2. Use each of the verbal intervention techniques presented in this chapter to help redirect the student to appropriate behavior in the following situations:

   (a) Student won't get started on a seat work assignment.

   (b) Student pushes her way to the front of the line.

   (c) Student talks to a friend sitting on the other side of the room.

   (d) Student lies about a forgotten homework assignment.

3. Under what circumstances, if any, would it be appropriate for a teacher to move directly to the third tier of the hierarchy: use of logical consequences? Justify your answer.

4. Develop logical consequences for each of the following misbehaviors:

   (a) Student interrupts while teacher is talking to a small group of students.

   (b) Student steals money from another student's desk.

   (c) Student copies a homework assignment from someone else.

   (d) Student squirts a water pistol during class.

   (e) Student throws spitballs at the blackboard.

   (f) Student physically intimidates other students.

   (g) Graffiti is found on the restroom wall.

5. List some common teacher verbal interventions that fall under the three types of ineffective verbal communication patterns.

6. Role-play the assertive delivery of "you have a choice."

7. When a teacher uses an aggressive response style, what feelings and behaviors are commonly elicited from the student? What effect does an aggressive response style have on overall teacher effectiveness in both the academic and management domains?

8. When a teacher uses an assertive response style, what feelings and behaviors are commonly elicited from the student? What effect does an assertive response style have on overall teacher effectiveness in both the academic and management domains?

9. **Principles of Teacher Behavior** After reading Chapter 9 and doing the exercises, use what you have learned to briefly describe your understanding of the implications of the principles listed at the beginning of the chapter for a classroom teacher.

Principle 1:

Principle 2:

Classroom Interventions for Working with Students Who Exhibit Chronic Behavior Problems

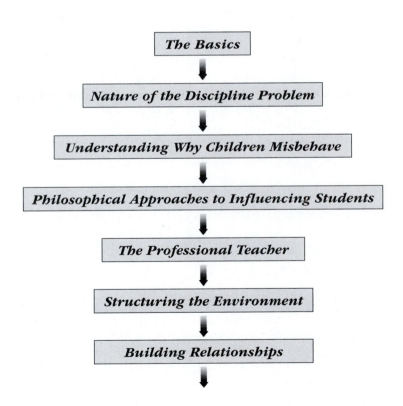

The Basics

Nature of the Discipline Problem

Understanding Why Children Misbehave

Philosophical Approaches to Influencing Students

The Professional Teacher

Structuring the Environment

Building Relationships

> ***Using Nonverbal Interventions to Influence Students to Behave Appropriately***
>
> ↓
>
> ***Using Verbal Interventions and Logical Consequences to Influence Students to Behave Appropriately***
>
> ↓
>
> ***Classroom Interventions for Working with Students Who Exhibit Chronic Behavior Problems***
> **The Dynamics of Chronic Disruptive Behavior**
> **Long-Term Problem-Solving Strategies**
> Relationship Building • Breaking the Cycle of Discouragement
> **Talking to Solve Problems**
> Receiving Skills • Sending Skills • Asking Authentic Questions
> **Short-Term Problem-Solving Strategies**
> Self-Monitoring • Anecdotal Record Keeping • Functional Behavior Assessment
> • Behavior Contracting

PRINCIPLES OF TEACHER BEHAVIOR THAT INFLUENCE APPROPRIATE STUDENT BEHAVIOR

1. When working with students who exhibit chronic behavior problems, teachers should employ strategies to resolve the problems within the classroom before seeking outside assistance.

2. Breaking the cycle of discouragement, in which most students who exhibit chronic behavior problems are trapped, increases the likelihood that the problems can be resolved within the classroom.

3. When teachers conduct private conferences and use effective communication skills with students who exhibit chronic behavior problems, the likelihood that the problems can be resolved within the classroom increases.

4. Interventions that require students to recognize their inappropriate behavior and its impact on others increase the likelihood that the problems can be resolved within the classroom.

5. Interventions that require students who exhibit chronic behavior problems to be accountable for trying to control their behavior on a daily basis increase the likelihood that the problems can be resolved within the classroom.

PREREADING ACTIVITY: UNDERSTANDING THE PRINCIPLES OF TEACHER BEHAVIOR THAT INFLUENCE APPROPRIATE STUDENT BEHAVIOR

Before reading Chapter 10, briefly describe your understanding of the implications of the principles for a classroom teacher.

Principle 1:

Principle 2:

Principle 3:

Principle 4:

Principle 5:

PREREADING QUESTIONS FOR REFLECTION AND JOURNALING

1. Think about and describe a student whom you have known and whom you would classify as exhibiting disruptive behavior over a long period of time. What factors influenced this student to behave inappropriately?

2. What behaviors on the part of the teacher are most important in working with students who exhibit chronic disruptive behavior?

INTRODUCTION

Research, as well as our own experience, indicates that the overwhelming majority of discipline problems (somewhere in the neighborhood of 97 percent) can be either prevented or redirected to positive behavior by the use of a preplanned hierarchy of non-verbal and verbal interventions (Shrigley, 1980). However, some students pose classroom discipline problems of a more chronic nature. These students continue to misbehave even after all preventive and intervention techniques, verbal and nonverbal, have been appropriately employed. They disrupt learning, interfere with the work of others, challenge teacher authority, and often try to entice others to misbehave on a fairly consistent basis. These are the students who prompt teachers to say, "If I could only get rid of that…Nikolai, third period would be a pleasure to teach." "Every time I look at that smirk on Jodi's face, I'd like to wring her little neck." "If that…Greg weren't in this class, I would certainly have a lot more time to spend on helping the other students learn."

These are the students, who come to mind when a teacher asks himself, "If I had to do it all over again, would I still choose to become a teacher?" These are the students that a teacher thinks about when he is driving home from school and passes the shopping mall that is advertising HIRING NOW FOR ALL POSITIONS. He thinks maybe he should apply; retail can't be that bad, after all; he almost majored in business in college. And, these are the students he thinks about when he reflects back upon his career and asks if it was worthwhile, and he answers yes because 10 years ago little Billy McCall was in his class. He remembers him. He was the student who challenged his authority. Just about every day, he called him a bitch more times than he wished to remember. He had him suspended twice and he twice failed his class. Last week, though, he stopped by his class and thanked the teacher for not giving up on him. He and handed him an invitation and said if he weren't busy next Saturday, maybe he'd like to come to his college graduation.

The authors of this text stress that teachers are highly qualified professionals, who, just like doctors and lawyers, apply a specialized body of knowledge to address challenging complex problems. Therefore, consider the following if there were no illness and people were born healthy and died at a ripe old age, what professionals would we not need? If everyone were law abiding, which professionals would we not need? Finally, if every student came to school motivated, well behaved, and with no behavioral or academic problems, what professionals would we not need? It is because students come to school with a myriad of behavior, academic, and motivational issues that we need professional teachers.

This chapter and Chapter 11 are for the teachers who work with the students who cause us to question what we are doing in the moment but also give us tremendous satisfaction over time.

THE DYNAMICS OF CHRONIC DISRUPTIVE BEHAVIOR

As Mr. Voman, the counselor, discovered when he talked to Jodi's teacher Ms. Kozin, Jodi had been a constant nuisance for the past month. The book-dropping incident was simply the straw that broke the camel's back. Jodi continually talked during lectures; forgot to bring pencils, books, and paper; refused to complete homework; didn't even attempt quizzes or tests; and reacted rudely whenever Ms. Kozin approached her, and it seemed as if it was getting worse. Ms. Kozin had tried nonverbal and verbal interventions, time-out, detention, and notes to parents. By the time Jodi accidentally dropped her book, Ms. Kozin was totally fed up with her.

CASE 10.1

"I Just Dropped My Book"

Jodi entered Mr. Voman's guidance office hesitatingly, sat down, and looked blankly at Mr. Voman.

MR. VOMAN: Well, Jodi, what are you doing here?

JODI: Ms. Kozin sent me out of class and told me not to ever come back. She told me to come see you.

MR. VOMAN: Why did she send you out of class?

JODI: I don't know. I just dropped my book on the floor accidentally!

MR. VOMAN: Now, come on, Jodi. Ms. Kozin wouldn't put you out of class just for that. Come on now. What did you do?

JODI: Honest, Mr. Voman, you can ask the other kids. All I did was drop my book.

MR. VOMAN: Jodi, I'm going to go and talk to Ms. Kozin about this. Wait here until I get back.

JODI: O.K., Mr. Voman. I'll wait here, and you'll see that I'm not lying.

Many, though not all, students like Jodi have problems that extend beyond school. Some have poor home lives with few, if any, positive adult role models. Some live in poverty. Some have no one who really cares about them or expresses an interest in what they are doing. Some simply view themselves as losers who couldn't succeed in school even if they tried. As a result, they act out their frustrations in class and make life miserable for both their teachers and their peers.

No matter how understandable these students' problems may be, they must learn to control their behavior. This may require that the teacher assume responsibility for teaching the student how to behave appropriately, which is consistent with this text's approach that you teach appropriate behavior (see Chapter 6). When students are lacking positive adult role models in their lives, it is often the case that no one has bothered to teach them how to behave appropriately, especially in difficult or challenging situations. Thus, if the teacher really expects students to behave positively, he must be willing to help the students acquire the knowledge and skills necessary to do so. If they do not, they are at risk of continued failure and unhappiness. Furthermore, although teachers are always concerned for the future of the student who is exhibiting disruptive behavior, they are also responsible for ensuring that misbehavior does not deprive the other students of their right to learn. Thus, chronic misbehavior must not be allowed to continue.

In attempting to work with students who exhibit chronically disruptive behavior, classroom teachers often fall into a two-step trap. First, they frequently give in to that natural, fully understandable, human urge to "get even." They scream, punish, and retaliate. When retaliation fails, which it is apt to, because the student who exhibits chronically disruptive behavior often loves to see the teacher explode, the teacher feels helpless and seeks outside assistance; that is, he turns the student over to somebody else. Often, such students are sent to an administrator or counselor and required to do some form of in-school or out-of-school suspension, which has many drawbacks that will be discussed later in this chapter.

Because outside referral removes the disruptive student from the class, the disruptive behavior does cease. However, this is usually a short-term solution because the student soon returns and, after a brief period of improvement, again disrupts the classroom. The severity and frequency of the misbehavior after a return to the classroom often increase. One hypothesis is that misbehavior increases because students view the referral either as a further punishment or as a victory over the teacher. When they view referrals as punishments, many students who exhibit chronic behavior problems retaliate as soon as they return to the classroom. When they view referrals as victories, these students often feel compelled to demonstrate even more forcefully their perceived power over the teacher. This back-and-forth behavioral display whereby the teacher publically reprimands the student, the student is removed from the classroom, the student returns to class and exhibits even more disruptive behavior is an example of a parallel process. In this case, both the teacher's and the student's pro-social self-esteem have been lowered and both are now trying to raise their self-esteem by displaying distorted power (see Chapter 3). For many reasons, including being a professional and having a higher level of cognitive and moral development than his younger students, it is the teacher's responsibility to stop the process (Levin and Shanken-Kaye, 2002).

Porter and Brophy (1988), in a research synthesis on effective teaching, strongly recommended dealing with chronic discipline problems within the classroom.

In a study of teachers' strategies for working with students who presented sustained problems in personal adjustment or behavior, teachers who were identified as most effective in dealing with such problems viewed them as something to be corrected rather than merely endured. Furthermore, although they might seek help from school administrators or mental health professionals, such teachers would build personal relationships and work with these students, relying on instruction, socialization, cognitive strategy training, and other long-term solutions. In contrast, less effective teachers would try to turn over the responsibility to someone else (such as the principal, school social worker, or counselor).

Contrary to popular belief, chronic behavior problems often can be resolved successfully within the confines of the regular classroom and with a minimum of additional effort by the teacher. When this occurs, everyone benefits. The student learns to control his behavior without loss of instructional time and without developing the negative attitudes that are often evident in students who have been excluded from the classroom. The teacher gains a more tranquil classroom and additional confidence in his ability to handle all types of discipline problems successfully. Finally, the other students in the class are again able to concentrate their attention on the learning tasks before them.

Alfie Kohn (2005) suggested that removing students from the classroom because of their behavior teaches them that they are valued only when they live up to the expectations of others. He claimed that temporarily ejecting a student from a class or from school for misbehaving is in effect telling everyone, the excluded student as well as those who stay, that everyone is part of this community only conditionally, thus creating an ultimately psychologically unsafe climate. In addition, handling chronic behavior problems within the classroom negates the possibility that these behavior issues will lead to an expulsion from school for the student. Often, repeated referrals for inappropriate behavior carry with them the eventual punishment of an out-of-school suspension. Many people applaud such punishments. They believe that eliminating the culprit from the school is a benefit for everyone. However, Sautner (2001) has identified multiple negative outcomes that appear to be associated with out-of-school suspensions. These include alienation from school, an increased dropout rate, increased academic failure, greater antisocial behavior, increased negative behavior upon returning to the school environment, and increased aggressive behavior. Therefore, handling the chronic behavior within the classroom may well prevent or at least postpone a distressing series of negative outcomes.

The remainder of this chapter is divided into three parts. The first part focuses on two long-term strategies for solving chronic behavior problems that are derived from referent authority. They are relationship building and breaking the cycle of discouragement and are presented first because they constitute essential tools for helping resolve the underlying issues that are influencing the student to engage in disruptive behavior.

The second part of the chapter, also derived from referent authority, focuses on talking with the student privately as a way to resolve the behavior problems. We believe that conversing honestly and openly with the student should always be a part of the teacher's plan for helping the student regain control of his behavior. Sitting down to discuss the problem openly results not only in a better relationship but may also result in a resolution that is acceptable to both the teacher and the student.

Even if an immediate resolution is not found, the groundwork for positive future communication has been laid.

The final section of the chapter focuses on four specific short-term problem-solving techniques, derived from expert authority, that may be used to solve chronic behavior problems. Student self-monitoring, a student-directed strategy; anecdotal record keeping, a collaborative management strategy; functional behavior assessment; and behavior contracting, a teacher-directed strategy, comprise the four short-term techniques. In contrast to relationship building, breaking the cycle of discouragement, and talking to solve problems, which are always used in working with students who exhibit chronic behavior problems, these short-term strategies may or may not be used depending on the specific situation, the student's needs, and the teacher's beliefs.

LONG-TERM PROBLEM-SOLVING STRATEGIES

Relationship Building

In Chapter 7, we examined the process of building student-teacher relationships as a proactive effort to reduce all types of misbehavior in both frequency and intensity. However, this relationship needs to be further developed for working with the students who are still exhibiting chronic disruptive behavior.

Without a doubt, the development of a positive relationship between the teacher and the student with a chronic behavior problem is one of the most effective strategies for helping such students. These students usually do not have positive relationships with their teachers or with adults in general. Indeed, teachers often tend to avoid interaction with such students. This is quite understandable. Students who exhibit chronic behavior problems are displaying distorted power (see Chapter 3) and are often very difficult to deal with. They disrupt the teacher's carefully planned learning activities. They sometimes intimidate other students and prevent their peers from engaging in classroom activities. They frequently challenge the teacher's authority and cause the teacher to doubt his own competence.

These doubts about competence arise from the misconception that the teacher can control a student's behavior. As we have noted continually in this text, the teacher can only influence and react to a student's behavior. He cannot control anyone's behavior except his own. If a teacher has the mistaken notion that his job is to control a student's behavior, he will feel that he is not as competent as he should be every time the student acts inappropriately. Thus, one of the first steps a teacher should take in working with students who exhibit chronic behavior problems is to recognize that his role is to help these students learn to control their own behavior. The teacher can be held accountable only for controlling his own behavior in such a way that it increases the likelihood that the students will learn and want to behave appropriately.

To accomplish this, the teacher must disregard any negative feelings he has toward the student and work at building a positive relationship with that student. Because feelings lead to actions, if a teacher has negative thoughts about a student that he cannot get beyond, he will likely act negatively toward the student. This will then put the teacher in a position that will greatly lessen his ability to influence the student to behave more appropriately. Understand that we are not suggesting that the teacher must like the student. This is not always possible. No teacher honestly likes every student whom he has ever encountered. However, a truly professional teacher, as hard as it may be, does not act on or reveal those negative feelings.

Our experience has given us two important insights about working with students who exhibit chronic behavior problems. First, teachers who look for and are able to find some positive qualities, no matter how small or how hidden, in students who exhibit chronic misbehavior are much more successful in helping those students learn to behave appropriately than those who do not. Second, the primary factor that motivated the vast majority of students who were at one time chronically disruptive to turn their behavior around was the development of a close, positive relationship with some caring adult. Case 10.2 illustrates the impact that a caring relationship can have on such an individual.

Of course, building positive relationships with students who exhibit chronic behavior problems is not always an easy task. Many of these students have a long history of unsuccessful relationships with adults. Because the adults in these

CASE 10.2

Darnell

Darnell, who was born to a single mother in a rundown, crime-ridden neighborhood, was raised by his grandmother, the one kind, caring, and protective figure in his early life. Despite her efforts to shield him, Darnell was exposed to drugs, street violence, and a variety of illegal activity while he was still in elementary school. In middle school, Darnell, who described himself at that age as full of anger and energy, became involved in petty theft and violent attacks on other adolescents and adults. As a result, he was sent to a juvenile detention facility and, after his release, assigned to Barbara, a juvenile probation officer.

Barbara was a streetwise veteran in her fifties who had worked with many troubled adolescents. As Darnell has said, "She did not take any crap." Barbara insisted that Darnell stop his aggressive behavior. She made it clear to him that she saw him as an intelligent young man who had the potential to be successful if he changed his behavior. Over the six-year period Darnell and Barbara worked together, Darnell changed dramatically. In Darnell's words,

"Barbara taught me how to take my anger and my aggression and turn them into positive forces, first on the basketball court and then later, much later, in the classroom." As a result of the close, positive relationship Barbara built, Darnell earned passing grades in school, stayed out of trouble, and became a good enough point guard to earn a scholarship to a small state college. He became a special education teacher and returned to his hometown to teach, hoping to make a difference in the lives of kids like him.

After returning, he saw the need to change the educational system itself but felt powerless to do so. After a few frustrating years, he left teaching and went on to earn a master's degree in counseling, a Ph.D. in curriculum, and a principal's certificate. Today, Darnell is a middle school principal in the inner city where he was raised. He lives in the city with his wife and young son and spends his time helping inner-city kids turn their energy and anger to useful purposes in much the same way as Barbara helped him.

relationships have ended up being abusive in one way or another, many of the students actively resist attempts to build positive relationships. Brendtro, Brokenleg, and Van Bockern (2002) suggested that the teacher who works with students with chronic behavior problems should think of the student's natural desire to form attachments with significant others as if it were a piece of masking tape and the significant others were walls. Each time the student begins to form a relationship with an adult, the masking tape sticks to the wall. Each time the relationship ends in a negative or hurtful way, the masking tape is ripped off the wall. This process of attachment and hurt is repeated several times. Eventually, the masking tape stops sticking. In other words, the desire to form attachments and relationships with adults is lost. In the eyes of the student, it becomes safer not to build any relationships at all than to risk another relationship that will result in hurt and disappointment.

Thus, teachers who want to build relationships with such students must be persistent, consistent, and predictable in their own behavior toward the student. They must search for positive qualities in the students and work at building the relationship without much initial encouragement or response from the student. As Brendtro et al. noted, the desire to build a relationship does not have to spring from a feeling of liking or attraction. The teacher simply has to choose to act toward the student in caring and giving ways. Over time, positive feelings of liking and attraction develop. Notice how Mike Egan, the veteran teacher in Case 10.3, proactively builds a

CASE 10.3

Relating to Evan

Mike Egan is a veteran elementary school teacher who generally gets along well with each of his students. On the first in-service day for teachers, Ms. Dorothy Powell, one of the third-grade teachers in his building, stops in for a visit. She notices Evan Blewitt's nametag on one of the desks and blurts out, "Wow, Mike, I am so sorry, but you are in for one long year! I had Evan last year and he ruined the entire atmosphere in my classroom. I think he probably spent more time in the office than he did with me." Mike does not respond to the negative nature of Dorothy's comments. Instead, he begins to ask questions about Evan. He finds out where Evan lives, what his family situation is like, what hobbies he has, what subjects he does well in, and if there are any students that he relates well with.

On the first day of school, Evan is one of the first students to arrive. Mike greets him at the door, shows him to his seat, and points out the other students who will be sitting at his desk set (one of them is Frank, a student with whom Evan gets along really well). Mr. Egan also tells Evan that he heard that Evan is interested in mixed martial arts (MMA). Although Mike confesses that he does not know much about that sport, he says that he would like to learn more about it and wonders if Evan might be willing to help him understand the basics of how points are scored during matches. Evan gleefully agrees and at recess seeks out Mr. Egan to begin tutoring him about MMA. Although Evan did exhibit some disruptive behavior from time to time during the year, his behavior was not remarkable in any negative way in fourth grade.

relationship with Evan. Although such dramatic results are not guaranteed, the efforts can be rewarding.

Bob Strachota (1996) called attempts to build positive relationships with students who have chronic behavior problems "getting on their side." He noted that teachers need to view themselves as allies rather than opponents of these students and has suggested several steps to help teachers do so. The first step is "wondering why." Strachota pointed out that many teachers become so preoccupied with techniques for stopping the misbehavior that they forget to ask fundamental questions such as, "Why is the student behaving in this way?" and "What purpose does it serve or what need does it fulfill?" Strachota's underlying assumption is that behavior is purposeful rather than random and directed at meeting some need even if the goal of the behavior is faulty or mistaken (see Chapter 3). If the teacher can identify the need, it is often possible to substitute a positive behavior that will result in fulfillment of the need.

The second step is to develop a sense of empathy and intimacy with the student. Have you ever found yourself in a situation in which you wanted to stop a behavior but couldn't get control of it? Have you ever yelled at your children using the same words as your parents, despite your promise to yourself that would never happen? Have you ever eaten too much or had too much to drink, although you vowed that you wouldn't? If you have, then you have a great opportunity to develop a sense of empathy with these students. If you can view yourself and the student in similar terms—wanting to stop a behavior but not being able to—you are much more likely to be able to work successfully with the student. Finding parallels between issues that you have struggled with and your student's struggle to control his own behavior enables you to reframe the problem in a much more productive way. Instead of being viewed as a control issue that threatens your sense of competence as a teacher and pits you against the student, reframing the problem allows you to see it as a teaching opportunity. You have the potential to help the student gain control over his behavior. In so doing, you become an ally and develop a much more accurate sense of empathy for what the student is experiencing.

The third step is to stay alert for cues and behaviors that reveal other aspects of the student's personality. Sometimes teachers become so riveted on the misbehavior that they do not look at other aspects of the student's behavior and personality. Students who pose chronic behavior problems have other aspects to their beings as well, but it takes self-control and persistence to focus on them. When a teacher is controlled and focused enough to see the student's personality and behavior in its entirety, he is often able to find positive and attractive aspects that can be used as a foundation for building a positive relationship.

Strachota's fourth and final step is for the teacher to monitor carefully his own behavior in interacting with the student. Strachota pointed out, "What's going on for me leaks out in the way I talk. I know what I sound like when I am happy, relaxed, curious, flexible, enthusiastic, etc. I know the difference when I feel tense, short, angry, controlling, hurried, sarcastic, or harsh" (1996, p. 75). Sometimes teachers unintentionally communicate negative feelings toward disruptive and low-achieving students (see Chapter 5). If a teacher listens closely to what he is saying and observes how he is behaving, he can avoid negative messages and instead offer positive, caring ones.

Our experience reinforces Strachota's belief that the teacher's mind-set is critical. In most chronic behavior situations, the teacher sees the student as an opponent in the conflict. Teachers who are successful in resolving chronic behavior problems see themselves on the student's side, working together to overcome the problem. The reader would probably laugh if a teacher saw a student having academic problems as an opponent. Instead, the teacher would likely search his experience and knowledge base and perhaps consult with more tenured professional peers to look for other ways to teach. The same parallels can be drawn with the student exhibiting chronic disruptive behavior. Instead of finding faults, try being on the student's side and phrase the issue to be education oriented, for example, "The student does not understand how to behave respectfully." It is the teacher's job to teach respect just as it is the teacher's job to teach math. This is another parallel process that can be summarized as how the teacher feels about a student is usually how the student feels about the teacher. It all starts with the teacher's feelings regarding the student.

Breaking the Cycle of Discouragement

Many students with chronic behavior problems suffer from low self-esteem and have a low success-to-failure ratio (see Chapters 3 and 11). Their need for a sense of significance or belonging, a sense of competence or mastery, a sense of power or independence, and a sense of virtue or generosity has not been fulfilled. As explained in Chapter 3, when these needs are not fulfilled, individuals take action to fulfill them. Unfortunately, the student with chronic behavior problems often takes actions that are inappropriate and negative. These negative behaviors are met with negative teacher responses, punishments, and consequences that further reduce the student's self-esteem and lead to further misbehavior, negative responses, punishments, and consequences. This cycle of discouragement, which is depicted in Figure 10.1, will continue until a teacher takes action to break it.

Students who fail to develop a strong sense of belonging are much more likely to be connected with a whole host of negative outcomes, including increased rates of failure, higher dropout rates, increased risk of teenage suicide, and an increased likelihood of criminal activity (Osterman, 2000). Thus, it is critical that each student feel a sense of belonging and connectedness to the teacher and to other students.

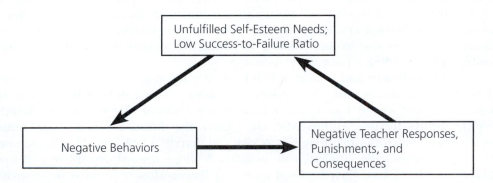

FIGURE 10.1   The Cycle of Discouragement.

To establish a strong sense of belonging on the part of all students, Kohn (2005) exhorted teachers to practice what he calls unconditional teaching. *Unconditional teaching* means that although the teacher does have high expectations for student behavior, the teacher's personal affection and concern for each student are not dependent on how the student behaves. They are given unconditionally to each student. The teacher's modeling of unconditional acceptance has been demonstrated to have a powerful impact on how the students in the class treat each other (Osterman, 2000).

Although it is entirely appropriate for students to receive negative messages about their inappropriate behavior and to experience the negative consequences of such actions, if that is all that occurs, the cycle of discouragement is simply reinforced. Suppose after reading this chapter, you walked into your kitchen and saw water pouring from underneath your kitchen sink. What would you do? Although you might prefer to close the kitchen door, pretend you never saw it, and go to a movie, that would not be the appropriate adult response. The appropriate response would be to shut off the water and then fix the leak. Shutting off the water is like applying punishment or consequences. It stops the water (the inappropriate behavior), but it does not fix the leak (the unfulfilled self-esteem needs). Although it is necessary to stop the misbehavior, the teacher must also find ways to meet those unfulfilled needs and break the cycle of discouragement.

Just as there are students who are caught in the cycle of discouragement, there are students who are caught in the cycle of encouragement. These students have a high success-to-failure ratio and are having their needs for pro-social feelings of significance, competence, power, and virtue met. As a result, they behave in positive and caring ways toward teachers and peers. These positive behaviors are reciprocated, and students are given the message that they are attractive, competent, and virtuous, resulting in the cycle of encouragement depicted in Figure 10.2. We believe that the appropriate way to solve chronic behavior problems is to break the cycle of discouragement by stopping the inappropriate behavior through intervention techniques *and,* at the same time, engaging in behaviors that will help meet the student's needs for feelings of significance, competence, power, and virtue. Together, these two actions result in the disruption of the cycle of discouragement, as shown in Figure 10.3.

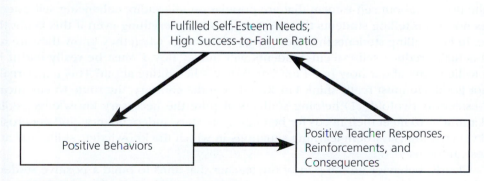

FIGURE 10.2 The Cycle of Encouragement.

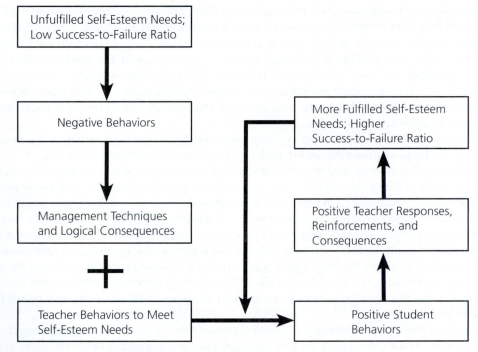

FIGURE 10.3 **Disrupting the Cycle of Discouragement.**

To accomplish this, teachers who are dealing with students with chronic behavior problems should ask themselves four questions:

1. What can I do to help meet this student's need for significance or belonging?
2. What can I do to help meet this student's need for competence or mastery?
3. What can I do to help meet this student's need for power or independence?
4. What can I do to help meet this student's need for virtue or generosity?

Obviously, the suggestions that follow are not the only possibilities. We know that teachers will use their own creativity to build upon and enhance these ideas. Contrary to the notions about self-esteem that are popular on talk radio, enhancing self-esteem does not mean telling students that they are good at everything even if this is not the case. In fact, telling students that they are good at things when they know they are not will actually reduce self-esteem. Students will think, "Boy, I must be really bad if he has to lie to me about how bad I am." or "What is he talking about? This paper really is not good. He must really think I'm stupid." On the contrary, the route to enhancing self-esteem is twofold: (1) helping students acquire the necessary knowledge, skills, and attitudes to meet their needs for belonging, mastery, independence, and generosity and (2) creating classroom learning situations in which the knowledge, skills, and attitudes can be used.

Clearly, behavior on the part of the teacher that aims to build a positive student-teacher relationship is one powerful tool for meeting a student's need for significance. Cooperative learning strategies (see Chapters 5 and 7) and other forms of group work help meet the student's need for feelings of belonging. Student teams that work together productively over time also can help the student develop a sense of group identity and belonging. Often, students who exhibit chronic behavior problems are not well liked by their peers. Thus, putting them in a student-selected group does not usually work and may result in the disruption of the group. The likelihood of positive group interaction can be increased greatly by the teacher's careful selection of the appropriate group for the student. The optimum group typically includes students who are good at controlling their own behavior, are sensitive to the needs of others, and can tolerate some initial conflict. It is also helpful if the teacher uses cooperative learning activities to teach students productive social skills (see Chapter 7).

At the elementary level, it is sometimes effective to place the student who exhibits chronic behavior problems in a responsible role, for example, message carrier. This often enhances the student's sense of belonging. In middle school and high school, finding clubs, intramurals, or other extracurricular activities or out-of-school activities (sometimes a job) in which the student has some interest and talent and then supporting the student's participation in this activity helps enhance the student's sense of belonging. At all levels, the teacher should make it a point to give the student attention and positive feedback when he engages in appropriate behavior.

The need for a sense of competence can be met by the use of encouragement as described in Chapter 3. Students who exhibit chronic behavior problems and their parents often receive only negative messages. Showing an interest in those things that the student values and making sure that you, as the teacher, recognize those strengths will help increase the student's sense of competence. Sometimes setting short-term goals with the student and then helping the student keep track of his progress in meeting the goals helps the student feel more competent.

At all times, feedback to the student with chronic behavior problems should emphasize what the student can do as opposed to what the student cannot do. Suppose, for example, that a student with chronic behavior problems takes a valid test of the material he was supposed to learn, makes a concerted effort to do well, and receives a 67 on the test. In most classrooms, the only message that the student would receive would be one of failure, which would reinforce the student's own feelings of incompetence. If we examine the situation more objectively, however, we can see that the student knows twice as much as he does not know. This does not mean that 67 is good or acceptable, but rather than communicating that the student is a failure, the teacher can point out that he has indeed learned and then use that limited success to encourage him to continue to make the effort to learn. Using encouraging communication, engaging the student in short-term goal setting, stressing effort and improvement, and focusing on the positive aspects of the student's behavior and performance can increase the student's sense of competence.

A student's need for a sense of power revolves around the need to feel that he is not simply a pawn on a chessboard. We all need to feel that we have control over the important aspects of our lives. When students are deprived of the opportunity to be self-directing and to make responsible choices, they often become bullies or totally dependent on others, unable to control their own lives. A teacher can enhance the student's sense of power by providing opportunities to make choices and by allowing the student to experience the consequences of those choices. As noted in Chapter 4, there is a wide range of classroom decisions in which, depending on the teacher's philosophy, the student can have a voice. When students are deprived of the opportunity to make choices, especially students with chronic behavior problems, they often become resentful and challenging of the teacher's authority. It is very important for the teacher not to engage in power contests with these students. Thus, the best course of action for the teacher is to find appropriate opportunities for these students to make responsible choices.

The need for a sense of virtue or generosity revolves around the need to feel that we are givers as well as takers. When we have a fulfilled sense of virtue, we realize that we are able to give to and nurture others. Elementary teachers often use "book buddies" and cross-grade tutoring opportunities to develop a sense of virtue among their students. Many secondary students have their sense of virtue fulfilled by participating in food drives, marathons, and walkathons for charities and other types of community service projects. Some of the most successful rehabilitation programs for juvenile offenders engage these adolescents in activities that are beneficial to others in the community (Brendtro et al., 2002). Although it is sometimes difficult to arrange classroom activities that tap into the need for a sense of virtue, peer tutoring and other opportunities to share talents can enhance a student's sense of virtue or generosity.

Lisa Delpit (2012) describes a specific type of cycle of discouragement that can entrap students who are culturally different from the teacher. The danger appears to be especially high for African American males. As explained in Chapter 4, Delpit argues that many Americans have unconsciously adopted a type of racism that sees black students as less capable than white students. The resulting lowered expectations (see Chapter 5) are communicated in subtle but powerful ways. Some African American males unconsciously internalize these stereotyped expectations and begin to doubt their own ability to succeed. The resultant decrease in their sense of competence can lead to acting out behavior that has a twofold purpose. It increases the students' sense of power and also diverts attention from the learning task at hand, enabling the student to avoid having to perform and risk not doing well. The acting-out behavior reinforces the teacher's low expectations, thereby creating a cycle of stereotype discouragement based on cultural differences. Breaking this cycle of sterotype discouragment requires creating a sense of belonging among the students, a sense that they belong in the club of scholars and achievers (Delpit, 2012, p. 20).

Before turning to techniques for influencing students who exhibit chronic behavior problems, it should be emphasized that relationship building and breaking the cycle of discouragement require commitment, persistence, patience, and self-control on the part of the teacher. These strategies will not turn things around overnight. Sometimes they do not result in any tangible benefits for several weeks or months. In fact, the behavior often gets worse initially. Students who have had abusive or abandonment experiences with adults will be resistant to your overtures. Their experience tells them that they need to be self-protective rather than trusting. As a result, they often react negatively in order to drive away adults who are trying to manipulate or con them. In addition, caring behavior on the part of adults in authority positions constitutes an anomaly for them. It creates cognitive dissonance. They are not sure how to interpret it. It seems too good to be true. While they are trying to sort out the dissonance, the safest behavior, in terms of protecting their egos, is to be resistant and negative. Persistent, caring behavior on the part of the adult is critical in helping such students learn to trust and to react positively. Persisting with them and ignoring the natural desire to get even or give up constitute the ultimate in professional behavior. It is extremely hard to do, but it is often the only thing that makes a real difference to students with chronic behavior problems in the long run.

TALKING TO SOLVE PROBLEMS

Holding private conversations with students who exhibit chronic behavior problems is a sine qua non of strategies designed to influence students to regain control of their behavior. Until the teacher takes time to sit down with the students to discuss their behavior and attempts to find ways to help the students behave in more productive ways, the teacher has not really employed the tool that may well be most influential of all. A private conversation or series of conversations with a student accomplishes several important goals: (1) it ensures that the student is aware that there is a problem that must be dealt with, (2) it is an initial step toward building a positive relationship with the student, (3) it is an important tool for helping the student take ownership for the problem and see it as his issue as opposed to viewing it as the teacher's problem, and (4) it can lead to innovative solutions to the problem that might not have occurred to the teacher alone.

Receiving Skills

During private conversations, the teacher needs to be aware of the student's perception of the problem and point of view in order to be sure that the intervention focuses on the actual problem. Suppose, for example, the student's chronic misbehavior is motivated by the student's belief that he doesn't have the ability to do the assigned work (e.g., as in the case of the stereotypic cycle of discouragement). Solutions that ignore the student's underlying feeling of incompetence are not likely to be successful in the long run. Therefore, it is important to be sure you receive the message that the student is sending. The following receiving skills will help ensure that you receive the student's message:

1. *Use silence and nonverbal attending cues.* Allow the student sufficient time to express his ideas and feelings and employ nonverbal cues such as eye contact, facial expressions, head nodding, and body posture (e.g., leaning toward the student) to show that you are interested in and listening to what he is saying. Most important, make sure these cues are sincere; that is, you really *are* listening carefully to the student.

2. *Probe.* Ask relevant and pertinent questions to elicit extended information about a given topic, for clarification of ideas, and for justification of a given idea. Questions such as "Can you tell me more about the problem with Jerry?" "What makes you say that I don't like you?" "I'm not sure I understand what you mean by hitting on you; can you explain what that means?" show that you are listening and want more information.

3. *Check perceptions.* Paraphrase or summarize what the student has said using slightly different words. This acts as a check on whether you have understood the student correctly. This is not a simple verbatim repetition of what the student has said. It is an attempt by the teacher to capture the student's message as accurately as possible in the teacher's words. Usually a perception check ends by giving the student an opportunity to affirm or negate the teacher's perception; for example, "So, as I understand it, you think that I'm picking on you when I give you detention for not completing your homework; is that right?" or "You're saying that you never really wanted to be in the gifted program anyway, and so you don't care whether you are removed from the program. Do I have that right?"

4. *Check feelings.* Feeling checks refer to attempts to reach the student's emotions through questions and statements. In formulating the questions and statements, use nonverbal cues (e.g., facial expression) and paralingual cues (voice volume, rate, and pitch) to go beyond the student's statements and understand the emotions behind the words. For instance, "It sounds as if you are really proud of what you're doing in basketball, right?" or "You look really angry when you talk about being placed in the lower section. Are you angry?"

Sending Skills

Individual conversations not only allow the teacher to be sure he understands the problem from the student's vantage point, but also allow the teacher to be sure the student understands the problem from the teacher's point of view. Using sending skills to communicate the teacher's thoughts and ideas clearly is a first step toward helping the student gain that insight. Ginott (1972) and Jones (1980) offered the following guidelines for sending accurate messages:

1. *Deal in the here and now.* Don't dwell on past problems and situations. Communicate your thoughts about the present situation and the immediate future. Although it is appropriate to talk about the past behavior that has created the need for the private conference, nothing is gained by reciting a litany of past transgressions.

2. *Make eye contact and use congruent nonverbal behaviors.* Avoiding eye contact when confronting a student about misbehavior gives the student the impression that you are uncomfortable about the confrontation. In contrast, maintaining eye contact helps let the student know that you are confident and comfortable in dealing with problems. Because research indicates that students believe the nonverbal message when verbal and nonverbal behavior are not congruent (Woolfolk and Brooks, 1983), be sure nonverbal cues match the verbal messages. Smiling as you tell the student how disappointed you are in his behavior is clearly inappropriate.

3. *Make statements rather than ask questions.* Asking questions is appropriate for eliciting information from the student. However, when the teacher has specific information or behaviors to discuss, he should lay the specific facts out on the table rather than try to elicit them from the student by playing "guess what's on my mind."

4. *Use "I"—take responsibility for your feelings.* You have a right to your feelings. It can be appropriate to be annoyed at students, and it can be appropriate to be proud of students. Teachers sometimes try to disown their feelings and act as if they were robots. Students must know that teachers are people who have legitimate feelings and that their feelings must be considered in determining the effects of the student's behavior on others.

5. *Be brief.* Get to the point quickly. Let the student know what the problem is as you see it and what you propose to do about it. Once you have done this, stop. Don't belabor the issue with unnecessary lectures and harangues.

6. *Talk directly to the student, not about him.* Even if other people are present, talk to the student rather than to parents or counselors. Use "you" and specifically describe the problem to the student. This behavior sends the student the powerful message that he, not his parents or anyone else, is directly responsible for his own behavior.

7. *Give directions to help the students correct the problem.* Don't stop at identifying the problem behavior. Be specific in setting forth exactly what behaviors must be replaced and in identifying appropriate behaviors to replace them.

8. *Check student understanding of your message.* Once you have communicated clearly what the specific problem is and what steps you suggest for solving it, ask a question to be sure the student has received the message correctly. It is often a good idea to ask the student to summarize the discussion. If the student's summary indicates that he has missed the message, the teacher has an opportunity to restate or rephrase the main idea in a way that the student can understand.

Asking Authentic Questions

The substance of the private conversation should be an open discussion between the teacher and student to identify the problem clearly and develop procedures for resolving it. The teacher should consider beginning the conversation with a brief description of the situation as he sees it and then posing a question about the situation to the student. The question should not be one to which the teacher already knows the answer. It should be something that is unclear or truly puzzling to the teacher. Strachota (1996) referred to this process as asking real questions of students. He suggested that students have a wonderful capacity and willingness to engage in solving authentic problems: "I can best help children take responsibility for their thinking and actions by helping them feel fascinated by life's dilemmas and then helping them feel that they have the power to go to work on these predicaments" (pp. 26–27). Asking real questions to which the teacher does not already know the answer opens up the possibility for the student to become a partner in the problem-solving process. It also enhances the likelihood that a novel solution can be found.

For example, a teacher who is faced with two students who simply seem to rub each other the wrong way on an ongoing basis could sit down with the two students and invite them to help him think through this dilemma: "How can it be that two well-intentioned and likeable individuals like yourselves just cannot seem to get along in this classroom?" An authentic question for a situation in which the teacher finds the student constantly antagonistic might be phrased something like this: "It seems to me that you and I are almost constantly doing things that aggravate the other person. I am not sure how we got to this point or what to do about it. I am wondering if you have any thoughts about that." If the teacher really allows the conversation to proceed naturally without leading it in a preconceived direction, it is likely that new insights about the student will emerge from the conversation. These new insights often point the way to innovative solutions. Of course, teachers who ask real questions must conceive of their role as collaboratively solving problems with students as opposed to imposing their own solutions. This requires a change in belief for many teachers. Strachota's rationale for the use of authentic questions is very powerful: "Since I believe that I cannot pass on the part of the truth that I know simply by telling it to a child, I must set up situations which allow me and her to explore together so that she can invent her own understanding. Therefore, my job becomes one of looking for the right questions rather than the right answers" (1996, p. 27).

Open pursuit of the authentic question might provide clear direction for the solution to the problem, making the use of short-term problem-solving techniques unnecessary. If the solution is found through the conversation, the teacher implements the solution and then continues to work on both relationship building and breaking the cycle of discouragement. If a solution is not found through the conversation process, the teacher can then turn to one of the four specific short-term problem-solving strategies that are described next.

SPECIFIC SHORT-TERM PROBLEM-SOLVING STRATEGIES

With these guidelines for talking about problems in mind, we can now consider four specific techniques for students with chronic behavior problems. Five assumptions underlie these techniques:

1. The number of students in any one class who should be classified as exhibiting chronic behavior problems is small, usually fewer than five. If there are more than five, it is a good indication that the teacher has not done all that could be done to prevent the problems from occurring.
2. The teacher is well prepared for each class, engages the students in interesting learning activities, and employs a variety of effective teaching strategies (see Chapter 5).
3. The expectations for behavior are clearly understood by students and enforced on a consistent basis (see Chapter 6).
4. The teacher intervenes with a preplanned hierarchy of nonverbal interventions, verbal interventions, and logical consequences when commonplace disruptions occur.
5. The teacher attempts to build positive relationships with students who exhibit chronic behavior problems and attempts to break the cycle of discouragement by helping them meet their self-esteem needs.

The teacher who is not aware of these assumptions may use short-term and long-term intervention techniques when their use is not appropriate or may use them in appropriate situations but fail to implement them correctly.

When several students exhibit chronic behavior problems, they usually fall into one of two categories—those who have the greatest potential for improving their behavior quickly and those whose behavior causes the greatest disruption. When several students with chronic behavior problems are in one class, the teacher may have to choose to work with one category over another. There are pitfalls in either choice.

Those with the greatest odds for quick improvement are usually the students with the least severe behavioral problems. Thus, even if the teacher succeeds in helping them, the general level of disruption in the classroom may remain quite high. On the other hand, those students who have the most severe and most disruptive behavior usually require the longest period of time to improve, but their improvement tends to have a more dramatic impact on the classroom.

There are no clear guidelines as to which category of students teachers should choose. It is really a matter of personal preference. If the teacher is the type of individual who needs to see results quickly in order to persist, he is probably better off choosing those students with the greatest likelihood for quick improvement. If, however, the more serious behavior is threatening to any individuals, the teacher must begin intervention with those students.

It must be noted that self-monitoring, anecdotal record keeping, behavior contracting, or functional behavior assessment probably will not be effective in influencing chronic behavior problems if the five assumptions underlying these techniques have not been met. If these assumptions have been met, then the teacher has done all that he can do to prevent behavior problems from occurring, and the following four intervention techniques have a reasonably high chance of success.

Self-Monitoring

Some students who exhibit chronic disruptive behaviors perceive a well-managed private conference as a sign of a teacher's caring and support. Some students leave the conference with a new understanding that their behaviors are interfering with the rights of others and will no longer be tolerated in the classroom. Given the nature and background of chronic behavioral problems, however, most students will need more intensive and frequent intervention techniques. The challenge is to design techniques that are congruent with the belief that students must be given opportunities to learn how to control their own behavior.

Self-monitoring of behavior is a student-directed approach that is often effective with students who are really trying to behave appropriately but seem to need assistance to do so. The use of self-monitoring can help establish an internal locus of control concerning behavior. The technique is usually more appropriate for elementary students who have extremely short attention spans or who are easily distracted by the everyday events of a busy classroom. Whereas self-monitoring can be effective with some older students, the teacher must consider the age appropriateness of the self-monitoring instrument that the student will use.

For self-monitoring to be effective, the instrument must clearly delineate the behaviors to be monitored and must be easy for a student to use. The student must also clearly understand the duration of the self-monitoring and the frequency of behavioral checks. Unfortunately, teachers occasionally design an instrument that is too cumbersome to use or is too time consuming. Thus, using the instrument actually interferes with on-task behavior.

In the beginning, the student may require teacher cues to indicate when it is time to check behavior and record it on the self-monitoring instrument. These cues may be private, nonverbal signals agreed upon by the teacher and the student. In the beginning, it is a good idea for the teacher to co-monitor the student's behavior using the same instrument. When this is done, the teacher and the student can compare their monitoring consistency and discuss the proper use of the instrument as well as the progress that is being made.

The effectiveness of self-monitoring relies heavily on how the use of the instrument is explained to the student. If self-monitoring is presented as a technique that students can use to help themselves with the teacher's assistance, support, and encouragement, the likelihood of improved behavior is high. When teachers have successfully communicated the purpose of the technique and stressed the possible positive outcomes, students have actually thanked them for the opportunity and means to demonstrate on-task behavior. On the other hand, if the intervention is introduced as a form of punishment, the likelihood of positive behavioral change is diminished.

Figure 10.4 shows a self-monitoring check sheet that Brittany Bird, an intern in the Penn State Elementary Professional Development School Collaborative, used with Kahlil, a third grader, to help monitor his completion of tasks during the school day. Kahlil was having difficulty getting his work done despite several teacher interventions to help him be successful. Before introducing the self-monitoring check

Date: _____

Part of the Day	Rating	Comments
Morning Work		
Math		
Languages arts		
Social studies/science		
End of the day jobs		

Rating System:
1—I did not finish all my work because I was talking to other people.
2—I did not finish all my work because I did not understand what to do.
3—I did not finish all my work because I didn't get started right away.
4—I finished all my work, but I was rushing so it is not my best work.
5—I finished all my work, and I am proud of it.

FIGURE 10.4   Self-Monitoring Check Sheet.

sheet, Brittany and Khalil discussed his behavior, the need to improve it, and his desire to do a better job. Brittany also made sure that Khalil understood the rating scale on the check sheet. Khalil rated himself after each activity, and he and Brittany discussed the ratings twice each day, at lunch and just before dismissal. After three weeks of self-monitoring, Khalil improved dramatically in his ability to complete his work.

As with any intervention that focuses on the improvement of chronic behavior, progress may be slow. Two steps forward and one step backward may be the best a student can do in the beginning. We must remember that chronic misbehavior does not develop in a day, and it will not be replaced with more appropriate behavior in a day. It is difficult to learn new behaviors to replace behaviors that have become ingrained and habitual. Therefore, the teacher must be patient and focus on improvements. It is usually best to work on one behavior at a time. For example, if a student continually talks to neighbors and calls out, the teacher and student should decide on which behavior to work on first. If the student is successful in managing the selected behavior, experience has shown that subsequent behaviors are more readily corrected.

As behavior improves, the teacher should begin to wean the student from self-monitoring. As a first step, once the teacher is convinced that the student is reliably monitoring his own behavior, the teacher stops co-monitoring and relies solely on the student's report. Next, as behaviors begin to improve, the teacher lengthens the period of time between self-checks. Finally, the teacher removes the student completely from self-monitoring. When this happens, the teacher uses the event to build self-esteem and self-control by making the student aware that he has changed his behavior on his own and should be quite proud of his accomplishments. Any corresponding improvements in academics or peer interactions should also be noted and tied to the student's improved behavior.

Figure 10.5 is a checklist that teachers can use to evaluate the self-monitoring procedures and instruments that they design.

1. Do the teacher and student clearly understand and agree on the behaviors to be monitored? _____ Yes _____ No

2. Is the time period for self-checks clearly specified? _____ Yes _____ No

3. Does the student understand how to use the instrument? _____ Yes _____ No

4. Have the teacher and student agreed on a meeting time to discuss the self-monitoring? _____ Yes _____ No

5. Is the instrument designed so that small increments of improved behavior will be noted? _____ Yes _____ No

6. Is the instrument designed to focus on one behavior? _____ Yes _____ No

FIGURE 10.5 Self-Monitoring Checklist.

Anecdotal Record Keeping

If the teacher either has tried self-monitoring or has decided not to try this technique because of philosophical objections or the student's refusal to make the required commitments, a second option, called *anecdotal record keeping*, can be used to work with chronic behavioral problems. This method, which is a collaborative approach to managing classroom behaviors (see Chapter 4), has been used successfully by student teachers and veteran teachers alike to handle a variety of chronic discipline problems at a variety of grade levels (Levin, Nolan, and Hoffman, 1985). It is based on the principles of Adlerian psychology, which state that changes in behavior can be facilitated by making people aware of their behavior and its consequences for themselves and others (Sweeney, 1981).

Anecdotal record keeping is usually most appropriate for middle and secondary students because students at these levels have better developed self-regulation. To employ the technique, the teacher merely records the classroom behaviors, both positive and negative, of a student who exhibits chronic disruptive behavior over a period of a few weeks. Although it is preferable to have the student's cooperation, anecdotal record keeping can be employed without it.

The record the teacher has made of the student's behavior and the measures that have been taken to improve that behavior form the basis for a private conference with the student. Nine guidelines should be followed in conducting this initial conference:

1. The teacher should begin on a positive note.
2. The teacher should help the student recognize the past behavior and its negative impact, showing the student the record of past behaviors and discussing it if necessary.
3. The teacher should explain that this behavior is unacceptable and must change.
4. The teacher should tell the student that he will keep a record of the student's positive and negative behavior on a daily basis and that the student will be required to sign the record at the end of class each day.
5. The teacher should record the student's home phone number on the top of the record and indicate that he will contact the parents to inform them of continued unacceptable behavior. (This option may not be useful for senior high students because parents are often not as influential at this age.)
6. The teacher should be positive and emphasize expectations of improvement.
7. The conference should be recorded on the anecdotal record.
8. A verbal commitment for improved behavior should be sought from the student. This commitment, or the refusal to give it, should be noted on the anecdotal record.
9. The student should sign the anecdotal record at the end of the conference. If the student refuses to sign, the refusal should be recorded.

After the initial conference, the teacher continues the anecdotal record, each day highlighting positive behaviors, documenting negative behaviors, and noting any corrective measures taken. Keeping this systematic record enables the teacher to focus on the behavior (the deed) rather than on the student (the doer; Ginott, 1972). The teacher reinforces the student for improved behaviors and, if possible, clarifies the connection between improved behaviors and academic achievement. Thus, the teacher "catches the student being good" (Canter and Canter, 2001; Jones, 1980) and demonstrates the concept of encouragement (Dreikurs, Grunwald, and Pepper, 1998). To illustrate the concept of student accountability, the teacher must be consistent in recording behaviors, sharing the record with the student, and obtaining the student's signature on a daily basis (Brophy, 1988). If the student refuses to sign the record on any day, the teacher simply records this fact on the record. Figure 10.6 is the anecdotal record used with one tenth-grade student over a three-week period. The technique succeeded after the intervention hierarchy had been utilized with little improvement in the student's behavior. Note that the teacher highlighted positive behaviors to "catch the student being good."

Although teachers may think that this technique will consume a lot of instructional time, it does not. If the documentation occurs in the last few minutes of class, perhaps when students are doing homework or getting ready for the next class, the two or three minutes required for it compare favorably to the enormous amount of time wasted by unresolved chronic discipline problems. Thus, this technique actually helps to conserve time by making more efficient use of classroom time.

In studying the use of anecdotal record keeping, Levin et al. (1985) requested teachers to log their views on the effectiveness of the procedure. Here are three representative logs by secondary teachers.

TEACHER'S LOG—ELEVENTH-GRADE ENGLISH

About a week and a half ago, I implemented the anecdotal record in one of my classes. Two male students were the subjects. The improvement shown by one of these students is very impressive.

On the first day that I held a conference with the student, I explained the procedure, showed him my records for the day, and asked for his signature. He scribbled his name and looked at me as if to say, "What a joke." On the second day, his behavior in class was negative again. This time, when I spoke to him and told him that one more day of disruptive behavior would result in a phone call to his parents, he looked at me as if to say, "This joke isn't so funny anymore." From that moment on, there was a marked improvement in his behavior. He was quiet and attentive in class. After class, he would come up to me and ask me where he was supposed to sign his name for the day. And he "beamed" from my remarks about how well behaved he was that day. Only one time after that did I have to speak to him for negative behavior. I caught him throwing a piece of paper. As soon as he saw me looking at him, he said, "Are you going to write that down in your report?" Then, after class, he came up to me with a worried expression on his face and asked, "Are you going to call my parents?" I didn't because of the previous days of model behavior.

I must say that I was skeptical about beginning this type of record on the students. It seemed like such a lengthy and time-consuming process. But I'll say what I'm feeling now. If the anecdotal record can give positive results more times than not, I'll keep on using it. If you can get one student under control, who is to say you can't get five or ten students under control? It truly is a worthwhile procedure to consider.

Student's Name _____

Home Phone _____

Date	Student Behavior	Teacher Action	Student Signature
4/14	Talking with Van Out of seat 3 times Refused to answer question	Verbal reprimand Told her to get back Went on	
4/16	Had private conference Rhonda agreed to improve	Explained anecdotal record Was supportive	
4/17	Stayed on task in lab	Positive feedback	
4/20	Late for class Worked quietly	Verbal reminder Positive feedback	
4/21	Worked quietly Wrestling with Jill	Positive feedback Verbal reprimand	
4/22	No disruptions Volunteered to answer	Positive feedback Called on her 3 times	
4/23	Late for class Left without signing	Detention after school Recorded it on record	
4/24	Missed detention	Two days' detention	
4/27	Stayed on task all class	Positive feedback	
4/28	Listened attentively to film	Positive feedback	
4/29	Worked at assignment well	Positive feedback	
4/30	Participated in class No disruptions Left without signing	Called on her twice Positive feedback Recorded it	
5/1	Conference to discontinue anecdotal records		

FIGURE 10.6 Anecdotal Record.

TEACHER'S LOG—TENTH-GRADE SCIENCE

Day 1

As a third or fourth alternative, I used an anecdotal record to help control the discipline problems incurred [sic] in my second-period class. Previously, I had used direct requests or statements (for example, "What are you doing? What should you be doing?" "Your talking is interfering with other students' right to learn," etcetera). The anecdotal record involved having one-to-one conferences with the four students. The conferences were aimed at reviewing the students' classroom behaviors and securing commitments from them for improved behavior. It was fairly successful, as I received a commitment from the four involved; and they, in turn, let the rest of the class in on the deal. In choosing the four students, I tried to pick a student from each trouble pair. Hopefully, this will eliminate misbehavior for both.

Day 2

The progress in my class with the anecdotal records was excellent today, as I expected. The four students were exceptionally well behaved. I will be sure to keep extra-close tabs on their progress the next few days to prevent them from reverting back to their disruptive behavior.

Day 3

My second-period class was again very well behaved. I did, however, need to put a few negative remarks (for example, talking during film) on the anecdotal records. I will continue to keep close tabs on the situation.

Day 4

My second-period class (anecdotal records) is quickly becoming one of my best. We are covering more material, getting more class participation, and having less extraneous talking. I did need to make a couple of negative remarks on the record; but on seeing them, the students should, hopefully, maintain a positive attitude and appropriate behavior.

TEACHER'S LOG—EIGHTH-GRADE SCIENCE

Day 1

I discovered a method with which to deal with some major discipline problems in one of my classes. It uses an anecdotal record, which is a record of student actions and student behaviors. I think it will probably work because it holds the student accountable for his his behaviors. If something must be done, the student has nobody to blame but himself.

Day 2

Today, I set up private conferences with anecdotal record students. I wonder if they'll show up—and if they do, how will they respond?

Day 3

Two students (of three) showed up for their anecdotal record conferences. The third is absent. Both students were very cooperative and made a commitment to better behavior. One student even made the comment that he thought this idea was a good one for him. The way things look; this will work out fairly well. We'll see...

Day 4
One of the students on anecdotal record has improved in behavior so much that I informed him that if his good behavior kept improving, I'd take him off the record next Wednesday. I think it will be interesting to see how his behavior will be; will it keep improving or will it backtrack again?

Implementing any new strategy may be difficult, and anecdotal record keeping is no exception. The teacher must expect that some students will be quite hostile when the procedure is introduced. Some may adamantly refuse to sign the record; others may scribble an unrecognizable signature. The teacher must remain calm and positive and simply record these behaviors. This action communicates to the student that he is solely responsible for his behavior and that the teacher is only an impartial recorder of the behavior. Student behavior will usually improve, given time. Because improved behavior becomes part of the record, the anecdotal record reinforces the improvement and becomes the basis for a cycle of improvement.

When the student's behavior has improved to an acceptable level, the teacher informs him that it will no longer be necessary to keep the anecdotal record because of the improvement in his behavior. It is important, as suggested earlier, to connect the improved behavior to academic success and improved grades if possible. It must also be made clear to the student that his fine behavior is expected to continue. Because continued attention is a key link in the chain of behaviors that turn disruptive students into students who behave appropriately, the teacher must continue to give the student attention when he behaves appropriately. If the student's behavior shows no improvement, it may be time to discontinue the process.

It can be quite difficult to decide when to stop recording behavior. There are no hard-and-fast rules, but there are some helpful guidelines. If the student has displayed acceptable behavior for a few days to a week, the record may be discontinued. If the student's behavior remains disruptive continuously for a week, the record keeping should be discontinued and the student told why. If the misbehavior is somewhat reduced, it may be advisable to have a second conference with the student to determine whether or not to continue record keeping.

Functional Behavior Assessment

The third short-term strategy for working with students who exhibit chronic behavior problems is *functional behavior assessment* (FBA), which is a teacher-directed strategy (Chapter 4) based on behavioral learning theory: "A functional behavior assessment simply means that someone skilled at observing behavior tries to determine the function (i.e., the motive) for the student's behavior" (Hall and Hall, 2003, p. 149). The intent of functional behavior assessment is to identify the purpose that the behavior serves either consciously or unconsciously for the student, the antecedents that provoke the behavior, and the consequences that maintain the behavior. Once the function, antecedent, and consequences have been identified, a positive behavior support plan can be developed for extinguishing the unproductive or disruptive behavior and replacing it with appropriate behavior. The behavioral support plan might take many forms, including but not limited to, altering the instructional environment and/or context in which the behavior occurs, teaching the student new social and academic skills, or modifying the consequences that follow the behavior. Modifying consequences could involve the use of behavior contracting (see the next section of this chapter).

Several assumptions underlie functional behavior assessment: (1) behavior is learned not innate, (2) behavior serves a specific purpose, and (3) behavior is related to the context in which it occurs (PaTTAN, 2008). The most common functions of behavior, according to Hall and Hall (2003), are to get or avoid attention, to become engaged in or avoid particular activities, to obtain or avoid certain objects or items, and to obtain or avoid sensory stimulation. According to training materials concerning FBA from the Pennsylvania Training and Technical Assistance Network (PaTTAN, 2008), functional behavior assessment is a data-gathering and analysis process that addresses the following questions:

1. How often does the target behavior occur and how long does it last?
2. Where does the behavior typically occur or never occur?
3. Who is present for the occurrence/nonoccurrence of the behavior?
4. What is going on during the occurrence/nonoccurrence of the behavior?
5. When is the behavior most likely/least likely to occur?
6. How does the student react to the usual consequences that follow the behavior?

Functional behavior assessment has been used most often with special needs students, and in fact, Chapter 14 of the Pennsylvania School Code, which focuses on special education, mandates the use of functional behavior assessment and positive behavior support as a prerequisite for exclusion of the special needs student from his educational setting (PaTTAN, 2008). Most often, a team of professionals that includes the special education teacher, regular education teacher, behavior specialist, and/or school psychologist, and other therapists collaborates in carrying out the FBA. It is helpful to include other individuals in the FBA process to share the workload but also to obtain a more comprehensive picture of the student's behavior that is less susceptible to bias than data that are collected by one person. Thus, we would suggest that you, as a classroom teacher, engage colleagues who have expertise in FBA to assist you in carrying out the process. If other professionals are not available to help, however, you can carry out much of the process independently, but doing so will require extra time and effort on your part.

The functional behavior assessment process consists of three parts: a pre-observation interview of individuals who have observed the student's behavior over time; direct observations of the student's behavior; and a summary that includes a hypothesis regarding the purpose or function of the behavior, the antecedent conditions under which it occurs, and the consequences that maintain or reward the behavior. The summary then serves as the basis for the development of the positive behavior support plan.

The pre-observation interviews are often conducted with the regular classroom teacher, the special education teacher, teachers of elective or special subjects such as physical education, parents, and others. The interviews may be conducted by the regular classroom teacher or by another team member. Although an interview is the recommended strategy for gathering data, an alternative technique would be to ask

1. Please describe the behavior that you are concerned about.

2. Could the behavior be related to any medical issue (for example, a medical condition or side effects of medication, etc.)?

3. Could the behavior be related to some physiological issue (for example, hunger, thirst, lack of rest, temperature, etc.)?

4. Are there certain circumstances that are typically or almost always present when the behavior occurs (for example, time of day, location of activity, type of activity, people present, etc.)?

5. Does the behavior seem to occur in response to certain stimuli (for example, noise level, tone of voice, demands of the activity, change in routine, number of people, etc.)?

6. Could the behavior be related to any skill deficits (for example, academic skills, social skills, communication skills, sensory processing, etc.)?

7. Does the behavior allow the student to gain anything (for example, preferred activities, peer or adult attention, items or objects, etc.)?

8. Does the behavior allow the student to postpone or escape anything (for example, nonpreferred activities, academic or social demands, etc.)?

9. Does the behavior provide stimulation or activity that is satisfying to the student?

FIGURE 10.7   Suggested Items for FBA Interview or Questionnaire.

the individuals just mentioned to fill out a questionnaire concerning the student's behavior. If the classroom teacher is engaged in the process alone, he might start by completing the questionnaire himself. Some of the questions that might be asked in an interview or on a questionnaire are listed in Figure 10.7.

The interview or questionnaire results create a measurable description of the behavior of concern and leads to a concrete and focused plan for data collection. The plan outlines the observation schedule including where, when, how often, and who will collect data. It is important to begin the data collection process by recording baseline levels of the behavior and its antecedents and consequences. The behavioral records should include the frequency and/or duration of the behavior and indicate time of day, location, activities occurring, and people present.

Four common recording strategies are used in collecting data. The choice of data recording technique depends on the behavior in question. *Event recording* engages the observer in documenting every occurrence of the behavior separately. The result is a record of exactly how many times the behavior occurs. It is a useful strategy for behavior that occurs fairly frequently in short bursts with a definite beginning and ending point. When the behavior in question occurs rapidly within a very short time period, event recording can be quite difficult, if not impossible. *Duration recording*, as the name implies, consist of recording the beginning and ending time of the behavior so that the duration of the behavior can be calculated. This strategy can be helpful when it is difficult to separate one instance of the behavior from the other or when the student engages in inappropriate behavior for lengthy periods of time. *Latency recording* refers to recording the interval between the time when the student is asked to initiate a behavior and when he actually starts the behavior. This strategy is particularly important when students attempt to avoid situations by finding ways to delay engagement in particular activities. Finally, *interval recording* or *time sampling* consists of recording behavior at preset intervals (e.g., every 15 seconds). Use of a time sampling strategy provides a record of both inappropriate and appropriate behaviors over a designated time period. The use of a combination of these strategies is often useful in capturing a comprehensive portrayal of a student's behavior. For example, it is possible to combine event and duration sampling by coding each occurrence of behavior and noting how long each occurrence lasts.

Once the data have been collected, the team members or the individual teacher analyzes the data. The analysis needs to address two key questions as accurately as possible:

1. How often does the behavior of concern occur and how long does it last?
2. What patterns can be identified concerning the occurrence and/or duration of the behavior?

The first question concerning the frequency and/or duration of the behavior is presented in a visual format, typically a graph that depicts the intensity of the behavior over time and may include comparisons with the same behaviors for peers of the student in question. The patterns that can be identified always include the antecedents of the behavior: the conditions (time of day, location or setting, activity, people, objects, etc.) that are typically present when the behavior occurs as well as the consequences that seem to maintain the behavior.

As noted earlier, the analysis culminates with a summary statement that consists of three key parts:

1. A description of the antecedents/circumstances—"When X occurs"
2. A description of the target behavior—"the student does this"
3. A description of the consequences—"to get/to avoid this"

For example, a summary statement might say, "When Justine is asked to engage in a creative writing activity, she engages in other tasks (sharpening her pencil, getting a drink, talking to other students, searching for materials) to avoid having to develop ideas on her own so that the teacher will provide help in coming up with ideas." Once the summary statement has been developed, the team or teacher develops a positive behavior support strategy to enable Justine to replace the inappropriate behavior with more productive behavior. Following are three general categories of positive behavior support:

1. *Antecedent strategies.* Adjusting the environment to reduce the likelihood of problem behavior occurring and to allow the student to be more independent and successful. Examples include modifying the curriculum, reorganizing the physical setting, and clarifying routines and expectations.

2. *Educative strategies.* Teaching replacement academic and social skills (teaching students how to ask to join a group to play or equipping a student with learning strategies that could be helpful in completing in-class activities).

3. *Consequence strategies.* Managing consequences to reinforce desired behaviors and withholding reinforcement following undesirable behavior (praise, access to reward, verbal redirect, loss of privilege; PaTTAN, 2008). Additional information concerning positive behavior support can be obtained from the National Technical Assistance Center on Positive Behavioral Intervention and Supports' website at *http://www.pbis.org/*

Given the hypothesis that Justine is using delaying tactics for the purpose of avoiding having to come up with her own ideas and to ensure that the teacher helps develop ideas, the team and/or the individual teacher can develop a strategy to extinguish the delaying tactics and replace them with a more productive strategy for getting started on the writing activity. An example of an antecedent strategy would be alerting Justine the day before a creative writing activity will be done in class so that she has time to brainstorm some potential ideas at home the night before. An example of an educative strategy for this situation would be to work with Justine independently on brainstorming techniques that would make it more likely that she could develop ideas for writing on her own with minimal or no teacher support. An example of a consequence strategy would be making sure that the teacher does not come to Justine's aid (withdrawing the reinforcement) to help her develop ideas during the writing activity. If she cannot complete the writing activity during the allotted time, it would have to be completed during her free time. Figure 10.8 provides a worksheet that can be used to develop the summary statement and to brainstorm positive behavior support strategies.

One of the strategies that can be used to provide positive behavior support is behavior contracting. We now turn our attention to this fourth short-term strategy for dealing with chronic behavior problems.

Behavior Contracting

Behavior contracting is a teacher-directed strategy (see Chapter 4) that can be used in conjunction with or independently of functional behavior assessment. This technique is grounded in the principles of operant conditioning, which state that a behavior that is reinforced is likely to be repeated and that a behavior that is not reinforced will disappear.

This technique involves the use of a written agreement, known as a *behavior contract*, between the teacher and student that commits the student to behave appropriately and offers a specified reward when the commitment is met. The contract details the expected behavior, a time period during which this behavior must be exhibited, and the reward that will be provided. The purposes of the contract

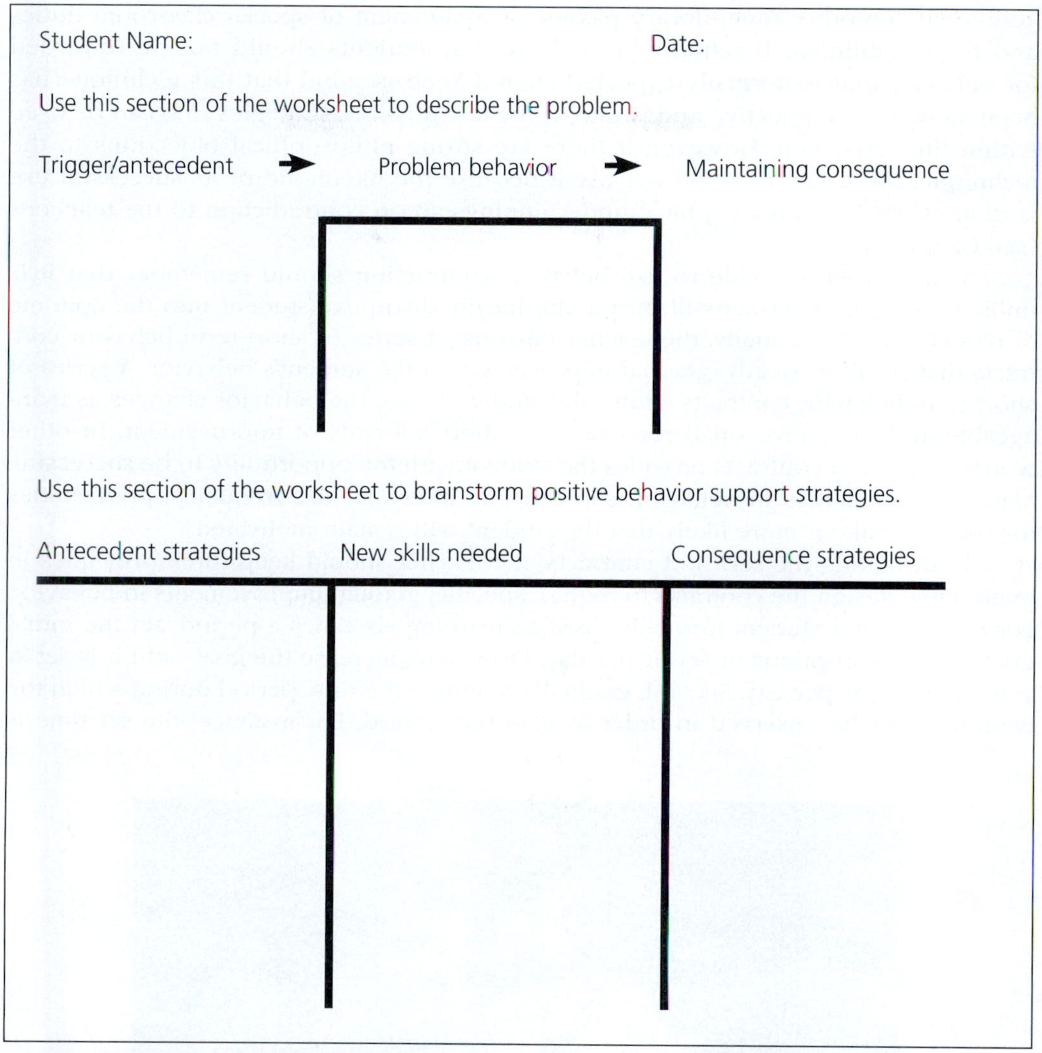

Student Name: _____   Date: _____

Use this section of the worksheet to describe the problem.

Trigger/antecedent ➔ Problem behavior ➔ Maintaining consequence

Use this section of the worksheet to brainstorm positive behavior support strategies.

Antecedent strategies   New skills needed   Consequence strategies

FIGURE 10.8 **Behavior Strategies Worksheet.**

are to influence behavior that is not influenced by normal classroom procedures, to encourage self-discipline, and to foster the student's sense of commitment to appropriate classroom behavior. Although behavior contracting can be used with students at any grade level, it is often more appropriate and effective with elementary and middle school students because older students often resent the obvious attempt to manipulate their behavior. This technique is frequently and effectively used in special education classes.

Because an integral part of behavior contracting is the use of rewards, often extrinsic, concrete rewards, some teachers may be philosophically opposed to the technique. These teachers often overcome their philosophical objections by replacing concrete, extrinsic rewards with those more focused on learning activities, such as additional computer time, library passes, or assignment of special classroom duties and responsibilities. Teachers who believe that students should not be rewarded for behavior that is normally expected should keep in mind that this technique has been shown to be effective and is one of the last possible strategies that can be used within the classroom. However, if there are strong philosophical objections to the technique, the teacher should not use it because the likelihood of its successful use is diminished if its philosophical underpinnings are in contradiction to the teacher's (see Chapter 4).

Teachers who decide to use behavior contracting should remember that it is unlikely that one contract will turn a chronically disruptive student into the epitome of model behavior. Usually, the teacher must use a series of short-term behavior contracts that result in steady, gradual improvement in the student's behavior. A series of short-term behavior contracts allows the student to see the behavior changes as manageable and to receive small rewards after short intervals of improvement. In other words, a series of contracts provides the student with the opportunity to be successful. Manageable changes in behavior, shorter time intervals, and frequent opportunities for success make it more likely that the student will remain motivated.

In designing the series of contracts, the teacher should keep three principles in mind. First, design the contracts to require specific, gradual improvements in behavior. For example, if a student normally disrupts learning six times a period, set the initial goal at four disruptions or fewer per day. Over time, increase the goal until it is set at zero disruptions per day. Second, gradually lengthen the time period during which the contract must be observed in order to gain the reward. For instance, the set time is

It is critically important to help parents believe that you all want what is best for their child.

one day for the first contract, a few days for the second contract, a week for the third contract, and so on. Third, move little by little from more tangible, extrinsic rewards to less tangible, more intrinsic rewards. Thus, a pencil or other supplies are the rewards under the first few contracts, and free time for pleasure reading is the reward under a later contract. Using these three principles takes advantage of a behavior modification technique called *behavior shaping* and gradually shifts management over the student's behavior from the teacher to the student, where it rightfully belongs.

Before writing the contract, the teacher should make a record of the student's past misbehaviors and the techniques that were used to try to ameliorate these misbehaviors. The teacher should use all available evidence, including documents and personal recollections, trying to be as accurate and neutral as possible. This record will help the teacher decide which specific behaviors must be changed and how much change seems manageable for the student at one time. It also ensures that all appropriate management techniques have been used before the implementation of the behavior contract process. Once the record is compiled, the teacher holds a private conference with the student. It is best to begin the conference on a positive note. The teacher should communicate to the student that he has the potential to do well and to succeed if he can learn to behave appropriately. In doing this, the teacher is employing the concept of encouragement (Dreikurs et al., 1998). The teacher should then attempt to get the student to acknowledge that his behavior has been inappropriate and to recognize its negative impact on everyone in the classroom. Stressing the effect of the student's behavior on others promotes the development of higher moral reasoning (Tanner, 1978). To help the student recognize that his behavior has been unacceptable, the teacher may want to use questions similar to these: "What have you been doing in class?" "How is that affecting your chances of success?" "How would you like it if other students treated you like that?" "How would you like it if you were in a class you really liked but never got a chance to learn because other students were always causing trouble?" Thereafter, the teacher should tell the student that his behavior, no matter what the explanation for it, is unacceptable and must change. This is followed by a statement such as "I'd like to work out a plan with you that will help you to behave more appropriately in class."

The teacher must clearly state how the plan works. Because a contract is an agreement between two people, the technique cannot be used if the student refuses to make a commitment to the contract. If, however, the student commits himself to improvements in classroom behavior for a specified period of time, some positive consequences or rewards result. The reward may be free time for activities of special interest; a letter, note, or phone call to parents describing the improvements in behavior; or supplies, such as posters, pencils, and stickers. The most important consideration in deciding which particular reward to use is whether or not it is perceived as motivating by the student. For that reason, it is often a good idea to allow the student to suggest possible rewards or to discuss rewards with him. If the student's parents are cooperative, it is sometimes possible to ask them to provide a reward at home that is meaningful to the student. At this point, the teacher should draw up the contract, setting forth the specific improvements in behavior, the time period, and the reward. Both the teacher and student should then sign the contract and each should receive a copy. In the case of young students, it is often a good idea to send a copy of the contract home to parents as well. The conference should end as it began, on a positive note. The teacher, for example, might tell the student that he is looking forward to positive changes in the student's behavior.

Figure 10.9 is an example of a behavior contract and a behavior contract checklist that teachers may use to evaluate the quality of contracts that they draw up. The sample contract was the third in a series between Jessica and her fifth-grade teacher, Ms. Jones. Before the behavior contract intervention, Jessica spent the vast majority of each day's 40-minute social studies period wandering around the room. The first two contracts resulted in her being able to remain seated for about half the period.

Once the contract is made, the teacher should record the behavior of the student each day in regard to the terms specified in the contract. At the end of the contract

---

1. *Expected Behavior*
Jessica remains in her seat for the first 30 minutes of each social studies period.

2. *Time Period*
Monday, February 27, to Friday, March 3.

3. *Reward*
If Jessica remains in her seat for the first 30 minutes of each social studies period,

    a. she can choose the class's outdoor game on Friday afternoon, March 3.

    b. Ms. Jones will telephone her parents to tell them of the improvement in Jessica's behavior on Friday afternoon, March 3.

4. *Evaluation*

    a. After each social studies period, Ms. Jones records whether Jessica did or did not get out of her seat during the first 30 minutes.

    b. Jessica and Ms. Jones will meet on Friday, March 3, at 12:30 P.M. to determine whether the contract has been performed and write next week's fourth contract.

Student _____

Teacher _____

Date _____

Behavior Contract Checklist

1. Is the expected behavior described specifically?	_____ Yes	_____ No
2. Is the time period specified clearly?	_____ Yes	_____ No
3. Has the reward been specified clearly?	_____ Yes	_____ No
4. Is the reward motivating to the student?	_____ Yes	_____ No
5. Is the evaluation procedure specified?	_____ Yes	_____ No
6. Has a date been set to meet to review the contract?	_____ Yes	_____ No
7. Has the student understood, agreed to, and signed the contract?	_____ Yes	_____ No
8. Has the teacher signed the contract?	_____ Yes	_____ No
9. Do both the teacher and student have copies?	_____ Yes	_____ No
10. Did the student's parents get a copy of the contract?	_____ Yes	_____ No

FIGURE 10.9   Third Contract between Jessica and Ms. Jones.

period, the teacher can use this record to conduct a conference with the student. If the student has kept his commitment, the teacher should provide the reward. If the student's behavior needs further improvement, the teacher can draw up a new contract that specifies increased improvement over a longer time period. If, at the end of the contract, the student's behavior has improved sufficiently to conform to final expectations, the teacher can inform the student that a behavior contract is no longer needed. If possible, the teacher should point out to the student the direct relationship between the improved behavior and the student's academic success in the classroom. The teacher also should make clear that he expects acceptable behavior and success to continue. Of course, the teacher must continue to give the student attention after the contract has ended. This consistent attention helps the student recognize that positive behavior results in positive consequences and usually helps maintain appropriate behavior over a long period of time.

If, at the end of the contract period, the student has not kept the commitment, the teacher should accept no excuses. During the conference, the teacher should assume a neutral role, explaining that the reward cannot be given because the student's behavior did not live up to the behavior specified in the contract. The teacher should point out to the student that the lack of reward is simply a logical consequence of the behavior. This helps the student see the cause-and-effect relationship between behavior and its consequences. If the student learns only this, he has learned an extremely valuable lesson.

At this point, the teacher must decide whether or not it is worth trying a new contract with the student. If the teacher believes that the student tried to live up to the contract, a new contract that calls for a little less drastic improvement or for improvement over a slightly shorter time frame may be worthwhile.

If the student has not made a sincere effort to improve, obviously the contracting is not working. It is time to try another option. Nothing has been lost in the attempt except a little bit of time, and the teacher has accumulated additional documentation, which will be helpful if it is necessary to seek outside assistance.

There is one final technique for the teacher to try when these classroom techniques do not work. This is the exclusion of the student from the classroom until he makes a written commitment to improve his behavior.

Prior to exclusion, the teacher tells the student that he is no longer welcome in the class because of his disruptive behavior, which is interfering with the teacher's right to teach and the students' right to learn. The teacher then tells the student to report to a specified location in the school where appropriate classroom assignments involving reading and writing will be given. The student is also told that he will be held accountable for the completion of all assignments in an acceptable and timely manner, the same as required in the regular classroom. The teacher stresses that the student may return to the classroom at any time by giving a written commitment to improve his behavior. This written commitment must be in the student's own words and must specify the changed behavior that will be evident when the student returns to the classroom. Of course, exclusion presupposes that the administration is supportive of such a technique and has made appropriate arrangements for the setting.

Our experience has shown that those few students who have been excluded from the classroom and have then made the written commitment and returned have remained in the classroom with acceptable behavior. Exclusion finally demonstrates to the student that his behavior will no longer be tolerated and that the entire responsibility for the student's behavior is on the student and only the student.

If a student does not make the written commitment within a reasonable period of time, usually no more than a few days, outside assistance (in the form of parents, counselor, principal, or outside agency) must be sought (see Chapter 11). If it is necessary to seek outside assistance, the teacher's use of self-monitoring, anecdotal record keeping, or behavior contracting will provide the documented evidence needed to make an appropriate referral.

Summary

This chapter discussed the strategies that can be used in working with students who exhibit chronic behavior problems. Two long-term strategies for resolving chronic problems—building positive relationships and breaking the cycle of discouragement—were described. In addition, four techniques for working with students with chronic behavior problems were introduced: self-monitoring, anecdotal record keeping, functional behavior assessment, and behavior contracting. Of these techniques, self-monitoring is most compatible with the student-directed philosophy; anecdotal record keeping is most compatible with the collaborative philosophy; and functional behavior assessment and behavioral contracting are most compatible with the teacher-directed philosophy. This chapter also discussed when, how, and with which students to employ these strategies and techniques. The communication skills needed for a private conference, an essential component of any strategy for working with students who have chronic behavior problems, were divided into receiving skills and sending skills. Finally, the technique of exclusion from the classroom, the final step between in-class teacher intervention and outside referral, was presented.

Exercises

1. Think of the teachers you had in school who were most successful in building positive relationships with students. What qualities did these teachers possess? How was their behavior toward students different from the behavior of teachers who were not good at building relationships? What implications do these differences have for building positive relationships with students who have chronic behavior problems?

2. This chapter presents several ideas for breaking the cycle of discouragement by helping to meet students' self-esteem needs. In each of the following four categories of self-esteem needs, suggest additional behaviors that a teacher might use to enhance student self-esteem: (a) the need for significance, (b) the need for competence, (c) the need for power, and (d) the need for virtue.

3. Form a triad with two other classmates. Designate a letter (A, B, or C) for each of you. Role-play three conversations between a teacher and a student who exhibits chronic behavior problems. In each role-play, the individual playing the teacher will create the scenario that has led to the conversation. During each conversation, the person who plays the role of teacher should practice using effective receiving and sending skills. The process observer will give feedback to the teacher on his use of effective communication. Divide the roles for the three conversations according to the following format:

	Person A	Person B	Person C
Conversation 1	Teacher	Student	Process observer
Conversation 2	Process observer	Teacher	Student
Conversation 3	Student	Process observer	Teacher

4. Design a self-monitoring instrument that is appropriate for elementary children and monitors (a) calling out, (b) talking to neighbors, and (c) staying focused on seat work.

5. This chapter classified self-monitoring as a student-directed approach to the management of chronic behavior problems. Do you agree? If so, what makes it a student-directed approach? If not, how should it be classified? If not, is it possible to have a student-directed technique to manage chronic behavior problems?

6. Should students who exhibit chronic behavior problems receive special rewards for behaviors that are typically expected of other students? Justify your answer.

7. Make a list of rewards under the regular classroom teacher's control that could be used in behavior contracts or functional behavior assessment for students at each of the following levels: (a) elementary, (b) middle or junior high, and (c) senior high.

8. Develop a list of learning-focused positive consequences that could be substituted for the use of concrete, extrinsic rewards in behavior contracts or functional behavior assessment.

9. Design an initial behavior contract for the following situation: Jonathan, a sixth-grade, middle school student who loves sports, has refused to do homework for the past three weeks, has started fights on three occasions during the past three weeks, and has disrupted class two or three times each day during the past three weeks.

10. We classify anecdotal record keeping as a collaborative approach to classroom management. Do you agree? If so, what makes it a collaborative approach? If not, how should it be classified?

11. Examine the sample anecdotal record in Figure 10.6. Explain whether you agree or disagree with the following decisions made by the teacher: (a) to continue the intervention after 4/23 and 4/24 or (b) to stop the record after 4/30. Justify your statements.

12. Which types of misbehavior constitute sufficient grounds for exclusion from the classroom? Justify your answer.

13. **Principles of Teacher Behavior** After reading Chapter 10 and doing the exercises, use what you have learned to briefly describe your understanding of the implications of the principles listed at the beginning of the chapter for a classroom teacher.

Principle 1:

Principle 2:

Principle 3:

Principle 4:

Principle 5:

11

Seeking Outside Assistance

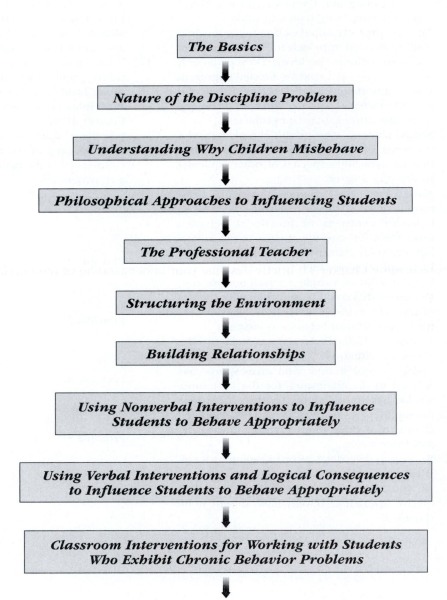

The Basics

Nature of the Discipline Problem

Understanding Why Children Misbehave

Philosophical Approaches to Influencing Students

The Professional Teacher

Structuring the Environment

Building Relationships

Using Nonverbal Interventions to Influence Students to Behave Appropriately

Using Verbal Interventions and Logical Consequences to Influence Students to Behave Appropriately

Classroom Interventions for Working with Students Who Exhibit Chronic Behavior Problems

Seeking Outside Assistance
**Understanding the Nature of Persisting Misbehavior • Recognizing
When Outside Assistance Is Needed • Making Referrals**
• Counselors • Administrators • School Psychologists
**• Working with Families • Alternatives to Suspension • Protecting
Students' Rights**

PRINCIPLES OF TEACHER BEHAVIOR THAT INFLUENCE APPROPRIATE STUDENT BEHAVIOR

1. Professional teachers recognize that some chronic misbehavior problems are not responsive to treatment within the classroom or are beyond their expertise and necessitate specialized outside assistance.

2. When outside assistance must be sought to manage a chronic misbehavior problem, the use of a multidisciplinary team is the most effective approach.

3. Family support and cooperation with the school is critical when attempting to work with a student who exhibits chronic behavior problems. Careful planning and skilled conferencing techniques are essential in developing a positive homeschool working relationship.

PREREADING ACTIVITY: UNDERSTANDING THE PRINCIPLES OF TEACHER BEHAVIOR

Before reading Chapter 11, briefly describe your understanding of the implications of the principles for a classroom teacher.

Principle 1:

Principle 2:

Principle 3:

PREREADING QUESTIONS FOR REFLECTION AND JOURNALING

1. How do you know when it is appropriate or necessary to obtain help from other people (families, administrators, counselors, etc.) in working with a student who exhibits behavior problems?

2. What are some important ideas to keep in mind in working with families to improve their child's behavior?

INTRODUCTION

Even when teachers employ all of the strategies suggested in this text to prevent, intervene in, and solve discipline problems, some students simply cannot behave appropriately without some type of specialized outside assistance or intervention. These students can be a continual source of frustration to the teacher and the other students in the classroom. Indeed, students who exhibit chronic behavior problems can so overshadow the positive educational climate of the classroom that a teacher can begin to question her professional competence. Thus, it is very important for teachers to acknowledge that there are certain circumstances under which they should and must seek outside support and expertise. In fact, the mark of a skilled professional is to recognize the limits of her expertise and to make the necessary and appropriate consultations and referrals without any sense of professional inadequacy.

Sometimes the first referral the teacher makes is to contact the student's family. It is helpful if the teacher has already begun to establish a positive relationship with the family early in the school year before any problems arise (see Chapter 7). If a behavioral issue requires contacting the family, the contact may be made through written correspondence or a phone conversation. If possible, a phone conversation is preferable because it allows for immediate two-way dialogue. Teachers should think about making this contact when (1) the misbehavior is a minor surface behavior that continues after the teacher has employed the strategies discussed in this text and (2) the teacher is confident that family input can play a positive role in ending the misbehavior. The contact should be made only after the student has been given a choice of improving her behavior or having her family informed of the behavior. Although it applies to all students, this caveat is especially important in working with middle and high school students. The teacher should point out the primary responsibility for controlling her behavior rests with the student, not her family. This in itself will often bring the desired change. If not, family contact is made and may result in consequences at home that are enough to motivate a change in school behavior.

At other times, the behavior is such that the teacher decides family contact will not be sufficient to remedy the problem and that she needs outside expertise to understand and work with the student. In these cases, family contact comes after consultation with other professional staff members. Consultation ensures that the student's family will have an adequate description of the problem, an explanation of the intervention strategies attempted, and a comprehensive proposed plan of action.

Whether family contact is the first step or a later step in seeking outside assistance, it is critical that the contact sets the stage for a cooperative home-school relationship. For this to occur, it may be necessary to overcome negative, defensive family perceptions and attitudes toward the school and/or the teacher. Thus, careful planning and preparation must precede any family contact. In addition to the student's family, the teacher may consult with the school's counselors, administrators, psychologists, learning specialists, and social workers. By doing this, specialized expertise is brought to bear on understanding and working with both the student who is displaying unremitting misbehavior and her family. In some cases, referrals outside the school may be necessary.

This chapter discusses the nature of persisting misbehavior, the point at which a teacher needs to seek outside assistance, preparing for and conducting family conferences, and the roles of other school staff members. The final section details behaviors that may not be disruptive but that teachers must be aware of because they may be symptomatic of other serious problems that require outside referrals.

THE NATURE OF PERSISTING MISBEHAVIOR

Chapter 3, which dealt exclusively with why children misbehave, noted that much of the daily disruptive behavior observed in children is characteristic of the developmental stages that all children go through and a normal reaction to society and recent societal changes. Obviously, some children display disruptive behavior more frequently or with more intensity than others, but again, most of this behavior is within the range of normal child and adolescent behavior and usually can be influenced through the techniques and strategies suggested in this text. However, some students display behaviors that resist all attempts at modification.

These students are often reacting to negative influences within their environment. These influences may be quite obvious and identifiable, or they may be rather subtle. When a teacher is trying to understand a long-term pattern of misbehavior, environmental influences must be viewed in a summative manner. Long-term behavior is not understood by examining one or two snapshots of specific environmental influences. A history of influences must be considered.

One concept that is especially helpful in understanding historical influences is the *success/failure ratio*, which is a ratio of the amount of success a student experiences in her daily life to the amount of failure she experiences. Most students exhibit adaptive, productive behavior and feel good about themselves when they are successful. Students who do not meet with a reasonable degree of success become frustrated and discouraged, and their behavior becomes maladaptive and destructive (Glasser, 1969). Although students with chronic behavior difficulties may appear hard and defiant, they are often very damaged and vulnerable. They are frequently encased in a negative and failure-oriented system of experiences, beliefs, and expectations that are highly resistant to normal classroom influences. These experiences have left them unresponsive to the normal classroom reinforcements intended to increase the success/failure ratio. What are the influences that cause students to have a low success/failure ratio?

Failure in the Classroom Environment

Some students simply are not or cannot find a way to be successful at school in academic, social, and/or extracurricular activities. For these students, school is a daily source of failure that significantly reduces their overall success/failure ratio. Success in school and behavior are so interrelated that it has been concluded that many misbehaving students do not feel successful in school (Wolfgang, 2008).

In some cases, careful observation and evaluation will uncover a learning or behavioral disability. The disability may have gone undiagnosed because it did not become apparent until the child moved toward higher grade levels, where behavioral expectations and the conceptual demands of the curriculum increased. These students are not involved or interested in what they learn. Their misbehavior serves as a protection from further hurt and feelings of inadequacy (Wolfgang, 1999). In other cases, students may possess personality traits that cause classmates to pick on or ignore them. The behavioral difficulties that these students display may be understood as an expression of their frustration and discouragement, which many times escalates into the observable behaviors of anger and retaliation. For these students, reward and gratification stem more from their success at focusing attention on themselves than from meeting appropriate behavioral and instructional objectives.

Failure Outside the Classroom Environment

Some students exhibit extreme behaviors that seem to have little to do with the day-to-day realities of the class environment. Extreme apprehension, distrust, disappointment, hurt, anger, or outrage is triggered in them under the most benign circumstances or with the slightest provocation. A teacher may find such a student reacting to her as if she were an abusive or rejecting family member, other adult, or peer.

These distorted emotional responses are reactions that often have been shaped outside the classroom and reflect problems that exist within the home and family or long-standing problems with peers. Some studies have concluded that 50 percent of children who experience behavior problems at school also experience them at home (e.g., Johnson, Bolstad, and Lobitz, 1976; Patterson, 1974). Some students with long-standing interpersonal relationship difficulties find the normal social pressures of the classroom too much to tolerate. Just as failure within the classroom lowers a student's perceived success/failure ratio, so does failure outside the classroom.

In some instances, initial failure outside the classroom actually has more impact on the student's perceived success/failure ratio than initial failure within the classroom. This occurs because the student's difficulties outside the classroom result in distorted, inappropriate classroom behaviors that cause additional experiences of failure within the classroom.

Failure as a Result of Primary Mode of Conduct

For some students, misbehavior seems to be the natural state of affairs. Their behavior seems to be an expression of their own internal tension, restlessness, and discomfort rather than a reaction to any apparent environmental influence. These students' difficulties emerge during the preschool and kindergarten years. Their teachers view them as immature, emotionally volatile, inattentive, demanding, overly aggressive, and self-centered. They are usually quick to react with anger to any sort of stress or frustration. Unfortunately, their behavior is too often explained simplistically as the natural expression of the "difficult child" temperament. For some, there is a significant improvement with age; for others, the problems intensify as negative reactions to home and school further reduce the success/failure ratio. Many of these children are eventually diagnosed with attention deficit hyperactivity disorder (ADHD) or oppositional defiant disorder (ODD).

WHEN OUTSIDE ASSISTANCE IS NEEDED

How does a teacher decide when to seek outside consultation or referral? Although there are no rules, two general guidelines can assist with the decision. First, referral is warranted when a teacher recognizes that a developing problem is beyond her professional expertise. When a true professional recognizes this, she acts to identify and contact specialized professional assistance. Second, the more deviant, disruptive, or frequent the behavior, the more imperative it is to make referrals. In other words, referral is necessary when

1. a student who displays disruptive behavior does not improve after the hierarchical interventions described in this text have been exhausted.
2. the hierarchical approach has resulted in improvement, but the student continues to manifest problems that disrupt either teaching or learning.

Some students are not discipline problems but show signs that may be symptoms of serious problems that require the attention of professionals with specialized training. Symptoms of social difficulty, illness, anxiety, depression, learning difficulty, abuse, substance abuse, suicide, and family discord become apparent to the knowledgeable and sensitive teacher. A more detailed discussion of these symptoms is included in a later section of this chapter.

THE REFERRAL PROCESS

When outside assistance is warranted, the teacher must have access to a network of school support personnel who are trained to cope with children with unremitting problematic classroom behavior. The first referral is most often to a counselor and/or an administrator (typically a principal in elementary school and an assistant principal at the secondary level). Contact with the counselor and/or the appropriate administrator helps ensure that families are not called in before the school has explored all the possible interventions at its disposal. Except for serious problems, families should be contacted only when it is apparent that the school has no other alternatives (Jones and Jones, 2006).

As was discussed in Chapter 7, families are apt to be responsive and cooperative if there is a history of positive family-teacher relationships. Have there been previous contacts by the teacher or the school with good news about their child or generally about curriculum and other school happenings? If so, and there is also a record of teacher and school interventions directed at the present problem, most families will be cooperative. Working closely with the families of students who exhibit chronic behavior problems is so critical that it will be discussed in depth later in this chapter. First, what role does the administrator or counselor play?

The Role of the Counselor

In schools with a counselor on the professional staff, the teacher contacts the student's counselor as soon as the decision has been made to seek outside assistance. The teacher should be prepared to present documented data on the student's misbehavior and all approaches the teacher has used in the attempt to manage the disruptive behavior. Anecdotal records, functional behavior analyses, and behavior contracts (see Chapter 10) are excellent sources for this information.

In difficult situations, a teacher may become stuck, repetitively applying strategies that do not work. As an outside observer, the counselor is quite useful. She is a neutral onlooker with a fresh view who may be able to suggest modifications in the strategies or techniques the teacher has tried. The counselor may want to explore further the student's behavior, the teacher's style, the nature of the teacher-student interaction, and the learning environment by visiting the classroom or by scheduling further conferences with the student and/or teacher, either alone or together. Once this has been done, the counselor may be able to provide objective feedback and offer suggestions for new approaches and/or work closely with the student to develop more acceptable behaviors.

The counselor can also help improve the strained teacher-student relationship by assisting the teacher and the student simultaneously. She can offer support to the teacher who must cope with the stress of teaching a child who exhibits chronically disruptive behavior, and she can discuss with the student classroom problems that arise from behavior, academics, or social interactions. Because the counselor has a thorough understanding of the viewpoints of both the teacher and student, she is able to act as an intermediary.

Often problems are adequately handled at the counselor level. However, when this is not sufficient, additional consultants are called on. They include an administrator, family members, or a school psychologist.

The Role of the Administrator

In many cases of chronic misbehavior, certain in-school strategies or decisions require the authoritative and administrative power of the principal or assistant principal. For example, decisions to remove a student from a classroom for an extended period of time, to change a student's teacher, and to institute in-school or out-of-school suspensions, which will be discussed later in this chapter, must be approved and supported by an administrator. An administrator's approval often is needed to refer a student to a learning specialist or the school psychologist.

Extremely deviant behavior may require action at the school district level. In cases of expulsion or recommendations for placement in specialized educational settings outside the school, the administrator will be expected to provide testimony at any hearings that may be held and thus must be thoroughly familiar with the student's history.

The Role of the School Psychologist

If there are indications that a student's problems are rooted in deeper and more pervasive personality disturbances or family problems, the clinical resources of the school psychologist should be sought. The initial role of the school psychologist is one of evaluation and diagnostic study. Although the school psychologist will apply independent observational, interview, and testing techniques, these are really an extension of the day-to-day data that have already been accumulated by the classroom teacher, counselor, and administrator. The results of the school psychologist's evaluative studies may lead to recommendations for further study, specialized programming, or referral to outside resources.

The Consultation Team

Once the counselor, an administrator, and possibly a learning specialist or school psychologist are involved, a consultative team has been created. Although a team approach is not formalized in many schools, it can be quite effective in delineating responsibilities and keeping the lines of communication open and clearly defined. The team approach facilitates group problem solving, offers a multidisciplinary perspective, and reduces the possibility that any one individual will become overburdened with a sense of responsibility for "the problem." As with any team, a leader is needed to coordinate the team's efforts. The counselor may be a good coordinator because she is thoroughly familiar with the student and has quick access to all members of the team.

Many school districts have come to realize that teachers cannot be expected to possess the expertise necessary to deal effectively with all the learning and behavior problems found in today's classrooms. To provide support in modifying these problems, school-based consultation teams that follow systematic models of assistance and/or intervention have been implemented. These teams are often referred to as intervention assistance teams, motivational resource teams, child study teams, and so on. In Pennsylvania, for example, all elementary schools are required to have instructional support teams. These teams, made up of classroom teachers, instructional support specialists, principals, family members, and others, work to modify the regular classroom environment to increase student achievement and improve behavior before a student can be referred for testing for possible placement in special education. At the secondary level, there are student assistance teams made up of teachers, counselors, principals, and others who provide assistance to students who are having serious personal, behavioral, or academic difficulties.

WORKING WITH FAMILIES

When it is apparent that the teacher and school have explored all the interventions at their disposal, the student's family should be contacted. It is essential to have the support and cooperation of the family in working effectively with students who exhibit chronic misbehavior. Unfortunately, familial contacts are often characterized by negative reactions and defensiveness on the part of the family and the teacher. It is imperative to minimize negativity and maximize positive support and cooperation. This takes careful planning and a great deal of skill in interpersonal interaction and conferencing techniques on the part of the consultative team members (Canter and Canter, 2001). As detailed in Chapter 7, if the teacher is proactive and started to build a positive relationship with the family before the problem really began, family contacts concerning surfacing problems are likely to result in much greater cooperation. Many teachers send a beginning-of-the-year letter home to families. This letter explains a little bit about the teacher and the teacher's academic and behavioral goals and hopes for the coming year. In addition to providing information about how to contact the teacher, the letter also spells out opportunities for family involvement in the classroom and suggestions for how families can help their child be successful. Many effective teachers follow up on this beginning-of-the-year letter with positive messages to families in the form of e-mails, telephone calls, and "good news notes."

When Families Should Be Contacted

Families should be contacted concerning behavior problems when the following conditions occur:

1. The student displays unremitting misbehavior after the teacher and the school have employed all available interventions.
2. The consultative team decides that the student needs a change in teacher or schedule.

3. The consultative team decides that the student should be removed from a class for an extended period of time or from school for even one day.

4. The consultative team decides that the student needs to be tested for learning, emotional, or physical difficulties.

5. The consultative team decides that outside specialists such as psychiatrists, physicians, and social workers are required.

The Importance of Working with Families

When the school has exhausted its alternatives in attempting to assist a student who exhibits chronically disruptive behavior to bring her behavior into appropriate boundaries, it is essential for the student's family to be contacted and made members of the consulting team. After all, whether or not a student exhibits disruptive behavior, all families have the right to be informed of their child's behavioral and academic progress. Furthermore, as this text has continually stressed, family support of the school has a major impact on a child's positive attitude toward school (Jones, 1980). When a student's family feels good about the teacher and school, the student usually receives encouragement and reinforcement for appropriate school behavior (Jones and Jones, 2006). Thus, families can be one of the teacher's strongest allies, which is particularly helpful when the student exhibits chronic behavior problems (Brookover and Gigliotti, 1988). support and cooperation must be cultivated by the teacher and other school staff members. To this end, schoolwide programs such as family visitation, back-to-school nights, parent-teacher organizations, parent advisory boards, and volunteer programs have been instituted. As noted earlier, and in Chapter 7, individual teachers complement these efforts by communicating positive aspects of children's schooling to their families through notes and phone calls, inviting families to call when they have any questions, and requiring students to take home graded assignments and tests.

Children with chronic behavior problems, especially when they are adolescents, are frequently not motivated or responsive to the encouragements a school can provide. Their families, on the other hand, can provide a wider variety of more attractive encouragements. Indeed, a system of home consequences contingent on school behavior can be an effective means for modifying classroom behavior (Ayllon, Garber, and Pisor, 1975). Such a system is illustrated in Case 11.1. Thus, because families, with few exceptions, care greatly about their children, they represent an interested party that can provide an inexpensive, continuous treatment resource to augment school efforts. The school's positive working relationship with families is often the most critical component for effectively influencing a student who engages in chronic misbehavior.

Understanding Families

For all the positive help families may be able to offer, many teachers and other school personnel feel uncomfortable contacting them, and many families harbor negative feelings toward their child's teachers and school. School personnel often complain that family contacts necessitate using time, usually before or after school, that could be put to better use. Teachers also complain that they often feel intimidated by families who think that teachers should be able to maintain control of their child without family help. Also because education is funded by tax dollars, they sometimes appear

CASE 11.1

To Drive, You Must Speak Spanish

Dawn is 15 years old. Her grades have gone from Bs to Ds in Spanish and social studies. The decline in academic performance results from inattentiveness and poor study habits. After the teacher and counselor speak to Dawn without any noticeable improvement, her parents are called.

During a conference, Dawn explains that she doesn't like Spanish or social studies and doesn't see why she needs these subjects anyway. Her teachers try to explain why these subjects are important, especially in today's world, but have little success. Finally her parents intervene and point out to Dawn that she has scheduled driver's education for the spring semester. If she expects to be able to drive, they say, she must demonstrate responsibility and discipline and one way to do so is to do well in all school subjects. They finally give Dawn a choice, either her grades improve or she will not be allowed to take driver's education or obtain her learner's permit.

Her teachers and parents keep in contact, and by the end of the fall semester Dawn's grades are again Bs.

to believe they should be able to judge and monitor teacher performance. However, as professionals, teachers and other school staff must not allow these feelings to jeopardize the opportunity to gain the support and cooperation of families.

If family contacts result in distrust, apprehension, and dissatisfaction for both families and teachers, efforts to assist the disruptive student probably will fail. In time, the family's sense of alienation from the school will be passed on to the child, further lessening the possibility of the school working with the family to find a means to redirect the student toward acceptable behavior. Therefore, the members of the consultative team must create an atmosphere that facilitates a change of negative family perceptions and assumptions into positive ones. This is more easily accomplished when team members understand the family's perspectives.

Many children who exhibit chronic misbehavior in school display similar behaviors at home. Often, their families have been frustrated by their own failures in influencing their child. Because many parents consider their children extensions of themselves and products of their parenting, they are not anxious to be reminded of how inadequate they have been. Sometimes, there has been a long history of negative feedback from teachers, counselors, and administrators that has created a feeling of powerlessness and humiliation. Because these families feel everyone is blaming them for their child's misbehavior, they are quite wary of any sort of school contact and react by withdrawing, resisting, or angrily counterattacking and blaming the school for the problems. This does not have to happen. Through careful planning and the use of proper conferencing skills, the school consultative team can gain the needed support and cooperation from families.

Recalling from Chapter 7 Hoover-Dempsey and Sandler (1997) suggest that three major factors influence a family's decisions about whether or not to become involved in their child's education. These are the family's role construction, sense of efficacy, and sense of school involvement.

Conducting Family Conferences

When the consultative team determines that conditions warrant family involvement, the counselor, who is often the coordinator, usually makes the first contact. The tone of this initial contact is extremely important in developing a cooperative working relationship. The counselor should expect some degree of defensiveness on the part of the family, especially if the student has had a history of school misbehavior. This attitude should be understood and not taken personally. The cause of the school's concern should be stated clearly and honestly. The climate of the conversation should be "How can we work as a team to best meet your child's needs?" rather than "Here we go again!" or "We've done everything we can; now it's up to you."

Once a conference has been scheduled, the team must decide who will attend the conference. Should all the members of the consultative team be in attendance? Should the student be at the conference? The answers depend on the particular problem, the amount of expertise needed to explain the situation and the approaches that have been tried, and who will need to be available to answer any questions that may arise. In addition, it must be kept in mind that the conference must be conducted in a positive manner that is least threatening to the family. This often means the fewer people present, the less threatening the conference appears to the family. In most circumstances, the counselor or administrator and the teacher conduct the initial conference. Unless the problem includes discussing behavior or other signs that indicate serious health, emotional, or legal problems, the student is usually present.

The counselor should begin the conference by introducing all in attendance, thanking the family for its willingness to attend, and outlining the goal of the conference. Throughout the conference, the counselor ensures that everyone has an equal chance to express her viewpoint. The counselor also looks for any signs that indicate that the conference is deteriorating into a debate or blaming session and acts rapidly to defuse the situation by directing the conference back to the major purpose of how best to meet the student's needs.

Obviously appropriate interpersonal and conferencing skills must be familiar to and practiced by all professionals in attendance. Some of these skills are to be friendly; to be supportive; and to use active listening, which includes paraphrasing to ensure proper understanding by all included (see Chapter 10). The teacher should be prepared to have some positive things to say about the student. Information should be elicited through the use of questions rather than directive statements aimed at the student or family. Neither the child nor the family should be attacked, disparaged, or blamed. However, sometimes families and the student attack, disparage, and blame the teacher or other school officials. If this occurs, it is important to remember that one does not defend one's professional competence with words, but with behavior.

One of the best means to demonstrate professional competence is through the use of previously collected data that illustrate and demonstrate the concerns of the school and the need for the conference. These data should include a history of objective and specific information about the student's behaviors and the actions taken by the teacher and the school to manage them. Anecdotal records are an excellent source for these types of data (see Chapter 10). The use of these data reduces the likelihood of the conference turning into a debate, illustrates that the problem is not exaggerated, and defuses any attempt by the family to suggest that the school did not take appropriate and necessary actions.

Throughout the conference, the family's and student's feelings, viewpoints, and suggestions should be actively solicited. The outcome of the conference, it is hoped, will be an agreed-upon course of action or the decision that the counselor will contact the family in the near future with a suggested course of action. The meeting ends on an optimistic note with a summary; a show of appreciation; and an encouraging statement that with both the home and school working as a team, a successful outcome is likely.

With some students, a decision may be made to try additional school and/or classroom strategies with little additional family involvement. This decision is usually a result of new information that allows the school to design additional appropriate strategies or because the family, like Sharon's mother in Case 11.2, clearly demonstrates its disinterest. Sharon's mother is atypical, not because she is disinterested but because she openly and honestly admits it. When families are disinterested, there is sometimes a tendency on the part of the school personnel to give up and adopt an attitude that "if they don't care, then we've done what we can." However, children should never be denied access to potentially effective school intervention programs because their families are disinterested, uncooperative, or unsupportive (Walker, 1979).

When it is apparent that family involvement will probably improve the child's behavior significantly or the family is interested in helping but there is evidence of a deficiency in parenting skills, increased family involvement will be requested. Many school districts now provide classes or employ family educators to work with families of children experiencing behavior problems in school.

CASE 11.2

"Won't Be Much Help"

Sharon is in eighth grade. Her behavior is perfect. She is of average intelligence, rarely absent, and well dressed and has some friends. She seems like the typical, happy eighth grader. However, she always asks one of her teachers if she can stay late to help with anything. If there is nothing for her to do, she just sits and talks. As the end of the first report period approaches, it appears that Sharon will receive all Ds and Fs.

Most of her teachers have spoken with her, and she has also been referred to the counselor. Throughout all of these sessions, she maintains that she is happy and nothing is wrong. Extra academic help is given but results in no improvement.

Before report cards are issued, a conference is scheduled with Sharon, her mother, the counselor, and her teachers. Sharon's mother arrives; she is well dressed and well spoken and seems somewhat concerned. She listens attentively to each teacher explain Sharon's poor academic performance. When they have finished, she states, "Sharon's dad left five years ago. I'm busy. I need to look after myself and get my life moving in the right direction. I have a career and I date a lot. Truthfully, besides buying her clothes and making sure she eats properly, I haven't much time for Sharon. I would truly appreciate anything you can do to help Sharon because I know I won't be much help. Is there anything else?"

A Question That Will Surely Be Asked

In thinking about the appropriate timeline concerning how best to work with students who exhibit chronic disruptive behavior, the authors as well as authorities on family-school dynamics agree that a best practice is contacting families early or even perhaps before the school year begins. This proactive effort is to develop positive family teacher relationships that are related to improved behavior and grades for all students. Additionally, this relationship is critical when the teacher is working with a student with a history of disruptive behavior.

However, there is no common agreement concerning the point at which families should be contacted in reference to student behavioral problems. Some experts and families support the notion that the family be notified at the first sign of any problem with their child. Others argue that making contact at the first sign of a problem is inappropriate because that does not give a student enough time to learn and overcome the difficulty before the family is brought into the situation. These same individuals also argue that waiting until the student is exhibiting chronic behavior is far too long. So they would suggest family contact at some point after behavior problems arise but before the student's behavior meets the criteria for chronic behavioral issues that we have outlined previously. In short, they argue not too early, but not too late. By the same token, they can't really stipulate any clear criterion for when the appropriate point for referral has been reached.

The authors of this text disagree. The disagreement is not about whether or not families should be informed by the teacher regarding disruptive behavior but when this contact should be made—at the first sign of a problem, at some intermediate but undefined point, or only later after the teacher and the other school professionals have attempted numerous interventions. Where you stand on this timing issue has to do with the long-term goals families and teachers have for their students. If the goal is compliance and obedience, then the first sign of disruptive behavior or the first sign of the student not doing what she is told warrants a call home. If the goal is self-control, then the student needs many more opportunities to learn self-control in many different contexts with the teacher's assistance. So when the family asks "Why weren't we notified earlier at the first signs of a problem?" the teacher needs to explain the concept of self-control and contrast it with the concepts of obedience and compliance, including the long-term benefits of being able to control one's own behavior.

ALTERNATIVES TO SUSPENSIONS

When a student's behavior reaches the level of being chronic, teachers and administrators begin to run out of interventions. It is at this point that many administrators begin to remove students from the classroom and school with out-of-school-suspensions. The rate of suspensions continues to rise. In the Chicago public schools more than 20,000 students were suspended, doubling the rate in less than a decade. African American children and students with special needs get more than their share being suspended disproportionally to their school population (Townsend, 2000).

No research indicates that suspensions have had a deterrent effect nor does the research support a change to more appropriate behavior on the part of those suspended (Skiba, Peterson and Williams, 1999). What research does support are the numerous negative outcomes of frequent suspensions. These include denial of access to learning opportunities while out of school, no follow-up learning opportunities such as special workshops on social skill development or anger management, greater dropout rates, and greater risk of running into legal issues because many of these students are on the street rather than in school.

Alternatives to suspensions are many, and all of them offer better outcomes than suspensions. These include learning modules on study skills, career exploration, problem solving to identify likely outcomes of certain behavior, restitution programs, community or school service, and special counseling groups. Likewise, peer mediation could be an option if the problem is between students or a teacher and a student.

As difficult as it might be for administrators to admit, suspensions are easy answers to tough problems; however, they send the message to the public that the school is tough on discipline and that the school has and maintains high behavioral expectations. The real challenge is not to suspend more students but to find alternatives that offer students better educational outcomes and help the students acquire alternative behaviors and thinking that can replace the inappropriate behaviors and thoughts that created the problems in the first place.

Suspensions are considered by the courts to be a serious punishment that denies the student a right to an education for a period of time. Therefore, the courts have afforded students certain rights if they face a suspension. If a student is given an in-school suspension for more than 10 days, the student has a right to an informal hearing usually held by the principal. The school must tell the student the reason for the suspension, give the student an opportunity to tell her side of the story, and notify the family in writing. For an out-of-school suspension for more than three days, the student has the same rights as just noted, and in addition, the hearing must be conducted within five days of the suspension and the student can bring witnesses.

SYMPTOMS OF SERIOUS PROBLEMS

Some students display symptoms of serious problems that may or may not be accompanied by disruptive and/or academic difficulties. These problems may be related to physical or emotional health or associated with an abusive home or with substance abuse. All of these areas may fall outside the expertise and domain of the school. An observant teacher often recognizes these symptoms and notifies the appropriate school official, usually the counselor, who then decides the proper step.

Some of the signs that may be significant include the following:

1. *Changes in physical appearance.*   Students may reveal their underlying problems through sudden changes in their physical appearance. Posture, dress, and grooming habits are reflections of underlying mood and self-image, and a student's deterioration in these habits should be noted with concern. More striking changes such as rapid weight loss or gain, particularly in light of the dramatic increase in eating disorders among high school students, should be investigated. Although unusual soreness, bruises, cuts, or scarring are signs of possible neglect or abuse, they may also indicate self-mutilation or other self-destructive tendencies.
2. *Changes in activity level.*   Teachers need to be aware of the significance of changes in activity level. Excessive tardiness, lethargy, absenteeism, and a

tendency to fall asleep in class may result from a variety of problems, including depression and substance abuse. Hyperactivity, impulsivity, lowered frustration and tolerance levels, and overaggressiveness may also represent the student's effort to deal with emotional unrest and discomfort.

3. *Changes in personality.* Emotional disturbances in children and adolescents are sometimes reflected in very direct forms of expression and behavior. The seemingly well-adjusted child who is suddenly sad or easily agitated or has angry outbursts not characteristic of her prior behavior should be closely observed and monitored.

4. *Changes in achievement status.* A decline in a student's ability to focus on her work, persist at her studies, or produce or complete work successfully is often an indication of the draining effects of emotional turmoil or significant changes in the home environment.

5. *Changes in health or physical abilities.* Complaints of not being able to see or hear, when it appears the student is paying attention, should be referred to the nurse for follow-up. Complaints of frequent headaches, stomachaches, dizziness, non-healing sores, skin rashes, and frequent bathroom use lead to concern for the student's health.

6. *Changes in socialization.* Children who spend most of the time by themselves, seem to have no friends, and are socially withdrawn are not often identified as problem students because their symptoms do not have a disturbing impact on the classroom. These students may drift from one grade to another without appropriate attention and concern. However, they often leave a sign of their underlying misery in their behavior, artwork, and creative writing samples.

In most cases of serious problems, schools are able to arrange for or make referrals to a host of specialized professionals, including psychologists, psychiatrists, nutritionists, medical doctors, social workers, and legal authorities. However, appropriate intervention rests with the aware and concerned teacher who must make the initial observations and referral.

LEGAL ASPECTS OF SEEKING OUTSIDE ASSISTANCE

Some legal issues must be considered to protect children's and family's rights when seeking outside assistance. Most school districts are aware of these laws and have developed appropriate procedures to abide by them.

The Individuals with Disabilities Education Improvement Act (IDEIA) and earlier versions all the way back to Public Law 94-142 require family consent before conducting any evaluation that might change the educational classification, evaluation, or placement of a child. *Evaluation* is defined as any selective procedure not used with all children in a school, class, or grade.

The release of student files is regulated by the Family Education Rights and Privileges Act (FERPA), also known as the Buckley Amendment (PL 93-380, as amended by PL 93-568). Briefly, schools may not release a student's records to outside sources without written consent from the family. This release must state the reasons for the release, the specific records to be released, and who will receive the records.

Many states also have laws that require teachers to report any signs of child abuse. Many of these have provisions that impose fines on school personnel who fail to meet this responsibility.

Students have specific rights in many areas, including freedom of expression, dress and grooming, corporal punishment, and student activities. Unfortunately, many of these rights are infringed upon by certain disciplinary actions taken by teachers and school administrators. These infringements usually go unnoticed or unchallenged. However, "when the infraction is of a very serious nature involving possible suspension or expulsion of the student, the legal rights of the student become of paramount importance" (Melnick and Grosse, 1984, p. 147). School officials must be aware of these rights and ensure that they are protected.

Summary

Some students simply do not experience the degree of success in the classroom that supports the development and maintenance of appropriate behavior. Their conduct problems remain unremitting despite the application of appropriate hierarchical strategies, or they show other signs and symptoms indicative of serious underlying disturbances. In these cases, some type of specialized or out-of-school assistance may be required.

A team approach, which may include the student, family, teacher, counselor, administrator, and outside specialists, is an effective means for expanded evaluation and for the development of specialized interventions that may extend beyond the normal classroom. The counselor typically plays the crucial role of team coordinator in communicating with and integrating the efforts of the family and in-school and out-of-school consultants. The support and cooperation of the family is critical to increase the likelihood of successful intervention. Any negative family attitudes must be defused. This is best accomplished through careful planning and the skilled use of conferencing techniques when working with families. Protecting students' rights throughout any process focused on addressing misbehavior is paramount.

Exercises

1. The student's success/failure ratio is an extremely important variable that influences student behavior. There are many areas in which students experience success and failure, including academic, social, and extracurricular areas. List several specific areas in a school setting in which students can experience success or failure.

2. Three important concepts are relevant to understand when working with students who exhibit chronic disruptive behavior. These concepts are listed below. Diagram or explain how each concept is related.

Success/failure ratio

Motivation = Expectation of Success × Value
Self-Esteem = Significance + Competence
+ Virtue + Power

3. The importance of success in specific areas depends on the student's age. Using the list of specific areas for success developed in exercise 1, rate each area's importance for students in elementary, middle, and senior high school.

4. Develop a list of symptoms that could be added to the list of potentially serious problems that

may warrant outside assistance. Be able to justify why each symptom should be included on the list.

5. Are there any dangers associated with using a list similar to the one developed in exercise 4? Before answering, consider areas such as contextual setting, duration and severity of behavior, and so on. If there are dangers, what can a teacher do to minimize them?

6. Even when students are not exhibiting behavioral problems, it is important for teachers to gain the support of families. In what ways can teachers develop such support?

7. Compose a beginning-of-the-school-year letter that you could send to families. In the letter, be sure to include information about yourself, your classroom, your hopes and goals for the coming year, and ideas about how families can become involved in supporting their child's success. Also include contact information so families can reach you. Make sure that the letter is free of educational jargon.

8. Sometimes teachers may decide to contact the families before consulting a student's counselor. When should families be contacted before the counselor?

9. In consultation with your instructor, contact a school (use your own school if you are presently teaching) and identify all the resources available to assist teachers with seriously misbehaving students.

10. Children with attention deficit hyperactivity disorder and oppositional defiant disorder are in mainstream classrooms. Research the behaviors these children exhibit and suggest or research strategies that are effective in influencing these children.

11. It has been said that if a teacher is a good teacher for difficult children, she will be an excellent teacher for all the children in her class. Explain what this means.

12. **Principles of Teacher Behavior** After reading Chapter 11 and doing the exercises, use what you have learned to briefly describe your understanding of the implications of the principles listed at the beginning of the chapter for a classroom teacher.

Principle 1:

Principle 2:

Principle 3:

13. Using concepts from Chapters 8 through 11, complete the fourth analysis of the iterative case studies.

Iterative Case Study Analyses

Fourth Analysis

Considering the concepts discussed in the Interventions for Common Behavior Problems and Interventions for Chronic Behavior Problems sections, Chapters 8 through 11, review your third analysis. What has changed and what has stayed the same since your last analysis? Once again, consider why the students may be choosing to behave inappropriately and how you might intervene to influence the students to stop the disruptive behavior and resume appropriate on-task behavior.

Elementary School Case Studies

"I don't remember" During silent reading time in my fourth-grade class, I have built in opportunities to work individually with students. During this time, the students read to me and practice word work with flash cards. One student has refused to read to me but instead only wants to work with the flash cards. After a few times I suggested we work with flash cards this time and begin reading next time. He agreed. The next time we met, I reminded him of our plan, and he screamed, "I don't remember. I want to do word cards." At this point, I tried to find out why he didn't like reading and he said, "There's a reason, I just can't tell you," and he threw the word cards across the room, some of them hitting other students. What should I do?

"Let's do it again" Cathy is in my third-grade class. Whenever I ask the class to line up for recess, lunch, or to change classes, Cathy is always the last to get in line. When she does, she pushes, shoves and touches the other students. When this happens I usually demand that all the children return to their seats, and we repeatedly line up again and again until Cathy lines up properly. I thought that peer pressure would cause Cathy to change her behavior but instead it has resulted in my students being late to "specials" and having less time for recess and lunch.

Middle School Case Studies

"It makes me look cool" I can't stop thinking about a problem I'm having in class with a group of 12-year-old boys. They consistently use vulgar language to one another and some of the shy kids in the class, especially the girls. In addition, they are always pushing and shoving one another. I've tried talking to them about why they keep using bad language when they know it's inappropriate. The response I get is that "it makes me look cool and funny in front of my friends." I have asked them to please use more appropriate language in the classroom, but that has not worked. I haven't even started to deal with the pushing and shoving. What should I do?

"My parents will be gone all weekend" One of my seventh-grade girls was passing notes to a boy two rows over. After the second note I made eye contact with her and it stopped for about half an hour. When I saw her getting ready to pass another note I went over to her desk and asked her to give me the note and told her that that the note passing had to stop. She looked very upset but she did give me the note. I folded it and put it in my desk drawer. When class ended she ran out of the room crying. My personal policy is not to read students' notes but, instead, give it back to the student at the end of class or throw it away. However, this time, maybe because of her reaction, something told me to read the note. It said, "Mike my parents will be away Saturday night, why don't you and John sleep over, it will be fun. I promise I'll do whatever you want me to do and that you and John can do anything you want to me." What should I as the teacher do?

High School Case Studies

"Homo" This past week I had a student approach me about a problem he was experiencing in our class. This eleventh-grade student had recently "come out" as a homosexual. He said he was tired and upset with the three boys who sit near him. These boys frequently call him a "homo" and a "fag" every time they see him, both in and out of class.

"Why don't you get out of my face?" A twelfth-grade student came up to me the first day of class and said, "My name is Ted. I don't want to be here, so just leave me alone and we'll get along just fine." I did not react to his comment but instead said "After you see what we will be learning, I think you will find the class interesting." Ted walked away and took a seat in the back of the room. Later that week I noticed Ted was reading a magazine while everyone else was working on an in-class assignment. Without making it obvious I walked by Ted's desk and quietly asked him to put the magazine away and to begin working on the assignment. Ted turned to me and said, "Maybe you don't understand; I asked you not to bother me. I'm not bothering you so why don't you get out of my face."

APPENDIX A

Analysis Inventory of Teacher Behavior that Influences Appropriate Student Behavior

The Analysis Inventory of Teacher Behavior is a tool that the classroom teacher can use to reflect upon her behavior used to influence appropriate student behavior with respect to prevention, causes, and solutions. The inventory presents questions teachers can ask themselves regarding the development of hierarchical plans for influencing appropriate student behavior. Part I of the inventory contains questions regarding the prevention of misbehavior. Part II contains questions regarding the resolution of misbehavior.

PART I: HAVE I DONE ALL I CAN TO PREVENT MISBEHAVIOR?

Chapter 1: The Basics

1. Do I consider how my behavior affects student behavior?
2. Am I familiar with the principles of teacher behavior that influence student behavior as presented in this book?
3. Do I employ a professional decision-making approach to influencing appropriate student behavior?

Chapter 2: Nature of the Discipline Problem

1. Do the behaviors I am trying to correct constitute discipline problems as defined in the text? Do they interfere with teaching or the rights of others to learn? Are they psychologically or physically unsafe? Do they destroy property?
2. Do my behaviors contribute to any discipline problems?
3. Do my behaviors maximize the time students spend on learning?
4. Do I deal with non-discipline behavior problems after the rest of the class is involved in the learning activities?

Chapter 3: Understanding Why Children Misbehave

1. Is the misbehavior a result of unmet physiological needs (e.g., nourishment, rest, temperature, ventilation, noise, lighting)?
2. Is the misbehavior a result of a lack of cultural synchronization that creates a negative learning climate?
3. Is the misbehavior a result of unmet safety and security needs (e.g., fear of other students, teachers, staff members, parents, other adults; insecurity about rules and expectations)?
4. Is the misbehavior a result of unmet needs for belonging and affection?
5. Do I provide opportunities for students to feel significant, competent, and powerful and to have a sense of virtue?
6. Is the misbehavior a result of a mismatch between the student's cognitive developmental level and instructional goals, tasks, or methods?

7. Is the misbehavior a result of a mismatch between the student's moral developmental level and my management plan?
8. Is the misbehavior a result of striving to meet the faulty goals of attention, power, revenge, or inadequacy?
9. Am I trying not to personalize students' misbehaviors?
10. Is the misbehavior a result of mobility of the student's family and that the student is in a new school?
11. Is the misbehavior a result of the student being bullied?

Chapter 4: Philosophical Approaches to Influencing Students

1. Have I analyzed which authority bases(s) I employ to influence appropriate student behavior.
2. Have I asked myself the nine basic questions to analyze which theories of teacher influence are consistent with my beliefs about teaching and learning?
3. Do I employ the authority base(s) that is(are) consistent with my beliefs about teaching and learning?
4. Are my teaching behaviors consistent with the authority base(s) and theories of influence I want to employ?

Chapter 5: The Professional Teacher

1. Do I make ongoing efforts to get to know my students as individuals and build positive relationships with them?
2. Do I plan my lessons to include findings from effective teaching research by

   Including an introduction?

   Clearly presenting the content?

   Checking for student understanding?

   Providing for coached and solitary practice?

   Providing for closure and summarization?

   Conducting periodic reviews?

3. Do I increase student motivation to learn by considering student interests, student needs, instruction novelty and variety, student success, student attributions, tension, feeling tone, assessment and feedback, and encouragement?
4. Do I communicate high expectations to all learners for learning and behavior by equalizing response opportunities, providing prompt and constructive feedback, and treating each student with personal regard?
5. Do I use questioning to involve students actively in the learning process by asking questions at different cognitive levels and using probing questions, wait time, a variety of techniques to elicit response, and a variety of positive reinforcements?
6. Do I maximize both allocated and engaged time in learning?
7. Do I teach for deep understanding, emphasizing topics that are important, at the appropriate developmental level, and related to students' lives and interests outside school?
8. Do I use cooperative learning activities that contain all three essential elements of cooperative learning?

9. Do I teach in ways that allow students to demonstrate their knowledge using all eight types of human intelligence?
10. Do I differentiate instruction to meet student needs?
11. Do I use personal goal setting and appropriate attributions for student success and failure to increase student motivation and promote positive feelings of self-efficacy?

Chapter 6: Structuring the Environment

1. Do I make my room physically comfortable by considering lighting, ventilation, and noise reduction?
2. Do I design seating arrangements to accommodate the various learning activities?
3. Does the seating arrangement ensure that each student can see the instructional activities, the teacher has close proximity to each student, and seats are not placed in high traffic areas or close to distractions?
4. Do I use my bulletin boards to recognize students and provide students with active participation?
5. Do I develop and teach procedures for everyday routines?
6. Do I analyze the classroom environment to determine the rules needed to protect teaching, learning, safety, and property?
7. Do I clearly communicate the rules and their rationales to students?
8. Do I attempt to obtain student commitments to abide by the rules?
9. Do I teach and evaluate student understanding of the rules?
10. Do I develop and enforce each rule with a natural or logical consequence?

Chapter 7: Building Relationships

1. Do I consider my students' cultural values, norms, and behavioral expectations in setting classroom rules and guidelines and in interpreting student behavior?
2. Do I use cooperative learning activities and teach social skills to my students in order to create group norms that will promote pro-social behavior and engagement in learning activities?
3. Do I employ referent and expert authority bases to demonstrate respect, care, and trust for my students?
4. Do I increase student expectations for success by helping them develop an internal locus of control?
5. Do I increase the value students place on outcomes of their efforts by helping them develop an internal value structure?
6. Do I proactively build positive relationships with students' families that encourage families to work as partners in the educational process?

PART II: AM I EFFECTIVELY RESOLVING MISBEHAVIOR?

Chapter 8: Using Nonverbal Interventions to Influence Students to Behave Appropriately

1. Do I meet the six prerequisites to appropriate student behavior?

   Am I well prepared to teach?

   Do I provide clear directions and expectations?

   Do I ensure student understanding of evaluation criteria?

Do I clearly communicate, rationalize, and consistently enforce behavioral expectations?

Do I demonstrate enthusiasm and encouragement and model expected behavior?

Do I establish positive relationships with students?

2. Do I effectively employ proactive intervention skills by changing the pace of instruction, removing seductive objects, boosting interest, redirecting behavior through nonpunitive time-out, reinforcing appropriate behavior, and providing cues?

3. Do I consider the five intervention guidelines when deciding which interventions to employ?

Does the intervention provide students with opportunities for self-control?

Is the intervention less disruptive than the students' behavior?

Does the intervention lessen the probability that students will become confrontational?

Does the intervention protect students and the teacher from physical or psychological harm?

Does the intervention maximize the number of management alternatives available to the teacher?

4. Do I effectively use the remedial intervention skills (planned ignoring, signal interference, proximity interference, and touch interference) in a hierarchical order?

Chapter 9: Using Verbal Interventions and Logical Consequences to Influence Students to Behave Appropriately?

1. Do I follow the guidelines for using verbal interventions?

Do I keep them as private as possible?

Do I make them brief?

Do I speak to the situation, not the person?

Do I set limits on behaviors, not feelings?

Do I avoid sarcasm and belittlement?

2. Do I monitor my verbal interventions for ineffective communication patterns?

3. Do I employ verbal interventions in a hierarchical manner (adjacent reinforcement, calling on the student, humor, awareness questioning, direct appeal, I message, positive phrasing, "are not for's," rule reminders, triplets, explicit redirection, broken record)?

4. Do I employ natural and/or logical consequences using "you have a choice"?

5. When I use consequences, do I consistently follow through or do I use them as threats?

Chapter 10: Classroom Interventions for Working with Students Who Exhibit Chronic Behavior Problems

1. Do I build positive relationships with students who exhibit chronic behavior problems?

2. Do I attempt to disrupt the cycle of discouragement and replace it with a cycle of encouragement?

3. Do I talk privately with students who exhibit chronically disruptive behavior?
4. Do I effectively use appropriate receiving skills during private conferences with students?

   Do I use nonverbal attending cues?

   Do I use probing questions?

   Do I check perceptions?

   Do I check feelings?

5. Do I effectively use appropriate sending skills during private conferences with students?

   Do I deal in the present?

   Do I make eye contact?

   Do I make statements rather than ask questions?

   Do I use "I" to relate my feelings?

   Am I brief?

   Do I talk directly to the students?

   Do I give the student directions on how to correct the problem?

   Do I check for understanding?

6. Do I ask authentic questions in talking with students about how to help them solve chronic behavior problems?
7. Have I reviewed the self-monitoring checklist to ensure that I have developed and employed an effective self-monitoring technique?

   Do the student and I understand/agree on behaviors?

   Is the time period specified?

   Does the student understand the instrument's use?

   Have the student and I agreed on a meeting/discussion time?

   Will the instrument facilitate the noting of small increments of progress?

   Does the instrument focus on one behavior?

8. Have I reviewed the guidelines for initiating and employing anecdotal record keeping to ensure that I have effectively implemented the procedure?

   Am I positive?

   Do I help the student recognize the past behavior and its negative impact?

   Do I explain that the behavior is unacceptable?

   Do I explain the anecdotal record-keeping procedure?

   Do I communicate an expectation for improvement?

   Do I attempt to obtain the student's commitment for improved behavior?

   Do I record the conference and obtain the student's signature?

9. Have I considered using functional behavior assessment to help deal with the behavior?

   Do I understand what purpose the behavior serves for the student?

   Do I know if the behavior allows the student to gain/avoid attention, items or objects, activities, or stimulation?

   Do I understand the conditions that are typically present when the inappropriate behavior occurs?

   Do I understand the consequences that help maintain the behavior?

   Have I collected or asked someone else to collect systematic data concerning the student's behavior?

10. Have I reviewed the behavior contract checklist to ensure that I have effectively developed and employed the behavior contract?

    Do I specify the behavior, time period, reward, and evaluation?

    Do I provide a motivating reward?

    Do I ensure that the student understands, agrees to, and signs the contract?

    Do I sign the contract?

    Do the student, the student's parents, and I get copies?

11. Do I exclude the student from the classroom and require a written statement of better behavior before allowing the student to return to class?

Chapter 11: Seeking Outside Assistance

1. Do I provide many opportunities for the student to be successful in the classroom?
2. Does the behavior warrant outside consultation?
3. Do I consult with a counselor or an administrator about the chronically misbehaving student?
4. Do I initiate contacts with families before problems begin?
5. Should families be contacted?

   Does the student display unremitting misbehavior?

   Has the consultative team decided that the student needs a change of schedule or teacher; should be removed from class or school for a period of time; should be tested for learning, emotional, or physical difficulties; should be referred to outside specialists?

6. Do I employ the behaviors that allow me to work positively with families and gain their support and cooperation?
7. Does the student show any behaviors or signs that may be symptomatic of other serious problems?

   Has the student undergone changes in physical appearance, activity level, personality, achievement states, health or physical abilities, or socialization?

8. Do administrators and I consider alternatives to suspensions?
9. Do I protect student rights?

APPENDIX B

General Guidelines for Working with Students with Special Needs

We, the authors, firmly believe that the teaching behaviors that are suggested throughout this text are effective for influencing appropriate behavior and academic success for *all* students. Students identified with special needs exhibit the same behaviors as students who are not identified with special needs; however, they may exhibit the behaviors to a greater degree, or at a higher level of intensity, or in a more unpredictable pattern. Therefore, it is useful for the classroom teacher to have some understanding of a variety of tools that might be especially effective in helping students with special needs to be successful. These same guidelines are also likely to be helpful for other students who are not identified as having special needs, but who struggle with controlling their own behavior.

Many texts that offer advice about dealing with students with special needs provide specific teacher behaviors that should be used with students in a specific special needs category; for example, for students identified with autism, do this, and for students identified with learning disabilities, do that. We see two problems with such lists. First, the differences in capabilities and behavior among individual students within the same special needs category can be just as great as the differences across special needs categories. Second, suggested behaviors may not be compatible with the teacher's philosophical approach to teaching as discussed in chapter 4, and may be uncomfortable for the teacher to follow.

Instead of offering specific behaviors or interventions for separate categories of special needs, we have chosen to offer general guidelines that may be helpful in thinking about working with students with special needs and all other students who struggle with behavior. These guidelines presuppose that the teacher is consistently modifying instruction to meet the student's needs and to enable the student to experience success. If this is not the case for any student, as noted in Chapter 8, then behavior problems will be a consistent feature of classroom life. Assuming that instruction has been properly modified, the following guidelines should prove helpful in increasing appropriate behavior:

1. Help the student develop a sense of significance/belonging in the classroom. Model a positive attitude of welcome and acceptance and also create opportunities for the students in the class to get to know one another and to work cooperatively. As noted in Chapter 10, relationships are a critical aspect of solving chronic behavior problems. It is important to establish a trusting, positive relationship, as early as possible in the school year, with each student, even those who have little self-control, and to find things about each student that you like.

2. Families of children with special needs typically have a better understanding of their child's behavior than teachers do. This is especially true in the early part of the academic year. Families often understand which situations and contexts are likely to help the student maintain self-control and those that make self-control more difficult. As students mature, they too become much more adept at understanding their own strengths and weaknesses. Two implications follow from these facts. First, involving students and families in the problem-solving process is critical, and, second, helping students with special needs understand and be able to label their own strengths and weaknesses is a powerful tool for helping them make better choices about behavior. Self-control is the ultimate goal.

3. Use the expertise of other specialists as part of the problem-solving process. Read the student's IEP carefully and consult regularly with special education teachers; school psychologists and counselors; physical, speech, and occupational therapists; and therapeutic support staff and paraprofessionals who work with the student. The benefits of a truly collaborative team approach to problem solving are tremendous.

4. Your ability as a problem solver will be the most important tool that you possess to help students to be successful in controlling their own behavior. Be a student of the student's behavior. Engage in informal functional behavior assessment on an ongoing basis, not just when a crisis occurs. Observe the student carefully and record as much information as possible about the student's behavior. Try your best to document those events and contexts that trigger inappropriate behavior and those events that lead to increased self-regulation. Investigate by collecting data about questions such as the following:

What times of day seem better for self-control?

What types of learning activities and materials seem to lead to better self-control?

What types of instructional groupings lead to better self-control?

What types of spaces and positions in the room seem to lead to better self-control?

What types of teacher interventions appear to lead to more appropriate behavior?

The better your understanding of the influence of context on the student, the better your ability to design situations that are likely to lead to more self-control.

5. Recognize and encourage positive behavior and effort whenever possible. Help the student keep track of progress in her behavior over time. Periodically take stock of progress together and help the student internalize feelings of success and pride. Formal functional behavior assessment can be very useful in this regard.

6. Teach to the student's strengths whenever possible and gradually move from strengths to areas of weakness. The teacher's goal in maximizing student success should be to use the teaching modalities (visual, aural, kinesthetic, tactile, and so on) that match the student's preferred ways of learning as much as possible. Remember the success/failure ratio is related to motivation. A history of success starts the cycle of high motivation. When the student is successful, her expectation of success increases, she is motivated to put forth more effort into studying, she meets with more success, and the cycle repeats itself. If possible, relate the student's successes to something the student can control such as effort.

However, it is also important to help the student acquire new ways of learning and to broaden the student's repertoire of learning capabilities. Therefore, when the student is experiencing success on a regular basis, gradually begin to challenge the student to learn in ways that may not be strengths. As you do so, watch the student carefully for signs of overload and frustration.

7. Make both instruction and your daily schedule predictable. Many special needs students function better when they are able to predict events that will occur and prepare themselves emotionally. A daily schedule or class agenda that is clearly visible, either on the board for all students to see or on the desk of an individual student, can be a powerful tool in helping the student control behavior. Obviously, the schedule will not always go according to plan, and students will have to learn to adjust, but predictability of events helps create a psychologically safe and comfortable environment for many students with special needs.

8. Keep instructions brief, clear, and to the point. If there is a long series of steps that students must follow in order to complete a given task, sequence the steps and introduce one or two at a time instead of giving all the directions at once. Try to provide more frequent feedback on the specific steps that make up the completed task, rather than solely focussing on the completed task. Try to provide instructions in multiple channels—for example, orally and visually.

9. Hold appropriate but high expectations by focusing on the quality of work that the student does rather than the quantity. Help the student clearly understand what high-quality work looks like by providing exemplars and rubrics, and by ensuring that students understand the criteria that you use to judge their work. Whenever possible, help students internalize standards for high-quality work by asking them to engage in self-evaluation by asking, "Does this work represent your best effort?" "If not, what can you do next time to improve?"

10. Work to make sure that students have the opportunity to learn the social skills that they lack in order to interact positively with classmates. The classroom teacher will probably not be able to do this alone. Collaboration with specialists who work with the students can often provide help and support in this area. Social stories and *skillstreaming*, a nine-step approach to teaching pro-social skills, have proven to be very effective strategies for teaching social skills directly (McGinnis, 1984).

11. Teach students self-management skills that they can use to gain or regain control when they experience problems. Breathing and relaxation techniques; anger management strategies, such as slowly counting to ten; or "stop, relax, and think," as well as nonpunitive time-out are tools that students can use to keep it together when things start falling apart. The specialist and classroom teacher should work together on helping the student acquire and use these skills. The specialist may be in a better position to actually teach the steps of the strategy, but the classroom teacher is more likely to be present when the strategy is needed. Thus, the classroom teacher's ability to cue the student to use the strategy and to help the student process the effectiveness of the strategy are critical components of enabling the student to use the tools effectively.

12. Use functional behavior assessment (FBA) and positive behavior support to help students with special needs learn to control their behavior when appropriate. Certain states may require that FBA and positive behavior support be employed before suspending or excluding students with special needs. Such actions are currently mandated by the Pennsylvania School Code (PaTTAN, 2008).

References

McGinnis, E. (1984). *Skillstreaming the elementary school child: A guide for teaching prosocial skills*. Champaign, IL: Research Press.

PaTTAN. (2008). *Functional behavior assessment mini-module training materials*. Pennsylvania Technical Training and Assistance Network. Retrieved from *http://www.pattan.net/*

APPENDIX C

Decisions and Tasks for Beginning the School Year

Although the manner in which each of the following tasks is carried out will differ depending on the individual teacher, the grade level, the subject area, and the teacher's beliefs about teaching, each teacher must spend time at the beginning of the school year thinking about and doing particular tasks that will get the year off to a good start. The following list of beginning-of-the-year tasks is designed to help you think about those decisions.

Before Students Arrive

____ Arrange the classroom learning environment, including general use of space, seating arrangement, traffic patterns, storage of materials and equipment, and bulletin boards and display areas.

____ Obtain class lists or a list of students whom you will be teaching.

____ Develop a general curriculum plan for the year, a block plan of activities for the initial unit, and detailed daily plans for the first week of school.

____ Make contact with students and their families before school begins if appropriate and possible.

____ Read student academic records, IEPs, health records, and collaborate with specialists who will be working with your students and decide how to use the information you gather in terms of classroom management, instruction, and grouping.

____ Decide on how you will develop classroom guidelines (teacher derived, cooperatively derived, student derived).

When Students Arrive

____ Establish a classroom community in which students know one another and in which they feel psychologically safe and comfortable.

____ Help students understand classroom guidelines, including both rules and procedures, beginning with those procedures that are needed immediately and moving toward those that will come into play later, and obtain student commitment to living up to the classroom rules.

____ Motivate students to be excited and interested in the academic content that they will be learning this year, focusing on students' expectation of success and value of what will be learned.

____ Begin to build self-esteem by considering how to impact students' significance, competence, virtue, and power.

____ Acquaint students with the physical layout of the room and help them understand how to acquire and use materials.

_____ Make sure that students are aware of any safety precautions and procedures including fire drill procedures.

_____ Make sure that families are kept in the loop and informed about expectations for students as well as how they can be involved in supporting their children so that they are successful.

REFERENCES

Chapter 1

Berliner, D. (1984). The half-full glass: A review of research on teaching. In P. Hosford (Ed.), *Using what we know about teaching.* Alexandria, VA: Association for Supervision and Curriculum Development.

Boyan, N. J., and Copeland, W. D. (1978). *Instructional supervision training program.* Columbus, OH: Merrill.

Brophy, J. (1988). Research on teacher effects: Uses and abuses. *The Elementary School Journal, 89,* 1, 3–21.

Charles, C. M., and Senter, G.W. (2010). *Building classroom discipline,* 10th ed. Upper Saddle River, NJ: Pearson/Prentice Hall.

Curwin, R., Mendler, A., and Mendler, B. (2008). *Discipline with dignity,* 3rd ed. Alexandria, VA: Association for Supervision and Curriculum Development.

Danielson, C. (2007). *Enhancing professional practice: A framework for teaching.* Alexandria, VA: Association for Supervision and Curriculum Development.

Dean, C., Hubbell, E., Pitler, H., and Stone, B. (2012). *Classroom instruction that works: Research-based strategies for increasing student achievement,* 2nd ed. Alexandria, VA: Association for Supervision and Curriculum Development.

Emmer, E. T., and Evertson, C. M. (2008). *Classroom management for secondary teachers,* 8th ed. Boston: Allyn and Bacon.

Evertson, C. M., and Emmer, E. T. (2009). *Classroom management for elementary teachers,* 8th ed. Boston: Allyn and Bacon.

Haberman, M. (1995). *Star teachers of children in poverty.* West Lafayette, IN: Kappa Delta Pi.

Kounin, J. S. (1970). *Discipline and group management in classrooms.* New York: Holt, Rinehart & Winston.

Marzano, R., Frontier, T., and Livingston, D. (2011). *Effective supervision: Supporting the art and science of teaching.* Alexandria, VA: Association for Supervision and Curriculum Development.

National Education Association. (2010). *Status of the American public school teacher, 2005–2006.* Washington, DC: Author.

Redl, F., and Wineman, D. (1952). *Controls from within: Techniques for treatment of the aggressive child.* New York: Free Press.

Shrigley, R. L. (1985). Curbing student disruption in the classroom—Teachers need intervention skills. *National Association of Secondary School Principals Bulletin, 69,* 479, 26–32.

Sweeney, T. J. (1981). *Adlerian counseling: Proven concepts and strategies,* 2nd ed. Muncie, IN: Accelerated Development.

Tauber, R. T., and Mester, C. S. (1994). *Acting lessons for teachers: Using performance skills in the classroom.* Westport, CT: Praeger.

Chapter 2

American Psychological Association. (2006). Classroom Management. Retrieved from *http://www.apa.org/education/k12/classroom-mgmt.aspx*

Baker, K. (1985). Research evidence of a school discipline problem. *Phi Delta Kappan, 66,* 7, 482–488.

Bauer, G. L. (1985). Restoring order to the public schools. *Phi Delta Kappan, 66,* 7, 488–490.

Black, S. (2001). When teachers feel good about their work student achievement rises. *American School Board Journal,* January.

Brendtro, L. K., Brokenleg, M., and Van Bockern, S. (1990). *Reclaiming youth at risk: Our hope for the future.* Bloomington, IN: National Educational Service.

Brophy, J. (1988). Research on teacher effects: Uses and abuses. *The Elementary School Journal, 89,* 1, 3–21.

Bushaw, W. J., and Lopez, S. J. (2011). Betting on teachers: The 43rd annual Phi Delta Kappa/Gallup poll of the public's attitudes toward the public schools. *Phi Delta Kappan, 93,* 1, 9–26.

Canter, L. (1989). Assertive discipline—More than names on the board and marbles in a jar. *Phi Delta Kappan, 71,* 1, 57–61.

Charles, C. M. (2002). *Building classroom discipline,* 7th ed. Boston: Allyn and Bacon.

Children's Defense Fund. (2002). *School safety issues basics.* Retrieved from *http://www.childrensdefense.org/ss_ssfs_basics.php*

Conradson, S., & Hernández-Ramos, P. (2004). Computers, the Internet, and cheating among secondary school students: Some implications for educators. *Practical Assessment, Research & Evaluation, 9*(9). Retrieved from *http://PAREonline.net/getvn.asp?v=9&n=9*

Coopersmith, S. (1967). *The antecedents of self-esteem.* San Francisco, CA: W. H. Freedman.

Curwin, R. L., and Mendler, A. N. (1980). *The discipline book: A complete guide to school and classroom management.* Reston, VA: Reston Publishing.

Curwin R. L., and Mendler, A. N. (1999). *Discipline with dignity.* Upper Saddle River, NJ: Merrill/Prentice Hall.

Dade County Public Schools. (1976). *Experiences of teachers and students with disruptive behavior in the Dade public schools.* Miami, FL: Author.

DeVoe, J. F., Peter, K., Kaufman, P., Miller, A., Noonan, M., Snyder, T. D., and Baum, K. (2004). *Indicators of school crime and safety: 2004* (NCES 2005–002/NCJ 205290). Washington, DC: U.S. Government Printing Office.

DiPrete, T., Muller, C., and Shaeffer, N. (1981). *Discipline and order in American high schools.* Washington, DC: National Center for Education Statistics.

Doyle, W. (1978). Are students behaving worse than they used to behave? *Journal of Research and Development in Education, 11,* 4, 3–16.

Dreikurs, R. (1964). *Children: The challenge.* New York: Hawthorn.

Elam, S. M. (1989). The second Gallup/Phi Delta Kappa poll of teachers' attitudes toward the public schools. *Phi Delta Kappan, 70,* 10, 785–798.

Emmer, E. T., Evertson, C. M., Sanford, J. P., Clements, B. S., and Worsham, M. E. (1989). *Classroom management for secondary teachers,* 2nd ed. Englewood Cliffs, NJ: Prentice Hall.

Evertson, C. M., Emmer, E. T. and Clements, B. S. (1994). *Classroom Management for Elementary Teachers.* 3rd ed. Allyn and Bacon, Needham Heights, MA.

Feitler, F., and Tokar, E. (1992). Getting a handle on teacher stress: How bad is the problem? *Educational Leadership, 49,* 456–458.

Feldhusen, J. F. (1978). Behavior problems in secondary schools. *Journal of Research and Development in Education, 11,* 4, 17–28.

Gallup, A. M. (1986). The 18th annual Gallup poll of the public's attitudes toward the public schools. *Phi Delta Kappan, 68,* 1, 43–59.

Haberman, M. (2004). *Teacher burnout in black and white.* The Haberman Educational Foundation. Retrieved from *http://www.eric.ed.gov/ERICWebPortal/search/detailmini.jsp?_nfpb=true&_&ERICExtSearch_SearchValue_0=EJ819913&ERICExtSearch_SearchType_0=no&accno=EJ819913*

Harris, L. (1984). *Metropolitan Life survey of the American teacher.* New York: Metropolitan Life Insurance Company.

Hawes, J. M. (1971). *Children in urban society: Juvenile delinquency in nineteenth century America.* New York: Oxford University Press.

Huber, J. D. (1984). Discipline in the middle school—Parent, teacher, and principal concerns. *National Association of Secondary School Principals Bulletin, 68,* 471, 74–79.

Hyman, I. A., and Perone, D. C. (1998). The other side of school violence: Educator policies and practices that may contribute to school misbehavior. *Journal of School Psychology, 36,* 1, 7–27.

Hyman, I. A., and Snook, P. A. (1999). *Dangerous schools: What we can do about the physical and emotional abuse of our children.* San Francisco: Jossey-Bass.

Iverson, A. M. (2003). *Building competence in classroom management and discipline,* 4th ed. Upper Saddle River, NJ: Merrill/Prentice Hall.

Josephson, M. (1998). *1998 report card on the ethics of American youth.* Los Angeles, CA: Josephson Institute of Ethics.

Josephson, M. (2002). *2002 report card on the ethics of American youth*. Los Angeles, CA: Josephson Institute of Ethics.

Josephson, M. (2012). *2012 report card on the ethics of American youth*. Los Angeles, CA: Josephson Institute of Ethics.

Kindsvatter, R. (1978). A new view of the dynamics of discipline. *Phi Delta Kappan, 59,* 5, 322–365.

Kounin, J. (1970). *Discipline and group management in classrooms*. New York: Holt, Rinehart & Winston.

Lalli, M., and Savitz, L. D. (1976). The fear of crime in the school enterprise and its consequences. *Education and Urban Society, 4,* 401–416.

Langdon, C. A. (1997). The fourth Phi Delta Kappa poll of teachers' attitudes toward public schools. *Phi Delta Kappan, 79,* 3, 212–221.

Langdon, C. A. (1999). The fifth Phi Delta Kappa poll of teachers' attitudes toward the public schools. *Phi Delta Kappan, 80,* 8, 611–618.

Langdon, C. A., and Vesper, N. (2000). The sixth Phi Delta Kappa poll of teachers' attitudes toward the public schools. *Phi Delta Kappan, 81,* 8, 607–611.

Levin, J. (1980). *Discipline and classroom management survey: Comparisons between a suburban and urban school*. Unpublished report, Pennsylvania State University, University Park.

Levin, J., Hoffman, N., Badiali, B., and Neuhard, R. (1985, April). *Critical experiences in student teaching: Effects on career choice and implications for program modification*. Paper presented to the Annual Conference of the American Educational Research Association, Chicago.

Levin, J., and Shanken-Kaye, J. (2002). *From disrupter to achiever: Creating successful learning environments for the self-control classroom*. Dubuque, IA: Kendall/Hunt.

Lippman, L., Burns, S., and McArthur, E. (2004). *Urban schools: The challenge of location and poverty*. Darby, PA: Diane Publishing Company.

Maag, J. W. (2004). *Behavior management: From theoretical implications to practical applications,* 2nd ed. Belmont, CA: Thomson Wadsworth.

Markow, D., and Scheer, M. (2003). *The MetLife survey of the American teacher, 2003, An examination of school leadership*. New York: Metropolitan Life Insurance Company.

Markow, D., and Scheer, M. (2004). *MetLife survey of the American teacher, 2004–2005, Transitions and the role of supportive relationships*. New York: Metropolitan Life Insurance Company.

Mennell, R. M. (1973). *Thorns & thistles: Juvenile delinquents in the United States 1825–1940*. Hanover, NH: The University Press of New England.

National Education Goals Panel. (1994). *The national education goals report: Building a nation of learners, 1994*. Washington, DC: Superintendent of Documents, U.S. Government Printing Office.

National Education Goals Panel. (2000). *Building a nation of learners*. Retrieved from *govinfo.libraryunt.edu/negp/reports/99rpt.pdf*

National Institute of Education. (1980). *Teachers opinion poll*. Washington, DC: U.S. Department of Health, Education and Welfare.

Robers, S., Zhang, J., and Truman, J. (2010). *Indicators of school crime and safety: 2010* (NCES 2011-002/NCJ 230812). Washington, DC: National Center for Education Statistics, U.S. Department of Education, and Bureau of Justice Statistics, Office of Justice Programs, U.S. Department of Justice.

Schlossman, S. L. (1977). *Love and the American delinquent: The theory and practice of "progressive" juvenile justice, 1825–1920*. Chicago: University of Chicago Press.

Schulte, B. (2002, Sept. 15). Cheatin', writin' & 'rithmetic. How to succeed in school without really trying. *The Washington Post*. Retrieved from *http://www.jhu.edu/~virtlab/misc/Cheatin.htm*

Shrigley, R. L. (1979). Strategies in classroom management. *The National Association of Secondary School Principals Bulletin, 63,* 428, 1–9.

Smith, O. B. (1969). Discipline. In R. L. Ebel, *Encyclopedia of educational research,* 4th ed. New York: Macmillan.

Stipek, D. J. (2001). *Motivation to learn: Integrating theory and practice,* 4th ed. Boston: Allyn and Bacon.

Thomas, G. T., Goodall, R., and Brown, L. (1983). Discipline in the classroom: Perceptions of middle grade teachers. *The Clearinghouse, 57,* 3, 139–142.

Vittetoe, J. O. (1977). Why first-year teachers fail. *Phi Delta Kappan, 58,* 5, 429.

Walker, H. M. (1979). *The acting-out child: Coping with classroom disruption.* Boston: Allyn and Bacon.

Walker, H. M., and Buckley, N. K. (1973). Teacher attention to appropriate and inappropriate classroom behavior: An individual case study. *Focus on Exceptional Children, 5,* 5–11.

Walker, H. M., and Buckley, N. K. (1974). *Token reinforcement techniques: Classroom applications for the hard to teach child.* Eugene, OR: E-B Press.

Walsh, D. (1983). Our schools come to order. *American Teacher, 68,* 1.

Wayne, I., and Rubel, R. J. (1982). Student fear in secondary schools. *Urban Review, 14,* 1, 197–237.

Wayson, W. W. (1985). The politics of violence in school: Doublespeak and disruptions in public confidence. *Phi Delta Kappan, 67,* 2, 127–132.

Weber, T. R., and Sloan, C. A. (1986). How does high school discipline in 1984 compare to previous decades? *The Clearinghouse, 59,* 7, 326–329.

Weiner, B. (1980). A cognitive (attribution)–emotion–action model of motivated behavior: An analysis of judgments of help-giving. *Journal of Personality and Social Psychology, 39,* 186–200.

Zabel, R. H., and Zabel, M. K. (1996) *Classroom management in context: Orchestrating positive learning environments.* Boston: Houghton Mifflin Company.

Chapter 3

Abi-Nader, J. (1993). Meeting the needs of multicultural classrooms: Family values and the motivation of minority students. In M. J. O'Hair and S. J. Odell (Eds.), *Diversity and teaching: Teacher education Yearbook 1.* Fort Worth, TX: Harcourt, Brace, Jovanovich.

Adler, I. (1966). Mental growth and the art of teaching. *The Mathematics Teacher, 59,* 706–715.

American Academy of Child & Adolescent Psychiatry, American Academy of Family Physicians, American Academy of Pediatrics, American Medical Association, American Psychiatric Association, and American Psychological Association. (2000). *Joint statement on the impact of entertainment violence on children.* Congressional **Public Health** Summit, July 26. Retrieved from *www.capalert. com/**violence**in**entertainment**.htm*

American Psychiatric Association. (2002). *Psychiatric effects of media violence.* Retrieved from *http://www.psych.org/public_info/media_violence.*cfm

American Psychological Association. (1993). *Violence and youth: Psychology's response,* Vol. 1. Washington, DC: Author.

American Psychological Association. (1996). *Violence and the family: Report of the American Psychological Association presidential task force on violence and the family.* Washington, DC: Author.

Anderson, C. A. (2003). Violent video games: Myths, facts, and unanswered questions. *Psychological Science Agenda, 16,* 5.

Anderson, C. A. (2004a). An update on the effects of playing violent video games. *Journal of Adolescence, 27,* 1, 113–122.

Anderson, C. A. (2004b). Violent video games: Myths, facts, and unanswered questions. *Science Briefs.* Washington, DC: American Psychological Association.

Atkin, C. (1983). Effects of realistic TV violence vs. fictional violence on aggression. *Journalism Quarterly, 60,* 4, 615–621.

Aud, S., Fox, M., and KewalRamani, A. (2010). Status and trends in the education of racial and ethnic groups (NCES 2010-015). U.S. Department of Education, National Center for Education Statistics. Washington, DC: U.S. Government Printing Office.

Bandura, A. (1973). *Aggression: A social learning analysis.* Englewood Cliffs, NJ: Prentice Hall.

Barton, P. E., and Coley, R. J. (2007). *The family: America's smallest school.* Princeton, NJ: Educational Testing Services.

Batsche, G. M., and Knoff, H. M. (1994). Bullies and their victims: Understanding a pervasive problem in the schools. *School Psychology Review 23*(2), 165–174.

Bayh, B. (1978). Seeking solutions to school violence and vandalism. *Phi Delta Kappan, 59,* 5, 299–302.

Benard, B. (1991). *Fostering resiliency in kids: Protective factors in the family, school and community.* Minneapolis, MN: National Resilience Resource Center.

Benard, B. (1995). *Fostering resilience in children.* New York: ERIC Clearinghouse on Elementary and Early Childhood Education. Retrieved from *http://resilnet.uiuc.edu/library/benard95.html*

Boon, H. J. (2010). School moves, coping, and achievement: Models of possible interactions. *The Journal of Educational Research, 104,* 1, 54–70.

Bowker, M. A., and Sullivan, M. (2010). Sexting, risky actions and overreactions. *FBI Law Enforcement.* Retrieved from *http://www.fbi.gov/stats-services/publications/law-enforcement-bulletin/july-2010/sexting*

Bureau of Justice Statistics. (1995). *Special report: Violence against women: Estimates from the redesigned survey* (NCJ-154348). Washington, DC: U.S. Department of Justice.

Callan, R. J. (1998). Giving students the (right) time of day. *Educational Leadership, 55,* 4, 84–87.

Cantor, J. (1999). *"Mommy, I'm scared": How TV and movies frighten children and what we can do to protect them.* New York: Harvest Books.

Cantor, J. (2002, April). *The psychological effects of media violence on children and adolescents.* Paper presented at Colloquium on Television and Violence in Society, Montreal, Canada.

Carnagey, N. L., and Anderson, C. A. (2004). Violent video games exposure and agression. *Minerva Psichiatrica, 45,* 1–18.

Center for Media and Public Affairs. (1999). *I'm okay, you're dead! TV and movies suggest violence is harmless.* Retrieved from *http://www.cmpa.com/pressrel/violence99.htm*

Charles, C. M., and Senter, G. W. (2004). *Building classroom discipline,* 8th ed. Boston: Allyn and Bacon.

Children's Defense Fund. (1997). *The state of America's children yearbook, 1997.* Washington, DC: Author.

Children's Defense Fund. (2002a). *Media violence.* Retrieved from *http://www.childrensdefense.org/ss_mvfs_medvio*

Children's Defense Fund. (2002b). *Child poverty: Characteristics of poor children in America—2000.* Retrieved from *http://www.childrensdefense.org/fs_cptb_child00.php*

Children's Defense Fund. (2002c). *Child poverty.* Retrieved from *http://www.childrensdefense.org/fs_chpov.php*

Children's Defense Fund. (2002d). *Child abuse and neglect.* Retrieved from *http://www.childrensdefense.org/ss_chabuse_fs.php*

Children's Defense Fund. (2002e). *Domestic violence and its impact on children.* Retrieved from *http://www.childrensdefense.org/ss_domviol_fs.php*

Children's Defense Fund. (2010). *American dream vanishing for 16.4 million children.* Retrieved from *http://www.childrensdefense.org/newsroom/cdf-in-the-news/press-releases/2011/american-dream-vanishing-for.html*

Clarizio, H. F., and McCoy, G. F. (1983). *Behavior disorders in children,* 3rd ed. New York: Harper & Row.

Coopersmith, S. (1967). *The antecedents of self-esteem.* San Francisco: W. H. Freeman.

Cotton, K. (1989). Expectations and student outcomes. Northwest Regional Educational Laboratory. Retrieved from *educationnorthwest.org/webfm_send/562*

Coy, D. R. (2001). Bullying. *ERIC/CASS Digest.* ERIC Clearinghouse on Counseling and Student Services. ED459405.

Dahl, R. E. (1999). The consequences of insufficient sleep for adolescents: Links between sleep and emotional regulation. *Phi Delta Kappan, 80,* 5, 354–359.

Delpit, L. (2012) *Multiplication is for white people.* New York: The New Press.

Department of Justice. (1993). *Bureau of justice assistance, family violence: Interventions for the justice system.* Washington, DC: Author.

DeVoe, J. F., Peter, K., Kaufman, P., Miller, A., Noonan, M., Snyder, T. D., and Baum, K. (2004). Indicators of school crime and safety: 2004 (NCES 2005–002/ NCJ 205290). Washington, DC: U.S. Government Printing Office, America. New York: Oxford University Press.

Dewey, J. (1916). *Democracy and education.* New York: Macmillan.

Dreikurs, R., Grunwald, B., and Pepper, F. (1982). *Maintaining sanity in the classroom: Classroom management techniques,* 2nd ed. New York: Harper & Row.

Dubelle, S. T., and Hoffman, C. M. (1984). *Misbehaving—solving the disciplinary puzzle for educators.* Lancaster, PA: Technomic.

Elliot, D. S., and Voss, H. L. (1974). *Delinquency and dropout.* Lexington, MA: Lexington.

Eron, L. D. (1982). Parent child interaction, television violence and aggression of children. *American Psychologist, 37,* 2, 197–211.

Eron, L. D., and Slaby, R. G. (1994). Introduction. In L. D. Eron, J. H. Gentry, and P. Schlegel (Eds.), *Reason to hope: A psychosocial perspective on violence and youth.* Washington, DC: American Psychological Association.

Feldhusen, J. F. (1978). Behavior problems in secondary schools. *Journal of Research and Development in Education, 11,* 4, 17–28.

Feldhusen, J. F., Thurston, J. R., and Benning, J. J. (1973). A longitudinal study of delinquency and other aspects of children's behavior. *International Journal of Criminology and Penology, 1,* 341–351.

Finkelhor, D., Mitchell, K. J., and Wolak, J. (2000). *Online victimization: A report on the nation's youth.* Durham, NH: Crimes Against Children Research Center.

French, J. R. P., and Raven, B. (1960). Social authority bases. In D. Cartwright and A. Zander (Eds.), *Group dynamics: Research and theory.* Evanston, IL: Row-Peterson.

Gabay, J. (1991, January). ASCD Update.

Gelfand, D. M., Jenson, W. R., and Drew, C. J. (1982). *Understanding child behavior disorders.* New York: Holt, Rinehart & Winston.

Gilliland, H. (1986). Self concept and the Indian student. In J. Reyhner (Ed.), *Teaching the Indian child.* Billings, MT: Eastern Montana College.

Glasser, W. (1978). Disorders in our schools: Causes and remedies. *Phi Delta Kappan, 59,* 5, 321–333.

Glick, M. (2011) *The instructional leader and the brain: Using neuroscience to inform practice.* Thousand Oaks, CA: Corwin Press.

Goertzel, V., and Goertzel, M. (1962). *Cradles of eminence.* Boston: Little, Brown.

Gorman, R. M. (1972). *Discovering Piaget: A guide for teachers.* Columbus, OH: Merrill.

Grand Rapids Institute for Information Democracy. (2000). Give us what we want? TV news and violence. *GRIID Report.* Retrieved from *http://www.mediamouse.org/resources/griid/reports/report-viol2000*

Hartman, C. (2002). High classroom turnover: How children get left behind, In Dianne M. Piche, W. L.Taylor, and R. A. Reed (Eds.), *Rights at risk: Equality in an age of terrorism.* Citizen's Commission on Civil Rights.

Howard, S., and Johnson, B. (1998, November). *Tracking student resilience.* Paper presented at the 1998 annual conference of the Australian Association for Research in Education. Retrieved from *http://www.aare.edu.au/98pap/joh98076.htm*

Huesmann, L. R., Moise, J., Podolski, C. P., and Eron, L. D. (2003). Longitudinal relations between childhood exposure to media violence and adult aggression and violence: 1977–1992. *Developmental Psychology, 39,* 2, 201–221.

Irvine, J. J. (1990). *Black students and school failure: Policies, practices and prescriptions.* Westport, CT: Greenwood.

Jessor, J., and Jessor, S. L. (1977). *Problem behavior and psychosocial development.* New York: Academic.

Johnson, J. G., Cohen, P., Smailes, E. M., Kasen, S., and Brook, J. S. (2002). Television viewing and aggressive behavior during adolescence and adulthood. *Science, 29,* 295, 2468–2471.

Kaiser Family Foundation. (2003a). *Children and the news: Coping with terrorism, war and everyday violence.* Menlo Park, CA: Author.

Kaiser Family Foundation. (2003b). *TV violence.* Menlo Park, CA: Author.

Kaiser Family Foundation. (2010). *Daily media use among children and teens up dramatically from five years ago.* Menlo Park, CA: Author.

Karplus, R. (1977). *Science teaching and the development of reasoning.* Berkeley: University of California Press.

Kerbel, M. (2000). *If it bleeds, it leads: An anatomy of television news.* Boulder, CO: Westview Press.

Kindsvatter, R. (1978). A new view of the dynamics of discipline. *Phi Delta Kappan, 59,* 5, 322–325.

Klite, P. (1999). TV news and the culture of violence. *Rocky Mountain Media Watch.* Retrieved from *http://bigmedia.org/texts6.html.*

Kohlberg, L. (1969). *Stages in the development of moral thought and action.* New York: Holt, Rinehart & Winston.

Kohlberg, L. (1975). The cognitive-developmental approach to moral education. *Phi Delta Kappan, 56,* 10, 610–677.

Kounin, J. S. (1970). *Discipline and group management in classrooms.* New York: Holt, Rinehart & Winston.

Kreider, R. M., and Fields, J. M. (2001). *Number, timing, and duration of marriages and divorces: Fall, 1996.* Current Population Reports, pp. 70–80. Washington, DC: U.S. Census Bureau.

Ladson-Billings, G. (1994). *The dreamkeepers: Successful teachers of African American children.* San Francisco: Jossey-Bass.

Levin, J., and Shanken-Kaye, J. (2002). *From disrupter to achiever: Creating successful learning environments for the self-control classroom.* Dubuque, IA: Kendall/Hunt.

Levine, V. (1984). Time use and student achievement: A critical assessment of the National Commission Report (College of Education, The Pennsylvania State University). *Forum, 11,* 12.

Lounsbury, K., and Mitchell, K. J. (2011). *The true prevalence of "sexting.".* Durham: University of New Hampshire, Crimes Against Children Research Center.

Maslow, A. (1968). *Toward a psychology of being.* New York: D. Van Nostrand.

Menacker, J., Weldon, W., and Hurwitz, E. (1989). School order and safety as community issues. *Phi Delta Kappan, 71,* 1, 39.

Murray, J. P. (1995). Children and television violence. *Kansas Journal of Law and Public Policy, 4,* 3, 7–14.

Nansel, T. R., Overpeck, M. D., Haynie, D. L., Ruan, W. J., and Scheidt, P. C. (2003). Relationships between bullying and violence among US youth. *Archives of Pediatrics and Adolescent Medicine, 157,* 4, 348–353.

Nansel, T. R., Overpeck, M., Pilla, R. S., Ruan, W. J., Simons-Morton, S., and Scheidt, S. (2001). Bully behaviors among US youth: Prevalence and association with psychosocial adjustment. *Journal of the American Medical Association, 285,* 2094–2100.

Nastasi, B., and Bernstein, R. (1998). Resilience applied: The promise and pitfalls of school-based resilience programs. *School Psychology Review, 27,* 3. Retrieved from *http://www.nasponline.org/publications/spr/index.aspx?vol=27&issue=3*

National Center for Education Statistics. (2000). *Condition of America's public school facilities: 1999* (NCES 2000-032). Washington, DC: Author.

National Center for Education Statistics. (2003a). *Overview of public elementary and secondary schools and districts: School year 2001–02* (NCES 2003-411). Washington, DC: Author.

National Center for Education Statistics. (2003b). *Indicators of school crime and safety: 2002* (NCES 2003-009). Washington, DC.

National Center for Education Statistics. (2005). *Indicators of school crime and safety: 2004* (NCES 2005-002). Washington, DC: Author.

National Center for Education Statistics. (2011). *Digest of national statistics, 2010* (NCES 2011-015). Washington, DC: Author. Retrieved from *http://nces.ed.gov/programs/digest/d10/*

National Center for Health Statistics. (2006). *National vital statistics report, 54,* 20. Washington, DC: Author.

National Center for Injury Prevention and Control. (1999). *The co-occurrence of intimate partner violence against mothers and abuse of children*. Center for Disease Control and Prevention. Retrieved from *http://www.cdc.gov/ncipc/factsheets/dvcan.htm*

Noddings, N. (1988, Dec. 7). Schools face crisis in caring. *Education Week*.

Nolin, M. J., Davies, E., and Chandler, K. (1995). *Student victimization at school: Statistics in brief*. Washington, DC: National Center for Education Statistics.

Olson, L. (2000a). Minority groups to emerge as a majority in U.S. schools. *Education Week, 20*, 4, 34, 35.

Olson, L. (2000b). Mixed needs of immigrants pose challenges for schools. *Education Week, 20*, 4, 38, 39.

Olweus, D. (1993). *Bullying at school: What we know and what we can do*. Oxford, UK: Blackwell Publishers.

Olweus, D. (2001). *Olweus' core program against bullying and antisocial behavior: A teacher handbook*. HEMIL-senteret, Universitetet i Bergen, N-5015 Bergen, Norway.

Olweus, D., and Limber, S. (1999). *Blueprints for violence prevention: Bullying prevention program*. Boulder: University of Colorado, Boulder, Institute of Behavioral Science.

Pace, B. (2001). Bullying. *The Journal of the American Medical Association, 285*, 2156.

Parke, R. D. (1978). Children's home environments: Social and cognitive effects. In I. Altman and J. F. Wohlwill (Eds.), *Children and the environment*. New York: Plenum.

Patchin, J. W., and Hinduja, S. (2006). Bullies move beyond the schoolyard: A preliminary look at cyberbullying. *Youth Violence and Juvenile Justice, 4*, 2, 148–169.

Pearl, D. (1984). Violence and aggression. *Society, 21*, 6, 15–16.

Pearl, D., Bouthilet, L., and Lazar, J. (Eds.). (1982). *Television and behavior: Ten years of scientific progress and implications for the eighties*, Vol. 2. Washington, DC: U.S. Government Printing Office.

Peled, E., Jaffe, P. G., and Edleson, J. L. (Eds.). (1995). *Ending the cycle of domestic violence: Community responses to children of battered women*. Thousand Oaks, CA: Sage.

Piaget, J. (1965). *The moral judgment of the child*. Glencoe, IL: Free Press.

Piaget, J. (1970). Piaget's theory. In P. H. Mussen (Ed.), *Carmichael's manual of child psychology*, Vol. 1. New York: Wiley.

Public Broadcasting System. (2002). *"Let's get married."* Frontline. Retrieved from *http://www.pbs.org/wgbh/pages/frontline/shows/marriage/etc/script.html*

Quiroz, H. C. (2002, April). *Understanding, preventing and responding to school bullying*. National School Safety Center, p. 8.

Rees, J. (2003). Children hurt more by TV news violence than soaps. *IcWales*. Retrieved from *http://icwales.icnetwork.co.uk/printable_version.cfm?objectid=134*

Resiliency Resource Centre. (2008). Available at *http://www.embracethefuture.org.au/resiliency/index.htm*.

Rice, M. L., Huston, A. C., and Wright, J. C. (1982). The forms and codes of television: Effects on children's attention, comprehension and social behavior. In D. Pearl, L. Bouthilet, and J. Lazar (Eds.), *Television and behavior: Ten years of scientific progress and implications for the eighties*, Vol. 2. Washington, DC: U.S. Government Printing Office.

Rice, P. F. (1981). *The adolescent development, relationships, and culture*, 3rd ed. Boston: Allyn and Bacon.

Rideout, V., Roberts, D., and Foehr, U. (2005). *Generation M: Media in the lives of 8–18 year olds*. Menlo Park, CA: Kaiser Family Foundation.

Robers, S., Zang, J., and Truman, J., (2010). Indicators of School Crime and Safety: 2010 (NCES 2011-002/NCJ 230812). National Center for Education Statistics, U.S. Department of Education and Bureau of Justice Statistics, Office of Justice Programs, U.S. Department of Fustice. Washington, DC.

Rosenthal, R., and Jacobson, L. (1968). *Pygmalion in the classroom: Teacher expectations and pupils' intellectual development.* New York: Holt, Rinehart & Winston.

Rutter, M. (1978). Family, area, and school influences in the genesis of conduct disorders. In L. Herson, M. Berger, and D. Shaffer (Eds.), *Aggression and anti-social behaviour in childhood and adolescence.* Oxford, UK: Pergamon.

Rutter, M. (1985). Resilience in the face of adversity: Protective factors and resistance to psychiatric disorder. *British Journal of Psychiatry, 147,* 598–611.

Sampson, R. (2002). *Bullying in schools.* Problem-Oriented Guides for Police Series. Washington, DC: U.S. Department of Justice.

Simmons, B. (1994, July/August). Violence in the air: Why do we show this stuff? *Columbia Journalismreview.* Retrieved from *http://archives .cjr.org/year/94/4/violence.asp*

Singer, J. L., Singer, D. G., and Rapaczynski, W. S. (1984). Family patterns and television viewing as predictors of children's beliefs and aggression. *Journal of Communications, 34,* 2, 73–89.

Smith, P. K., Pepler, D., and Rigby, K. (Eds.). (2004). *Bullying in schools: How successful can interventions be?* Cambridge, UK: Cambridge University Press.

Stinchcombe, A. L. (1964). *Rebellion in a high school.* Chicago: Quadrangle.

Stipek, D. J. (2001). *Motivation to learn, from theory to practice,* 4th ed. Boston: Allyn and Bacon.

Strizek, G. A. Pittsonberger, J. L., Riordan, K. E., Lyter, D. M., and Orlofsky, G. F. (2006). *Characteristics of schools, districts, teachers, principals, and school libraries in the United States: 2003–04 schools and staffing survey* (NCES 2006-313 Revised). U.S. Department of Education, National Center for Education Statistics. Washington, DC: U.S. Government Printing Office.

Sweeney, J. J. (1981). *Adlerian counseling proven concepts and strategies,* 2nd ed. Muncie, IN: Accelerated Development.

Tanner, L. N. (1978). *Classroom discipline for effective teaching and learning.* New York: Holt, Rinehart & Winston.

Toffler, A. (1970). *Future shock.* New York: Random House.

U.S. Bureau of the Census. (2001). *U.S. adults postponing marriage, Census Bureau reports.*

U.S. Census Bureau (2004). *Geographical mobility: Population characteristics March 2002 to March 2003.* U.S. Department of Education.

U.S. Department of Health and Human Services. (2007). *Child maltreatment 2005.* Administration on Children, Youth and Families. Washington, DC: U.S. Government Printing Office.

U.S. Department of Health and Human Services. (2011). *Child maltreatment 2010.* Administration for Children and Families, Administration on Children, Youth and Families, Children's Bureau. Available from *http://www.childwelfare.gov/ systemwide/statistics/can.cfm.*

U.S. General Accounting Office. (1994). *Elementary school children: Many change schools frequently, harming their education,* Washington, DC: Author.

Visher, E. B., and Visher, J. S. (1978). Common problems of stepparents and their spouses. *American Journal of Orthopsychiatry, 48,* 252–262.

Vossekuil, B., Reddy, M., Fein, R., Borum, R., and Modzeleski, W. (2002). *Final report and findings of the safe school initiative: Implications for the prevention of school attacks in the United States.* Washington, DC: U.S. Department of Education, Safe and Drug Free Schools Program and U.S. Secret Service, National Threat Assessment Center.

Weaver, R. (2005). Showing them the love—and money. *NEA Today, 23,* 5, 7.

Weaver, R. (2006). Schools' changing faces. *NEA Today, 25,* 1, 7.

Werner, E. (1993). *Overcoming the odds: High risk children from birth to adulthood.* Ithaca, NY: Cornell University Press.

Werner, E., and Smith, R. (1992). *Overcoming the odds: High-risk children from birth to adulthood.* New York: Cornell University Press, 1992. ED 344 979.

Whitmire, R. (1991, October). Educational declines linked with erosion of family. *The Olympian, 1.*

Withall, J. (1969). Evaluation of classroom climate. *Childhood Education, 45,* 7, 403–408.

Withall, J. (1979). Problem behavior: Function of social-emotional climate? *Journal of Education, 161,* 2, 89–101.

Ybarra, M. L., and Mitchell, K. J. (2004). Youth engaging in online harassment: Associations with caregiver-child relationships, Internet use, and personal characteristics. *Journal of Adolescence, 27,* 319–336.

Chapter 4

Alberto, P., and Troutman, A. (2012). *Applied behavior analysis for teachers,* 9th ed. Upper Saddle River, NJ: Merrill/Prentice Hall.

Berne, E. (1964). *Games people play: The psychology of human relations.* New York: Avon.

Cameron, J. (2001). Negative effects of rewards on intrinsic motivation—a limited phenomenon: Comment on Deci, Koestner, & Ryan. *Review of Educational Research, 71,* 1, 29–42.

Cangelosi, J. (2008). *Classroom management strategies: Gaining and maintaining students' cooperation,* 6th ed. New York: Wiley.

Canter, L., and Canter, M. (2007). *Assertive discipline: Positive behavior management for today's classrooms,* rev. ed. Santa Monica, CA: Canter Associates.

Charles, C. M., and Senter, G. W. (2010). *Building classroom discipline,* 10th ed. Boston: Allyn and Bacon.

Charney, R. (2002). *Teaching children to care: Classroom management for ethical and academic growth, K–8,* rev. ed. Greenfield, MA: Northeast Foundation for Children.

Crowe, C. (2009) *Solving thorny behavior problems: How teachers and students can work together.* Greenfield, MA: Northeast Foundation for Children.

Curwin, R., Mendler, A., and Mendler, B. (2008). *Discipline with dignity,* 3rd ed. Alexandria, VA: Association for Supervision and Curriculum Development.

Curwin, R., and Mendler, A. (1999). Zero tolerance for zero tolerance. *Phi Delta Kappan, 81,* 2, 119–120.

Dean, C., Hubbell, E., Pitler, H., and Stone, B. (2012) *Classroom instruction that works: Research-based strategies for increasing student achievement,* 2nd ed. Alexandria, VA: Association for Supervision and Curriculum Development.

Deci, E., Koestner, R., and Ryan, R. (2001). Extrinsic rewards and intrinsic motivation in education: Reconsidered once again. *Review of Educational Research, 71,* 1, 1–28.

Delpit, L. (2012) *Multiplication is for white people.* New York: The New Press.

Denton, P., and Kriete, R. (2000). *The first six weeks of school.* Greenfield, MA: Northeast Foundation for Children.

Developmental Studies Center. (1996). *Ways we want our class to be: Class meetings that build commitment to kindness and learning.* Oakland, CA: Developmental Studies Center.

Dreikurs, R. (2004). *Discipline without tears: How to reduce conflict and establish cooperation in the classroom.* New York: Wiley.

Fay, J., and Funk, D. (1995). *Teaching with love and logic: Taking control of the classroom.* Golden, CO: Love and Logic Press.

Forton, M. B. (1998). Apology of action. *Responsive Classroom, 10,* 1, 6–7.

French, J. R. P., and Raven, B. (1960). The bases of social power. In D. Cartwright and A. Zander (Eds.), *Group dynamics: Research and theory.* Evanston, IL: Row-Peterson.

Ginott, H. (1972). *Between teacher and child.* New York: Wyden.

Glasser, W. (1992). *The quality school: Managing students without coercion.* New York: Harper/Collins.

Glick, M. (2011). *The instructional leader and the brain: Using neuroscience to inform practice.* Thousand oaks, CA: Corwin Press.

Gordon, T. (1989). *Teaching children self-discipline at home and in school.* New York: Random House.

Harris, T. (1969). *I'm O.K., you're O.K.: A practical guide to transactional analysis.* New York: Harper & Row.

Kerr, M. M., and Nelson, C. M. (2005). *Strategies for addressing behavior problems in the classroom,*

5th ed. Upper Saddle River, NJ: Merrill/Prentice Hall.

Kohn, A. (2006). *Beyond discipline: From compliance to community,* 2nd ed. Alexandria, VA: Association for Supervision and Curriculum Development.

Lasley, T. J. (1989). A teacher development model for classroom management. *Phi Delta Kappan, 71,* 1, 36–38.

Lepper, M., and Green, D. (1978). *The hidden costs of reward: New perspectives on human motivation.* Hillsdale, NJ: Erlbaum.

Martella, R., Nelson, J., Marchand-Martella, N., and O'Reilly, M. (2011).*Comprehensive behavior management: Individualized, classroom and schoolwide approaches.* Thousand Oaks, CA: Sage Publications.

Nelson, J. (2006). *Positive discipline,* 3rd ed. New York: Ballantine Books.

Putnam, J. & Burke, J. (1992) *Organizing and managing classroom learning communities.* New York: McGraw Hill

Stipek, D. (2002). *Motivation to learn: Integrating theory and practice,* 4th ed. Boston: Allyn and Bacon.

Strachota, R. (1996). *On their side: Helping children take charge of their learning.* Greenfield, MA: Northeast Foundation for Children.

Wolfgang, C. (2008). *Solving discipline problems: Methods and models for today's teachers,* 7th ed. New York: Wiley.

Chapter 5

Anderson, L. M. (1989). Classroom instruction. In M. C. Reynolds (Ed.), *Knowledge base for the beginning teacher.* New York: Pergamon.

Armstrong. T. (1994). *Multiple intelligences in the classroom.* Alexandria, VA: Association for Supervision and Curriculum Development.

Aspy, D., and Roebuck, F. (1977). *Kids don't learn from people they don't like.* Amherst, MA: Human Resource Development Press.

Bandura, A. (1997). *Self-efficacy: The exercise of control.* New York: W. H. Freeman.

Blythe, T. (1998). *The teaching for understanding guide.* San Francisco: Jossey-Bass.

Brandt, R. (1993). On teaching for understanding: A conversation with Howard Gardner. *Educational Leadership, 50,* 7, 4–7.

Brophy, J. E. (1987). Synthesis of research strategies on motivating students to learn. *Educational Leadership, 45,* 2, 40–48.

Brophy, J. E. (1988a). Educating teachers about managing classrooms and students. *Teaching and Teacher Education, 4,* 1, 1–18.

Brophy, J. E. (1988b). Research on teacher effects and abuses. *Elementary School Journal, 89,* 1, 3–21.

Brophy, J. E. (1993). Probing the subtleties of subject matter teaching. *Educational Leadership, 49,* 7, 4–8.

Brophy, J. E., and Good, T. L. (1986). Teacher behavior and student achievement. In M. C. Wittrock (Ed.), *Handbook of research on teaching,* 3rd ed. New York: Macmillan.

Callahan, J., Clark, L., and Kellough, K. (2006). *Teaching in the middle and secondary schools,* 8th ed. Upper Saddle River, NJ: Merrill/Prentice Hall.

Cleveland, K. P. (2010). *Teaching boys who struggle in school: Strategies that turn underachievers into successful learners.* Alexandria, VA: Association for Supervision and Curriculum Development.

Dean, C., Hubbell, E., Pitler, H., and Stone, B. (2012). *Classroom instruction that works: Research-based strategies for increasing student achievement,* 2nd ed. Alexandria, VA: Association for Supervision and Curriculum Development.

Delpit, L. (2012). *Multiplication is for white people.* New York: The New Press.

Dreikurs, R. (2004). *Discipline without tears: How to reduce conflict and establish cooperation in the classroom.* New York: Wiley.

Duke, D. E. (1982). *Helping teachers manage classrooms.* Alexandria, VA: Association for Supervision and Curriculum Development.

Emmer, E., Evertson, C., and Worsham, M. (2003). *Classroom management for secondary teachers,* 6th ed. Boston: Allyn and Bacon.

Evertson, C. M. (1989). Classroom organization and management. In M. C. Reynolds (Ed.), *Knowledge base for the beginning teacher.* New York: Pergamon.

Feathers, N. (1982). *Expectations and actions.* Hillsdale, NJ: Erlbaum.

Fusco, E. (2012). *Effective questioning strategies in the classroom: A step by step approach to engaged thinking and learning, K–8.* New York: Teachers College Press.

Gardner, H. (1996). Multiple intelligences: Myths and messages. *International School Journal, 15,* 2, 8–22.

Gardner, H. (2004). *Frames of mind: The theory of multiple intelligences.* New York: Basic Books.

Glick, M. (2011). *The instructional leader and the brain: Using neuroscience to inform practice.* Thousand Oaks, CA: Corwin Press.

Good, T. L. (1987, July–August). Two decades of research on teacher expectations: Findings and future directions. *Journal of Teacher Education,* 32–47.

Good, T., and Brophy, J. (2008). *Looking in classrooms,* 10th ed. Boston: Allyn & Bacon.

Hunter, M. (1982). *Mastery teaching.* El Segundo, CA: TIP Publications.

Jensen, E. (2005). *Teaching with the brain in mind,* 2nd ed. Alexandria, VA: Association for Supervision and Curriculum Development.

Johnson, D. W., Johnson, R. T., and Holubec, E. J. (1993). *Cooperation in the classroom,* rev. ed. Edina, MN: Interaction Book Company.

Kagan, S. (1994). *Cooperative learning.* San Juan Capistrano, CA: Resources for Teachers.

Karweit, N. (1984). Time on task reconsidered: Synthesis of research on time and learning. *Educational Leadership, 41,* 8, 32–35.

Lewis, S. G., and Batts, K. (2005). How to implement differentiated instruction: Adjust, adjust, adjust. *Journal of Staff Development, 26,* 4, 26–31.

Lieberman, A., and Denham, C. (1980). *Time to learn.* Sacramento: California Commission for Teacher Preparation and Licensing.

Marzano, R. (2007). *The art and science of teaching: A comprehensive framework for effective instruction.* Alexandria, VA: Association for Supervision and Curriculum.

Marzano, R., Frontier, T., & Livingston, D. (2011). *Effective supervision: Supporting the art and science of teaching.* Alexandria, VA: Association for Supervision and Curriculum Development.

Osterman, K. (2000). Students' need for belonging in the school community. *Review of Educational Research, 70,* 3, 323–367.

Pintrich, P. R., Marx, R. W., and Boyle, P. (1993). Beyond conceptual change: The role of motivational beliefs and classroom contextual factors in conceptual change teaching. *Review of Educational Research, 63,* 2, 167–200.

Prawat, R. S. (1993). From individual differences to learning communities. *Educational Leadership, 49,* 7, 9–13.

Rosenshine, B., and Stevens, R. (1986). Teaching functions. In M. C. Wittrock (Ed.), *Handbook of research on teaching,* 3rd ed. New York: Macmillan.

Rosenthal, R., and Jacobson, L. (1968). *Pygmalion in the classroom: Teacher expectation and pupils' intellectual development.* New York: Holt, Rinehart & Winston.

Rothstein-Fisch, C., and Trumbull, E. (2008). *Managing diverse classrooms: How to build on students' cultural strengths.* Alexandria, VA: Association for Supervision and Curriculum Development.

Shepard, L., Hammerness, K., Darling-Hammond, L., and Rust, F. (2005). Assessment. In L. Darling-Hammond and J. Bransford (Eds.), *Preparing teachers for a changing world: What teachers should learn and be able to do.* San Francisco: Jossey-Bass.

Shulman, L. S. (1987). Knowledge and teaching: Foundations of the new reform. *Harvard Educational Review, 57,* 1–22.

Slavin, R. E. (1989–90). Research on cooperative learning: Consensus and controversy. *Educational Leadership, 47,* 4, 52–54.

Stipek, D. (2002). *Motivation to learn: Integrating theory and practice,* 4th ed. Boston: Allyn and Bacon.

Sweeney, T. J. (1981). *Adlerian counseling: Proven concepts and strategies,* 2nd ed. Muncie, IN: Accelerated Development.

Tomlinson, C. (2005). Traveling the road to differentiation in staff development. *Journal of Staff Development, 26,* 8–19.

Tomlinson, C. A., and Edison, C. C. (2003). *Differentiation in practice: A resource guide for differentiating curriculum.* Alexandria, VA: Association for Supervision and Curriculum Development.

Tomlinson, C., and Imbeau, M. (2010). *Leading and managing a differentiated classroom.* Alexandria, VA: Association for Supervision and Curriculum Development.

Wang, M. C., and Palinscar, A. S. (1989). Teaching students to assume an active role in their learning. In M. C. Reynolds (Ed.), *Knowledge base for the beginning teacher.* New York: Pergamon.

Weinstein, R. S. (2002). *Reaching higher: The power of expectations on schooling.* Cambridge, MA: Harvard University Press.

Wiggins, G., and McTighe, J. (1998). *Understanding by design.* Alexandria, VA: Association for Supervision and Curriculum Development.

Wilen, W. W. (1986). *Questioning skills for teachers,* 2nd ed. Washington, DC: National Educational Association.

Wineburg, S. (1987). The self-fulfillment of the self-fulfilling prophecy. *Educational Researcher, 16,* 9, 28–36.

Wiske, M. (1998). What is teaching for understanding? In M. Stone Wiske (Ed.), *Teaching for understanding: Linking research with practice.* San Francisco: Jossey-Bass.

Chapter 6

Brady, K., Forton, M., Porter, D., and Wood, C. (2003). *Rules in school.* Greenfield, MA: Northeast Foundation for Children.

Brophy, J. (1988a). Educating teachers about managing classrooms and students. *Teaching and Teacher Education, 4,* 1, 1–18.

Brophy, J. (1988b). Research on teaching effects: Uses and abuses. *The Elementary School Journal, 89,* 1, 3–21.

Canter, L. (1989). Assertive discipline—More than names on the board and marbles in a jar. *Phi Delta Kappan, 71,* 1, 57–61.

Canter, L., and Canter, M. (1992). *Assertive discipline: Positive behavior management for today's classroom.* Santa Monica, CA: Lee Canter & Associates.

Clarizio, H. F. (1980). *Toward positive classroom discipline,* 3rd ed. New York: Wiley.

Clayton, M., and Forton, M. (2001). *Classroom spaces that work.* Greenfield, MA: Northeast Foundation for Children.

Curwin, R. L., and Mendler, A. N. (1999). *Discipline with dignity.* Upper Saddle River, NJ: Merrill/Prentice Hall.

Dayton Public Schools. (1973). Corporal punishment: Is it needed? *Schoolday, 5,* 1, 4.

Delpit, L. (1995). *Other people's children: Cultural conflict in the classroom.* New York: The New Press.

Dreikurs, R. (1964). *Children: The challenge.* New York: Hawthorne.

Dreikurs, R. (2004). *Discipline without tears: How to reduce conflict and establish cooperation in the classroom.* New York: Wiley.

Dreikurs, R., Grunwald, B. B., and Pepper, F. C. (1998). *Maintaining sanity in the classroom, Classroom management techniques,* 2nd ed. New York: Taylor and Francis.

Emmer, E. T., and Evertson, C. M. (2008). *Classroom management for secondary teachers,* 8th ed. Boston: Allyn and Bacon.

Epstein, C. (1979). *Classroom management and teaching: Persistent problems and rational solutions.* Reston, VA: Reston.

Evans, G., and Lovell, B. (1979). Design modification in an open-plan school. *Journal of Educational Psychology, 71,* 41–49.

Evertson, C. M., and Emmer, E. T. (1982). Preventive classroom management. In D. L. Duke (Ed.), *Helping teachers manage classrooms.* Alexandria, VA: Association for Supervision and Curriculum Development.

Good, T., and Brophy, J. (1997). *Looking in classrooms,* 4th ed. New York: Longman.

Hansen, S. J. (1992). *Schoolhouse in the red. A guide-book for cutting our losses: Powerful recommendations for improving America's school facilities.* Arlington, VA: American Association of School Administrators.

Heitzman, A. J. (1983). Discipline and the use of punishment. *Education, 104,* 1, 17–22.

Hopkins, E. (1998). Hard hat area: The deteriorating state of school buildings. *Education World.* Retrieved from *http://www.educationworld.com/a_admin/admin/admin089.shtml*

Howell, R. G., Jr., and Howell, P. L. (1979). *Discipline in the classroom: Solving the teaching puzzle.* Reston, VA: Reston.

Hyman, I. A., and Snook, P. A. (1999). *Dangerous schools: What can we do about the physical and emotional abuse of our children?* San Francisco: Jossey-Bass.

Johnson, D. W., Johnson, R. T., and Holubec, E. J. (1993). *Cooperation in the classroom,* 6th ed. Edina, MN: Interaction Book Company.

Johnson, S. M., Bolstad, D. D., and Lobitz, G. K. (1976). Generalization and contrast phenomena in behavior modification with children. In E. J. Mash, L. A. Hamerlynck, and L. C. Handy (Eds.), *Behavior modification and families.* New York: Brunner/Mazell.

Jones, V. F., and Jones, L. S. (2012). *Comprehensive classroom management: Creating communities of support and solving problems,* 10th ed. Boston: Allyn and Bacon.

Kamii, C. (1991). Toward autonomy: The importance of critical thinking and choice making. *School Psychology Review, 20,* 3, 382–388.

Kazdin, A. E., and Bootzin, R. R. (1972). The token economy: An evaluative review. *Journal of Applied Behavior Analysis, 5,* 343–372.

Kohn, A. (1999). *Punished by rewards.* Boston: Houghton Mifflin.

Levin, J., and Shanken-Kaye, J. (2002). *From disrupter to achiever: Creating successful learning environments for the self-control classroom.* Dubuque, IA: Kendall/Hunt.

Lewis, L., Snow, K., Farris, E., Smerdon, B., Cronen, S., and Kaplan, J. (2000). *Condition of America's public school facilities: 1999* (NCES 2000-032). Washington, DC: National Center for Educational Statistics.

Madsen, C. H., Becker, W., and Thomas, D. R. (1968). Rules, praise and ignoring: Elements of elementary classroom control. *Journal of Applied Behavior Analysis, 1,* 139–150.

Rinne, C. H. (1984). *Attention: The fundamentals of classroom control.* Columbus, OH: Merrill.

Schneider, M. (2002). *Do school facilities affect academic outcomes?* Washington, DC: National Clearinghouse for Educational Facilities.

Sweeney, T. J. (1981). *Adlerian counseling, proven concepts and strategies,* 2nd ed. Muncie, IN: Accelerated Development.

Walker, H. M. (1979). *The acting-out child: Coping with classroom disruption.* Boston: Allyn and Bacon.

Chapter 7

Abi-Nader, J. (1993). Meeting the needs of multicultural classrooms: Family values and the motivation of minority students. In M. J. O'Hair and S. J. Odell (Eds.), *Diversity and teaching: Teacher education yearbook 1.* Fort Worth, TX: Harcourt, Brace, Jovanovich.

American Federation of Teachers. (2007). Building parent teacher relationships. *Readingrockets.* Retrieved from *http://www.readingrockets.org/article/19308/*

Banks, J., Cochran-Smith, M., Moll, L., Richert, A., Zeichner, K., LePage, P., Darling-Hammond, L., and Duffy, H. (2005). Teaching diverse learners. In L. Darling-Hammond and J. Bransford (Eds.), *Preparing teachers for a changing world: What teachers should learn and be able to do.* San Francisco: Jossey Bass.

Cummins, J. (1986). Empowering minority students. *Harvard Educational Review, 17,* 4, 18–36.

Darsch, M., and Shippen (2004). A model for involving parents of children with learning and behavior problems in the schools. *Preventing School Failure, 48,* 3, 24–35.

Davis, K. S., and Dupper, D. R. (2004). Student-teacher relationships: An overlooked factor in school dropout. *Journal of Human Behavior in a Social Environment,* (1–2), 179–193.

Gathercoal, F. (1998). Judicious discipline. In R. E. Butchart and B. McEwan (Eds.), *Classroom discipline in American schools: Problems and possibilities for democratic education*. Albany: State University of New York Press.

Gregory, A., and Ripski, M. (2008). Adolescent trust in teachers: Implications for behavior in the high school classroom. *School Psychology Review 37,* 3, 337–353.

Henderson, A. T., & Berla, A. (Eds.). (1997). *A new generation of evidence: The family is critical to student achievement*. Washington, DC: National Committee for Citizens in Education.

Irvine, J. J. (1990). *Black students and school failure: Policy, practices, prescriptions*. Westport, CT: Greenwood.

Jackson, S. A. (2001, April). *A study of teachers' referrals to the school counselor*. Paper presented at the annual meeting of the American Educational Research Association, Seattle, WA.

Johnson, D. W., Johnson, R. T., and Holubec, E. J. (1993). *Cooperation in the classroom,* 6th ed. Edina, MN: Interaction Book Company.

Kochman, T. (1981). *Black and white: Styles in conflict*. Chicago: University of Chicago Press.

Ladson-Billings, G. (1994). *The dreamkeepers: Successful teachers of African American children*. San Francisco: Jossey-Bass.

National Research Council. (2004). Committee on Increasing High School Students' Engagement and Motivation to Learn. *Engaging schools: Fostering high school motivation to learn*. Washington DC. National Academies Press.

Ogbu, J. (1988). Class stratification, racial stratification, and schooling. In L. Weis (Ed.), *Class, race and gender in American education*. Albany: State University of New York Press.

Osterman, K. (2000). Students' need for belonging in the school community. *Review of Educational Research 70,* 3, 323–367.

Rothstein-Fisch, C. and Trumbull, E. (2008). *Managing diverse classrooms: How to build on students' cultural strengths*. Alexandria, VA: Association for Supervision and Curriculum Development.

Stipek, S. (2006). Relationships matter. *Educational Leadership, 64* 1, 45–49.

Townsend, B. (2000). The disproportionate discipline of African American learners: Reducing suspensions and expulsions. *Exceptional Children, 66,* 3, 381–392.

U.S. Department of Education, Office for Civil Rights. (1993). *1990 Elementary and Secondary School Civil Rights Survey: National summaries*. Washington, DC: Author.

Chapter 8

Brophy, J. (1988). Educating teachers about managing classrooms and students. *Teaching and Teacher Education, 4,* 1, 1–18.

Canter, L. (1989). Assertive discipline—More than names on the board and marbles in a jar. *Phi Delta Kappan, 71,* 1, 57–61.

Haberman, M. (1995). *Star teachers of children in poverty*. West Lafayette, IN: Kappa Delta Pi.

Huber, J. D. (1984). Discipline in the middle school—Parent, teacher, and principal concerns. *National Association of Secondary School Principals Bulletin, 68,* 471, 74–79.

Kounin, J. (1970). *Discipline and group management in classrooms*. New York: Holt, Rinehart & Winston.

Lasley, T. J. (1989). A teacher development model for classroom management. *Phi Delta Kappan, 71,* 1, 36–38.

Levin, J. (1980). *Discipline and classroom management survey: Comparison between a suburban and urban school*. Unpublished report, Pennsylvania State University, University Park.

Redl, F., and Wineman, D. (1952). *Controls from within*. New York: Free Press.

Shrigley, R. L. (1980). *The resolution of 523 classroom incidents by 54 classroom teachers using the six step intervention model*. University Park: Pennsylvania State University, College of Education, Division of Curriculum and Instruction.

Shrigley, R. L. (1985). Curbing student disruption in the classroom—Teachers need intervention skills. *National Association of Secondary School Principals Bulletin, 69,* 479, 26–32.

Thomas, G. T., Goodall, R., and Brown, L. (1983). Discipline in the classroom: Perceptions of middle grade teachers. *The Clearinghouse, 57,* 3, 139–142.

Weber, T. R., and Sloan, C. A. (1986). How does high school discipline in 1984 compare to previous decades? *The Clearinghouse, 59,* 7, 326–329.

Chapter 9

Bandura, A. (1997). *Self-efficacy: The exercise of control.* New York: W. H. Freeman.

Brophy, J. (1988). Educating teachers about managing classrooms and students. *Teaching and Teacher Education, 4,* 1, 1–8.

Canter, L. (1989). Assertive discipline: More than names on the board and marbles in a jar. *Phi Delta Kappan, 71,* 1, 57–61.

Canter, L., and Canter, M. (2001). *Assertive discipline: Positive behavior management for today's classrooms,* 3rd ed. Los Angeles, CA: Canter Associates.

Dreikurs, R., Grunwald, B. B., and Pepper, F. C. (1998). *Maintaining sanity in the classroom: Classroom management techniques,* 2nd ed. New York: Taylor and Francis.

Ginott, H. (1972). *Between teacher and child.* New York: Peter H. Wyden.

Glasser, W. (1969). *Schools without failure.* New York: Harper & Row.

Glasser, W. (1992). *The quality school: Managing students without coercion.* New York: HarperCollins.

Gordon, T. (1989). *Teaching children self-discipline at home and in school.* New York: Random House.

Lasley, T. J. (1989). A teacher development model for classroom management. *Phi Delta Kappan, 71,* 1, 30–38.

Levin, J., Nolan, J., and Hoffman, N. (1985). A strategy for the classroom resolution of chronic discipline problems. *National Association of Secondary School Principals Bulletin, 69,* 7, 11–18.

Rinne, C. (1984). *Attention: The fundamentals of classroom control.* Columbus OH: Merrill.

Saphier, J., and Gower, R. (2008). *The skillful teacher,* 6th ed. Carlisle, MA: Research for Better Teaching.

Shrigley, R. (1985). Curbing student disruption in the classroom—Teachers need intervention skills. *National Association of Secondary School Principals Bulletin, 69,* 7, 26–32.

Valentine, M. R. (1987). *How to deal with discipline problems in the school: A practical guide for educators.* Dubuque, IA: Kendall/Hunt.

Chapter 10

Brendtro, L., Brokenleg, M., and Van Bockern, S. (2002). *Reclaiming youth at risk: Our hope for the future,* 2nd ed. Bloomington, IN: National Educational Services.

Brophy, J. (1988). Educating teachers about managing classrooms and students. *Teaching and Teacher Education, 4,* 1, 1–18.

Canter, L., and Canter, M. (2001). *Assertive discipline: Positive behavior management for today's classrooms,* 3rd ed. Los Angeles, CA: Canter Associates.

Delpit, L. (2012) *Multiplication is for white people.* New York: The New Press.

Dreikurs, R., Grunwald, B. B., and Pepper, F. C. (1998). *Maintaining sanity in the classroom: Classroom management techniques,* 2nd ed. New York: Harper & Row.

Ginott, H. G. (1972). *Teacher and child.* New York: Macmillan.

Hall, P. S., and Hall, N. D. (2003). *Educating oppositional and defiant children.* Alexandria, VA: Association for Supervision and Curriculum Development.

Jones, V. F. (1980). *Adolescents with behavior problems.* Boston: Allyn and Bacon.

Kohn, A. (2005). Unconditional teaching. *Educational Leadership, 63,* 1, 20–24.

Levin, J., Nolan, J., and Hoffman, N. (1985). A strategy for the classroom resolution of chronic discipline problems. *National Association of Secondary School Principals Bulletin, 69,* 479, 11–18.

Levin, J. & Shanken-Kaye, J. (2002). From disrupter to achiever: Creating successful learning environments for the self-control classroom. Dubuque, IA: Kendall hunt.

Osterman, K. (2000). Students' need for belonging in the school community. *Review of Educational Research, 70,* 3, 323–367.

PaTTAN. (2008). *Functional behavior assessment mini-module training materials.* Pennsylvania Technical Training and Assistance Network. Retrieved from *http://www.pattan.k12.pa.us/resources/request.aspx?UniqueID=04525*

Porter, A. C., and Brophy, J. (1988). Synthesis of research on good teaching: Insights from the work of the IRT. *Educational Leadership, 45,* 8, 74–83.

Sautner, B. (2001). Rethinking the effectiveness of suspensions. *Reclaiming Children and Youth, 9,* 4, 210–215.

Shrigley, R. L. (1980). *The resolution of 523 classroom incidents by 54 classroom teachers using the six step intervention model.* University Park: Pennsylvania State University, College of Education, Division of Curriculum and Instruction.

Strachota, R. (1996). *On their side: Helping children take charge of their learning.* Greenfield, MA: Northeast Foundation for Children.

Sweeney, T. J. (1981). *Adlerian counseling: Proven concepts and strategies.* Muncie, IN: Accelerated Development.

Tanner, L. N. (1978). *Classroom discipline for effective teaching and learning.* New York: Holt, Rinehart & Winston.

Woolfolk, A., and Brooks, D. (1983). Nonverbal communication in teaching. In E. W. Gordon (Ed.), *Review of research in education, 10.* Washington, DC: American Educational Research Association.

Chapter 11

Ayllon, T., Garber, S., and Pisor, K. (1975). The elimination of discipline problems through a combined school-home motivation system. *Behavior Therapy, 6,* 616–626.

Brookover, W. B., and Gigliotti, R. J. (1988). *Parental involvement in the public schools.* Alexandria, VA: National School Boards Association.

Canter, L., and Canter, M. (2001). *Assertive discipline: Positive behavior management for today's classrooms,* rev. ed. Los Angeles, CA: Canter Associates.

Glasser, W. (1969). *Schools without failure.* New York: Harper & Row.

Hoover-Dempsey, K., and Sandler, H. (1997). Why do parents become involved in their children's education? *Review of Educational Research, 67,* 1, 3–42.

Johnson, S. M., Bolstad, O. D., and Lobitz, G. K. (1976). Generalization and contrast phenomena in behavior modification with children. In E. J. Marsh, L. A. Hamerlynck, and L. C. Handy (Eds.), *Behavior modification and families.* New York: Brunner/Mazell.

Jones, V. F. (1980). *Adolescents with behavior problems.* Boston: Allyn and Bacon.

Jones, V. F., and Jones, L. S. (2006). *Comprehensive classroom management: Creating positive learning environments for all students,* 8th ed. Boston: Allyn and Bacon.

Melnick, N., and Grosse, W. J. (1984). Rights of students: A review. *Educational Horizons, 62,* 4, 145–149.

Patterson, G. R. (1974). Intervention for boys with conduct problems: Multiple settings, treatments and criteria. *Journal of Consulting and Clinical Psychology, 42,* 471–481.

Skiba R. J., Peterson, R. L., and Williams, T. (1999). The dark side of zero tolerance: Can punishment lead to safe schools? *Phi Delta Kappan, 80,* 5, 372–381.

Townsend, B. (2000). Disproportionate discipline of African American children and youth: Culturally-responsive strategies for reducing school suspensions and expulsions. *Exceptional Children, 66,* 381–391.

Walker, H. M. (1979). *The acting-out child: Coping with classroom disruption.* Boston: Allyn and Bacon.

Wolfgang, C. H. (2008). *Solving discipline problems,* 7th ed. Boston: Allyn and Bacon.

INDEX